Author of *The Peace Race* and Professor of Industrial Engineering at Columbia University, Seymour Melman has been carrying on an impressive and unrelenting one-man debate with the White House and the Pentagon, parts of which have been read into the *Congressional Record*. In OUR DEPLETED SOCIETY he strongly urges immediate conversion from arms to peace-time production, since our defenses have already reached the level of multiple overkill. Mr. Melman's picture of the losses resulting from the colossal overdevelopment of military power includes the alienation of millions of children from productive work, and statistics of mental and physical depletion that will horrify every American who reads this book.

The author cites tragic instances that have occurred because we did not have the foresight to prepare our weapon technicians and industries for production cut-backs and cutoffs. He further specifies several cities and states as probable economic disaster areas if conversion to civilian industry is not begun. While Mr. Melman's predictions have seldom proved wrong, he does reveal how we can correct our situation by marshaling our manpower, retraining it, and putting it to work in new jobs and new markets that have been sadly neglected.

Mr. Melman's thesis will undoubtedly offend many people, among them a large proportion of the American Medical Association, those who profit from the sale of military equipment to underdeveloped countries, and those who find it easier to produce goods abroad than to utilize efficient methods of production and organization in this country. Coming from one of our foremost authorities on industrial development, this candid criticism of our present policies is certain to become one of the nation's most hotly debated issues.

Our Depleted Society

Other Books by the Same Author:

Dynamic Factors in Industrial Productivity
Inspection for Disarmament (*Editor*)
Decision-making and Productivity
The Peace Race
No Place to Hide (*Editor*)
Disarmament: Its Politics and Economics (*Editor*)

Seymour Melman

Our
Depleted
Society

Holt, Rinehart and Winston

New York   Chicago   San Francisco

Grateful acknowledgment is made to the following for permission
to reprint selections in this book:

Ben Segal, "A Labor Leader's Lament," *War/Peace Report*, June,
1964.
Benjamin Spock, "Our Policies Shape the Next Generation," in *"A
Strategy for American Security,"* Lee Service, Inc. 48 East 21st
Street, New York 10, N. Y. April, 1963.
Erich Fromm, *The Sane Society,* Holt, Rinehart and Winston, 1955.
The Engineers Joint Council, "The Nation's Engineering Research
Needs, 1965–1985, A Summary Report and Subcommittee Re-
port," May, 1962.
Suki Ports, "Educational Disaster Area," *West Side News,* July 9,
1964.
Robert L. Bartley, "Scientist Shortage, Space, Military Work Cut-
ting into Research for Civilian Economy," *The Wall Street
Journal,* August 9, 1963.
Senator Gruening, "Exporting Trouble," *The Nation,* October 6,
1962.
Irving Bluestone (UAW), "Problems of the Worker in Industrial
Conversion," International Arms Control Symposium, University
of Michigan, December 19, 1962.

Designer: Ernst Reichl
85660-0115
Printed in the United States of America

To my dear father Abraham Melman,
a lifelong independent of firm convictions,
who does not necessarily subscribe to
a single viewpoint in this book.

Preface

This book is an economic audit of the price that America has paid for twenty years of cold war. It is also a proposal of what may be done to repair the damage that has been caused at home and abroad. It is essentially a statement of the conditions of life, public and private, that have been caused by long priority to guns instead of butter, and by the sustained failure to differentiate between economic growth that is healthy and that which is parasitic. This economic analysis is independent of particular ideology or political justification. Its validity does not depend upon political consensus.

Almost all the data of this book pertain to the United States. But the analysis is applicable to every country which has long endured large military spending.

It is likely that the Soviet Union has experienced a parallel process of depletion. That fact, once understood, will help to establish common ground for international agreement toward curtailing the arms race and the space marathon. For disarmament and the establishment of alternative security systems will then be understood as the indispensable act for rehabilitating depleted parts of American and Soviet society. Similar reasoning applies to other industrialized countries, especially to Great Britain.

For the underdeveloped countries, the conclusion from this book is clear: These nations will have no chance to begin catching up with the industrialized part of the world until they start converting their own military budgets into economic-development capital. So long as the less-developed nations continue to enlarge their own military forces and budgets they will continue to choke off their own economic development.

The final test of a security policy is the well-being of our people, while our country is secured against physical destruction. The weight of evidence now shows that because of the military use of nuclear power physical safety can no longer be purchased—at any price. Meanwhile, the continued, massive quest for the now-unattainable military shield has been using up so much of our treasure and our talent as to deplete the very quality of life in our country. In a word: The military quest for security has become self-defeating. We have not yet faced up to this new fact, and to the instruction that it gives to devise alternatives to military-based security policies.

Despite the broader relevance of the analysis of depletion, I have written this book mainly as a critique of American policy. As Americans our first responsibility is to our own country. I hope the analyses given here will support the understanding that the well-being of the American people urgently requires the end of the Cold War and a turn toward productive use of American resources.

In the preparation of this book I have had the benefit of critical comment from Professor John E. Ullmann, Terence McCarthy, Dr. George Papas, Dr. Emanuel Ghent, Dr. Julius Marmur, David Dreiblatt, and Murray Mohl. Mr. Morris Forgash generously gave me permission to publish a summary prospectus of A Bank for Economic Acceleration, a highly original world economic development plan.

Miss Dolly Gattozzi and Mrs. Eloise Segal graciously applied their editorial talents to improving the manuscript. Mrs. Marion Krebser did yeoman work in researching several parts of the book.

The mechanical preparation of the manuscript was considerably facilitated by the generous co-operation of Susan Alexion and Mrs. Nita Hagan.

My dear wife, Clarice, was a constant source of constructive comment and sustaining support during the preparation of this volume.

I wish to acknowledge here the great debt which all of us owe to William Perk, of Southern Illinois University, for his highly original analyses of the overkill aspect of military power. His analyses are essential for the formulations of alternatives to security policies that breed a depleted society.

                                                        S.M.

Contents

Appendix

Our Depleted Society

1

Behind the Mask of Success

Once upon a time the United States was the standout performer, world-wide, as a vigorous, productive society, exceptionally strong in basic industries and in mass-producing consumer goods. American design and production methods set world standards in many fields.

These qualities have been the basis for a confident ideology which proclaims that the combination of technical excellence and money-making incentives is the key to growing affluence for all.

But the United States now is the scene of a drama different from that implicit in her confident ideology. A process of technical, industrial, and human deterioration has been set in motion within American society. The competence of the industrial system is being eroded at its base. Entire industries are falling into technical disrepair, and there is massive loss of productive employment because of inability to hold even domestic markets against foreign competition. Such depletion in economic life produces wide-ranging human deterioration at home. The wealthiest nation on earth has been unable to rally the resources necessary to raise one fifth of its own people from poverty. The same basic depletion operates as an unseen hand restricting America's relations with the rest of the world, limiting foreign-policy moves primarily to military-based initiatives.

This deterioration is the result of an unprecedented concentration of America's technical talent and fresh capital on military production. While United States research programs for civilian purposes are grossly understaffed, and many industries do virtually no research at all, more than two thirds of America's technical researchers now work for the military. We have constructed the most awesome military organizations in human history, with the actual power to destroy what we call civilization on this earth, a power which rational men dare not use. Military extravagance has been undermining the world value of the dollar and with it the world-banking position of the United States.

The price of building colossal military power, and endlessly adding to it, has been the depletion of American society, a process now well advanced in industry, civilian technology, management, education, medical care, and the quality of life. The prospect of "no future" has become a permanent part of government security policies that depend mainly on the threat of using nuclear weapons. Never before were men made to feel so powerless, so incapable of having a voice over their own fate.

The action necessary to restore United States competence as a productive society will be an urgent issue in American life until at least 1985. The pathology of and the cure for the depletion process is what this book is about.

Many Americans are probably unprepared for such formulations. That is because the ordinary, well-regarded criterion for judging a society—making more money—tells us that America is successful, even allowing for the existence of the poor.

Economic growth has been widely trusted as the yardstick of well-being with too little attention given to the quality of the growth, to economic health. Growth can include parasitic and malignant processes, as well as those that are healthy and productive. Depletion in America, like the increasing inability of many industries to hold their own in competitive markets, is mainly the result of parasitic growth. Replacing this with productive growth is the essential process of reconstruction for America.

By the test of income and the value of goods and services produced, the United States, in 1963-64, was clearly the front-running nation in the world. During 1964 the total value of all goods and services produced in the United States (Gross National Product) was over $600 billion.* In 1963, the average value of goods and services per person in the United States was $3,000.

What has become critical for America is the quality of this economic growth. How much is healthy and how much is parasitic? Which parts add to the level of living and to further production, and which parts deplete the quality of life?

The Federal Government's Selective Service Administration, since the Second World War, has maintained a set of minimum standards, physical and educational, for acceptability of men into the armed forces. By these standards, 30% of the young men examined by Selective Service during the Second World War were rejected. Twenty years later, in 1963, the same standards produced a rejection rate averaging 50%. The meaning of this danger signal for deterioration in physical and educational competence among our youth was appreciated by senior officials of the Federal Government, and President Kennedy named a commission to study this development.

In 1950, for every 100,000 Americans, there were 109 physicians in practice. By 1955, this number declined to 102; in 1960 it was 98; and by 1963, there was a further drop to 97. During the same period, the United States imported physicians trained elsewhere in the world. And so 1,600 foreign physicians came to the United States in one year, 1963, representing the equivalent output of 16 medical schools. Their presence has saved the United States from a sharp crisis in medical services. From 1950-63, there were modest increases in the number of doctors graduated in the United States. But they fell far short of the growth in population, with the result that the availability of medical service in this nation has declined.

In the wealthiest country in the world, 1,500,000 school children attend grossly overcrowded classes and schools. Twenty-two million Americans are classified as "functionally illiterate," not having completed eighth-grade education. The following is an

* All data sources used in this book are listed, by chapter, at the end of the book.

inventory of teacher needs in the elementary and high schools of the nation as of September, 1964:

Needs most likely to be met:

1. To replace those leaving	134,000
2. To serve increased enrollment	54,000

Needs which have not been met and are most likely to continue:

3. To relieve overcrowding and eliminate half-day sessions	30,000
4. To give instruction and services not now provided	20,000
5. To replace the unprepared	10,000
Total need, September, 1964	248,000
Number of available graduates of 1964	130,000
Estimated shortage	118,000

This National Education Association estimate of the number of teachers required does not even begin to cope with the problem of satisfactory education for our functional illiterates, essential job retraining, and the vast problem of helping millions of Americans overcome disadvantages of segregated education.

Where are the potential physicians and the potential teachers?

An announcement by the Atomic Energy Commission gives us a clue. On December 26, 1964, the AEC publicized a program to recruit for management, technical, engineering, and accounting intern training programs outstanding college students receiving degrees in June of 1965. In the technical-intern program, for which a master's degree or equivalent in science or engineering is required, the starting salary is $7,950 per year and increases to $8,935 per year—all of this within the framework of an AEC job-training program.

Compare this with the position of teachers and physicians after five years of college training. During 1964, the average teacher's salary in American elementary and secondary schools was $5,963. The starting salary was obviously less than that. I do not know of any school system with a program of teacher internship that approaches the salary level offered by the Atomic Energy Commission. What is the status of a physician in training after five years of college? At that point, he is looking forward to another five years of medical school and hospital training—at no salary at all while a student, and at bare subsistence salary while an intern.

The program announced by the Atomic Energy Commission illustrates the system of rationing by salary which has been operated in the United States, and which has siphoned off a large proportion of talented young people to the service of the defense-space complex. Similar salary differentials between military and civilian work show up in various engineering fields. Military contractors, or the National Aeronautics and Space Administration, offer substantially higher rewards, thereby attracting many of the most talented people.

Whatever worth may be attached to the defense and space program, this much is clear: The work of these men, when completed, does not, by its very nature, contribute to economic health, or to further production. From an economic standpoint defense work only expends manpower and materials. That is why the growth of defense work is parasitic growth, regardless of the fact that the workers buy groceries and services with their salaries. Since we use about two thirds of our prime technical research talent for military-oriented work, the result is a short supply of comparable talent to serve civilian industry and civilian activities of every sort.

Money and manpower continue to be poured into military and related work, creating a superabundance of killing power without precedent. The armed forces of the United States now have six times as many intercontinental missiles and intercontinental airplanes as the Soviets. The U.S. strategic aircraft and missiles alone are able to deliver explosive power equivalent to 6 tons (12,000 pounds) of TNT per person on this planet. But the overkill continues to be piled up. Defense and space budgets continue to take more than half of our tax-dollars each year. Now that we have 6 tons of TNT per person in our strategic missiles and aircraft alone, have we become more secure than when we had only 1 ton of TNT per human being on earth? Will we become more secure when we can deliver 8 or 10 tons of TNT per human being?

There is little doubt about other effects from the incessant and costly pile-up of overkill in America's armed forces. By draining the finite stock of technical talent, the overkill program has depleted our education and health services. The rationing of talent plus capital has resulted in the depletion of entire basic industries in the United States—reducing employment of every sort for Americans, making the United States incompetent in important industrial areas, compelling reliance on foreign sources of supply, and contributing to decay in the quality of our lives by closing off many possible opportunities for productive employment for our young people.

Americans must begin to face the bitter fact that, in many areas of industrial technology, the United States has already become second-rate and that this condition promises to be epidemic if the present concentration of talent and capital on piling up overkill is continued.

In order to learn how to design and operate really high-speed railroad systems it is now necessary to send a technical mission to Japan to see how it is done. Ditto to Poland and Russia to learn about advanced fishery technology. Similarly, European countries, after the Second World War sent productivity teams to the United States to observe technological methods which they might usefully apply to improve the productiveness of their own industry.

America's twenty major shipyards in 1964 had under construction only 40 merchant ships, totaling 615,000 tons. In the Soviet Union, 673 merchant ships totaling 6,450,000 tons were under construction, or under order. The merchant fleet of every major maritime country in the world—except our own—has been expanding during the last twenty years. In the United States, and in the United States alone, there has been a persistent decline in the size of the merchant fleet and a failure to replace aging vessels.

Merchant vessels are important, complex industrial products. They are required in large numbers by a major industrial society that exports $25 billion worth of goods, as does the United States. In other major maritime countries, between 30% and 50% of the foreign trade is carried by ships under the nation's flag. But of the goods flowing from the United States, only 9% is now carried in American flag ships. This means a decline in jobs for American seamen and declining employment in shipbuilding; it also feeds back into many other industries. Ships require engines, turbines, generators, instruments of many sorts, steel plates, cargo-handling equipment, navigation devices and communications equipment—all, in turn, the product of diverse industries. The decline of shipbuilding therefore means a decline in production and employment in all of these different industries.

Why has the United States shipbuilding industry not been a competent producer of merchant ships? American and foreign shipowners still buy ships, but they do not buy them in the United States. The essential reason is this: The American shipbuilding industry has been unable to compete with the costs and prices of shipbuilders abroad.

Many are quick to say that this uncompetitiveness is due to the high wages paid to American workers. The dramatic fact, however, is that the automobile industry in the United States pays the highest automobile wages in the world, and has also been producing in its low-price lines the cheapest cars in the world measured in price per pound of fabricated vehicle. This was made possible in the auto industry by sustained application of modern production engineering, but it has not been done in the ship-building field. This means that the shipbuilding industry has not been introducing in the design of the product and the method of manufacture the technology that would enable it to offset the wages to American workers by high productivity of labor and capital.

During the Second World War, Henry Kaiser operated ship-yards at Richmond, California, where 7 million tons of merchant ships valued at $1.8 billion were manufactured in an astonishingly short time and at remarkably low cost. Seven hundred Liberty ships, each of about 10,000 tons capacity, were produced at an average cost of 13¢ per pound of vessel. Ships were launched at the rate of one per day. High-productivity manufacturing techniques were widely applied by the Kaiser shipyard operation. Deckhouses were prefabricated; large sections of ships were built upside down and on continuous line operation to enable simplified working by 300,000 new welders—including a large contingent of former housewives, drugstore clerks, and the like. What happened to all of these high-productivity techniques? Apparently these ideas were promptly scrapped by the shipbuilding industry at the end of the war and we were left with an industry that has become technically retarded.

In the United States a shipbuilding worker was paid about $3.05 an hour in 1964. In Sweden the wage to shipbuilding workers was $1.62 an hour. This means that in order to be competitive with Swedish shipyards American firms must install and utilize production methods which would make the man-hours of American workers about twice as productive as those of Swedish workers.

This is feasible from an engineering standpoint, but the managers of America's shipbuilding industry have not done it. They have been oriented primarily to serving the United States Navy as a principal customer. Ships for the Navy, like destroyers, are produced at a cost of about $5 per pound, and Polaris submarines at $12 per pound. By contrast, a commercial tanker must be manufactured at a cost of 20¢ per pound, or less if possible. By concentrating on military work where cost is of lesser importance, and by concentrating technical talent in the cost-doesn't-matter department as well, the shipbuilding industry has become commercially noncompetitive on the world market. This condition will not be altered until there is a transfer of talent and capital from the military to the civilian sphere.

Until now, there has been no major intervention by any private or public body to save the American shipbuilding industry. From the side of the Government, the major requirement—building up defense—is being satisfied. That is where the talent and the capital have been going. The fiction that the private shipbuilding firms should fend for themselves in a competitive market is maintained despite the fact that the Government, through the Defense

Department, has long been the main customer and thereby the main decision-maker for the size and the character of American shipbuilding firms.

Americans have grown up believing in the technological superiority of American industry. We are due for a rude awakening, for the depletion that is visible in the shipbuilding field is also visible in an array of other American industries, notably those that produce basic industrial goods of many sorts.

Americans have believed that our nation is so wealthy and so productive that there is no possible contradiction between massive military buildups and growing affluence for all. The United States can afford guns *and* butter; besides, doesn't defense spending put money into circulation? This was learned from three years of U.S. involvement in World War II—an experience different from twenty years of Cold War. The contradiction between guns and butter is now real and measurable. Our able young men cannot, at once, be trainees for the Atomic Energy Commission and physicians in training; they cannot be teaching the young and also designing missile components. The salary money spent by the missile builder goes into circulation, but that does not in the least add to the stock of talent available for civilian work that needs to be done. "Guns" take away from "butter" even in the United States.

National concentration on the production of overkill, which gives priority to talent and capital for the military sphere, has produced in many industries a deterioration so severe that they are virtually at a terminal condition in terms of economic and technical competence. The point of no return for an industry is reached when it becomes difficult to estimate how long it would take to restore it to economic health. We are approaching that point in the shipbuilding industry and the issue now is: How much second-rate industry is the United States prepared to suffer as the price of accumulating overkill without limit? How much loss of productive employment should be tolerated? How dependent on foreign countries for the supply of industrial goods should the United States become?

Our economists are quick to remind us that it is efficient to buy things from the cheapest producer. Altogether reasonable. But this rule of reason does not give us instruction about what to do when the noncompetitiveness of American industry has become epidemic, and results in major withdrawals of American firms from productive work in this country.

If the epidemic of noncompetitiveness spreads, we will be left with unassailable leadership in the design and manufacture of Polaris submarines, gadgets, and slick packaging. This direction is the way to an incompetent society, and that is where we are heading fast.

Priority to military and space buildups has continued—despite the fact that the ceaseless pile-up of weapons has, for a long time, not even made military sense.

2

Overkill: The Drain on America

A human being or a community can be destroyed only once. This is a limit of military power, and no conceivable technological break-through is going to change that. But the defense budgets and military policies of the United States embody a denial of these propositions, in the form of the weapons and the forces in being and in preparation.

In 1965 more than 7,000 nuclear warheads are carried by the 1,400 intercontinental missiles and the 2,000 long-range-bombing aircraft of U.S. armed forces. Each of these 7,000 warheads is capable of destroying a city. The warheads range in size from less than 1 million tons of TNT-equivalent to explosives whose power is equivalent to that of 20 million tons of TNT, and more. The 3,400 strategic aircraft and missiles of the U.S. armed forces can carry about 19 billion tons of TNT-equivalent, or about 6 tons for each human being on earth.

Apart from these there are more than 25,000 "tactical" nuclear warheads whose average explosive force is 100,000 tons of TNT-equivalent, or 5 times the power of the bomb that destroyed Hiroshima in World War II. These tactical warheads are encased in short-range missiles, artillery shells, and bombs, or fashioned into various sorts of nuclear demolition kits. The tens of thousands of nuclear warheads that Secretary of Defense Mc-

Namara declared that the military had during 1963 are carried by an array of short-range aircraft, and in missiles of every description: ground-to-ground, ground-to-air, air-to-air, and air-to-ground. This stockpile of strategic and tactical nuclear weapons is being increased constantly.

How much military power is represented by this stockpile? The bomb that destroyed the city of Hiroshima and took the lives of about 100,000 people in August, 1945, had the power of 20,000 tons of TNT-equivalent. A standard boxcar on American railroads can carry about 20 tons of TNT. In other words, the bomb used to destroy Hiroshima had explosive power equivalent to the TNT that could be carried in 10 freight trains, each made up of 100 freight cars, each car carrying 20 tons of TNT. By similar reckoning, a warhead of 1 megaton—that is, 1 million tons of TNT-equivalent—has the explosive power equivalent to the TNT carried by 500 freight trains each of them with 100 carloads of TNT.

We can try to visualize the present power of the U.S. strategic nuclear stockpile in another way. Suppose a Hiroshima-size bomb had been exploded every day of every year for the last 1,965 years, or since the birth of Christ. The combined force of all of these explosions would be just over 14,000 megatons; this is only 70% of the destructive capability now encased in the U.S. long-range bombers and missiles alone.

Nuclear military power involves a factor of concentration of destructive capability that has no precedent in human experience. In wars fought with bullets, the idea of overkill has been held to mean having more bullets than enemy soldiers. There were, in fact, more bullets than soldiers in World War II. But it was technically impossible to deliver the firepower of billions of bullets and shells and bombs at once place and at one time. Now this is possible, owing to the concentration of energy-release by nuclear weapons. One large missile or bomber-load of warheads produces an energy-release greater than the cumulation of explosives used from 1939 to 1945 on several continents. A single 10-megaton warhead load means an explosion equivalent to 10,000,-000 tons or 20,000,000,000 pounds of TNT. As the photographs of Hiroshima show, the fast release of two tenths of 1% of this much explosive force at that place, at one time, produced, not damage or partial destruction, but atomization of 100,000 people, scorched earth, and durable damage to the genes of many survivors. The present warheads are immensely more powerful than the one used at Hiroshima. That is the meaning of overkill.

The Department of Defense of the United States employs 3.7 million people, of whom 2,680,000 are in the uniformed forces. These forces include 16 elaborately equipped Army divisions, 1,987 ships of the Navy, of which 620 are warships, 28,000 aircraft of all types, and 30,000 to 40,000 missiles of all varieties and sizes armed with nuclear warheads. Stockpiles of raw material for potential military use are valued at $8.5 billion. The armed services use 340,000 buildings. The total property value of the installations and equipment exceeds $171 billion.

These numbers are so large as to defy visualization. I will therefore elaborate one aspect of U.S. military power: the strategic delivery forces. The intercontinental aircraft and missiles of the United States probably account for about one third of the military spending during the last years. Here is an estimate of

	Number of Vehicles	Yield in Millions of tons of TNT-equivalent per Vehicle (megatons)	Total Yield in Millions of tons of TNT-equivalent (megatons)
B-52 Bombers	630	20	12,600
B-47 Bombers	225	10	2,250
B-58 Bombers	80	20	1,600
Atlas Missiles	60	3	180
Titan II Missiles	54	10	540
Minuteman Missiles	800	1	800
Skyhawk A-4D Navy Aircraft	1,000	1	1,000
Skywarrior A-3D Navy Aircraft	150	1	150
Polaris Submarines	464	1	464
(29 with 16 missiles each)			
	3,463		19,584 (megatons)

the principal U.S. strategic nuclear-weapons system operational in 1965. Bear in mind that this enumeration includes only the delivery vehicles with intercontinental range; it does not include the largest number of aircraft and missiles—which have less than intercontinental range.

This tabulation brings up to 1965 an estimate of the U.S. nuclear forces that was originally prepared for the report "A Strategy for American Security," which several colleagues and I published in 1963.*

All told then, U.S. armed forces in 1965 included 3,400 strategic delivery vehicles with the destructive capability that totaled 19,000 million tons of TNT-equivalent. Just what this means in terms of military power is almost beyond comprehension. A 1-megaton warhead (1 million tons of TNT-equivalent) is capable of destroying most cities by its blast, radiation, and fire effect, which can extend across an area 24 miles in diameter. Therefore, the 3,400 U.S. strategic delivery vehicles must be considered in relation to the 140 cities with populations of 100,000 or more in the Soviet Union, or the 370 cities of this size in the entire Sino-Soviet bloc.

There is no way of giving reliable numerical statements of the military power contained in these strategic weapons. No one has ever seen a nuclear war and therefore no one is able to say what size of error is involved in a particular estimate of nuclear military power. Nevertheless some reckoning can be made. Let us assume, for example, that for some combination of reasons 90% of the U.S. forces' strategic aircraft are destroyed and 75% of the intercontinental missiles are lost. Here is an estimate of the residual strategic delivery capability.

* Seymour Melman (ed.), "A Strategy for American Security," Lee Service, 48 East 21 Street, New York, New York (50¢).

This sort of tabulation represents a system that is being constantly altered; some vehicles are being retired—like the B-47 bombers that numbered 600 in 1963 and the Atlas and Titan I missiles that were ordered dismantled by June 30, 1965; others are being added—like the Minuteman and Polaris; and altogether new types of strategic vehicles are being produced—like the 1700 TFX (F-111) planes, each able to carry the equivalent of 10 megatons between continents.

	Vehicles	Total Warhead Power in Megatons (Million Tons TNT-Equivalent)
10% of 225 B-47 bombers	22	220
10% of 630 B-52 bombers	63	1,260
10% of 80 B-58 bombers	8	160
10% of 1150 Navy Aircraft	115	115
25% of 54 Titan missiles	13	130
25% of 60 Atlas missiles	15	45
25% of 464 Polaris missiles	116	116
25% of 800 Minutemen missiles	200	200
Total	552 vehicles	2,246 megatons

The 552 vehicles that remain after the assumption of massive attrition are still almost 4 times the number of Soviet cities with populations of 100,000 or more.

It is also possible to estimate the size of this destructive power by taking into account the demonstrated capability of a nuclear device of 20,000 tons of TNT-equivalent, the bomb that killed 100,000 people at Hiroshima.* Let us refer to 100,000 people

* In order to estimate the destructive capability of U.S. strategic forces I assumed that 20,000 tons of TNT-equivalent in the Hiroshima bombing destroyed 100,000 people. Since no one has ever observed a nuclear war, all forecasts concerning the effect of the use of nuclear weapons on a large scale involve estimations for circumstances where the error of estimate cannot be known. Gauging the number of fatalities at Hiroshima involves this problem.

The U.S. Atomic Energy Commission (*The Effects of Nuclear Weapons*, 1962, p. 550) says that casualties at Hiroshima included 68,000 killed. The U.S. Strategic Bombing Survey reporting on *The Effects of Atomic Bombs on Hiroshima and Nagasaki* (1946, p. 15), stated:

. . . the exact number of dead and injured will never be known because of the confusion after the explosion. Persons unaccounted for might have been burned beyond recognition in the falling buildings, disposed of in one of the mass cremations of the first week of recovery, or driven out of the city to die or recover without any record remaining. No sure count of even the pre-raid population existed. Because of the decline in activity in the two port cities, with constant threat of incendiary raids, and formal evacuation programs of the Government, an unknown number of inhabitants had either drifted away from the cities or been killed by 20,000 tons of TNT as one "Hiroshima unit"; the megatonage deliverable by U.S. strategic forces can be calculated in terms of "Hiroshima units." In these terms, the 140 Soviet population centers of 100,000 or more comprise approximately 500 "Hiroshima units."

On the assumption of 90% attrition of aircraft and 75% attrition of strategic missiles, the resulting overkill factor would be about 220 times on the main population-industrial centers of the USSR. If the assumption of attrition were relaxed to 50%, then the overkill rate on Soviet industrial-population centers would be more than 1,000 times.

As noted above, all such calculations embody unknown errors of estimate, and there is no way of verifying such numbers. In the event of a nuclear war it is doubtful that the survivors, if any, would be either competent to master or would be interested in such arithmetic. What is important is this: In the realm of overkill, there is no difference between an overkill of 1, or 2, or 220, or 1,000. The United States has been spending billions of dollars to overkill—that is, to do an impossible thing.

---

removed according to plan. In this uncertain situation, estimates of casualties have generally ranged between 100,000 and 180,000 for Hiroshima . . . the Survey believes the dead at Hiroshima to have been between 70,000 and 80,000.

A Japanese study on *Atomic Bomb Injuries* (Nobuo Kusano, Ed. 1953, p. 60) accounted for 92,000 dead and missing by February 2, 1946, and further stated:

. . . these figures do not include the deaths among the army in the city. According to information published later by Hiroshima City the number of dead, including those in the military employees and Army, and the injured who died in the meantime, is estimated at 210,000 to 240,000. Another estimate put the number of dead as 270,000.

The effect of a warhead like that used on Hiroshima is influenced by many factors—for example, population density, which is much higher in large modern cities. Deaths traceable to the Hiroshima bombing are still occurring and are not counted. Since estimates of deaths at Hiroshima range from 68,000 to 270,000, I regard the figure of 100,000 fatalities at Hiroshima as one reasonable yardstick for estimating the destructive power of nuclear weapons.

On the Soviet side, too, nuclear-weapons systems are numerous enough to give the Soviets charter membership in the international overkill club. The following is an estimate of Soviet strategic systems as of 1965:

	Number of Vehicles	Yield (megatons)	Total Yield (megatons)
Strategic Missiles	200	10-30	3,200
Strategic Bombers	190	20 (est.)	3,800
Missile Submarines	120	.5 (est.)	60
(40 with 3 missiles each)			
	510		7,060 (megatons)

Match the estimated 510 strategic nuclear-weapon vehicles in the Soviet arsenal with 132 U.S. cities having populations of 100,000 or more. Even if we assume a hypothetical 50% attrition of Soviet delivery vehicles, the remaining 205 would be more than competent to destroy all these communities. The overkill capability of 7 billion tons of TNT-equivalent in the Soviet strategic vehicles can also be reckoned in terms of "Hiroshima units." Again assuming a 50% loss of these delivery vehicles, the residual Soviet megatonage would have an overkill factor of more than 100 on U.S. population-industrial centers. Again, I emphasize that there is no way of "knowing" what the overkill factors in nuclear war "really" could be. Such proof is humanly and militarily needless.

The final meaning of the military power that now resides in American and in Soviet hands was described by Secretary of Defense McNamara in November, 1964. He stated:

As President Johnson pointed out only recently, the total number of Americans killed in battle from the Revolution until today is a little over 526,000 people. A full-scale nuclear exchange between the United States and the USSR would kill 100 million Americans during the first hour. It would kill an even greater number of Russians. I doubt that any sane person would call this "victory." Every President in the nuclear era has stated emphatically his belief that there can be no victors in a full-scale nuclear war.

Despite such frank and honest statements, the present plans of the Department of Defense include major additions to the nuclear strategic stockpile: a system of the new F-111 aircraft (once called TFX) with intercontinental range, involving 1,700 new airplanes, each capable of carrying the equivalent of 10 megatons, thereby adding a potential 17,000 megatons to the 19,000 now deliverable; 300 additional Minuteman missiles are now programmed; the Polaris submarine fleet is to have 12 additional vessels carrying a total of 192 additional strategic missiles; and all of this is apart from the continuous expansion of the stockpile of tactical nuclear warheads and their delivery vehicles, which, according to the Secretary of Defense, already number in the "tens of thousands."

In a statement to the Congress in February, 1963, Secretary of Defense McNamara summarized the meaning of the United States-USSR overkill confrontation in these terms:

As the events of last October [1962] have so forcefully demonstrated, the expanding arsenals of nuclear weapons on both sides of the Iron Curtain have created an extremely dangerous situation not only for their possessors but also for the entire world. As the arms race continues and the weapons multiply and become more swift and deadly, the possibility of a global catastrophe, either by miscalculation or design, becomes ever more real.

More armaments, whether offensive or defensive, cannot solve this dilemma. We are approaching an era when it will become increasingly improbable that either side could destroy a sufficiently large portion of the other's strategic nuclear force, either by surprise or otherwise, to preclude a devastating retaliatory blow. This may result in mutual deterrence, but it is still a grim prospect. It underscores the need for a renewed

effort to find some way, if not to eliminate these deadily weapons completely, then at least to slow down or halt their further accumulation, and to create institutional arrangements
which would reduce the need for either side to resort to their
immediate use in moments of acute international tension.

The United States and the Soviet Union, as the two great nuclear powers, are the nations most directly endangered by these
weapons and, therefore, have a great mutual interest in seeing
to it that they are never used. But until we can find a safe and
sure road to disarmament, we must continue to build our own
defenses. . . .

In my statement a year ago, I pointed out that "as the Soviet
Union hardens and disperses its ICBM force and acquires a
significant number of missile launching submarines (as we must
assume that they will do in the period under discussion) our
problem will be further complicated." There is increasing evidence that this is the course the Soviet Union is following. . . .

A very large increase in the number of fully hardened Soviet
ICBM's and nuclear-powered ballistic missile launching submarines would considerably detract from our ability to destroy
completely the Soviet strategic nuclear forces. It would become
increasingly difficult, regardless of the form of the attack, to
destroy a sufficiently large proportion of the Soviet's strategic
nuclear forces to preclude major damage to the United States,
regardless of how large or what kind of strategic forces we
build. Even if we were to double and triple our forces we would
not be able to destroy quickly all, or almost all, of the hardened ICBM sites. And even if we could do that, we know no
way to destroy the enemy's missile launching submarines at
the same time. We do not anticipate that either the United
States or the Soviet Union will acquire that capability in the
foreseeable future. . . .

Mr. McNamara used a double standard in stating: "Until we
can find a safe and sure road to disarmament, we must continue to
build our own defenses." He characterizes the present arms race

as unsafe and uncertain, while specifying that the road to disarmament must be safe and sure. Americans have yet to understand
that no present or conceivable policy is risk-free.

Most important, the realities and military implications of our
nuclear-ringed world clash with the traditional understanding that
the industrial power of the United States can be used to develop
military superiority and thereby to build a base for national security. That military superiority is no longer purchasable *at any
price* is a conclusion Americans are finding very hard to take. I
think the reaction that greeted Mr. McNamara's reasoning in the
Armed Services Committee of the House of Representatives is
illuminating. In the following exchange Mr. McNamara is ques-
tioned by Congressman Gerald Ford of Michigan:

MR. FORD: When do we reach this period of mutual deterrence which is a "grim prospect"?

SECRETARY MCNAMARA: I think that date on which we reach
it is difficult to pinpoint with any accuracy because in part deterrence is a frame of mind.

I cannot open the mind of the Soviet leaders. The point I
tried to make and which point I worded very carefully was expressed by the sentence: "We are approaching an era when it
will become increasingly improbable that either side could
destroy a sufficiently large portion of the other's strategic nuclear force . . ."

That I think we can demonstrate by comparing the relative
change in our strategic nuclear forces versus the estimated relative change in the Soviet forces.

MR. FORD: Why must we assume that this is going to come
to pass?

SECRETARY MCNAMARA: Well, I have not assumed it. I have
said, "We are approaching an era when it will become increasingly improbable." I do not assume it is coming to pass. I believe we are approaching that era.

MR. FORD: Why do we have to approach that era? Are we so
unimaginative, lacking in skill and diligence, to permit this to
be upon us relatively soon?

SECRETARY MCNAMARA: I do not believe we are either unimaginative, or lacking in skill, but I do believe that a careful assessment of the probable increases in the Soviet nuclear power as estimated by the experienced intelligence evaluators in our Government indicate that power will increase in such ways, particularly in such types, that there will not be a possibility for us to build a force that can destroy that power to such a degree that there will not remain elements so large as to cause severe damage to our Nation in retaliation for our destructive effort directed against that power.

MR. FORD: In other words, you are saying that for technical reasons, scientific, engineering reasons, we have to assume that we are moving into an era of mutual deterrence. . . .

I refuse to believe—and I think this has been the traditional attitude of the American people—that we must concede that we cannot be sufficient militarily, that we must accept a position that is a grim prospect. I have never known us to assume that or to believe that or to concede that in the past. Why are we doing it now?

SECRETARY MCNAMARA: I am not certain I understand what you refuse to accept.

MR. FORD: I refuse to accept that the competence, the quality, and technical skill of the American people as a whole is insufficient to prevent this grim prospect from taking place which you describe.

SECRETARY MCNAMARA: If by that you mean you refuse to believe that with the ability and imagination which we possess we cannot develop a sure means to destroy the missile launching submarines, then I can only disagree with you, because I have carefully considered this problem with the best minds and the best brains in the Defense Department, with the best minds and the best brains in the scientific community, on which the Defense Department draws for technical assistance and counsel, and I have found no one who states that they anticipate it will be possible in the next several years.

(Statement off the record.)

SECRETARY MCNAMARA: It appears to me my conclusion is

justified, and I see no evidence to support any conclusion to the contrary.

MR. FORD: Your statement that we are facing this grim prospect is predicated on weapons systems in being and those that are in the process of being procured and produced. Is that correct?

SECRETARY MCNAMARA: It is predicated on our weapons systems in being, the known technology in our possession that will affect weapons systems development over the next several years, available inteligence on Soviet weapons systems in being, and the best possible estimates of the probable further development of Soviet weapons systems between now and the date we are discussing, that is to say, 1968.

MR. FORD: Do we have any weapons systems of any kind that are being funded in this budget to preclude this grim prospect?

SECRETARY MCNAMARA: We have a series of development projects underway. Off the record.

(Discussion off the record.)

MR. FORD: This acceptance that we are in a period of grim prospect, I must admit shocks me. I repeat, as I said a few minutes ago, I refuse to concede that the ingenuity and the industry of 180-some million Americans cannot be channeled to preclude this grim prospect from being on the doorstep of the United States. I am surprised that we concede it. This is what you are telling us.

SECRETARY MCNAMARA: Mr. Ford, yesterday you quite properly pointed out the danger of underestimating one's opponent. I would simply emphasize today that I share your sentiments. I think you seriously underestimate our opponent if you believe that between now and the period we are talking about the ingenuity of the American people can develop certain techniques and systems such as so to destroy the Soviet nuclear forces to such an extent as to leave surviving such a small force that it could not accomplish severe damage when directed against this Nation. I know of no responsible person, including our leading military advisers, and including our leading scientific and engineering consultants, who would share your conclusion.

MR. FORD: I am not underestimating the enemy. I am just disappointed that we are not willing to gamble on our own competence and come up with some weapons systems both offensive and defensive that would prevent this from taking place.

SECRETARY MCNAMARA: Again, I do not believe it is a question of gambling or not gambling. It is a question of concentrating the scientific and engineering know-how of our Nation upon a very serious problem. We have so concentrated it, and we have not found the solution.

Behind the drama of this confrontation is the technological transformation in military power caused by the application of nuclear energy. Let me briefly restate the facts. On the offensive side the matter is straightforward: Adding to overkill capability has no military meaning. Neither people nor communities can be killed more than once. On the defensive side the concentration factor in nuclear energy release frustrates all conceivable defensive technologies. Defensive efficiency of 99% is not known and is not predictable. Even if it were obtained, placed against an overkill factor of 100 or more, even 99% defense is not good enough. A residual overkill of one is quite sufficient.

Jerome Weisner and Herbert York, science advisors to the Kennedy and Eisenhower administrations respectively, have put the matter in the following terms. During the Second World War, defensive interception of 10% of the attacking Luftwaffe over England gave a victory to the defense. This was so because of the limited destructive power involved. A 10% interception rate meant that a bomber could deliver only 10 payloads of high explosives on the average; the sum of these explosives was not militarily significant enough to be worth a 10% rate of loss. According to Weisner and York:

In warfare by thermonuclear missiles, the situation is quantitatively and qualitatively different. It is easily possible for the offensive to have in its possession and ready to launch a number of missiles that exceeds the number of important industrial targets to be attacked by, let us say, a factor of ten. Yet, the successful delivery of only one warhead against each such target would result in what most people would consider an effective attack. Thus, where an attrition rate of only 10 percent formerly crowned the defense with success, a penetration rate of only 10 percent (corresponding to an attrition rate of 90 percent) would give complete success to the offense.

This change of advantage in favor of the offensive in nuclear war marks the termination of meaningful military advantage among nations, each of whom is equipped with major nuclear offensive ability. America's 3,400 strategic missiles and planes are not "more effective" than the USSR's 510. Both can overkill, and the numerical differences in such forces have lost military— or any human—meaning.

Classically, wars have been won when one side destroyed the military capability of the other. Then the victor could take control of the society of the loser. Such possibilities are frustrated by the condition of nuclear strategic parity: Each major nuclear power becomes competent to destroy the society of the other, regardless of differences in the numbers of weapons, and independently of who strikes first. These conditions define the termination of war-making as a workable proposition among great powers. The same reasoning defines the creation of additional nuclear military power as an exercise in futility, on its own account and for the entire human race.

One of the articles of faith that most Americans have lived by during recent years is that having nuclear weapons really protects us, and that having more of them means that we just have that much more protection. The idea that nuclear weapons protect probably had its origin in our understanding of how the Second World War ended.

Most Americans, officials and private citizens, have believed that the surrender of Japan in World War II not only followed but was *caused by* the dropping of the two atomic bombs on Hiroshima and Nagasaki. The bombs were to show the Japanese that further fighting was hopeless. Americans felt that dropping the bombs had saved the lives of possibly a million Americans and as many Japanese who would have been lost in massive landings and fighting on the Japanese homeland. Therefore, it was reasoned, the dropping of the bombs on Hiroshima and Nagasaki, while regrettable, nevertheless was a necessary act to persuade the Japanese Government that there was no alternative but to surrender.

However, after the Second World War, American scholars were able to examine the detailed records of the Japanese Government and interview Japanese officials. It was discovered that the Japanese Cabinet included a group that wanted to end the war as well as a group that was determined to fight a battle to the death for the defense of the Japanese home islands. From the records of their discussions that became available to American scholars, it was learned that the dropping of the atomic bombs *had caused no change in the alignment of the "pro-war" and the "pro-peace" groups in the Japanese Government.* The decisive proximate factor in the surrender of Japan was the United States Government's modification of "unconditional surrender."

To most Japanese the Emperor and the Imperial House were more than civil institutions. They were sacred within the context of Japanese religion. Accordingly, a surrender that doomed the Emperor was unthinkable, and Japanese leaders were prepared to organize a defense-to-the-death of the home islands. Surrender that included agreement to spare the Imperial institution was thinkable. The United States Government, upon inquiry from the Japanese Government, implied that the Emperor was not slated for automatic removal, but that the authority of the Emperor and of the Japanese Government should "be subject to the Supreme Commander of the Allied Powers." This concession met the Japanese political leaders' minimum terms for surrender, which was promptly agreed upon.

It appears that even the actual use of the bombs did not have the decisive persuasive effect that Americans have long believed. In Japanese eyes, the war, as a military operation, was understood to be lost long before atomic bombs were dropped. But unconditional surrender was unthinkable so long as that meant removal of the Emperor. The place of the Imperial House in Japanese culture and society has no counterpart at all in the culture of the United States. Americans did not, probably could not, perceive the role which this issue played in Japan.

The significance of this understanding of the end of World War II for today is this: The Japanese surrender is not a sufficient basis for assuming that vast quantities of atomic weapons necessarily protect the United States. We have assumed that simply the threat of destruction implied in the wielding of nuclear weapons would serve as a competent deterrent to actions by other governments against the United States.

Having confidence in this theory, Americans have paid an enormous price in material goods and in the quality of their life to purchase a security system whose basis is that the possession and wielding of masses of nuclear weapons would indeed guarantee security. We have had two tests for the validity of this reasoning. First, the surrender of Japan. The assumption has been that this was caused by the nuclear demonstrations of overwhelming military power, namely on Hiroshima and Nagasaki. We now have strong grounds for doubting the conventional assumption that this was caused simply by superior military power. Second, we had the experience of the nuclear confrontation over Soviet missiles in Cuba. Americans and Russians faced the bedrock reality of nuclear armaments: Each side could destroy the other, and neither side could defend itself against the attack of the other. The United States, in October, 1962, had overwhelming numerical nuclear superiority vis-à-vis the Soviets. This fact and the Soviets' knowledge of it, did not deter them from attempting to emplace nuclear-armed medium-range missiles in Cuba.

Several things have become clear about nuclear weapons: First, if used on two sides in war, nobody wins; second, their use by one side (as against Japan) does not necessarily control the political decisions—even about surrender—of the other side; third, overwhelming numerical overkill in nuclear weapons does not decisively deter political or nuclear military moves by America's opponents, or by the United States itself.

Some Pentagon strategists responded to this impasse with the scheme of "prevailing" at the close of nuclear war operated with priority to destruction of enemy weapons. But "prevailing" means having more missiles left than the enemy even though the country is devastated. Who would operate the remaining weapons? Who would care?

Strategic theories took a new turn: Let the nuclear arsenal, and conventional forces, be so devised as to give military and political commanders a great array of options concerning which weapons to use under particular situations; let the use of these weapons be regulated through highly centralized control. Nuclear weapons could then be launched, if their use is unavoidable, in controlled salvos so aimed as to persuade an enemy that it is in his best interests to curtail a nuclear war and come to terms.

These speculations on the use of nuclear warheads as a super-persuader rest upon unrealistic assumptions. The destructiveness of nuclear weapons virtually excludes the likelihood of retaining reliable control over tens of thousands of planes and missiles from control centers which are themselves subject to massive attack. Is Washington, D.C., supposed to be immune to nuclear attack, permitting the President to dash for his helicopter en route to one of the central command posts? Could both Soviet and American leaders respond to a major nuclear exchange by sitting back and considering in a detached way (with the help of computers) whether it was worth while to continue? This involves assumptions about human nature, availability of information, and the capabilities of human beings under extreme tension that simply go beyond any human experience.

All of the strategic reasoning for waging a "successful nuclear war" neglects this fact: While we have been successfully buying "more bang for a buck," the Soviets have been buying "more ruble for a ruble." We have both succeeded.

The chairman of the Senate Armed Services Committee has warned against these theories of "controlled counter-force" nuclear war as altogether misleading. Senator Richard Russell stated on April 11, 1962:

There have been some estimates and some so-called mathematical computations of the casualties that would result from a nuclear war under various assumptions, including a positive attempt by the adversaries to limit targeting in military installations and facilities. I have no hesitancy in saying, however, that to me these extrapolations, or projections, or hypotheses, are exceedingly unrealistic. In my opinion, if nuclear war begins, it will be a war of extermination.

The Pentagon, however, continues to press for ever more costly additions to the overkill stockpile.

Many Americans have yet to learn that a population can be killed only once, and that adding to overkill cannot add to military security.

Professors Weisner and York have summarized the nature of the big-power arms race:

> Both sides in the arms race are thus confronted by the dilemma of steadily increasing military power and steadily decreasing national security. *It is our considered professional judgment that this dilemma has no technical solution.* If the great powers continue to look for solutions in the area of science and technology only, the result will be to worsen the situation. The clearly predictable course of the arms race is a steady open spiral downward into oblivion.

None of this is altered by the various deterrence theories. Nuclear deterrence strategies are two-sided: In a confrontation, each side is encouraged by its deterrence theory to assume that the other will be rationally deterred from acting. The possibility of a collision is thereby accelerated because each side feels free to act in the confidence that the other has been rationally deterred. The Cuban missile crisis of October, 1962, was one chilling experiment involving these possibilities. In the Japanese surrender of World War II we *know* that Japanese rationality was not the same as ours.

I have appended to this chapter a schematic statement of the essential nature of the military transformation that has been wrought by the introduction of nuclear weapons.

Given the United States and the Soviet Union examples of how to behave, many other nations also seek nuclear military power. This objective becomes ever more feasible as the technologies involved are simplified and reduced in cost. In October, 1964, Secretary of Defense McNamara pointed out that American nuclear warheads ". . . cost anywhere from roughly half a million dollars on up, perhaps, to a million dollars.

"We anticipate in the years ahead, because of advances in nuclear technology, the cost of nuclear weapons will fall dramatically," Mr. McNamara went on. "As it falls, and as the technology becomes simpler, we can expect more and more nations to acquire capability for both developing and producing such weapons.

"You can imagine the danger that the world would face if 10, 20 or 30 nations possessed nuclear warheads instead of the four that possess them today."

Moreover, there are no plausible grounds for expecting new nuclear powers to be stymied in using their nuclear armament because of limited numbers and varieties of delivery vehicles. Americans need to become accustomed to the idea that technological capabilities usually involve a large number of alternatives. Our attention has been focused on the more complex and costly military alternatives. But nuclear warheads could, for example, be delivered (placed in position for use) by the relatively simple device of building a large nuclear warhead into an underwater mine and carrying it in any ocean-going vessel to the three-mile limit off a seacoast. Such warheads could be triggered by remote control. Having no motion that discloses their presence, they would not be detectable by the elaborate, costly, early warning systems that were designed to warn the United States of bomber and missile attacks from the direction of the USSR. Such underwater nuclear warheads could generate catastrophic tidal waves and lethal water-borne fallout along American coasts, and the technological capability for doing this is probably within the reach of countries that either now have, or soon could have, nuclear warheads. This includes China.

During the four years 1961-64, the budget of the Department of Defense exceeded the rate of military spending during the

Eisenhower years by a total of $30 billion. The military professionals, as well as the members of Congress who review and vote on military budgets, were caught up in a fruitless search for military advantage despite the technological revolution in the military art that has been brought about by nuclear power. They have not been able to face up to the new condition that the search for military advantage has become an exercise in futility. It is no wonder then, that the Office of the Assistant Secretary for the Air Force issued a memorandum in 1964 declaring that ". . . the overkill concept . . . is now haunting the Pentagon."

In February, 1964, Secretary of Defense McNamara presented his annual statement on defense affairs to the Committee on Armed Services of the U.S. Senate. When Mr. McNamara completed his introductory report and the section on strategic systems, he turned to the Committee and invited questions. Senator Russell, the Chairman of the Committee, responded:

CHAIRMAN RUSSELL: From your analysis . . . Mr. Secretary, our forces have almost reached the number under the overkill theory that the Columbia University group predicted.

SECRETARY McNAMARA: Yes Sir. I think that we have almost reached that point. I say "almost" because I don't think we are there yet, and we are proposing therefore the procurement of 50 additional MINUTEMAN silos in the fiscal 1965 budget.

CHAIRMAN RUSSELL: I never have believed, of course, that we could possibly foresee every intangible that might be involved. Man never has been able since the day of the bow and arrow, to predict exactly what is going to happen in any war that has ever been fought.

There will be some matters overlooked that will undoubtedly arise.

SECRETARY McNAMARA: I fully share that view, Mr. Chairman.

It appears that members of Congress are troubled by the appearance of overkill and its meaning—military, economic and political. Article 1, Section 8 of the Constitution of the United

States assigns to Congress the ". . . power to . . . provide for the common defense and general welfare of the United States. . . ." As Congressmen and other Americans perceive that a limit has been reached in meaningful military power, the question arises: Should defense budgets be continued at the same levels?

Americans have become so accustomed to huge military budgets that our sense of proportion has been dulled. For the fiscal year 1964, for instance, the defense budget request totaled $56.7 billion. But how much is that, really? Comprehension glimmers if we consider that only three European countries—France, West Germany, and the United Kingdom—had total outputs of goods and services of greater money value than the U.S. defense budget for 1964. Our understanding grows when we learn that the 1964 defense budget of $56.7 billion exceeded the combined budgets of the entire Federal Government, for all purposes, for the period 1933-39. And comprehension is stunned by the realization that the new spending for military purposes during fiscal year 1964 was twice the amount spent on education of every sort by the Federal, state, and local governments combined: that is, for the education of 50 million Americans.

Ordinarily, the defense budget has been willingly supported on the grounds that it produces a priceless result, national security; the ability of the nation to be autonomous, self-governing, to conduct itself according to the values and standards that it prefers. While military power serves this purpose, the American people are overwhelmingly in favor of sizable military expenditures, so long as it can be shown that this is the most practicable course for getting the desired result and that other reasonable methods are not available. But national security is one thing; overkill is another matter altogether.

What has been the cost of overkill to American society?

The pile-up of meaningless military capability is a form of expensive busy-work. Its cost is not only the budgeted money for these purposes, but also the shoddy education system, the poor housing, the neglected medical-care needs, the polluted streams —in short, the whole array of depletion at home and abroad due to the productive activity foregone because of the concentration of talent and capital and materials in the military sphere.

The 1964 defense budget of $56.7 billion included the budgets of the Department of Defense, the Atomic Energy Commission, and the military-assistance program overseas. With the sparse data available to the public on the Department of Defense budget, I have attempted to estimate the portion of the budget that consists of additions to the overkill stockpile. The essential idea is this: Removing the sums that add to overkill should leave a remainder sufficient to operate and maintain the military establishment as it exists. Such a maintenance-of-present-forces budget was calculated. It totaled $34.2 billion, or $22 billion less than the Administration budget in 1964. Here is the comparison between these two budgets, using the titles that appear in the budget of the United States Government:

Major Military Functions	Administration Budget (1964) (millions of $)	Maintenance-of-Present-Forces Budget (millions of $)
Military personnel		
Present programs	$13,235	$13,235
Pay increase	900	900
Operation and Maintenance	11,792	11,792
Procurement	16,725	5,725
Research, Development, Test	7,262	262
Military construction	1,232	—
Family housing	734	734
Civil defense	300	—
Military assistance	1,480	480
Atomic Energy Commission	2,893	1,093
Defense-related Activities		
Strategic materials stockpile	28	—
Selective Service	38	38
Emergency preparedness	82	—
Totals	$56,702	$34,260

I want to indicate immediately that the limited information available from published sources does not enable anyone outside of the Defense establishment to do a detailed analysis of the cost of overkill in the 1964 budget. The best I could do with more detailed categories than those I show above was to estimate a range of possible budget reductions totaling $16.45 to $25.65 billion. I presented these suggested reductions to the Committees on

Armed Services of the House of Representatives and the Senate with the proposal that they be used as guides in the sort of detailed examination for which these Committees are responsible.

In the maintenance-of-present-forces budget, the Personnel and Operations and Maintenance proposals of the Administration are left intact, while Procurement is slated for a cut of $11 billion. The rate of spending for long-range missile production, research, testing, and development was running close to $7 billion a year. (This does not include aircraft and other types of delivery vehicles such as Polaris submarines and other naval vessels.)

Major reduction is recommended for the Research, Development, and Test item on the grounds that there is no conceivable technological break-through that could end the nuclear stalemate. Furthermore, it is no longer reasonable to expect that improvement in a military system as a whole could result from a sum of detailed improvements such as a better rifle, a better engine, missiles that would land a calculated 50 yards closer to their targets. Fifty yards does not count for much when the warhead atomizes everything within one mile of its center.

Research and Development also includes more than $1 billion for military astronautics and related equipment. This is apart from the $5 billion budget of the National Aeronautics and Space Administration. The military item is for spending by the Air Force, mostly in an effort to find some role for the military in space where, apart from designing and launching observation satellites, no one has been able to define a meaningful role. Putting nuclear bombs in orbit is an incredibly dangerous exercise and, in any case, delivering warheads is done more cheaply and more reliably from one place on earth to another, rather than launching them from outer space. But the Air Force, accounting for about half of the military budget, is a political power to be reckoned with; it has been able to command substantial sums to be used in an effort to discover new military goals for itself, even while its classic function as an operator of military aircraft has decreased in importance because of the development of missile technology.

It seems reasonable to curtail new military construction on the grounds that by 1963 the Defense Department already had 341,-

000 buildings within the United States alone. The civil-defense item is cut out on the ground that the civil-defense concept is technically faulty and politically dangerous. [See data and analysis in S. Melman, *No Place to Hide,* Grove Press: New York, N.Y., 1962.] Military assistance deserves major reduction or combination with other activities.

The Atomic Energy Commission budget is slated for major reduction on the grounds that the operation of its weapons-producing factories at Hanford, Washington, Paducah, Kentucky, Oak Ridge, Tennessee, and elsewhere, cost $1.8 billion a year. In 1963, it was disclosed that the AEC already had in stock surplus fissionable material valued at about $1 billion. Further operation of these factories for the military is the most obvious sort of waste.

The sum of these calculations is a sharp reduction in a military budget designed to be responsive to the simple provision of not adding further to overkill. This is not in any sense a disarmament budget insofar as it does not reduce, but rather maintains, existing military power.

It is difficult to comprehend the magnitude of possible expenditures for military purposes were we to follow the escalating recommendations of the various armed services. Some officers have pressed for a $15 billion program for the development and construction of antimissile weapons systems, despite the fact that such systems would be doomed to ineffectiveness for technical reasons. No conceivable defensive system could overcome the offensive advantage that is inherent in the number and power of nuclear weapons, in relation to population-industrial centers. Such a program, however, would require the construction of a major shelter system to try to protect the population from the radioactive fallout caused by the antimissile warheads bursting overhead. A large-scale shelter system for the United States would cost about $300 billion and would not work. All told, the recommendations of the military enthusiasts could easily lead to an annual military budget of $175 billion. I have shown the composition of such a budget and its policy meaning in Column 1 of the chart on "The Structure of Alternative Security Policies and Budgets," which you will find in the back of this book. (Appendix B.)

The prospect of more elaborate and more costly military technologies has, predictably, excited those people who try to forecast the future of particular industries. In 1963 the U.S. Department of Labor, for example, forecast growth in the electronic industry from 1961 to 1970. Out of an estimated $306 million of increased annual sales during that period, 61% is supposed to be due to growth in the military and space markets. Large-scale spending for defense purposes over a long period has generated intense economic dependency in the important military-industrial areas. In Los Angeles, for example, 42.6% of all manufacturing employment during 1961 was tied directly or indirectly to orders from the Department of Defense and the National Aeronautics and Space Administration.

Perhaps we can get a more meaningful view of the cost of defense and overkill if we think of their price in terms of dwelling, schools, and medical-care items. Here are some illustrations:

One TFX airplane, $5,000,000.

> = 13 elementary schools, or
> 570 dwelling units in low rent public housing projects, or
> 278 hospital beds.

One Polaris Submarine with 16 missiles, $122,600,000.

> = 331 elementary schools, or
> 6,811 hospital beds, or
> 13,723 dwelling units in low rent public housing.

Military Space Program (Military Astronautics and Related Equipment) 1965 estimate, $1,283,714,000.

> = 71,317 hospital beds, or
> 3,469 elementary schools, or
> 143,688 dwelling units in low rent public housing.

Civil Defense Budget for Fiscal Year 1965, $358,000,000.

> = 40,071 dwelling units in low rent public housing projects, or
> 967 elementary schools, or
> 249 secondary schools, or
> 19,900 hospital beds, or
> 32,545 nursing home beds, or
> 795 miles of highway in rural areas, or
> 223 miles of highway in urban areas.

Atomic Energy Commission, Nuclear Weapons Program 1965, $1,800,000,000.

= 4,864 elementary schools, or
201,477 dwelling units in low rent public housing projects, or
100,000 hospital beds.

Based upon:

elementary school $370,000
secondary school $1,433,000
1 mile rural road $450,000
1 mile city road $1,600,000
1 hospital "bed" $18,000
1 nursing-home "bed" $11,000
1 low-rent apartment $8,934

How did we ever reach a level of defense spending that amounts to more than half of the Federal budget? I doubt that it is possible to answer this question properly with the information now available to the public. Still, we can begin to understand by examining the list of military "gap" crises: the bomber gap, the missile gap, the conventional forces gap, and the latest, the counterinsurgency gap.

During the mid-1950's there was widespread clamor in the United States over a predicted bomber gap. On the assumption that the Soviets could and would devote very large industrial resources to constructing many hundreds of long-range bombers, it was held that the United States must set up an elaborate early-warning system as well as a counterprogram of long-range bomber construction. The multibillion dollar North American Air Defense network (NORAD) was established, and a large heavy-bomber program was organized and funded.

By 1961, there was a great outcry in the United States over a predicted missile gap. This discussion played an important role in the 1960 Presidential election. President Eisenhower and his Defense Secretary, Thomas S. Gates, Jr., denied the existence of a missile gap, but the political atmosphere in the United States at that time made the missile-gap claim seem plausible.

The purveyors of the missile gap could build on fifteen years of Cold War suspicion, the popular dismay over the Soviet's sputniks, and the fear that U.S. military pre-eminence was about to be lost to the Soviets. The cooler heads in responsible positions —including President Eisenhower and his Secretary of Defense— who perceived the nuclear revolution in military power, were unable, even with their firm, matter-of-fact reassurance, to persuade the American people that there was no gap.

The condition in 1965 is summarized by the estimates I have given here of the number of strategic delivery vehicles available to the United States and the Soviet Union. The United States has a numerical preponderance of 6 to 1.

At what point did the United States Government have firm information concerning the actual size of Soviet bomber forces and Soviet missile forces? Looking back over the last fifteen years, we find important clues that bear on this question.

On May 1, 1960, Francis Gary Powers was shot down over the USSR in a U-2 reconnaissance plane. These flights had been taking place since 1956. President Eisenhower's Defense Secretary Gates pointed out on June 2, 1960, with respect to the U-2 flights: ". . . from these flights we got information on airfields, aircraft, missiles, missile testing and training, special weapons storage, submarine production, atomic production and aircraft deployment . . . all types of vital information."

Soon after the U-2 flights over the USSR ceased, United States technology made possible a satellite, orbiting 125 miles above the earth's surface, containing cameras capable of differentiating objects 3 inches apart. The SAMOS reconnaissance satellites produced a very large number of highly detailed photographs of the Soviet Union and other areas. Mr. Howard Simons, staff reporter of The Washington *Post*, published a very informative article on December 8, 1963, concerning "Our Fantastic Eye in the Sky." The SAMOS satellites, he wrote, "helped American intelligence officials reassess and down-grade previous estimates of Soviet intercontinental ballistic missile strength; that is, to show that the so-called 'missile gap' was non-existent."

Here is another clue. During the spring of 1963, a series of news dispatches from Moscow reported on the trial and execution of Mr. Oleg Penkovsky, a senior Soviet science official who had been functioning for some time as a Western intelligence agent. Mr. Penkovsky, it was reported, had dispatched 5,000 frames of microfilm to the West.

Taking this evidence together, it is plausible to infer that by 1957 (after a year of U-2 flights) the United States Government was in possession of detailed information concerning Soviet bombers and Soviet missiles. This was certainly the case by 1960-61, which means that the aircraft and missile programs originally prompted by fear of a Soviet advantage were carried through to completion and were not cut back even *after* defense officials had in their possession hard information from multiple sources that defined the quality and size of the overwhelming American numerical advantage in both aircraft and missiles.

Let us now take a close look at the "conventional forces gap." Since the end of the Second World War the understanding has been widespread in the West that Soviet conventional forces were overwhelmingly more numerous than our own. In an address to the Economic Club of New York on November 18, 1963, Secretary of Defense McNamara reported that the actual number of active Soviet divisions was less than half the widely reported figure of 160-175 divisions. "Furthermore," he said, "what remains is a large number but even that is misleading. . . . United States divisions have about twice as many men in the division unit and its immediate combat supporting units than comparable Soviet divisions. A United States mechanized division has far more personnel and maneuvering units, far more in armored cavalry, far more engineers, far more signals, far more light armored personnel carriers, and far more aircraft available in support than Soviet divisions." The Warsaw Pact forces, he indicated, total about 4.5 million men, as against the armed forces of NATO countries, which exceed 5 million. "In Central Europe," he said, "NATO has more men and more combat troops on the ground than does the Bloc. It has more men on the ground in West Germany than the Bloc does in East Germany. It has more and better tactical aircraft, and these planes on the average can carry twice the payload twice as far as their Soviet counterparts." In a word: as of 1963, at least, there clearly was no conventional-forces gap.

From 1960 to 1965, very much was made of an alleged lack of American preparation in the field of "counterinsurgency" forces. One of the early actions of the Kennedy Administration was the rapid development of several Special Forces units trained in counter-guerrilla warfare tactics.

What makes guerrillas successful is their personal dedication; their technical ability to melt into a surrounding population; and finally, popular support of their activities from the surrounding population. When the nature of guerrilla warfare is defined in these terms, the intimate involvement of primarily political issues and political problems becomes apparent. From the description of the essential nature of successful guerrilla operations, it is quite clear that military-professional training for countering a guerrilla-style operation by military-technical methods is a futile exercise.

When the conditions required for guerrilla success are satisfied, then even overwhelming military power in opposition can be resisted for a long time by guerrilla forces. That is borne out by the German Army's massive and futile campaign against Jugoslav guerrillas during World War II, and by the inability of American-equipped South Vietnamese forces to subdue the Vietcong. In both cases a small number of men fought against major military forces on the strength of their readiness to take high personal risk and their ability to melt into the background population— as individuals or as groups. In this context political backing from the surrounding population is the key factor. Military-tactical considerations play a part, but not a controlling part. Nevertheless, the Army's Limited Warfare Laboratory has concentrated on streamlined balloons, portable landing platforms for helicopters in jungles, leech repellents, antiambush devices, gliders to be towed by helicopters, improved air-to-ground rockets, and similar devices.

The dismal warfare in South Vietnam has afforded a critical experiment in the viability of the military counter-insurgency theory. The idea that "our" guerrillas should be trained to fight "their" guerrillas makes no sense on military or political grounds. The political conflicts represented by guerrilla activity cannot be resolved as a form of military-tactical exercise. Insofar as military methods are being applied to essentially political issues, the counter-insurgency programs are a case of mistaken identification and misplaced emphasis.

Why this plague of defense gaps developed is a problem for the future, when one might hope for more information on the interior working of the Defense Department, various trade associations, and the calculations of political parties. These defense gaps are probably the joint product of concern for national security coupled with press agentry, constraints on military intelligence, industrial lobbying, and struggles for government appropriations favoring one or the other military service. Apart from the politics of the defense gaps, what is crucial for this analysis is that they all proved to be fictions and costly at that.

The available evidence supports the inference that from about 1957 on—that is, after a year of U-2 flights—the Government of the United States was well informed, as Defense Secretary Gates stated, concerning Soviet aircraft and missile capability. Accordingly, the escalation of American defense budgets to the levels that produced the current enormous United States preponderance in overkill capability must be understood as the economic toll taken by these gap fictions. The cost includes the research, development, production, operation and maintenance of the U.S. overkill weapons and forces that exceed the Soviet stockpile. For 1964 I estimated that the overkill component of the defense budget was about 40%—not including operation and maintenance of these forces in being. From 1957-1965 the increments to defense budgets owing to nonexistent gaps could hardly be less than one fourth to one third of the defense budgets through that period. Total defense spending from 1957 to 1965 was $440 billion. Therefore, the direct spending on overkill that was prompted by the fictitious gaps amounted to between $110 to $146 billion.

This is not the total cost to American society. We must take into account the fact that the labor and capital resources that were used to produce this stock of overkill materiel could have been used to produce other goods and services for America, of equal money value. This means we must add to the estimate of direct cost an equal amount to take into account the value of goods and services foregone. The cost of the missile and bomber gaps to the United States was therefore between $220 and $290 billion.

Even if it should be shown one day that this estimate is overstated, the order of magnitude is probably correct. The use of such enormous resources for accumulating overkill military power goes far to explain how it is that the United States is beset by a pervasive depletion process.

In February, 1964, *Fortune* reported that the uranium-mining industry, which delivers the raw material for the warhead factories of the Atomic Energy Commission, "now drains $480 million a year from the Federal Treasury. By 1970, when the AEC's buying program is scheduled to end, the government will have spent $5.7 billion here and abroad; more than half of this outlay has occurred since 1958 when the AEC already knew that its appetite for the stuff was sated. There are now tens of thousands of atomic weapons in the United States arsenal and 350,000 kilograms of U-235 available for civilian nuclear-powered plants. In the face of this glut, government support obviously cannot go on indefinitely."

I would agree; but it has gone on long enough to cost the people of the United States, for this single item alone, $2.8 billion since 1958, when it was known that even the most extravagant of the military requirements, including the overkill buildup, had already been satisfied.

From 1953 to 1963 the Department of Defense canceled 63 major weapons projects that had been in the research or development stage. These contracts for never-completed aircraft, missiles, ships, and ordnance cost American citizens $6,816,000,000. During 1964 the Defense Department canceled the Mobile Medium Range Ballistic Missile scheme that cost $100 million, the Pluto nuclear engine for missiles after an outlay of $196 million, and the B-70 bomber project after spending $1.6 billion. The grand total for all this materiel found to be technically useless or otherwise unnecessary has been $8,712,000,000.

The B-70 bomber project produced two planes weighing

500,000 pounds each. The combined cost of the two planes has thus been $1,600 per pound of aircraft. Gold has long been priced at $560 per pound.

But the pile-up of weaponry continues. After all, the men who hold senior positions in private and public life reached adulthood at a time when "more military power" and "winning a big war" were phrases that still meant something. As the discussion between Secretary McNamara and Congressman Ford disclosed, it is really difficult for men reared in this tradition to comprehend the new condition where the use of even conventional military power by the United States carries the danger of escalation to nuclear conflict in which there can be no winner.

Two years after General Dwight D. Eisenhower left the White House with his historic warning about the growth of a military-industrial complex, he told the National Association of Manufacturers (December 7, 1962):

> ... When fifty billion dollars, in the name of security, is found in our annual budget, it behooves us all to demand explanations of how and why such sums are spent.
>
> Too much can, in some cases, be as bad as too little.
>
> There is the danger also that we may encourage a false belief that military expenditures accelerate a healthy corporate, regional, even national prosperity.
>
> Such a belief is now seemingly accepted by many despite the recognized fact that military growth and spending, beyond the proper demands of security, is sterile in promoting sound, economic progress and is ultimately destructive of creative, productive enterprise.
>
> The military-industrial complex—an unavoidable phenomenon of our situation today—must never be allowed to exercise a domination over American life.
>
> Surely we must be concerned that American industries in particular do not become so acutely dependent for their very existence upon defense contracts that they fail to protest expenditures that, in their judgment, exceed the needs of the nation.
>
> Our intellectual strength, manifested principally in the wid-

est and deepest possible education of our young people, in a nation-wide network of educational institutions and research laboratories and in an increasing command over our environment, is as essential to the nation's strength and vitality, and therefore to security, as is military power. . . .

THE NUCLEAR REVOLUTION IN MILITARY POWER*

Conventional (Pre-Overkill) Military Assumptions	Strategic Changes Due to Overkill Capability
1. Addition to offensive capability increases military power (or deterrence).	1. Addition to offensive capability in the overkill range does not add to military power (or deterrence): overkill of 1000 is not greater than overkill of 100, or 1.
2. Defensive systems can effectively protect sufficient numbers to insure an on-going society.	2. All defensive strategies and technologies can be saturated, overwhelmed or evaded by variety and quantity of offensive power. A 99% effective defense against overkill of more than 100 leaves overkill.
3. With plausible technological breakthroughs the shores of the United States can be shielded against military assault.	3. See proposition 2.
4. With sufficient nuclear delivery capability, the military power of the USSR could be destroyed and the U.S. spared a counterblow.	4. Hardened missile sites and submarine based missiles on both sides renders this strategy inoperative.
5. A nuclear war would be composed of a series of calculated, controlled nuclear weapons exchanges.	5. Major portion of military communication networks would be destroyed. Under stress of combat some military and civilian leaders could be expected to react independently, releasing the nuclear weapons at their command. (For example, the Commander of a Polaris Submarine has control of 16 missiles carrying the equivalent of 16 megatons of TNT.)

* These notes were prepared in collaboration with Alan L. Madian.

THE NUCLEAR REVOLUTION IN MILITARY POWER (Continued)

Conventional (Pre-Overkill) Military Assumptions	Strategic Changes Due to Overkill Capability
6. For military security a lead must be held in all relevant research and technology, together with a preponderance of military material.	6. This assumption is nullified by propositions 1 and 2 (above).
7. The total strength of our military system is maximized by improving the strength of each component.	7. Our total military power cannot be defined as the sum of the parts. Suboptimization—making a better warhead, a better antimissile missile, a better vehicle—is the prevailing approach of the Department of Defense, despite its nullification by propositions 1 and 2 (above).
8. We must be competent to cope with all military contingencies.	8. The United States is a wealthy society but not an infinitely wealthy society. For example, incomplete protection from fallout, which could cost 250 to 300 billion dollars, can be gained only at the expense of generating economic weakness which, in turn, weakens the security of the United States.
9. The United States must be prepared to absorb a nuclear first strike and have sufficient reserve power to strike back, punish the aggressor, and stop hostilities.	9. In 1960, Dr. Jerome Weisner advised that studies by the U.S. Army and Navy indicated that 200 secured missiles would be an adequate deterrent. We now possess 1,378 such missiles. The assumption that we need additional weapons to destroy Soviet missiles and allied weapons overlooks the relatively small Soviet delivery capability (and the relatively invulnerable hardened sites, and Soviet Polaris-type submarines). The Soviets would have to use their entire strength in a first blow in order to minimize the power of the counterattack. Our counterattack on military targets would be on empty holes.

THE NUCLEAR REVOLUTION IN MILITARY POWER (Continued)

Conventional (Pre-Overkill) Military Assumptions	Strategic Changes Due to Overkill Capability
10. Pre-eminent military power is the decisive requirement for successful conduct of American foreign policy.	10. When potential opponents each possess more than 100 times overkill, neither can be pre-eminent. Over 600 million Chinese went under Communist rule while the West had a nuclear monopoly. Industrial-economic power Is crucial for shaping the social and political systems of developing nations.

3

Profits Without Productivity

In 1959, "A group of foreign businessmen was touring the Underwood typewriter plant in Hartford, Conn. A workman turned from the assembly line and asked, 'You guys Italians?' One of the visitors nodded. 'You here to learn how to make typewriters?' The reply was soft but firm: 'No. We are here to teach you.' " The visitors were in fact members of the new top management team which Olivetti of Italy sent over to refurbish the Underwood firm.

The United States typewriter industry is an example of what can happen when the depletion of metal-working production equipment and technique continues over a long period of time. There are a number of important typewriter factories in the New England area, which once supplied virtually all the typewriter requirements of the United States. However, by 1963, about 60% of the typewriters sold in America were being imported.

One of the major typewriter-producing factories in the United States is housed in a graceful, old, multistory factory that is a fine specimen of late nineteenth-century New England textile-mill architecture. While a beginning was recently made toward modernizing this plant, the manufacturing continued with machinery that will soon qualify for museum status; while painting was done with ultramodern automatic equipment, the factory continued making small parts on lathes turned by overhead belts just like those in illustrations of the early Industrial Revolution. The management of this firm, over a long period, withdrew profits and did not reinvest in new production equipment. Research and development were substantially neglected and newer developments in production were not introduced. The firm relied on the stockpile of "Yankee know-how" and mechanical ingenuity that was available among its foremen and skilled workers. That class of production technique is not adequate for producing efficiently enough to absorb modern wage rates, while manufacturing a quality product at a price low enough to sell. I think it noteworthy that the Olivetti company of Italy purchased one of the major American typewriter firms, Underwood, and immediately began modernization of its factories and methods; but certainly the interests of Olivetti, with its Italian-based operation, will also be served by supplying its American sales organization with products from its home-based factories. Profits will probably be sustained from sales in the United States, but an important part of the production base of Olivetti-Underwood is not in this country.

Among the depleted industries the pattern varies: profits from U.S. sales while production is done abroad by foreign firms buying into American companies; American firms maintaining a production base in the United States, but putting fresh capital abroad; profitability maintained for a few firms that service a government market—as in shipbuilding—while the whole level of activity of the industry declines; general decline in an industry owing to long-standing management failure to invest enough in new technology—as in fishery industries, railroads. The common feature of all the depleted industries is less work in the United States.

The one industry which may be said to be most basic to a society utilizing metal and machines is the machine-tool industry. Machine tools are usually understood to include all those machines that remove metal in the form of chips, or that shape metal by pressing it between dies. The products of this industry, the lathes, milling machines, drills, and the like, are the machines which are used to manufacture all other machines.

In 1963, the United States reached the position of operating the oldest stock of metal-working machinery of any industrial country in the world. In that year 64% of American machine tools were ten years old, or older. The figure for West Germany was 55%, for the Soviet Union about 50% (a declining percentage), while the American stock continues to age.

Here is a portrait of antiquity in American production. The percentage of machines in use that was twenty years old or older in 1963:

	%
Machine Tools	20
Ships and Railroad Equipment	41
Construction, Mining, Materials Handling	25
Precision Instruments and Mechanisms	15
Electrical Equipment	16
Automobiles	23
Office Machines	14
Special Industry Machinery	28

Since 1925 the McGraw-Hill organization has been conducting national "inventories" of the machine tools and other equipment in American industry. The following data show the proportion of metal-cutting machines in American industry found to be ten years old or older at the indicated times:

1925........44	1945........38
1930........52	1949........43
1935........67	1953........55
1940........72	1958........60
1963........64	

The growing age of the machine tools in use in American factories means that 2.2 million basic manufacturing machines are not being replaced by newer equipment that could incorporate many technical improvements. The replacement is not made because the firms using the existing machine tools are unable to justify investment in new machines except when the savings from their introduction will pay off the initial cost of the machine within a period of perhaps four to five years, or even sooner.

This means that it is not enough for new machines to have a higher output per hour of use, that is, greater productivity. It means that it is also necessary for the new machine's price to be low enough to permit higher physical productivity to be registered in the form of a lower production cost—almost immediately. Owing to relatively high production costs, the prices of machine tools during the last decade have been too high to be attractive to machine-tool users on a large scale. The result is that the demand for American built machine tools has been so low that the metal-working machinery stock of the United States industry has been aging. The net effect of this stagnation, relatively speaking, is that the metal-working industries of the United States have a less efficient set of basic production machines available to them than would be the case if machine tools produced here were lower in price.

The high cost of producing machine tools in the United States can be traced to the market for machine tools which has been classically unstable. This instability has made it difficult for the machine-tool makers to introduce high efficiency operations into their factories. Therefore, the instruments of mass production are being fabricated in factories that do not themselves use mass-production techniques. In order to preserve the position of single firms, managements attempt to diversify the products produced, and to differentiate their own product design from those of other firms. As a result the firms of this industry become involved in producing small quantities of many products. This raises the cost of manufacturing and becomes the basis for a high selling price. At the same time, standardization is not pursued by the managements of the machine-tool industry because that would open up the possibility of customers securing attachments or parts from other firms. Indeed, to my knowledge, there has been no extensive study of the cost-saving that might be obtained in the machine-tool industry if standardization were to be widely practiced.

In October, 1959, I produced a report for the European Productivity Agency on "The Productivity of Operations in the Machine-Tool Industry in Western Europe." The recommendations for defining major new avenues for improving productivity in the European machine-tool industry, given in that report, apply equally well to the United States. At that time they included projected studies for discovering what proportion of machine tools could be constructed from standardized components; the possibility of building machine tools on the basis of standardized modules; devising methods for formulating and adapting design standards; defining the cost and productivity of alternative production systems for the manufacture of machine tools; problems of controlling quality on precision components in small and large quantity production; and finally, possible methods for offsetting market fluctuations in order to insure stable production conditions in this industry. The crucial fact is that no studies along these lines have been carried out, either in Western Europe, or in the machine-tool industry in the United States, where this report was widely circulated. This means that there has not even been a serious attempt to discover the possibilities for productivity improvement and cost reduction along the recommended lines.

In the last decade the American machine-tool industry has been very active in developing its overseas operation. The principal firms of the industry are involved in investment in Western Europe and elsewhere, and in licensing arrangements with foreign firms, which often enable American firms to import machine tools manufactured in Western European plants for sale through the American firms' sales organization. An examination of any current issue of the machine-tool industry's principal trade journal *American Machinist* discloses that advertising by foreign machine-tool firms has increased in importance during this period.

While the American machine-tool industry has invested in manufacturing facilities overseas, the American market for machine tools has come to include the Government as a principal customer. By 1957, it was estimated that the Federal Government owned about 15% of all the machine tools in the country and thereby became the largest single owner of such equipment, valued at about $3 billion.

The headquarters of the National Machine-Tool Builders' Association was once in Cleveland, a long-standing center of the metal-working industries; but the headquarters have been moved to Washington, D.C., which, although not a metal-working center, is now the location of the industry's principal customer. Major sales to the Department of Defense and the Atomic Energy Commission have the effect of discouraging emphasis on cost reduction in the manufacture of machine tools. For the armed services, desirous of buying machines with particular capability, have tended to give cost consideration secondary importance. Since the Department of Defense has become the single largest customer for the machine-tool industry, the industry is thereby made less sensitive to pressures from other customers for reducing the prices of its products.

At the same time the machine-tool industry of the United States has had and continues to have a world-wide reputation; the quality of its product is widely respected. Nevertheless, failure to produce quality products at low prices, because modern production techniques are not used in its operation, has the effect of leaving U.S. metal-working industries without the flow of higher efficiency machines at modest prices which U.S. industry must have to maintain a major productivity advantage over foreign competitors—and thereby offset higher wages to American workers. If, in a given industry, U.S. wages per hour are twice those of European workers, then, in order for the American factory to be competitive, its man-hours must be twice as productive as those of the Europeans. This is only possible if the productivity margin is maintained by constant replacement with more productive equipment. That is why the slowdown in machinery replacement and an aging stock of metal-working machinery is a danger signal for the economic viability of a whole sector of American industry.

On Sunday, January 5, 1964, the New York *Times* ran a full-page ad boldly titled "Trains vs. Planes." The text of the ad, under a page-wide photograph of a fast-moving streamliner train read:

You might think planes have the edge. Not entirely true. The new Hitachi Superexpress streaks down the tracks at a phenomenal 155 miles per hour.

When the Superexpress goes into operation in late 1964 it will equal total airline time on the Tokyo-Osaka run, 320 miles in only three hours! A new era in railroading is about to begin.

Add to the speed the convenience of one carrier, no to and from airport travel, no waiting. You go downtown to downtown in one comfortable seat. The Superexpress achieves what many experts believed impossible—trains that effectively compete with aircraft.

The Superexpress is guided by electronic control in the train, a motorman, and a supervisory control room in Tokyo. The train automatically increases speed when the line is clear, slows down or stops when the line is not clear. The human error factor is eliminated.

This is only one example of Hitachi versatility in industry, any industry. Hitachi manufactures more than 10,000 basic products from turbines and generators to transformers and trains. Anything powered by electricity and a few things that are not.

Hitachi brings you the finest first. Look for the name and buy with confidence.

There are 215,000 miles of principal railroad trackage in the United States. But the sort of capability implied in the Hitachi ad is not part of recent American experience. Both the volume and the quality of railroad service on the whole, have been deteriorating, not improving.

An examination of journals that report on railroad developments around the world shows that in Western Europe, the Soviet Union, and in the Far East, the railroads, far from being abandoned, are being intensively developed with respect to the speed and quality of both freight and passenger service. The Italian State Railway expects to raise the maximum of its top electric train to 112 miles per hour in the near future. In West Germany 1,988 miles of main rail line are being converted to standards necessary for high-speed operations, 124 miles per hour, for passenger travel. The investment for rebuilding the lines is estimated at about $416,000 per mile. In 1965 British Railways is going to institute 75-mile-per-hour fast freight flyers between the principal cities of the British Isles. British Railways is stimulating vacation and tourist travel by "car-sleeper" trains. You drive your automobile onto a flat car, and then you ride in the sleeper. In Australia, the rail system is being unified and rebuilt and the two principal cities, Melbourne and Sydney, are linked by high-speed train systems. In France, railroad timetables show 38 point-to-point runs timed at better than 75 miles per hour. The total mileage of these fast rail runs adds up to 5,597—more than double the United States total.

The decay of the railroad system in the United States has imposed high costs for freight and passenger travel because people and freight can be carried much more cheaply by rail than by private motor vehicle.

There is no development in the United States that parallels the new Japanese express. It is perfectly obvious that this would be a superior transportation service between major American cities. But American railroads, and their equipment suppliers, Westinghouse, General Electric, General Motors, *et al.*, have become technologically inert. Innovations have been few and far between. And so deterioration of the railroads has continued; the public is serviced with more expensive transportation, while the number of railroad employees has dropped from 1,200,000 in 1950, to 700,000 in 1962.

What is the cause of this inertia? After all, alternative technical ideas are readily available. Why are they not applied?

From the standpoint of investing fresh industrial capital, the easiest way is to purchase a going, successful enterprise. Thereby, managerial, marketing, and production competence is bought in one package. Next in line of difficulty is the investment of new funds in new manufacturing facilities, in new "growth" industries. Under these conditions the investing management takes responsibility for the detailed equipment of plant, the organization of management, of staff, the training of a work force, and the development of markets.

The most difficult management situation is the technical renewal and reorganization of existing industrial operations. When the designs of products are changed, and new manufacturing methods are introduced, this immediately implies a requirement for learning new occupational skills by managers, engineers, foremen, and workers. Re-equipping factories, learning new skills, and regrouping job responsibiiities on a large scale are the most difficult sorts of tasks for an industrial management. But this is precisely the requirement in the whole range of basic American industries which have operated for a long time and whose competent functioning is essential for a productive society.

In the absence of strong encouragement and assistance for industrial updating by industry associations, by government, and by journals of opinion, it is no wonder that the managers of many industrial firms have sought easier ways of handling the investment of their funds, thereby making it possible to earn profits on investment while not advancing the productivity of many of America's basic industries. After all, advancing productivity is not a conventional yardstick of business success. If a firm shows "growth" and profits, its management is usually regarded as competent.

The firms in these industries have lacked the industrial engineering staffs and allied specialists needed for continuous technical and managerial review and renewal. The firms in civilian machinery industries that are economically and technically healthy have generally had this self-renewal tradition.

The sewing-machine industry offers a good example of how money-making and basic economic deterioration can go hand in hand. The Singer Company operates a factory in Elizabethport, New Jersey, that has a special claim for distinction. It is the last place in the United States where household sewing machines are manufactured. About 10,000 people worked there in 1947. By 1964 about 3,000 workers were left to man a factory composed of primarily antiquated manufacturing equipment.

Aged equipment, together with rather old-fashioned engineering and operating methods, have been used to produce fine sewing machines, but at high cost and high price.

Yet, at the same time, *Fortune* magazine wrote about the "Spryer Singer" in December, 1963, acclaimed recent sales of

$631 millions and profits of $29.2 millions, and declared the Singer of today a company ". . . aggressively looking to the future instead of resting on its past."

Where did all this money come from? Classically, we understand that new wealth must be created by someone's productive work. The financial vigor of the Singer firm contrasts with the declining quantity and relatively low efficiency of its American production operations in the sewing-machine field.

All the sewing machines needed in the United States used to be manufactured by American factories. By 1964 about 1½ million sewing machines were sold for American home use, but some 66% of them were imported, mainly from Japan and Western Europe. How did this happen? Let us understand that no great technological breakthroughs have been scored in sewing-machine design for many years. Is it possible that the level of wages paid to American workers makes the economic production of sewing machines impossible in the United States? That cannot be the case since sewing machines enjoy a market of about 1,500,000 units per year in this country, and that surely is a market for mass-production manufacturing. In the case of the automobile industry, the record is that with the highest wages in the world to automobile workers, the major U.S. firms are still able to produce cars at the lowest price per pound of fabricated vehicle in the world. What makes this possible is high productivity of labor by means of mechanization and systematic organization of the work. What happened to the United States sewing-machine industry?

The essential weakness of the Singer operation in Elizabethport is this: In order to produce sewing machines that are competitive with the output of Japanese workers, paid one sixth of United States wages, it is essential that productivity in the U.S. plants exceed the productivity of operations in Japan by a factor as much as five times as large. But such productivity has been made impossible by the failure of the Singer management to install modern high-productivity equipment which could indeed produce up to the desired level. The production workers in Elizabethport operate a stock of largely aged equipment. For example, 40% of their foundry equipment was twenty years old or more by 1963. Nationally, only 5% of foundry equipment was that old. Of the metal-cutting machine tools in the factory 80% were over twenty years old, as contrasted with 37% of that vintage in U.S. manufacturing as a whole.

Furthermore, redesigning of the product (to simplify its manufacture) has been neglected. For example, the Singer Company has had no standardization system for components that makes use of conventional screw threads. The firm manufactures its own screws, and the tools for making them to special dimensions. This is costly and technically wasteful. In another era this may have seemed a shrewd way to generate a captive spare-parts business, but by the middle of this century it became clear that the manufacture of parts in relatively small quantities made production costs too high. Singer has 91 colors for their machines, and over 80,000 different parts in inventory. There are about 100 sorts of flat, metallic washers with less than 1″ outside diameter. The Singer Company, and its former U.S. competitors, have not bothered to do the job of standardization now being done so competently by the Japanese sewing-machine industry.

How did the Singer Company develop its strong financial position under such conditions of depleted technical efficiency?

The Singer Company and its reputable sewing machines have been household words in the United States and other countries for over a century; Singer employs 81,000 people in 95 countries. Since the Second World War the Singer Company has expanded in the following ways: New sewing-machine factories have been erected abroad; production of new products have been undertaken abroad, either directly, or by other firms, to Singer's order; sewing machines and other products produced abroad have been sold there and also imported into the United States for sale through Singer's far-flung retailing organization. Finally, within the United States, Singer has bought up several going concerns, including several in the "space age" industries.

By 1953 Singer factories for sewing machines were located in 6 countries. Thereafter, an expansion program was set in motion to manufacture in 16 countries, with 12 additional assembly plants and parts factories in various lands. In Western Europe, and in the Far East, Singer undertook the sales of various household appliances manufactured there to its requirements. These included vacuum cleaners, washing machines, refrigerators, hi-fi equipment, typewriters, and TV sets.

Sewing machines made in Singer's plant in Scotland are imported for sale in the United States; so are portable typewriters made in Europe. In 1963, on the West Coast, Singer began to market Japanese-made TV sets carrying the Singer name. No sophistication in production methods is required to use low-wage labor for making products to sell competitively in the United States.

At the same time, the Singer management has bought up companies in the United States in various fields: military cameras, textile machinery, electrical and electronic instruments, and data processing machines. All the firms involved, of which the Friden business-machines firm is most important, were successful operations when Singer bought them. *Fortune* in December, 1963, reported that these non-sewing-machine firms made up about 20% of Singer's sales in 1962, and contributed 25% of the firm's total profits.

The formula for financial success adds up to this: expansion of production and sales abroad; expansion of ownership in the United States; expansion of sales in the United States, based upon overseas production with low-wage labor; *contraction* of sewing-machine production within the United States, owing to failure to offset U.S. costs by improved productivity.

By the conventional tests of financial success the Singer record is entirely commendable. By the test of participation in a viable American production system, the Singer record is calamitous.

If this sort of pattern were the performance of a few firms, a rarity, a set of exotic contrasts, then there would be little point in pursuing this analysis. But the combination of financial success and decaying productive capability has become a far-ranging pattern that threatens the viability of the American industrial system at its base.

The shipbuilding and ship-operating industries are good illustrations of managements that are financially successful while contributing to industrial depletion.

The United States still possesses one of the largest merchant fleets in the world, but between 1955 and 1963, it was the only major merchant fleet in the world that declined in size while all others registered considerable growth. The principal maritime countries of the West increased the tonnage of their merchant fleets from 72 to 96 million gross tons between 1955 and 1963, while American tonnage declined from 25 to 22 million gross tons. Exactly what is the nature of the incapacity that seems to have seized the American merchant marine?

Recently constructed Swedish shipyards, equipped to build vessels of the largest size, are highly mechanized; closed-circuit television is used for central control of internal movement of steel plates, and the like. In one of the yards a vessel is assembled inside a building. As each section of the ship is built, mainly from prefabricated assemblies, it is pushed out of the building into a dock area by hydraulic jack. Then work begins on the next section, and then the next, in a continuous pattern, until, like toothpaste squeezed out of a tube, the whole vessel is in the outdoor dry dock from which it is finally floated. By such methods it has been possible to produce a ship of the largest merchant class (a 36,000-ton ore carrier) in 27 weeks, working only one shift. Compare this with the customary 40 weeks spent doing the same job by conventional methods.

Unfortunately, the point of all this is that the semiautomated shipyard is located in Sweden, not the United States, and further, that the plausible methods of modern production engineering that have been applied in the Swedish yard do not exhaust the possibilities of further technological refinements in the art of shipbuilding. And virtually none of this is going on in American shipyards.

In 1964 the United States attained the distinction of operating the world's oldest oil-tanker fleet. The tanker fleets of other countries, notably that of the Soviet Union, with an annual increase of 29% since 1953, have been growing while the American fleet has been diminishing. In 1962 only 9% of the ocean-borne cargo of the United States was carried by vessels of American registry, as against 43% in 1954. The U.S. performance in 1962 was the lowest per cent among the principal maritime countries of the West; the merchant marine of France carried 59% of its cargo; Denmark, 23%; Sweden, 33%; and the United Kingdom, 52%.

Why is the merchant marine of the United States declining? Basically, because the cost of building merchant ships in the United States has been about twice the cost of building similar ships elsewhere in the world. Three important factors contribute to the incompetence of U.S. commercial shipbuilding: the system of subsidies to shipbuilders and ship operators; the dominance of naval shipbuilding in the United States; and, finally, the failure of the shipbuilding industry to make use of modern design and production-engineering techniques.

The subsidy system for shipbuilders and ship operators follows a remarkable pattern. Under the Merchant Marine Act of 1936, provision was made for a differential construction subsidy for vessels of American registry to be used in the foreign commerce of the United States. This subsidy may not exceed 55% of the cost of the vessel, which means that if you are the prospective buyer of a commercial vessel, you go to a naval architect in the United States and commission a set of drawings for a vessel to your specifications. You then proceed to get a quotation on the price of building such a vessel from an American, and a foreign, shipbuilder. If you want the vessel built in the United States, you can get the difference between the American quoted price and the foreign quoted price from the Federal Government. This will amount to about 50% of the U.S. quoted price, because shipbuilding costs are twice as high in the United States as elsewhere. Obviously, this style of operating cannot offer much incentive to the American shipbuilding industry to improve the efficiency of its operation and make the changes necessary to improve productivity and thereby equal overseas ship costs and prices.

Then there are the operating subsidies. An operating differential subsidy is given to American ship operators to place American vessels on a parity with those of foreign competitors. This is based on the difference between "the fair and reasonable cost of insurance, maintenance, repairs, and wage and subsistence of officers and crews, and the estimated costs of the same items if the vessels were operating under foreign revenue." Such payments are authorized by the Merchant Marine Act of 1936. At the same time, the Act provides that any profits made by the ship operator in excess of 10% of the capital employed are to be shared 50-50 between the ship operator and the Federal Government. This subsidy system does not apply to domestic trade.

In 1963, the construction subsidy cost the Federal Government $91,996,000. The operating subsidy cost the Federal Government $220,677,000 in 1963.

In 1963, in the various navy yards of the United States, 90,000 men were employed; 118,000 men worked in the private shipbuilding industries. However, about 60% of the tonnage under construction in the private shipyards has recently consisted of naval vessels. Accordingly, we may estimate that about 47,000 men were employed in commercial shipbuilding in 1963, while 161,000 men were employed in military shipbuilding. The number of men working in commercial and naval work is important because of the sharp difference in the costs of ship construction in each case.

The Polaris-type submarine has become an important class of naval shipbuilding. These vessels, excluding major weapons, are built at the cost of about $12 per pound. On the other hand, large oil tankers constructed in the United States cost about 20¢ per pound. This dramatic difference in cost between naval and commercial vessels also defines the gap in the style of design and methods of construction.

The essential point is that in naval construction, cost considerations take a definite second place, while for commercial vessels, cost considerations must be paramount as the criterion requisite to their construction. A production manager in one of the major shipbuilding firms once put the contrast between the two types of shipbuilding to me as follows: "If I were asked to construct naval vessels in the same shipyard with commercial vessels, the first thing I would do is erect a very large fence between the naval and commercial sections of the yard. I would regard this as essential to prevent contamination of the standard of work in each case by the other."

The methods of designing and building commercial vessels in the United States are so anachronistic that a cautious estimate points to the possibility of reducing the manufacturing costs of commercial vessels by 30%. A more adventurous exploration of technological possibilities, already encompassed by other industries, leads to a possible 50% reduction of shipbuilding costs. The latter case would make the elaborate Federal subsidy system unnecessary, and American shipbuilders would once more be competitive in the world shipbuilding market. At the same time, this cost reduction would be an incentive for American shipping firms to purchase and use American-built ships. Both developments would cause expanded employment in the shipbuilding industry, and in ship operations, even though more sophisticated productivity techniques would be used both in the construction and operation of commercial vessels.

However, the possibility for substantially improved productivity in shipbuilding awaits reorganization of methods within the industry. The principal commercial shipbuilding firms still do virtually no research on ship design. Neither do they operate substantial design organization. The naval architects who design ocean-going vessels operate as a separate profession, removed from the shipbuilding industry itself. This is like having a chemical industry with no chemists on the staff, or an electric-power industry without electrical engineers.

Further, the technique of standardizing ship components is virtually unknown. There is no active shipbuilding standardization movement in the United States. A contrast may be seen in Japan where the shipbuilding industry has a vigorous program of standards development. The Japanese industry has published a major volume depicting its standards for ship structure as an instrument for industry-wide advertising throughout the world.

Since research and development in shipbuilding in the United States is concentrated in the naval field, one might expect the state of the art to develop rapidly in the naval-vessel direction, while the technology of commercial shipbuilding, design, and construction remained stagnant; and that is exactly what has been happening. The result is that even construction subsidies of as much as 50% have not been sufficient to turn the American shipbuilding industry into a vigorous builder of commercial vessels.

As a result of these several factors—depending upon Government subsidies, more money and imagination invested in naval construction, and a technology of design and production unsuited to cost conditions—the American shipbuilding and ship-operating industries are reaching a terminal condition of depletion. Mr. Ralph E. Casey, President of the American Merchant Marine Institute, warned in March, 1964, that unless major policy decisions were made soon, the United States must prepare to lose more than half of its merchant fleet in a very few years. He pointed out that in 1945, with 5,000 ships, the United States operated the largest merchant fleet in the world. By 1953 the number had dropped to 1,258, and ten years later to 983. Mr. Casey's warning was directed to the Congress, pressing the Federal Government for even greater subsidies and more Federal funds to sustain the merchant marine in its present style of operation.

But the point is rather that the technological and economic renewal of the merchant marine, and the shipbuilding industry, requires a fundamental change away from a style of operation that has up until now generated economic and technical depletion. This change is required *before* the introduction of new technology and fresh productive capital. Such an orientation has yet to be considered seriously by the shipbuilding industry or the merchant-marine operators.

The United States fishing industry, with 3,000 aging and relatively inefficient fishing vessels, is closely linked to the depletion process in the shipbuilding industry. Modern, large capacity trawlers operating in fleets around ocean-going fish-processing vessels are unknown to America. Elsewhere in the world, trawler fleets of modern design operate with high efficiency to produce an increasing stock of fish food from the world's oceans. In the past ten years the United States has dropped behind Peru, Communist China, and Soviet Russia and now ranks fifth among the fishing nations. The tendency is for the American fishing fleet to decrease in size while the total market for fish grows. As a result, the value of U.S. fishery imports during the period 1953-63 has exceeded exports by more than $3 billion.

A hopelessly inefficient fishing fleet cannot hold the world market, or even serve the domestic American market. But there is no American center, or institute, or set of firms now practicing design for, or construction of, modern fishing vessels. The technological talent that might be applied to this function has been substantially pre-empted by naval design and naval ship construction. Therefore, American fisheries which provided employment for 263,000 men in 1950 could employ only 217,000 by 1962. Like the merchant marine and major shipbuilding industries, the fishery and fishing-craft-construction industry could provide an increasing volume of employment because of the predictable expansion of the market for fish products. But the men and the capital required for this industry have instead been given strong incentive either to move abroad and operate with low-cost labor in foreign countries, or to abandon the industry altogether. The fishing industry is therefore in decline at the very same time that the market for its product in the United States is rapidly expanding and being supplied, increasingly, by imports.

The American aircraft industry which has produced outstanding commercial planes like the DC-3, the Boeing 707, and the DC-8 has also developed technically exotic airplanes like the XB-70, a six-engine jet that is expected to fly at 2,000 miles per hour. Built largely of stainless steel, this plane cost the United States Government $1.6 billion for two prototype planes that have no defined mission.

Reflecting the depletion of civilian product competence in the aircraft industry are the efforts of the Federal Aviation Agency to encourage the design of an air transport that would excel in safe short hauls. In aviation circles it is widely appreciated that the best plane ever produced for this class of work was the DC-3. These aircraft, first built in the 1930's, are still used around the world, and pilots say that it is one of the safest planes ever built.

In 1964 the Federal Aviation Agency asked aircraft firms to

submit bids for designing a successor to the DC-3; and the Agency set aside $300,000 as an award to be divided among three firms to prepare detailed design specifications for such an aircraft. There is a remarkable contrast between the government allocation of $300,000 for the design of a safe, competent, commercial aircraft, as against an expenditure of 1.6 billion dollars for the design of the XB-70—a design that will probably never be used for more than the two prototype models already constructed. It is significant that the seven American firms who submitted bids for the successor to the DC-3 did not include its original designer and builder, the Douglas Aircraft Corporation. During the last decades Douglas has become primarily involved in the design and manufacture of missiles and space vehicles.

The industrial depletion process is characterized by declining markets, stationary or declining employment and failure to apply modern technology to the relevant industry, either in design or manufacture. Other industries, such as printing machinery, water turbines, ceramics, and textile machinery, also disclose a pattern of depletion. Such industries and their firms need not be unprofitable. For example, while many features of the machine-tool industry may be subject to criticism, the performance, financially speaking, has been of acceptable quality. The same may reasonably be said of many American railroads, which have continued to pay satisfactory interest rates even while the process of production depletion has been going on.

The characteristic combination of depletion of production, coupled with the maintenance of good profit levels, is found in many of the machinery and allied industries of the United States. This is crucially important since, in an industrial society, the competence of these industries reflects the production competence of the society as a whole. The technical stagnation noted in many American machinery-producing industries is not caused by some inherent quality of their product, but rather by the absence of a self-renewal process—available internally or encouraged from the outside. A healthy industry such as road-building equipment operates in the United States at costs and prices that make it competitive worldwide. Many American-produced appliances are solidly competitive in the whole world market. Fractional-horse-power motors are produced in the United States at a cost and price that make them competitive.

But America's scientific-equipment industry, while growing in the volume of its sales, is, like the typewriter industry and the shipbuilding industry tending to rely increasingly on overseas production of its product. In December, 1964, the New York *Times* reported that Dr. Edward E. Sheldon had received an American patent for his invention of an electron X-ray microscope. This development improves the electron microscope and eliminates much extra work for the technician who operates this research tool. The new device is to be manufactured in Japan for distribution in the United States by an American instrument firm. It is noteworthy that the pages of *Science* magazine, the journal of the American Association for the Advancement of Science, are filled with advertising from many foreign firms, even though the United States-based scientific-instruments industry has had a large and growing market for such products.

We have become accustomed to thinking of the electronics industry as one of the really outstanding areas of technological development in the United States. However, the fact is that the evolution of the transistor-type radio, although based on techniques that were largely developed in the United States, was actually carried out by the electronics industry of Japan. This is probably the first case of a major appliance that was not initially developed in the United States.

Do high wages necessarily mean high costs and high prices?

In response to economic incentives, American agriculture has drawn upon varied technological capability to make possible production of foodstuffs in prodigious volume at low cost. Research support from the agricultural experiment stations, new developments by farm-machinery firms and the chemical industries—all of these made possible the growth of U.S. agricultural productivity to the point where U.S. farm products are the single largest class of U.S. exports able to hold their own and then some in many world markets.

Again, the point is not that the United States can or should function as an autarchic economy. Rather, I regard these data as evidence against the proposition that a high wage automatically means high product cost and price. What counts is the wage and other cost per unit of product. Essentially, the choices in methods available in modern technology make it feasible to offset high labor and capital costs by efficient methods in production and organization. High wages can be combined with low prices.

But making this happen takes some doing; capital, management talent, and technical skills must be systematically applied in a self-renewal process. During the 1950's and 1960's, capital has been available in large amounts in the United States. On the other hand, important kinds of managerial talent and technical skills have been in short supply.

During the last decade, there has been a growing alarm over reduction in employment owing to mechanization and automation in industrial and other kinds of work. The depleted industries manifest decline in employment not because of change in the way the work is done, but *because of the decline in the total amount of work performed by these industries in the United States.* The growing reliance on imports, in industries integral to an industrial system, has resulted in a decline in employment in the United States. This decline is unrelated to whether or not the factories supplying the United States from abroad were owned by American firms.

Our economists have tended to view the decline of a firm or an industry as part of an ordinary and recurring process of the decay and growth of the enterprise. The assumption has been that if a given management is not competent to meet the market demand for a product, another management will in due course recognize opportunity, move into the field, and serve the market anew. This natural process of economic correction has been substantially checkmated by the development of government-controlled industries and markets dominated by the military sphere of society. By offering superior salaries that could be absorbed by selling to Federal defense agencies, the military contractors, and their nonprofit adjuncts, have absorbed a massive proportion of the available technological talent. At the same time, capital has been attracted to the new rapid growth of defense and space industries. The result is that the normal process of correction of economic depletion has been rendered inoperative.

Another aspect of the depletion process is the growth of dependence on foreign sources of supply. Here again, economists have tended to view this as an essentially desirable pattern when it occurs for particular firms and industries. The reasoning has been: If foreign sources of supply are more economic, then those suppliers should be drawn upon. Let each country produce and sell what it is naturally competent to do. In that way, there will be an international division of labor and everyone will be served from sources of supply that are most efficient. Thereby every country will stand to benefit. The awkwardness of the present problem, however, arises from the fact that the depletion of American industries has not been a spotty, random affair, relegated to a few firms. Instead, the process of depletion has been concentrated in the class of machinery-producing industries which lie at the base of any modern industrial system. The conventional economist's view does not take into account our present condition, under which industrial depletion has become epidemic, and the "natural" economic correction process frustrated by the unavailability of fresh capital and technological talent. While depletion in industry has been spreading, the public is reassured by reports of general economic growth. At the same time talent, capital, and society-wide attention have been lavished on the defense and space industries.

The American way of using up productive capital and talent has not been followed in the countries of the Common Market. Here is the contrast with the United States in 1960:

	United States	Common Market
Military Spending as % of GNP	9.2	4.2
Machinery and Equipment as % of GNP	5.4	10.2

The Common Market countries have enjoyed healthy economic growth and full employment.

Many people, including some engineers, have concluded that

the depleted industries are those concerned with "unsophisticated" products and technologies, and might just as well be located abroad. These industries, badly needed for a healthy economy, have not been given technological updating in product design or production methods.

The repair of our depleted industries requires investment of fresh productive capital and the broad application of science and technology for sustained internal self-renewal. Since the carriers of the necessary knowledge are our engineers and scientists, how can we escape the question: Where have our engineers and scientists been working?

4

Cold-War Science and Technology

During a 1962 Senate-committee discussion on how the United States uses its technical talent, Senator Hubert Humphrey burst forth with this critique:

In Germany, 85%—85 cents out of every research dollar is private, and less than 15 per cent goes into military and space. Eighty-five cents of that goes into the civilian economy, so that today the German plant competition for world markets of civilian goods is being automated, modernized, equipped in the latest and best fashion, and new products are developing, while we are developing new wrappings. We are the greatest packagers in the world. We package them beautifully. We have an artistic capacity second to none in cellophane wrappings, foils, and so forth, but the German is developing the thing inside the package.

In Japan, it is about 85 to 15 again. That is a rough estimate. Eighty-five cents out of every research dollar is private and going into the civilian economy, with huge capital investments going into the Japanese civilian economy.

In England, which also has a low rate of economic growth, as does our country, 60 cents out of every research dollar is governmental and goes into military and space, atomic energy, and 40 cents out of that research dollar goes into the private sector. . . .

This poses some problems here . . . the fact is that scientific manpower, technological and scientific research, moneys and the facilities, attract capital, because that is where the money is to be made; that is where the new product is to come from; there is where you need the new plant, the new facility. . . .

What is happening to our civilian economy as we plow more and more of our scientific personnel, our brains, into the military and into space and into atomic energy for military purposes? Where are we going to end up in this trade competition with these Belgians and these Dutch, who are clever, and the Germans who are very clever, who are spending more money for civilian aspects and will develop products cheaper, better, and more serviceable? Our rate of economic growth is nothing to be proud of. Look at the Italians, who put very, very little money into military—very, very little. We are paying the cost of their military expenditures. They put 90 cents of their research dollar into the civilian economy. They talk about a miracle of Italian economy. It proves that if you put enough brains to work on something with money, you get it done.

Humphrey's worry about the nation as a whole is underlined by the troubles of firms which cannot find needed research talent. These are civilian industries—the part of American industry that has not shared in the cost-hardly-matters affluence of the defense contractors.

On August 9, 1963, the *Wall Street Journal* reported:

. . . Top research men in industry reason this way: Frantic bidding, by space and military contractors, for scientists and engineers is creating a big shortage for industry. This scarcity, along with the skyrocketing salaries it is provoking, is bringing almost to a halt the hitherto rapid growth of company-supported research. This development hampers efforts to develop new products and processes for the civilian economy.

And it's not just the moon race they question. In general,

they wonder about the wisdom of the nation's continually increasing concentration of research effort on Government-sponsored projects.

Samuel Lebner, vice president of Du Pont Company, puts
it this way: "Government research programs serve as a brake
on research in the private sector." Even if corporations had
unlimited money to spend, they could not find the personnel
to expand research indefinitely, Mr. Lebner says.

. . . The space program alone could gobble up nearly all of
the 30,000 new professional workers expected to enter research this year if Commerce Department calculations are correct. Personnel working on Government research contracts
rose 317% to 190,000 between 1954 and 1961, while industry increased its private research payrolls only 30% to
130,000.

While the need for technical manpower is expanding, the
growth in supply is slowing. The demand for new engineers
alone now runs close to 60,000 a year, but only about 33,700
will be graduated this year, down from as many as 38,134 in
1959. While accurate figures are not available, the situation
appears to be nearly as acute in the physical sciences such as
chemistry and physics.

Not surprisingly, many companies report they are falling far
short of their goals in their recruiting drives.

Xerox Corporation which is trying to expand its research
and development in line with booming sales of its office copiers,
fell short of its 1962 goal by about one-third and so far this
year is lagging by about the same amount. Du Pont says it
probably will get only 75% to 80% of the 1,100 new technical graduates it is seeking this year. Adds the research manager of a major oil producer: "Like most companies, we
haven't met our goals. The growth rate in our department has
been up and down with the availability of technical personnel
and right now it's down."

Many companies also are faced with the problem of holding present staffs against recruiting for Government projects.

"A major space contractor put a lab right next to one of ours in Los Angeles and hired away 20% of our staff at a 15% premium," complains Borg-Warner's Mr. Collier. . . .

. . . Minneapolis-Honeywell Regulator Co. says unfilled openings for technical specialists have forced delay of its study of the nature of flame, which it considers vital to its basic heat control business. According to Mr. Lebner of Du Pont, in recent months three of the company's 12 industrial departments have said "they can't push as rapidly as they're being urged because they don't have the people." Joseph C. Wilson, President of Xerox, says lack of personnel last year meant "we didn't get to start some projects we wanted to."

Not all companies attribute slower growth in research and development directly to unfilled jobs. Many say big expansions can't be justified at this time by the profit possibilities from research. Part of this concern over profit potential reflects rising research costs, stemming primarily from the bidding up of salaries. . . .

These criticisms come from firms with major reputations and large and continuing budgets for research and development. Du Pont, Xerox, and Minneapolis-Honeywell, are the sort of firms that normally serve as magnets for high-grade research talent. These are not the complaints of small firms.

The rationing of engineers and scientists into military and allied activities takes place by means of systematic salary differentials that were disclosed in June, 1963, by the American Society of Mechanical Engineers. A survey of engineering salaries showed that for an engineer with 10 years' experience, machinery-producing industries pay $9,300 on the average, while the aerospace industries pay $11,500, on the average.

By 1963, two out of three research scientists and engineers were working directly or indirectly for the space or defense agencies of the Federal Government.

What has been the impact of this concentration? From 1940-52, there was a continuous relationship between growth in research performed by industry, and growth in Gross National Product. From 1952 onward, there was a sharp break with the previous pattern. Although spending for research rose steeply after 1952, there was a sharp drop in the related rate of growth in total goods and services produced. The reason for this is that an overwhelming part of the research increase was for military and space programs. Spending in these spheres differs fundamentally from spending in the civilian area of the economy, because the military goods and services, whatever worth may be attached to them, do not contribute to further production.

Even though those doing military research use their pay to function as consumers, the product of their working time, once created, does not, like civilian products, become an input for further production. Therefore, as research became more and more militarily oriented after 1952, there was no parallel rate of general economic growth.

Officers of the Federal Commerce Department have become sensitive to the technological side of the industrial depletion process. They know that Japan and Europe, free of the space and defense effort borne by the United States, are gearing their technical resources to industrial needs. Sitting in technological backwaters, as a result, are entire U.S. industries like textiles and apparel, food processing, building and construction, machine-tool, forging, and the machinery industry generally.

By 1963 some of President Kennedy's associates were aware of technological deficiencies in major civilian industries. Dr. J. Herbert Holloman, Assistant Secretary of Commerce, found that:

Switzerland, Sweden, Japan, and West Germany each spend a larger percentage of their resources (labor force or Gross National Product) on Research and Development that aids the civilian economy than does the United States. Furthermore, . . . in West Germany, the number of scientists and engineers engaged in Research and Development that benefits the civilian economy is a much larger fraction of the labor force than is the case in the United States.

At present, only the largest firms in the largest industries can afford to maintain the technical capability that leads to new products, processes and improved productivity. In many other important industries, the individual firms are so small and the profit margins so limited that it is next to impossible for them to hire and support the technical staff which would be needed to develop and apply new, complex technology for their industry.

Such segments of the economy are the textile, lumber, leather, wood and clay products, machine-tools, foundries and casting, and the railroads industry. These segments have not supported or performed much Research and Development, and, consequently are neither well-situated to participate in the advances in technology generated by the other Research and Development efforts (industrial as well as military), nor to maintain their relative economic strength internationally. These industries have often been vulnerable targets for foreign competition.

How did this happen? Research and development spending in the United States totaled $6.4 billion in 1955, and grew to $20 billion by 1964. Out of the Gross National Product for 1964, $20 billion was expended for research and development and $15 billion of that was an expenditure of the Federal Government. The figure indicates that without formal planning Research and

FEDERAL RESEARCH AND DEVELOPMENT BUDGETS, 1940–1965 ($ Millions)

Fiscal Year	Department of Defense	National Aeronautics and Space Administration	Atomic Energy Commission	Health, Education, Welfare	National Science Foundation	Office of Scientific Research and Development
1940	26	2		3		
1945	513	24	859*	3		114
1950	652	54	221	40		
1955	2,630	74	385	70	9	
1960	5,654	401	986	324	58	
1965 (est.)	7,107	4,990	1,557	796	204	

* Manhattan project

Development have been undergoing a process of nationalization.

This growth period has been characterized mainly by the expansion of the military and space programs. In 1964, five government departments in the table accounted for 96% of all Federal research spending. In the Federal Government, during the period 1950-65, research and development expenditures by the Department of Defense grew tenfold, from $652 million to $7 billion. In the space field, the growth from 1950 to 1965 was hundredfold, from $54 million to $5 billion. The Atomic Energy Commission budgeted $221 million for research and development in 1950, and $1.5 billion in 1965. Other research and development activities grew during this period. While the proportional change in the nonmilitary fields is significant, the magnitude of sums spent is drastically different. Thus, research for health, education, and welfare grew from $40 million, in 1950, to $800 million, in 1955. Expenditures by the National Science Foundation, established to sponsor research, especially in basic science and related fields, grew from $1 million in 1952, to $204 million in 1965. By 1965, however, about 90% of the Federal Government's outlays for research and development lay in the military and related fields.

While the Government's budgets for military and allied research have been booming, there has been no parallel proportionate growth in the number of trained people available. A House of Representatives Committee on Government Research in 1964 noted: "It is significant that the number of individuals capable of performing this urgent development increases by only 7% annually, while the annual growth in Federal research and development expenditures has averaged 15%." This contrast measures the rationing pressure that has been exerted on the research and development manpower sources of the country through the growth of government expenditures in these fields.

The growing concentration of engineering talent in government-directed defense and space programs is sharply revealed by the impacts on technological developments in many fields. This subject was explored by an eminent committee of the Engineers' Joint Council in its report on "The Nation's Engineering Research Needs, 1965-1985." Published in 1962, this report has a table of contents that reads like an analysis of the relatively depleted sectors of technology in American society.

First, the committee noted that there is a significant imbalance in the national technical effort. Many industries have been left without resources for developing their technology either in terms of products or production methods.

Second, the committee found that there has been relatively little increase in research on energy and raw material resources. (I am told by colleagues in electrical engineering that it is hard to find university teachers for fields like power engineering, which have been left aside while electronics burgeoned.) Research into urban environmental problems has been substantially neglected. The same is true for national and metropolitan transportation systems. In that context, for example, the depletion of the railroad system is particularly notable. The engineering of hospital and medical services has not been developed, although a reasonable understanding of the problem indicates that many economies can be made, and are even essential, if competent medical care is to be provided for all citizens. For example, there is no excuse for nurses spending a substantial part of their work time in essentially unproductive activity.

Educational services have been neglected. The technological problems of developing nations receive fragmentary attention in various universities. Furthermore, the EJC report notes that many possible applications of engineering to biological systems are yet to be explored.

Finally, they note that there are problems of engineering education and technical information involving, for example, how to operate many large libraries as the number of books and journals riscs at a geometric rate.

The EJC, in its detailed report on how research and development resources are used in the United States, drew this conclusion:

> The needs of people and society are not given sufficient attention in the allocation of research and development funds.

Non-defense agencies do not have research and development programs that relate broadly to their entire mission or that reflect the enormous impact of technology on the lives of people and social organizations. It has been far easier to win support for an $80-million-dollar program on high energy physics, than $10 million dollars for research and development on national transportation problems. It has been far easier to win support for a $30-million-dollar program in atmospheric sciences than $5 million dollars for research and development on problems of aid to the developing countries. The need-oriented problems associated with the impact of technology on society and the revolution of rising expectations do not conform to the patterns associated with man's scientific knowledge of the physical world. Yet, orderly empirical engineering developments have been possible in the absence of a comprehensive theoretical science. Need-oriented research and development programs could make contributions to the alleviation of problems raised by the spread of technology in the modern world.

The Council went on to specify:

The importance of maintaining a competitive technological position to contribute to growth of the national economy is not recognized in the current allocations for research and development. Civilian industry is expected to assure the growth of the civilian economy. Research and development for industries that serve the general economy must compete for a share of the national research and development resources. The aggressive programs for research and development that have been generated to advance the defense or quasi-defense programs are attracting many of the most competent individuals. These programs are dynamic, clearly focused on matters in the national interest, and performed on the brilliantly lighted stage of national awareness. United States industries' place in international economic competition is being threatened by foreign technological advances. . . .

This report, though representing the work of a distinguished committee, distributed in the name of the Engineers' Joint Council, and representing all the engineering societies in the United States, has received virtually no attention, even in the journals of the societies. My experience also suggests that professors of engineering themselves are virtually unaware of the very existence of this report, let alone of certain of its detailed findings.

A rather striking example of environmental depletion, and the neglect of technological development, was pointed out by the EJC report in respect to air pollution and its threat to health:

Relative to cancer three very important facts have been established: (1) cancer producing agents are present in the air we breathe; (2) concentrates of urban smog have produced cancer in animals; (3) the lung cancer rate in our largest cities is twice as high as the rate in nonurban areas. It must also be noted that in England where the atmosphere is highly polluted the lung cancer rates are much higher than in the United States.

In areas of high pollution, chronic bronchitis occupies a high place as a fatal disease. It is the opinion of the medical profession in England that the high rate of bronchitis which exists there is the result of the higher degree of air pollution. It is also the considered opinion of medical experts in the United States that chronic bronchitis is on the increase in the United States.

It has also been fairly well established that ozone scars the lungs of animals when they breathe sublethal doses for several months. Other experiments show that it may also affect the enzyme systems of the respiratory tract. Results of recent research show that aerosols intensify the harmful effects of sulfur dioxide.

And further, the EJC found that:

The U.S. Public Health Service has found that cities having high air pollution indices tend to show high rates of incidence and death rates due to heart disease. The oxides of sulfur in concentrations found in community air makes breathing more difficult. This forces weakened hearts to work harder. Furthermore certain invisible pollutants such as ozone injure the lining of the lungs. This results in permanent scars and causes chronic labored breathing. It is a matter of record that deaths from heart disease tripled during the London smog of 1952.

The economic losses owing to air pollution are described in the EJC report as

. . . staggering. Reliable data place this cost at $65 per capita annually. This loss results from the destruction of crops and livestock; the deterioration of metals; the enormous waste of unburned by-products of combustion, increased cleaning costs, and reduced property value. During the periods of smog, illumination costs are increased and automobile accidents increase. It is doubtful if an estimate of the losses due to reduced work efficiency, the total cost of medical care and added insurance costs has as yet been made.

Competent research for reducing or eliminating air pollution can be purchased for a price which would be a small fraction of the economic waste that it causes.

Medical research in various fields has gone undone because of the channeling of finite technical resources into the aerospace and defense spheres. For example, one of the central restrictions that confronts investigators in medicine, chemistry, biochemistry, and microbiology is the inability to make direct observations of the structure and behavior of molecules. Therefore experimental methods in these fields rely on ingenious methods of indirection for making inferences about molecular structure and changes. The limits of micro-observation have been the limits of the electron microscope. Yet, there have been no research programs addressed to major development of the electron microscope or to related techniques, to magnification and observation at the molecular level as a general problem. The discovery of means for direct observation at the molecular level would accelerate understanding of the nature of the human cell, of its complex biochemistry. The relevant technology could therefore be instrumental for developing new knowledge on the nature of growth, for solving medical mysteries like the source of cancer and the mode of treating it. More broadly, the ability to "see" at the molecular level would undoubtedly reinforce our ability to extend the human life span. Colleagues in the biological sciences advise that there has been no concerted effort to "break" the present constraint on direct micro-observation.

For a contrast between areas of wealth and depletion in the technological sphere, one may turn to a class of technology which, because of its closeness to the military art, suffers from none of the defects we have delineated elsewhere. I refer to the development of the supersonic transport, discussed in aero-space industry circles as a potential $10 billion market. During the last decade, aircraft manufacturers have grown more ambitious, now wishing to develop planes capable of speeds up to or greater than 2,000 miles per hour. Such swift aircraft, designed primarily with government funds, would make it possible to travel from New York City to a European capital within an hour and a half to two hours.

In an enthusiastic article, *Fortune* magazine, February, 1964, suggested that there could be a major world-wide market for supersonic aircraft on the order of the magnitude of 600 or more planes. Furthermore, *Fortune* argued that not only a large market but also national prestige is at stake. However, the considerable publicity given to the development of the supersonic aircraft by the technical press and the newspapers of the country did not consider some of the problems concomitant with the development and use of such aircraft. An analysis by B.K.O. Lundberg, Director-General of the Aeronautical Research Institute of Sweden, entitled "The Supersonic Threat," pointed out that on grounds of safety and economy, there are grave doubts attached to supersonic aircraft. In regard to safety, Lundberg offered the following considerations:

". . . Hail and rain may be present in clouds up to at least 75,000 ft. Collision with hail at supersonic speed can undoubtedly be

catastrophic; even flying through heavy rain might be serious."
For the first time in the history of transportation ". . . passengers
will be carried in a vehicle whose crew is virtually blind." Speeds
of 2,000 miles per hour (33 miles per second) would not allow
adequate time for reaction to whatever might be perceived by the
human eye.

Another major hazard facing the SST's is structural fatigue.
"Friction of the air on wings and fuselage will produce aerody-
namic heating and hence thermal stresses. . . . These effects will
will be far more complex and difficult to predict than in the case
of subsonic aircraft."

In the course of the development of the supersonic aircraft, one
of the striking conditions that came to the fore was the problem
of the so-called sonic boom. This is the shock wave produced by
the passage of an aircraft traveling faster than the speed of sound.
The sonic boom would be induced along the whole trail of the
aircraft traveling at supersonic speed.

After some discussion an experimental program on sonic
boom was carried out in the Oklahoma City area, during July and
August of 1964. A correspondent of the London *Economist,*
reporting on the experiment in Oklahoma City, disclosed the following: "At times the flood of complaints reached 500 a day,
mostly in the form of telephone calls to the Federal Aviation
Agency. It is responsible for the decision to treat Oklahoma City
as one big laboratory in an effort to discover whether 2,000 miles-
an-hour supersonic transports will be tolerable to those on the
ground. In addition to answering most of the complaints, the
FAA has so far paid out nearly $10,000 in damages, mostly small
sums, to compensate householders for cracked windows or walls.
Three claims for personal injury have been settled for a total of
only $330."

The urgent publicity given to a supersonic aircraft program
with multi-billion-dollar government subsidies contrasts with the
recent effort of the Federal Aviation Agency to attract aircraft
manufacturers to a design competition for planning a successor
to the DC-3 aircraft. A 50-man evaluation team found that none
of the designs from American firms warranted spending $100,000

in taxpayer's money on them. Accordingly, at this writing, there seems to be the imminent possibility that awards for the design of a successor to the DC-3 will have to be made to non-U.S. aircraft firms.

The effect of our concentration on military research and development is notably seen in the case of our industrial experience. During 1964, 90% of almost $15 billion of Federal research expenditures were made by the Department of Defense, the Atomic Energy Commission, and the National Aeronautics and Space Administration. The bulk of the activity contracted by these agencies took place in industrial firms. In January, 1963, the electronics, aircraft, and missile industries together employed 146,-000 engineers and scientists for research and development. This number exceeded the combined total number of persons engaged in research in the chemical industries, the petroleum industries, the steel industries, all the machinery-producing industries, and the automobile industries.

Another indication of the concentration on military-related research and development is that the number of scientists and engineers per 1,000 employees in the aircraft and missile industry was 101, or four times the comparable ratio of 23 per 1,000 employees for all other manufacturing industries combined.

The difference between the military and civilian industries is further amplified by the fact that much larger outlays for research and development are made per research and development employee within the military industries than within in the civilian industries.

Parallel to the virtual "nationalization" of control over research and development funds and their disposition, in the United States, is the evolution of a pattern of rather sharp concentration of research and development activity in the larger firms of particular industries. This process of concentration is promoted by the large proportion of industrial research that is government financed. The importance of Federal support ranges from 47% of the research done in the first eight firms of the primary metals industries to 93% of the research done by the major firms in electronics and related industries.

Competing for the defense market has led to remarkable patterns in the use of technical manpower. About 18% of the aerospace industry's top scientific and engineering talent has been working on proposals for *new* business rather than concentrating on existing contracts. And about 75% of this effort is spent on proposals that are rejected by the Government. The cost of efforts on competitive proposals frequently exceeds the value of the contract awarded.

The massive growth in Federal research budgeting since about 1950 has transformed the relationship between the university and the Federal Government.

In the table below, we already see the dependence of the universities on the Federal Government for their research funds by 1959-60. Leading, in this field, is the Massachusetts Institute of Technology. Of the MIT budget of $80.3 million, $65.6 million

FEDERAL RESEARCH IMPACT ON UNIVERSITY BUDGETS (1959–1960)

Institution	Total University Expenditures ($ Millions)	Federal Funds for Research ($ Millions)	Federal % of University Budgets
Cal. Tech	71.9	60.1	83.5
MIT	80.3	65.6	81.8
Princeton	40.6	30.6	75.3
U. of Cal., San Diego	11.1	7.4	67.0
Chicago	114.1	72.8	63.8
Stanford	35.0	14.4	41.1
Cornell	63.8	21.9	34.3
Michigan	73.8	20.5	27.8
Harvard	68.3	16.4	24.1
Iowa State	27.3	6.6	24.1
U. of Cal., Berkeley	53.0	8.6	16.4
Notre Dame	8.1	1.2	15.7
UCLA	54.2	7.6	14.0
Penn. State	45.5	6.0	13.3
Louisville	7.0	.9	13.0
Syracuse	18.3	2.3	12.9
Tulane	14.2	1.7	12.5
U. of Cal., Davis	17.9	2.0	11.2
Wyoming	7.4	.5	7.5
Indiana	43.2	2.3	5.5

or 81.8%, was accounted for by grants from the Federal Government. At the California Institute of Technology, with $71.9 million expended for all purposes, 83.5% or $60.1 million was derived from the Federal Government. At Princeton University, $30.6 out of $40.6 million total expenditure for all general purposes, or 75.3%, was accounted for by funds received from the Federal Government.

National dependence of this sort inevitably carries with it a degree of decision-power over what is done at universities which, however restrained, is nevertheless an inroad on the university's liberty to pursue freely the development of useful knowledge and to make it available for the use of mankind. To "pursue freely" means to make one's own choices about what is important research. The presence of vast Federal research programs constitutes a set of decisions about what is important, based upon particular political-military policies rather than the investigator's own choices about what will advance knowledge.

The economy of the university is being seriously compromised, and many people within its community are much concerned by this development. I think it especially useful to note the consequences of financial dependence, along these lines, in two universities that are important in their own right; this growing dependence also illustrates the organization of science for the Cold War, and its impact on the university and the related community.

The Massachusetts Institute of Technology and Stanford University are outstanding institutions in respect to developments in engineering and the sciences.

In 1963 Jesse E. Hobson, Vice-President of Southern Methodist University, and one-time chief executive officer of Stanford Research Institute, related this tale to a Congressional committee:

... Stanford University has become one of the great universities of the United States and of the world. Stanford's budget this year will be nearly $60 million with almost one-half of that coming from grants for research, almost entirely from agencies of the Federal Government. Only $9 or $10 million will come from student tuition and fees, and there will be additional income from an industrial research park development on the Stanford campus, amounting to more than $1 million, as well as additional income from the operating surplus of Stanford Research Institute. Stanford University has about 9,000 students, of whom 3,500 are working for advanced degrees and 5,500 are undergraduates. There are now 5 Nobel laureates on the staff of Stanford University (as well as 5 multimillionaires —staff members who have become multimillionaires through their participation in developments on the peninsula); about 200 Ph.D.'s are awarded each year by the university and there are 400 graduate students in electronics alone of which number at least 175 are employed full time in local industry. The endowment of Stanford University now stands something like $200 million with the expectation that it will amount to more than $250 million within the next year or two.

Stanford Research Institute now has a full-time staff of more than 2,000, and it will have income from research contracts this year amounting to nearly $35 million so that the total grant and contract income and support to Stanford University and Stanford Research Institute will be well over $60 million. Stanford Research Institute now has a net worth of $12 million, at least $8 million of which has been earned as surplus income on its own operations and something like $4 million which has been contributed by industry and business in order to make these research services possible and available. I do not know the total industrial employment on the peninsula nor the total amount of sales of new companies or of existing companies attracted to that area, but the sales will probably amount to $2.5 to $3 billion. Many of these companies were started by staff members, students, and graduates of Stanford University —such well-known companies as Hewlett Packard Co., Varian Associates, and many others which are well known and highly successful now. Other new companies have been started by former employees of Stanford Research Institute such as Granger Associates, Raychem, and others. Still other companies—General Electric, IBM, Lockheed, etc.—have moved research laboratories and manufacturing operations to the community to take advantage of the consulting services, the students, research assistance, and opportunities for higher education available in that community. It is interesting to me that the tax rate in the city of Palo Alto has declined from $1.50 per $100 in 1950 to 80 cents per $100 today—in spite of the fact that there are many more public schools, better schools, better libraries, better parks, and outstanding community services. . . .

It was early in the war [World War II] when the Federal Government decided to locate four of its key research laboratories at Harvard University and Massachusetts Institute of Technology in Cambridge.

The decision—based on the outstanding science and engineering departments at the two institutions—proved to be the fountainhead for New England's later dominance in the R&D field.

The radio research laboratory and the psycho-acoustic laboratory were established at Harvard, and the famed radiation laboratory and servomechanism laboratory were located at MIT.

Outstanding scientists, engineers, and graduate students from throughout the Nation joined the staffs of these laboratories—and many remained in the area after the war. The staff of the radiation laboratory, for example, numbered more than 4,000 at one time.

Both Harvard and MIT turned to local industry for assistance in producing the numerous electronic devices that the laboratories developed. The Raytheon Company, for instance, was utilized to produce magnetrons, the first ship-borne radar, and other such equipment. Many smaller companies also helped, and in doing so, they developed skills which they continued to exploit after the war.

When the war ended, a number of these campus military R&D efforts were terminated. However, at the insistence of the Department of Defense, the institutions continued their research in certain areas. In doing so, they were able to retain some of the most promising researchers on their faculties.

It was this young group that created a dynamic and creative research climate that attracted many of the Nation's most able students and spearheaded the industrial "spin-off" that followed.

At the same time, the Air Force and the Navy started several laboratories to capitalize on the wartime reservoir of scientific and engineering manpower that had migrated to New England —and liked the cultural, recreational, and intellectual attractions of the area.

Meanwhile, many scientists and engineers with ideas—and little or no money—found financial backing and launched scientifically oriented companies in electronics, nuclear physics, biology, medicine, metallurgy, operations research, meteorology, and other fields.

The region received another shot in the arm following the Korean conflict when the Department of Defense asked MIT to work on the Nation's air defense problems at Lincoln Laboratory. The Government went to MIT because of the reputation of its faculty in advanced electronics technology, and particularly computer and radar design.

A new building was constructed near Route 128 to house the Lincoln Laboratory, and satellite industries followed— forming the nucleus for the approximately 400 companies that currently line a 20-mile stretch of the highway.

The speed with which this buildup occurred is shown clearly in the surveys conducted by the Massachusetts Department of Commerce of industrial development along Route 128:

COMPANY FACILITIES

Year	In Operation	Under Construction
1955	39	14
1957	140	18
1958	209	17
1960	258	19
1961	306	28
1962	385	11

Among the scientifically oriented companies that have located in the area are High Voltage Engineering, Mitre, Instron, Itek, Minneapolis-Honeywell Electronic Data Division, Polaroid, National Research Corp., Raytheon, Dumont Laboratories, Sylvania, Baird-Atomic, Tracerlab-Keleket, RCA, Microwave Associates, Power Sources, Infrared Industries, and Geophysics Corp. of America.

Many Harvard and MIT faculty members and graduate students either have served as consultants to these companies or have helped form them. As a result of this close collaboration, many of the discoveries made in the university laboratories were applied almost immediately in industry, thereby further strengthening the area's position.

The elaborate development of government-sponsored research facilities at the universities has not occurred without serious rearrangement of the university structure in the United States as a whole. For example, in the fiscal year 1962, ten institutions received 39% of the Federal Government's total university expenditures on research and development. One result has been the concentration of talented young men within the ten large universities, drawn there by the facilities and the attraction of sheer growth rate; the attraction of superior academic personnel, both at the faculty and assistant level; and the concomitant pattern of attraction of students. One of the consequences of this, noted by those concerned with education in the United States, is that the medium-sized and the smaller academic institutions in the United States (there are 2,000 colleges and universities in this country), have been deprived of competent personnel, especially in the sciences. The smaller institutions, without large staffs and large laboratories, and without the funds to create them, cannot attract Federal contract awards.

At the same time, the universities that have been favored by large research contracts have found them a not-unmixed blessing. Many universities have complained to Congressional committees that the payments to them for indirect costs of research have been short of the actual costs incurred by the university. Of course, it is generally understood that there is no single, "correct" solution to the problem of indirect costs, which must be arbitrarily designated. For example, there is really no way of measuring what proportion of the operating cost of a major university library should be attributed to personnel performing research under government contract.

In the government-research-oriented universities there have been problems of imbalance between teaching and research, between basic and applied research, between science and the humanities. There has been a disproportionate growth of the physical sciences over the last decades. There has been great difficulty in attracting competent students into the various fields of the humanities. None of these departments can command the research contracts, the assistantships, or grants-in-aid that have been available to students in the fields of engineering and sciences. Thus there is a concentration of talent and money, if not of meaningful values for our society, in the high-government-supported technical universities; at the same time medium-sized and smaller institutions are at a disadvantage in getting and holding talented faculties because of lack of funds. The teaching function can hardly escape a degree of depletion wherever the performance of contract research is given sustained top priority for the time of senior professors.

Finally, it should be re-emphasized that even in the research institutions receiving very large government funds, there is the hard-to-measure impact of mission-oriented research, dependent on government contracts, as contrasted with the tradition of free-wheeling non-mission-oriented explorations.

In a volume entitled *The Uses of the University*, Clark Kerr, President of the University of California, indicated: "The University has become a prime instrument of national purpose. This is new. This is the essence of the transformation now engulfing our universities. Basic to this transformation is the growth of the knowledge industry which is coming to permeate government and business and to draw into it more and more people raised to higher and higher levels of skill."

On the face of it, Clark Kerr's description would seem to reflect a widening level of scientific and technical competence, measured in terms of the amount of activity and, by implication, of the functional knowledge produced. What is not accounted for, without careful analysis, is the necessary differentiation between research and development on behalf of the Department of Defense and allied agencies, as against research and development for human needs, or for the civilian economy, as understood broadly. In the case of research done primarily on behalf of the defense-space complex, one must understand that the knowledge there produced does not, except in rare cases, contribute to further production in American society. The ordinary assumption that the elaboration of science and technology will provide the base for expanding productivity within a society is abridged when a major part of research and development activity is carried on in behalf of the military functions.

The idea of a "knowledge industry" is a travesty on the process of inquiry. There is no conceivable way of specifying a standardized, routine, repeated set of acts, out of which new knowledge may be produced—not even in explicitly applied research where a preferred result is formulated in advance.

During the last decade, many Americans who have followed this concentration of research into the defense and space fields have been very concerned with the question as to whether or not there is a transfer of knowledge, or a spillover of knowledge, from the military to the civilian sector of the economy.

The National Aeronautics and Space Administration has sponsored a number of major investigations into this question. A report that the Denver Research Institute did for NASA listed a possible array of "spin-offs" from the missile-space program. I find it noteworthy that in their judgment "intangible spin-off is far more important than tangible spin-off." That leaves the ordinary reader in some difficulty, since if the spin-off is intangible it is difficult to observe or measure. One can only speculate as to what may be its nature or to its possible effect. Although NASA has been somewhat embarrassed at raising the issue of civilian spin-off from its space research, we may expect further discussion from them on this matter. The burden of judgment, in scientific circles, among people in the universities, and in industry is that derived civilian effects from space or defense research will be of modest dimension. One person noted that one might concentrate on the civilian research field in the hope that the spin-off toward space activity would be of a magnitude great enough to justify the civilian activity in terms of the space effect.

The Director of Research at the General Electric Company, Dr. Guy Suits, made the following judgment on this matter:

... a popular misconception has somehow come into being that defense-oriented research and technology determine, or at least are primary factors in, the advance of non-defense industry. If this were so, the tail would certainly be wagging the dog. . . .

It is also a fact that there is an extensive and mutually beneficial interaction between defense technology and non-defense technology; in some fields the two are so interwoven as to defy separate identification. Illustrative cases are electron tube and semi-conductor technology. The field of computer development might fit into this category also.

However, I have the impression that, in view of the remarkably large magnitude of defense research, development and evaluation, there has been a surprisingly small amount of technological by-product which has provided non-defense consumer and industrial products and services.

On the same subject the verdict of the Engineers' Joint Council is clear:

... There is much evidence that spill-over from military research to the civilian economy does not occur very frequently. Accordingly, the military program must be recognized as utilizing a large fraction of the most talented individuals in research and development in the country and of denying to the civilian economy the services of these individuals. As the national problems relating to the growth of the civilian economy increase in intensity and complexity, the consequences of allocating such a large fraction of the national research talent to defense must be given careful consideration.

Until now, the dominant issue among Americans, with respect to the governmental budget for science and technology, has not been: What should the money be best spent for? Rather, the point has been: Which defense contractor should get the money? Is our state getting its "fair share"?

However, the contest about who should receive the Government's contracts has proceeded on the assumption that, wherever these contracts are allotted, they produce not only direct revenue, but indirect, long-range, economic growth. There is no question that salaries received in factories or laboratories and spent in shops for services, in a given region, will provide a livelihood for the people operating such shops.

Nonetheless, major governmental military-research spending, with its regional and industrial concentration, has not produced healthy national economic growth. The growing suspicion that this is indeed the case has been troubling many senior military men and their civilian advisors.

At the military-budget hearings during 1964, before the Committee on Armed Services of the House of Representatives, Admiral Coates, of the Office of Naval Research, gave testimony concerning civilian benefits from the military program. The Admiral was discussing the research program for the development of methods for separating the uranium isotope U-235—one of the processes used in the production of material for the first atomic bomb. He commented that "an interesting but rather insignificant and trivial accomplishment that has come out of this program is the greaseless fry pan. This is interesting because the work done at the Naval Research Laboratory was for a dry lubricant for very cold applications and coincidentally someone has found a hot application out of the same thing. The program was to develop a method for coating steel with Teflon."

This contribution from the Naval Research Laboratory will surely be appreciated by all grateful greaseless fry-pan users. The issue remains: In what degree do such—or grander—by-product results justify military-space-research outlays of $13 billion each year?

The response of conventional wisdom has been: What of it? Isn't the United States the richest country in the world? Why can't we have both guns and butter—with trips to the moon for good measure?

The ability of a society to enlarge its capacity for money spending must be differentiated from limitations on the number of people with special talents. The very nature of money is that its quantity is almost indefinitely expansible; the amount of money in use can be enlarged by printing more money, by extending credit, by granting loans. The same cannot be said for the number of qualified persons available for certain work. That number is finite, for there is in particular areas, a finite number of people with particular capabilities or potential to become particularly skilled persons. The most crucial allocation of resources to the defense-space complex has been the assignment of two thirds or more of the nation's finite stock of technical researchers to these efforts. This has effectively depleted the civilian economy at many points.

During the years of World War II, guns and butter did increase together in the United States, because the war effort made use of the enormous and unused capacity of factories and manpower that had been idled by the Great Depression. The long-drawn-out Cold War has diverted high-grade talent from civilian work. One man cannot at the same time be a designer of merchant ships and a researcher on rocket airframes. By favoring rockets we have automatically chosen guns rather than butter.

The domination of the defense agencies over funds for science and technology has produced distortions in the very processes integral to the successful performance of inquiry itself. Included in the long tradition of science is agreement that the unfolding of new knowledge proceeds best when investigators themselves decide what are preferred next steps in inquiry, and when there is free dissemination and open discussion of the methods of investigation as well as the results. These practices, interacting, place controls (knowledgeable constraints) on the design of investigation and on the validation of results.

Within the context of a many-sided Cold War contest, political and military considerations have been used to decide on experiments whose results include long-range effects on man and on the physical universe itself.

For military reasons, the United States Government in 1958

and 1962 conducted high-altitude nuclear explosions to gauge the effects on radio communication. These and other experiments were conducted without benefit of open discussion of the experimental design, and the results include long-lasting contaminating effects on the Van Allen Belt.

Such government-sponsored experiments, performed by men in government employ, have generated disquiet in the scientific community. A firm warning against such violations of scientific procedures was given by a committee of the American Academy of Sciences in a report (December, 1964) on *The Integrity of Science*. The violation of the essential procedures of science, they warned, can only produce deterioration in the productivity of science and its serviceability on behalf of man.

The space program, featuring a manned landing on the moon (the Apollo program), is a major demonstration of how Cold War pressures operate on science and technology. The manned moon landing will cost between $20 and $40 billion—let us say $30 billion. From the standpoint of scientific return, little is expected from this effort. The space program includes launching a series of satellite vehicles around the moon as well as various instrumented, unmanned lunar landings that will produce a long array of scientific information. The incremental contribution of the manned landings to science will be "geological exploration" —though prior unmanned vehicles are scheduled to take core samples of the moon crust and return them to earth. Why then a $30 billion manned landing?

The record discloses that the decision by President Kennedy to race for a lunar landing was a political decision for a political purpose, and had little relation to purely scientific considerations. The Space Science Board, established by the National Academy of Science in 1958, gave manned lunar landing low priority in a schedule of space-science activities.

After the disastrous Bay of Pigs adventure and subsequent Soviet space flights, President Kennedy gave the man-on-the-moon project political priority. Since then about 75% of the $5.2 billion 1964 space budget has been used in pursuit of this program.

From the standpoint of science there has been a warping effect from this decision, as defined by the report on *The Integrity of Science:*

In general, scientific observations required for the planning of the manned landing are now assigned higher priorities than other studies which are of greater scientific interest but not essential to the development of the technology needed for the Apollo project. Therefore, the pattern for development of scientific research in space has been altered significantly by the essentially political decision to undertake the Apollo program.

This procedure is seriously at variance with important precepts of scientific experimentation and technology. The preferable order of events is: basic scientific investigation, technological application based on the resultant basic knowledge, social use of the technological innovations. In the Apollo program this sequence has been reversed, so that a program for a particular technological achievement has been committed, even as to the date of its accomplishment, in advance of the orderly acquisition of the related basic knowledge. The Apollo program, in its present form, does not appear to be based on the orderly, systematic extension of basic scientific investigation.

We are also, all of us, sponsoring a gamble with the lives of the men aboard. However much money, talent, and time is devoted to doing things the best-known way, it remains that an estimated 22,000 separate acts must be carried off without flaw in performing the projected manned earth-moon-earth journey. Even a very small percentage of error could produce tragedy.

There are now substantive reasons for doubting that man can survive after space flight over an extended period. Professor Marcel Florkin of Liege University, a member of the international scientific Committee on Space Research, announced on December 23, 1964, that the consensus among scientists was that weightless flight by man would be impossible for more than five or six days. He indicated that Soviet scientists had produced photographs showing abnormalities in human cell division attributable to the sustained weightlessness some of their astronauts have experienced. Normal cell division is a vital life process, and abnormal division can be lethal. In Project Apollo the astronauts landing on the moon will be weightless for less than three days on each leg of the journey. A third man, in a moon-orbiting vehicle while his colleagues land, would be weightless about a week.

The Space Science Board, on November 17, 1964, issued a new policy recommendation on research in space. With respect to manned moon exploration the Board wrote:

Aware of the parallel criteria of scientific and intellectual importance *and* of significance to the national interest, the Board summarizes its recommendations on the primary national objectives in the field of space science for the 1971-1985 period as follows: *Exploration of the planets with particular emphasis on Mars*

(a) This objective includes both physical and biological investigations, and especially the search for extraterrestrial life.

(b) The experimentation should be carried out largely by unmanned vehicles while the solution of difficult biomedical and bioengineering problems proceeds at a measured pace so that toward the end of this epoch (1985) we shall be ready for manned planetary exploration.

(c) Alternatives to the Mars and planetary exploration goal—(i) extensive manned lunar exploration (possibly including lunar base construction) and (ii) major manned orbiting space station and laboratory program—are not regarded as primary goals, because they have less scientific significance. However, both have sufficient merit to warrant parallel programs but of lower priority.

Professor Polykarp Kusch of Columbia University and Nobel Laureate in Physics, commented on the Apollo crash program from the standpoint of classically understood requirements for competent inquiry:

It is my belief that the present space program attempts too much too fast. There is not enough time for profound thought, for imagination to play over the demanding problems that occur. Someone has said to me, in a discussion of the space program, that the attempts that are being made to explore space are similar to those that would have been made had the physicists of the prewar era attempted a program of research involving a billion-volt proton accelerator. The scientific ideas that allow us presently to build such machines had not yet appeared; conceivably that machine could have been built, but only with very much greater difficulty than present machines propose. The important problems that have engaged in mind and efforts (sic) of the generation of physicists now in their prime were too dimly understood to allow the kind of effective inquiry currently undertaken. Much of the auxiliary gear that is central to the observation of high energy phenomena had not yet been invented. Finally, the extraordinarily effective guidelines that the theorists of physics develop had not yet begun to appear. (June 10, 1963, to the U.S. Senate, Committee on Aeronautical and Space Sciences.)

Meanwhile, spending $5 billion a year in one set of projects stirs up the economy of the localities that are directly involved. The space agency estimates that 20,000 firms and 300,000 people eventually will be involved in the project: $2 billion each year in direct salaries alone. Already 130,000 men are working on the spacecraft program itself; 20,000-40,000 substantial homes have been built near the $150 million Houston, Texas, Manned Space Center.

In 1962 Dr. Hugh L. Dryden, Deputy Director of NASA, stated that by 1970 one fourth of American scientists and engineers would be engaged in space activities. Skeptics may note that in July, 1964, a random sample of 2,000 members of the American Association for the Advancement of Science showed 12% of them receiving Federal support related to space activities. Meanwhile the space program appetite for technical talent cannot be satisfied—even at the cost of depleting many American activities. With relatively high-paying jobs as a lure, space contractors have been attracting foreign scientists and engineers.

About 43,000 scientists and engineers have come to the United States since 1949, thereby imposing our priorities on other nations.

Why this massive space effort? James E. Webb, Director of the National Aeronautics and Space Administration has declared:

> Far more is involved in the Apollo program than the propaganda or prestige value of insuring that an American is first to set foot on the moon. Rather, we are concerned with the strength and the image of the United States as the acknowledged leader in all areas of science and technology.
>
> Exploration of the moon has been selected as the focal point of our present efforts in space partly because, by its very nature, it commands worldwide public interest. But it also has been selected because it is the first major objective in which we have an excellent chance of being first, because it promises to add to our knowledge of the laws of nature, the forces mankind strives to understand and use, the origin of the universe, and because its accomplishment requires mastery of a broad spectrum of science and technology on which a growing capability to operate in space and increase efficiency on earth must rest.
>
> Those who view the lunar program simply as a "propaganda" effort fail to grasp that not only our prestige, but our capacity for constructive international leadership, our economic and military capacity for technological improvement, depend upon our ability to achieve acknowledged superiority in science and technology, and to use this capability in our own behalf and that of our allies.
>
> With a billion people already allied against us, and the uncommitted and emerging nations weighing events that will affect their own future welfare, the United States must present the image of a can-do nation, with which they can confidently align their futures.

Two sets of issues are at stake here: first, the meaning of the space program for science; second, the political significance of the effort. The space agency's 1964 budget for basic research

was about twice the budget of the National Science Foundation
—whose responsibility for encouraging science is broadly defined. While the space agency's spending for basic research will
surely produce new knowledge in the fields that are tackled, it
remains that the space projects, as defined, set constraints to what
the agency is interested in. These constraints are automatically
understood both by the agency's administrators and by the scientists who apply for grant funds. Consequently, the scientists, seeking success in their applications for funds, ask themselves: What
is NASA interested in? Asking that question is a distortion of
the priority that free inquiry needs. For the integrity of science
the investigator must be free to ask: What do I think is the next
research step for unfolding new knowledge in a field that is interesting to me and to other scientific colleagues?

On the political side, concern for America's total strength
should take into account the depleting effects caused elsewhere
by the concentration of talent and capital in defense-space work.
The manned lunar landing as a mark of constructive international
leadership may be gauged against alternatives such as acting to
reduce hunger or developing and building good quality mass-
produced housing that is desperately needed at home and abroad.
A Civil Rights bill or murder without punishment in the American South are more influential than space shots in affecting the
judgment of most of mankind about the moral or political merits
of American society.

There is little warrant for the prediction that the Apollo project could be decisive politically—in winning "the battle for the
minds of men." American political positions in Asia and Africa
are not controlled by the success of space projects. Soviet decisions to move toward profit incentives in industry and agriculture
have little to do with rank in an international rocket weightlifting
contest. The movement of Eastern European countries toward
greater autonomy and less Soviet control is not determined by the
crash program for lunar landing.

In my judgment the "space race" altogether is a form of pseudo-
challenge. It is an evasion of the substantive issues which deeply
concern most of the people of the earth: How can one organize
and act for rapid economic development, so that the potentials of

science and technology can be realized for man? Which social order best combines efficiency with human freedom?

How shall we look to ourselves after spending $30 billion on an operation that we shall see as a seven-day TV spectacular? It will be spectacular, and we can only admire the display of technical ingenuity and the bravery of the astronauts. But will it be worth $30 billion? Won't we and many millions of people throughout the world wonder: What sort of society is this that could devote so much wealth to so trivial a purpose?

Dr. Warren Weaver, distinguished mathematician and former president of the American Academy of Science, has drawn up this shopping list as an alternative to spending $30 billion on the Apollo program:

	Cost ($ billions)
10% yearly salary raise for 10 years to all U.S. teachers	9.8
$10 million to each of 200 small colleges in U.S.	2.0
Complete 7-year fellowships to train 50,000 scientists and engineers, at $4,000/man/year	1.4
$200 million to create 10 new medical schools	2.0
Build and endow complete universities, with liberal arts, science, engineering, medical and agricultural faculties, in each of 53 nations	13.2
Establish 3 new foundations, like the Rockefeller Foundation	1.5
For public education on science	.1
(or the cost of a manned lunar landing) =	$30.0

Serious doubts about the wisdom of the space race have not been restricted to some leading scientists or particular political parties. Democrats have affirmed that being first in productive achievement on earth is more significant—politically and humanly—than being first on the moon. When the 1964 NASA budget was under consideration in the Congress, a staff paper of the Senate Republican Policy Committee asked:

> Is it more important to have a man on the moon than to conquer cancer which will take the lives of over 40 million Americans now living?

Is being first more important than insuring an adequate water source for our great metropolitan centers?

Is a fistful of lunar dust meaningful to the 17 million Americans who, we are told, go to bed hungry each night?

President Kennedy, too, touched on this problem, when he wrote in his Economic Report to the nation for 1963, that the United States has "paid a price by sharply limiting the scarce scientific and engineering resources available to the civilian sectors of the American economy."

5

Firms Without Enterprise

The National Aeronautics and Space Administration gave one of America's leading military electronics firms a contract to devise an advanced form of electrocardiograph for use by Colonel Glenn on his space flight. The machine was constructed. It was attached to the Colonel while he orbited the earth, and it performed admirably. The marketing department of this company decided that its new electrocardiograph, which gives more information about heart function than ordinary machines, might be sold to the medical profession. So the firm prepared a machine for demonstration for a heart specialist.

The equipment was boxed in an available container, a military type (sturdy olive drab), and carried off to the doctor's office. There a demonstration of the machine's capabilities was given, and the physician was genuinely impressed. He turned to the marketing men and asked, "Has the AMA approved this machine?" The marketing men were a bit nonplused, thinking to themselves: What does the American Management Association have to do with all this? The doctor soon made it clear to them that it was approval by the American Medical Association that was of interest to him. No, the machine had not been shown to any formal body of the Medical Association. The physician then asked: "Is the firm prepared to take out a $1 million liability insurance policy on the use of this machine so that if a doctor's patient should suffer some mishap while he was attached to this machine, the doctor would be covered for medical liability?" The company men, as they reported it, were rather upset: "Do you mean," they said to the doctor, "that you want us to pay for a $1 million liability policy while we are selling you this advanced machine for a mere $6,500?" The heart specialist clarified the point for the military technicians, explaining that such insurance coverage was conventional for medical machines.

Then there is the matter of the $6,500 price which made this machine exactly ten times as expensive as the ordinary, first-rate electrocardiograph machine already being used by physicians. The high price of the machine made it unattractive to the doctor. When the marketing man in charge of this venture told me his story, I asked, "Before you saw the physician and set this price, did you find out how many pieces of equipment in a modern hospital might cost $6,500 or more?" "No," he said, "no attempt was made to get such information."

The end of the tale is that the marketing department of the military-electronics firm gave up on the whole affair, and decided to try to turn their new machine over to a company already established in the medical-instrument field.

This incident is characteristic of the behavior of many military-industrial firms during the last few years. From time to time, engineers and others on their staffs decided that some particular product might be commercially marketable. Whereupon, efforts were made in that direction and, with rare exception, they failed. A regular pattern was to be discerned: These companies, and their employees, no longer had the capability to design, manufacture, and sell to the civilian markets. Long experience in servicing the defense agencies of the Government, under conditions where cost had been a secondary matter, resulted in a trained incapacity, among many military-industrial firms, and their staffs, to operate in a civilian market.

Management of the ordinary sort of industrial firm, in the civilian field, involves deciding on what shall be produced, how it will be produced, in what quantity, and how to dispose of the product.

Before all this, the management must also gather the capital and organize the human and technical resources required for production. The ability to do all these things is the essential nature of "entrepreneurship," or, in more recent usage, enterprise. The inability of military-industrial managements to do work within this range has caused them to become the chiefs of firms without enterprise.

The private firm raises capital from its own surpluses, the result of previous activity, or by means of loans from banks, or by inviting the general public to invest in securities. One of the principal differences between the procedures of the private firm and the military-industrial firm is that the larger military-industrial firm has drawn heavily upon Government as a source of capital. Thus, Federal defense agencies have become the principal owners of metal-working machinery in the United States. The Department of Defense itself owns 341,000 buildings within the United States (some proportion of these are factory buildings). These buildings encompass almost 2 billion square feet of floor space, and their value, taken together with the attached land, and facilities, amounts to almost $37 billion.

What should be produced? In a civilian firm, this decision is based on an estimate of the market, the functional requirements to be met by the product, an estimate of its ability to attract purchases at an acceptable price. In a military-industrial firm, of course, the Department of Defense makes the principal decision about the nature of the product to be produced. Very often, the Department of Defense invites advice from the research and allied departments of principal military contractors. Study contracts are issued for research to be done on possible new weapons systems. The research reports are submitted to the Department of Defense and provide a basis for decisions about what should be produced.

Research and development is one of the key activities in an industrial firm, since it affects and shapes the technical position of the firm among its competitors. In a civilian-oriented enterprise, decisions about industrial research are based upon the characteristics of civilian products and their sales potential. Those performing such research for the civilian firm have access to the general body of literature in the areas of science and technology. Further, the amount of money spent on research by the firm must be controlled by the amount the sale of the product brings. In the case of the military-industrial firm, new technology is freed from cost restraint, for new military technology is justified as an end in itself, and so cost considerations take a back seat. In addition, there is no built-in restraint in military industry to determine what is a reasonable level of expenditure for research affecting new military technology. Since refined methods in the military art are regarded as important for attaining and holding military advantage, great pressure has built up behind research into new military techniques.

In the aerospace industries, for example, the level of spending per research engineer and scientist in the larger companies reached the level of $55,700 per man, while in all American industries combined, the equivalent figure was $34,700 per research engineer. Finally, military-industrial research is segregated from civilian research because of access to a "classified" body of literature unavailable to civilian researchers. This, of course, involves the operation of libraries of classified information under special security controls.

The structure of management in the military firm, and its cost, are significantly different from structure and cost in a civilian firm. While there has been a tendency toward growth in the relative cost of management in all industry during the last half century, restraints on administrative costs of the sort operative in civilian firms do not appear to be dominant in the military-industrial enterprise. A good illustration of an aspect of this condition is found in an electronics firm I visited in 1963. This firm was in the unique position of producing an instrument whose working parts were assembled on a chassis in two different departments. One department packaged the equipment in a case for civilian use; the second department packaged it in containers for military use. The main production operation therefore included both civilian and military shipments. However, in this plant (all under one roof) two separate management offices were maintained. The military administrative office included function-aries not found on the civilian side. In order to meet the requirements of the Department of Defense the defense section included a property officer, security officers and guards, a contract administrator, contract lawyers, contract auditors, contract negotiators, contract re-negotiators, and contract-termination specialists. Also, the firm employed a larger number of technicians in the military administrative section than in the civilian counterpart. The result was that the overhead rate on direct costs on the civilian side was 80%, while the overhead charge on the military side was 135%. In military-industrial firms administrative costs have reached hitherto unknown heights.

How should a product be produced? In a civilian enterprise the production methods chosen are usually those that minimize costs while turning out a functionally satisfactory and salable item. In a defense-oriented enterprise, the operating characteristics of the product take first importance. Indeed, there is sustained pressure for "improving" the product in detail, while cost considerations take a definitely secondary role.

In order to meet the requirements of firms that are asked to undertake the production of new products, the Department of Defense has long practiced the pattern of writing contracts which pay the contracting firm for all the costs incurred, and in addition, pay the firm a profit over and above the cost. This sort of contract inevitably involves an incentive to maximize and not minimize costs. In an effort to hold down costs of military materiel, the Defense Department has tried to shift to contracts based on a fixed price, or contracts that include an incentive toward lower costs. In each case, however, the prior cost experience in these fields was the available basis, or standard, for setting the fixed price, or for setting the level of costs to serve as the target for an incentive system. Where the experience of cost-plus-profit is the basis for setting fixed price, the experience biases the decision in favor of high costs as a basis for setting a fixed price. In the case of incentive-type contracts, the target cost has again been the subject of bargaining. In this case the military-industrial firm is given an incentive to set the target cost as high as possible so that an incentive could be readily earned by operating under the target cost. (At this point, I think many people who know something about methods of industrial management in the USSR will feel they are on partly familiar ground. Their intuition is probably correct, and can be checked out by an examination of two books that treat this style of Soviet industrial management. I recommend Joseph S. Berliner, *Factory and Manager in the USSR*, Harvard University Press, 1957; and, David Granick, *The Red Executive*, Doubleday, 1960.)

Industrial relations are a most important function of the civilian industrial manager, since the level of wages has an important effect on the competitive position of the firm. Therefore, industrial relations are treated as a major part of management's concern, in the effort to protect the firm's competitive position. Among military-industrial firms, however, the situation is rather different. There, the customer (the Department of Defense), is the one who pays. Accordingly, in many military-industrial firms, the custom has developed of consulting with the Department of Defense before new contract arrangements are concluded. Through such arrangements the management of the military-industrial enterprise becomes merely the nominal contracting party with the labor union, because the crucial decisions on these matters are made by the Government-customer.

Decisions on how much to produce are made in the civilian firm on the basis of estimates of markets and the relation of costs and price. The Department of Defense, however, decides for the military-industrial management.

Marketing strategy is a primary function for the civilian manager, as disposition of the product is his responsibility. For the military-industrial firm, all of this is subordinate to the customer's decision, and the Department of Defense decides on shipments, their timing and quantity, to suit its convenience.

Customer relations in the civilian enterprise have an essentially commercial basis, notwithstanding a degree of applied personal leavening. In the military-industrial enterprise, however, the critical considerations in customer relations are a combination of technical and political considerations. On the technical side, there is the requirement of demonstrated competence to produce particular goods, with cost again of secondary importance. The political aspect of military customer relations involves not only the personnel of the Department of Defense, but also members of Congress and other public officials. Recently the custom has developed of permitting Members of Congress to make the first public announcements of the award of new contracts in their respective districts or states. Some Members of Congress devote a considerable part of their working time to helping military-industrial enterprises in their districts secure particular contracts. This involvement in contract competition culminated in the remarkable spectacle of the long-drawn-out 1964 hearings on the so-called TFX aircraft in which the principal issue was never, "Should this plane be produced?" but only, "Who should have gotten the contract?"

In a civilian firm, the most efficient utilization of the equipment and labor force is characteristically obtained under conditions of stable operation—where the rate of output is not permitted to vary widely. By contrast, the military-industrial enterprise is best enabled to enlarge, adding to research staff and production facilities, under conditions of instability, of major changes in the work done and the products produced. These changes became the opportunity for increasing research and production staffs and for drawing on fresh Government capital for these purposes.

In the private, civilian firm, the main criterion for the investment of productive capital is an estimate of the future activity and earnings of the particular enterprise. Forecasting the future condition of the market involved is thereby a primary requirement of its management. On the military side, however, judgments about investments must necessarily be based almost exclusively on current earnings. Estimates of future conditions must be based primarily on contracts already in hand. Beyond the terms of the contract, the future of the enterprise is not in the hands of its management but lies rather with the officers of the Federal Government's defense agencies.

The ways of birth and death of enterprise differentiate the civil-

ian from the military firm. In the case of the private firm, both
starting and terminating an enterprise are based primarily on
private decision. In the military sphere, however, the birth of an
enterprise may be a private decision or a Government agency's
decision, or a mixture of the two. The Air Force, for example,
initiated the formation of special firms based in California to
supervise the detailed management of many missile contracts.
A privately owned firm, though heavily engaged in contract work
for a government agency, can be legally terminated by decision
of its management. But managements are not oriented toward
terminating their enterprises. Rather, there is a strong drive in
every industrial management to continue and to expand the operation of the firm. The more critical test of the unique characteristic of the military-industrial enterprise is the reaction of such
a firm to the sort of grave financial difficulty that could ordinarily
result in the termination of a private enterprise. By decision of
the Department of Defense, for example, particular firms can be
made unsinkable, financially speaking. A case in point is the General Dynamics Corporation, which has for many years been the
number one military-industrial contractor in terms of the volume
of work done. One of the divisions of this firm is the Convair
aircraft group with principal factories in San Diego and Fort
Worth. The Convair Division undertook the design and manufacture of the Convair 880 airplane. This enterprise, in competition with the 4-engine jets of Boeing and Douglas, produced
long-delayed aircraft at costs that netted General Dynamics a
loss of about $440 million. The same division of the same firm
was subsequently awarded the multi-billion-dollar Air Force contract for the manufacture of the highly controversial TFX airplane. The effect of this contract award was certainly to sustain
the firm as an available military contractor.

Both the location and primary function of top management
differ sharply in the civilian as against the military-industrial
enterprises. In the private firm, the final veto in decision-making
is usually found in the most senior officers of the firm itself. This
final veto power pertains to virtually the whole range of operations of the firm. Not so in the military-oriented enterprise; there,

final veto power is located in the Department of Defense or in the other governmental agencies to which the firm is beholden, and the principal duties of top management in this case are to maintain satisfactory relations with the government agencies.

In some military-industrial enterprises, the managers resemble the men in charge of a subdivision of a major central-office firm, rather than the operators of autonomous enterprises. These managers operate nominally independent firms; they do not, however, perform those functions classically understood as entrepreneurship, management, or enterprise.

Another aspect of operating that differentiates the military-industrial firm from the civilian one is the role of the union. Classically, the trade union, in the realm of private industrial enterprise, has functioned as an autonomous organization of workers, housing among them an evolving process of mutual decision-making. This is expressed in the contract relations between union and management which have developed, in ever greater detail, the terms of worker employment. Because of the important decision-making role of the Federal Government agencies, the trade union, in military-industrial enterprises, has entered into unique relationships with both local management and the decision-making group in the Federal Government. Union officers, in these firms, have often become important participants in the marketing function. Union leaders have learned to use political contacts and political methods to help get preference in the allocation of contracts to their enterprise. This has involved delegations to the Department of Defense, and the establishment of Washington offices, an important part of whose business is to lobby at the Department of Defense and in the Congress in favor of procurement programs for their industries and to see that contracts are allocated to their firms.

For some unions, the growth of defense industries has afforded a major area of job and membership expansion. This has taken on special importance owing to job losses in depleted industries, and those resulting from automation. Three of the principal unions in the AFL-CIO—the United Automobile Workers, the International Union of Electrical Workers, and the International

Association of Machinists—are heavily involved in the aerospace and the military-electronics industry.

The development of a pattern of political participation on behalf of contract soliciting has resulted in a functional commitment to defense industry. This has had varied results for unions: union reluctance, as among many defense managers, to plan for conversion from military to civilian industry; concern for the level and continuity of military contracts; and finally, an inability, resulting from inner tension, to confront the problems of reorganizing depleted American industries. To the extent that such pressures operate among defense managements and unions, both are hard put to find ways to participate effectively in reconstructing depleted industries or repairing the human damage due to restricted budgets for the human care of human beings.

6

The High Cost of
Discarding People

During 1963, 532,000 young men, registrants of the Selective
Service System, were examined for potential military service. Exactly 50% of them were found unacceptable: of these 24% were
medically disqualified; 21.6% failed the mental test; 3.1% failed
the mental test and were also medically disqualified; and 1.3%
were ruled out "administratively."

From Colonel George H. Walton (USA), formerly Planning
officer of the Selective Service System, we learn that during the
Second World War the average rejection rate for all reasons was
about 30%. A 50% rejection rate in 1963, without a change of
standards, would seem to represent a massive deterioration in the
educational and physical competence of the young people of
American society. (A Report to President Kennedy estimated
that 33% of our youth would not meet Selective Service standards. I am using actual draft records.) In *The Saturday Evening
Post* (December 8, 1962), Colonel Walton wrote:

> . . . Five years ago, when I was assigned to Selective Service
> and first encountered the facts on draft rejection, I refused to
> believe that the situation could really be as bad as the figures
> indicated. Two possible explanations occurred to me: that the
> draft standards had been steadily raised or that young men
> were deliberately failing their exams to dodge military service.

Only after much study of the problem did I become convinced that both these conjectures are false.

. . . Examining the cases of 14,556 such men, I gave special attention to those who were rejected because they had failed the written test. It seemed incredible to me at the time that so many men could possibly flunk it. But after I had gone over their classifications questionnaires . . . I was forced to the conclusion that they were literally unable to read and comprehend some of the simplest questions. In many cases the questionnaires had even been filled out by persons other than the youths whose scrawled signatures appeared on the forms. Letters from a large number of them were either illegible or incoherent, or both.

Among the states of the Union, the lowest rate of rejection was 32% in Utah, while the highest percentage, 67.3% rejected, was in Mississippi. So the best showing is made by a state in which one out of three of the young people are educationally and physically incapacitated; in the worst as many as two out of three of the teen-agers examined are found to be medically or educationally below standard.

The list of states whose rejection rate in 1963 for combined medical and educational factors exceeded the national average of 50% is worth examining:

State	Rejection Rate	State	Rejection Rate
Mississippi	67.3	Arizona	56.7
Louisiana	67.1	Georgia	55.9
Alabama	66.1	Tennessee	55.8
District of Columbia	63.0	Maryland	55.5
South Carolina	62.6	Virginia	55.4
West Virginia	62.6	Washington	54.4
Maine	61.4	New Jersey	54.3
Arkansas	58.9	Texas	52.9
New Mexico	58.9	Nevada	52.1
Massachusetts	58.8	Hawaii	51.6
North Carolina	58.4	Kentucky	50.8
Florida	57.9	Vermont	50.1

It is significant that, in addition to strong representation from the economically underdeveloped states of the Old South, the list of high disqualification areas includes the District of Columbia, Massachusetts, Nevada, New Jersey, Vermont, and West Virginia. Massachusetts and New Jersey are both heavily industrialized Northern states and do not share a history of regional economic deprivation with the states of the South.

During 1963, President Kennedy ordered an investigation into this matter, and the report, called "One-Third of a Nation" found a direct relationship between draft rejection and substandard income. By August, 1964, the Congress was asked to appropriate $16 million for an experimental program of special education and physical rehabilitation of volunteers rejected by the Army. This program was to involve about 11,000 men.

These discussions have not included reference to the young women of the country. It would seem plausible to assume that the forces making for educational and physical deprivation would be operative among women as well. But virtually no attention seems to be paid to that half of the population. The implication appears to be that their physical and educational competence is of little importance.

How did all this deterioration happen? During the last 30 years the United States is supposed to have become more and more a "welfare state." It is a fact that many laws pertaining to social security, labor, health, full employment, housing, and the like have been enacted. But how much of our energy and our resources have we really devoted to aspects of human welfare that ordinarily fall in the public domain?

In 1939 the Federal Government spent $8.8 billion for all purposes. Out of this amount, the total expenditure for education, health, labor, welfare, housing, and community development was $3.7 billion, or 42.5%. Spending by the Federal Government is expected to be $100 billion or more by fiscal year 1965, and expenditures for the whole set of human-welfare items is estimated at $7.2 billion, or about 7%. Obviously, a drop from 42 to 7% marks a sharp decline in that proportion of the Federal Government's budget used for human welfare purposes. Of course, from 1939 to 1963 there has also been a sharp change in the purchasing power of money. Professor Emile Benoit, of Columbia University's School of Business, has calculated the amount spent per person for all nondefense purposes, by the Federal Government, and has expressed these expenditures in terms of the dollar's value in 1963. By his reckoning, $83 per person was spent in 1939; $75 was spent in 1953; and only $56 in 1963. Furthermore, nondefense buying by Federal and state, as well as local government, has declined from 17% of the value of all goods and services (Gross National Product) in 1939, to 12% by 1963.

During the quarter-century 1940-65, expenditures by the Federal Government grew tenfold, from $9 to $100 billion. This growth has been dominated by military spending, which has not only added to total outlays, but has also grown at the expense of many nonmilitary activities. That is parasitic growth, for its effects are felt in many facets of our national life: in poor medical services, in overcrowded schools, and in declining employment in many industries left to deteriorate technically and economically.

Infant mortality is a sensitive indicator of medical care. The infant-mortality rate measures the death of infants under one year of age per 1,000 live births. In 1963, the infant-mortality rate in the United States was 25.2. By this reckoning the United States ranked about twelfth among countries of the world. The following countries had lower reported infant-mortality rates: Czechoslovakia, Denmark, Finland, Hungary, Republic of Korea, Lebanon, Netherlands, New Zealand, Norway, Sweden, and the United Kingdom. In Sweden, the infant mortality rate was 15, and in Korea and Lebanon, the rates were respectively 13.2 and 13.6 in recent years. The records for the United States in 1962 show that the infant-mortality rate was 22.3 for white, but 41.4 for nonwhite Americans.

For an appreciation of these, as well as other data in this chapter, it is important to keep in mind the fact that in terms of the value of goods and services produced, in total and per person, the United States ranks far ahead of any other country in the world. Of course, this includes military and related goods and services. In 1961 the per-capita value of products in the United States was $2,831, while for the same year, Sweden, the wealthi-

est country in Europe, had an average per-capita income of
$1,777. But Swedish society gives much more attention to the
physical care of its people, since the Swedish infant-mortality rate
in 1963 was 15 compared to 25 for the United States.

Dental care is recognized as an important part of preventive
medicine. Among poor families of America 60% of the children
ages 5 to 14 have never been to a dentist. Among the white children of this age the figure is 22%, and among the nonwhite in
the United States, 63%. (See chart, p. 119.)

The supply of physicians has been diminishing. In February,
1963, the Surgeon-General of the United States told a committee
of Congress that "whereas in 1930 each family physician—including general practitioners, internists, and pediatricians—had
a potential patient load of 1,300, today that potential load has
reached 1,900. By 1970 it will certainly be well over 2,000, . . .
over the past 10 years the output of our medical schools has
lagged behind population growth. The physician-population ratio
has stayed almost constant . . . because foreign-trained physicians
have filled such a large part of the gap between population growth
and medical-school output. If it were not for the foreign-trained
physicians the ratio of physicians to population would have
dropped almost ten per cent below the present level." The United
States has been importing 1,600 foreign physicians annually. The
number of graduates from medical schools is about 7,700 a year.
At the present rate of development, 9,000 a year would be graduated by 1975. However, in order to have a ratio of physicians to
population in 1975, similar to the one that we had in 1959, we
should have at least 11,000 medical graduates per year.

If the national number of physicians in practice is to be held
to the California level, one to 770 of population—while eliminating the disgraceful drain on foreign countries and producing
a surplus to help the developing countries—the United States
output of physicians must soon be raised to 22,000 a year. An
even larger gap between supply and requirement applies to den-
tists. A minimum period of from 5 to 7 years is required for the
establishment of a new dental or medical school.

At the end of 1963 the American Medical Association re-

Children, Aged 5 to 14, Who Have Never Been to a Dentist

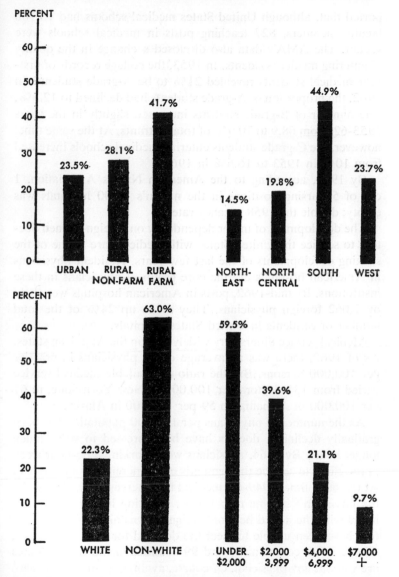

Source: U. S. Department of Health, Education and Welfare; Welfare Administration, Division of Research, 1964.

119

ported that, although United States medical schools had 13,700 faculty members, 827 teaching posts in medical schools were vacant. The AMA's data also disclosed a change in the quality of entering medical students. In 1953, the college records of first-year medical students revealed 21% to be A-grade students. In 1962, the proportion of A-grade students had declined to 12.5%. The number of B-grade students increased slightly in the years 1953-62, from 68.9 to 70.9% of total entrants. At the same time, however, the C-grade students entering medical schools increased from 10% in 1953 to 16.6% in 1962.

By 1964, according to the American Nurses Association, 1 out of 5 nursing positions in the nation's 7,100 hospitals was empty; double the 1958 vacancy rate.

The development of major dependency on foreign-trained doctors to service the United States with medical care is one of the striking developments of the last few years. Resident physicians in American hospitals are the core group of physicians in these institutions. By mid-1962, posts in American hospitals were held by 7,062 foreign physicians. They made up 24% of the total number of residents in United States hospitals.

Medical service differs very widely among the American states. As of 1963, there was an average of 97 physicians in practice per 100,000 persons. But the ratio of available medical service varied from 135 doctors per 100,000 in New York State, to 61 per 100,000 in Alabama, to 59 per 100,000 in Alaska.

As the number of physicians per 100,000 population has been gradually declining, doctors have been pressed to work much longer hours. By 1964, physicians were working a 60-hour week in the effort to service the demands of an increasing patient load. At the same time, 1949-61, medical fees increased by 52% while the physician's income rose 126%. Working harder and longer hours with the added help of foreign interns and residents, doctors have been unable to meet the demand for medical services. About 3,000 communities and 99 counties in the United States are without any physician. Of course, availability of medical care is severely rationed by income. Thus it is reported that in Cook

County Hospital, which services an important part of the Chicago poor, about half of the pregnant patients have not seen a doctor before coming to the hospital in labor. The hospital is heavily overloaded in terms of its designed capacity. Thus the mortality rate among infants there runs about three times the rate in the best Chicago hospitals, servicing the affluent part of the population.

Many details about medical service in the United States read like selections out of a horror story, for together with greatly improved capacity for coping with many diseases there are severe restraints on medical service imposed by a lack of people trained to do the work. In 1964, the fiftieth annual congress of the American College of Surgeons reported that half the ambulances in the United States are run by undertakers. There is a good chance, the report stated, that a patient taken to a hospital in an ambulance will be delivered in the same vehicle and by the same people who on other occasions transport coffins, containing corpses, from the hospitals' back door. "There is a question whether the best medical emergency services are rendered under these conditions," the report concluded.

The great cities of the United States are the site of both the best and the worst aspects of medical care. New York City, one of the great medical centers of the world, includes Harlem Hospital, which New York City's Commissioner of Health, Dr. Trussel, recently described: "In a city as rich in resources as New York, injured people should not have to sit on benches for lack of stretchers; should not have fractures left unset for five days for lack of physicians; should not lie on stretchers on the floor for lack of beds—yet all this and much more occurred."

Thus the United States, the country with the highest income per capita in the world, which should be able to produce a surplus of physicians for export to other countries, is short of physicians to care for its own people.

A valuable insight into the social cost of disease was given by the President's Commission on Heart Disease, Cancer and Stroke (1964). They found that the calculable cost of these ailments (cost of treatment and value of work-time lost) to the nation in 1962 was $31.5 billion. Even a modest 10% improvement in these fields could produce savings to the community of $3 billion—equivalent to the cost of 300,000 new dwellings for city families.

By contrast with medical services the whole set of defense-related sciences, lavishly funded by the Federal Government, has opened up opportunities for relatively rapid rise in status and income for able people, without necessarily involving the long and costly period of training, and the hard work demanded of the physician during that period, and after. At the same time, the medical profession, through its principal organization, the American Medical Association, has concentrated its public efforts on restricting governmental aid to the impoverished to help pay for their medical expenses, rather than acting vigorously and imaginatively to increase the number of American physicians. In so doing, the AMA acts out the venerable trading stratagem of restricting supply relative to demand. There can be little doubt of the close connection between the sharp rise in physicians' income and the limited number of licensed physicians.

In the sphere of public health, we have permitted an accumulation of problems that will become extremely difficult and costly to handle on a crash-emergency basis. An example is atmosphere pollution, which is becoming both widespread and serious. In June, 1964, Doctor Eric J. Cassell, a member of Cornell University's Department of Public Health, reported on New York's air-pollution problem. Essentially, he found the air-pollution situation in New York City far worse than the most pessimistic prognoses had anticipated. During the so-called killer fog that occurred in London in 1952, severe and sustained air pollution accounted for the deaths of 4,000 people. At that time, the sulfur-dioxide content of the air rose to 7/10 of a part per million. Dr. Cassell found that New York City's level exceeds that almost every month. In March, 1963, he said, the sulfur-dioxide content of air in New York City briefly reached a level of 3 parts per million, a figure he termed "incredible."

One contrast with depletion in medical care is afforded by the "space-medicine" budget of the National Aeronautics and Space Administration. By 1964, space medicine accounted for an annual outlay of about $41 million. This amount of money is enough to finance complete training programs for about 1,500 medical students, which would be a 20% increase over recent rates of M.D. graduation.

Another phase of the deterioration of our American youth is our failure to achieve functional literacy, and allied elementary education.

The public schools, high schools, and colleges of the country are filled to beyond their capacities, mainly because of a rise in population. As of 1960, among Americans aged 25 and over, 22 million had completed less than 8 years of schooling. Comprising 22% of the American population age 25 and older, this group contained the "functional illiterates" of American society.

"Functional illiteracy" is not the same as "illiteracy." An illiterate is "a person who cannot both read and write a simple message either in English or any other language." The ability to read and write is now shared by nearly all persons of fourteen years or older. Today's relatively small number of illiterates is concentrated within the older age groups. Because of the demands of present-day family, community, and national life, such a restricted definition of illiteracy is of limited usefulness. Today the concept of "functional illiteracy" is more meaningful, a condition that can be attributed to a low educational attainment, delineated by the completion of less than eight years of schooling.

The accompanying chart offers a good profile of the location and size of the functional-illiteracy problem: Only the state of Utah has fewer than 10% of its age-twenty-five-and-over citizens in the functional-illiteracy group. Every other state, including the most industrial and affluent, has a high rate of functional illiteracy.

The number of functional illiterates in the United States is closely connected with the resources we are willing to devote to the problem of education in our country. The National Education Association has reported on the average salaries paid to teachers

Persons 25 and Over with Less Than 8 Years of Schooling

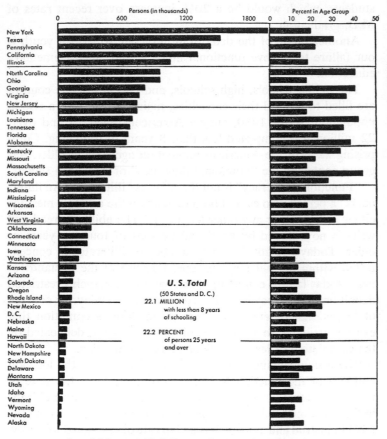

U. S. Total

(50 States and D. C.)

22.1 MILLION
with less than 8 years
of schooling

22.2 PERCENT
of persons 25 years
and over

Source: U. S. Department of Health, Education, and Welfare based on 1960 census data
supplied by the U. S. Department of Commerce, Bureau of the Census.

in public schools (1962-63), and the expenditure per pupil in both elementary and secondary schools. The data shown below are for the 16 most populous states:

States	Teachers' Salaries	Spending Per Pupil
California	$7,050	$516
New York	6,950	645
Michigan	6,444	447
Illinois	6,360	526
New Jersey	6,308	556
Indiana	6,150	405
Massachusetts	6,075	465
Ohio	5,750	422
Pennsylvania	5,660	464
Wisconsin	5,650	467
Florida	5,450	347
Texas	5,300	379
Missouri	5,289	405
North Carolina	4,975	297
Virginia	4,950	335
Georgia	4,637	298
National Average	$5,735	$432

The average salary, $5,735, paid to classroom teachers, obviously places the teaching profession quite low on the scale of financial rewards for various occupations. This is less than the average annual earnings of production workers in manufacturing industries. This low pay to teachers, coupled with the national average spending of $8.30 per week per pupil in public schools, helps to explain the number of functional illiterates in our population.

Children are sensitive to the adult community's indifference to their education, and they respond by quitting, in large numbers, the schools where overcrowding, over-large classes, and poor facilities, indicate to them how little the community cares for them. One third of the students attaining the fifth grade have not been completing high school. Drop-outs along the way number one million per year. Some time after the drop-out rate and the dropouts' subsequent unemployment began to be a national scandal, studies were made of the characteristics of the drop-out students.

It was discovered that half of the drop-outs had IQ's of average or greater than average capacity, and that 80% of them would have been capable of absorbing a high-school education or pushing work at the college level.

America's large cities are the site of massive deterioration in the quality of public- and secondary-school education.

Here is an account of the sadder aspects of education in one area of New York City that was published in *The Morningsider,* a newspaper addressed to the Morningside Heights neighborhood of that city. The school districts discussed include neighborhoods predominantly Puerto Rican and Negro.

. . . For the parents of the 40,000 children who attend the 25 public schools in districts 10 and 11, the school picture is that of an "educational disaster area." Our oldest school, built in 1883 (the "new wing" was added in 1910), contains 1,700 children. It is a five-story structure, without regular gym or auditorium facilities, and with but one bathroom, located off the cafeteria in the basement.

We have several buildings constructed in the "H" shape that was popular at the turn of the century. In one such building, we are fortunate to have a librarian full time. But the school lacks a library. The woman uses a supply closet and carries the books out each day. The request for library trucks is still part of the backlog of millions of dollars of "new" furniture orders. Conversely another school has a library that is underutilized because it has no licensed librarian. These buildings will be replaced soon. "Soon" is four or five years hence, for thousands of children close to their entire elementary school experience.

If these were but isolated examples of obsolete buildings that will be replaced, the story might contain some hope, but the situation in our newest buildings is equally as appalling.

One of these is a junior high. It is without a nurse full time and a wooden chair serves for children who become ill because a cot is not available. Our newest school opened so over-

crowded that the entire fifth grade has been left behind in the
old building until additional space is found. . . .

In addition to the shortage of licensed teachers (other than
substitutes) who are experienced and good, our schools are
faced with the following handicaps (to mention but a few):

Inadequate professional services—medical, social, etc.

"Crash" remedial programs (after school) with no money
for supplies.

Lunchroom floors that are mopped only three times a year.

An insufficient number of Spanish-speaking personnel to
facilitate good family-school communication.

Once young people begin to feel they are not valued by the
community, it is altogether reasonable to expect some portion of
the more aggressively endowed individuals to rise in open rebellion. The growth rate of juvenile delinquency cases in the courts
is one indicator of a wholesale rebellion against communities
which cynically demand that the young comply with moral codes
that place a high value on human life, although the adult community itself fails to behave according to these standards.

The young men and women who grow up physically incompetent and functionally illiterate become the unemployables of
our highly industrialized society. They are social castoffs. The
human as well as the economic meanings of this process are just
beginning to be understood. Millions of young men and women
are filled with resentment at being treated badly—a condition
they know could be changed in this wealthiest country of the
world. When this resentment flows over, we reap the bitter har-
vest of self-destructive and socially damaging behavior, such as
alcoholism among the young, narcotics addiction, and juvenile
delinquency on an epidemic scale. The human cost of this destructiveness is without measure.

It is worth while to compare the degree to which various nations discard their basic human assets by unemployment. For
the year 1962, the following were the unemployment rates in
the United States, Western Europe, and Japan, adjusted by the

United States Bureau of Labor Statistics to comply with the
United States Government's definition of unemployment:

United States	5.6%
France	1.8
Germany	0.5
Great Britain	2.8
Italy	3.2
Japan	1.0
Sweden	1.5

The United States has been tolerant of unemployment rates
which in other countries would generate crises of confidence in
their governments. Switzerland and Germany have *imported* hundreds of thousands of workers since World War II.

By giving low priority to the amount of technical talent and
money to be used for the care of human beings and their participation in productive work, American society has been sacrificing
future generations. Unemployment has been intense among young
people in the United States. Among job-seeking youth, not 5%
but 15% were unemployed in 1964 by official count. Within this
national youth average there was a major difference between
Negroes and others, for among Negroes the unemployment rate
for male teen-agers seeking work by 1964 was 25% and more.
A. Philip Randolph, veteran President of the Brotherhood of
Sleeping Car Porters, in June 1964, pointed out that Negro teen-
agers were dropping out of high school "at the bewildering rate
of as high as 75% in most metropolitan centers." He indicated
that these teen-agers "therefore, are ineligible to become ap-
prentices to learn skilled trades requiring a high school diploma."

The economic cost of the alienation of millions of people in
their youth and adulthood from productive work can be partially
estimated. The most expensive capital investment of a society is
for the rearing of its adult workers. In the United States, I estimate this cost as follows: $1,000 a year as a minimum for living
expenses, from birth through age 18; $430 a year as the average
cost of education per year from age 6 through 18; and, finally,
from age 13 through 18 I estimate an additional requirement of

about $1,000 per person per year over and above minimum maintenance. By this rule of thumb, the cost of rearing an adult worker to physical and educational competence, through age 18, amounts to $29,590.

How many people are "unemployed" in our country? The official, 1964, count of unemployed amounted to between 5 and 6 out of every 100 civilians. This only encompassed the number of people actually registered and seeking work with employment offices. But there are additional men and women who no longer seek work, having given up hope. These are the "invisible" unemployed who are formally "not in the labor force." To these must be added the full-time equivalents of those able to find only part-time work. Altogether, a 1964 report of the United States Senate's Subcommittee on Employment and Manpower reported estimates of the "real" unemployment rate at between 7 and 9% of the potential labor force. Out of a civilian labor force of 72.8 million in 1964, this meant between 5.1 to 6.5 million out of work.

Let us assume the average cost of rearing each of these unemployed through the age of 18 was $29,590; by this reckoning they represent an unused investment of $150 to $192 billion. The value of these discarded "human capital" assets exceeds the total available productive wealth of many entire countries. The President's Council of Economic Advisors estimates that the loss in goods and services produced as a result of a 5.5% as against 4% rate of unemployment is between $30 and $40 billion per year.

There is no measure of the economic and human loss to our country owing to the drop-out of 40% of all who enter college, and the inability or unwillingness of 30% of the high-school seniors in the 80 to 90 percentile of their classes to enter college.

Once created, blighted people and blighted areas of cities and towns cost us dearly, just for "maintenance." In Sacramento, California, the city's Planning Commission reports that blighted areas recently comprised 20% of the population on 8% of the land. While paying 12% of the city's taxes, they took 50% of the health budget, 41% of police, and 25% of fire protection. The same 20% of the population accounted for 26% of the city's fires, 36% of the juvenile delinquency, 42% of adult crime, and 76% of the tuberculosis cases. Variations on this theme appear all over the United States. It is a plausible inference that the improvement of neglected people and blighted neighborhoods would reduce many classes of local government costs.

The cost of sustained parasitic growth in our country is not even measured by the large budgets for overkill. We suffer the penalty of depleted bodies and minds. What sort of country will we become if we continue to neglect our children, our youth, and the quality of our lives, while lavishing talent and money on moon voyages ($5 billion a year), on ever more nuclear bombs that no one needs ($1.5 billion a year), on two B-70 bombers that have no mission ($1.6 billion), on parasitic economic growth that makes it unfeasible to rescue 9,000,000 American families from dwellings that would be marked for replacement in an under-developed country?

7
Selling Sovereignty
to Save the Dollar

Hardly anyone knows that the United States Government has gone into the business of selling armaments to many countries of the world. The sales organization is located in the Pentagon and is called the Office of International Logistics Negotiations. The man in charge of this operation is Mr. Henry Kuss, Deputy Assistant Secretary of Defense. Secretary Kuss's operation exceeded $1 billion in 1963 and was aimed at a larger volume of sales during 1964.

Under Secretary Kuss's direction is a group of men, with sundry helpers, in charge of weapons sales to various countries of the world. Here is the list of the Secretary's assistants and the countries which are their respective sales territories:

Germany	Mr. Gownley
	Mr. Chadwick
	Col. Crosswhite
	Mr. Tosti
Austria	Mr. Stevens
Israel	
Lebanon	
Saudi Arabia	
Sweden	
United Kingdom	Mr. Feigl
France	
India	
Switzerland	

Italy	Mr. Fede
Argentina	
Brazil	
Canada	
Chile	
Mexico	
Peru	
Spain	
Venezuela	
Iran	Mr. Cain
Iraq	
Jordan	
Libya	
Pakistan	
Portugal	
Burma	Mrs. Clay
Ecuador	
Ethiopia	
Greece	
Malaysia	
Philippines	
Republic of South Africa	
Turkey	
Japan	Mr. Alne
Belgium	Mr. Hodgson
NATO	
Netherlands	
Australia	Mr. Felker
Denmark	
New Zealand	
Norway	

How did the United States Government get into the wholesale weapons-merchandising business? It started as part of an effort to protect the value of the dollar.

After the Second World War the wry jokes that Americans enjoyed telling about themselves included a line of humor about all the gold in Fort Knox. Since the United States was left industrially intact after the Second World War, there was a vast influx of foreign orders for every sort of goods necessary to the restoration of the countries of Western Europe that had been heavily damaged by the long years of combat. Part of these goods was bought and paid for in gold bullion from the Treasury of each country. For a time it seemed as though virtually all the monetary gold stock of the world was flowing rapidly to Fort Knox. It was embarrassing. Here we were shipping out all sorts of useful goods, and what did we get in return? Gold bricks that piled up in the vaults.

The jokes continued until 1949-50. In 1949 the United States Treasury had a gold stock valued at $24.4 billion. After that the Fort-Knox-gold line of humor faded. By the end of 1964, the United States gold stock was reduced by $9 billion to $15 billion to meet the claims of foreign creditors. This was no subject for humor. For the fall in the U.S. gold reserve is part of a process that has piled up claims against U.S. gold abroad, far exceeding the ability of the Treasury to redeem in gold. This condition threatens the international value of the dollar, has had a strong impact on the foreign and domestic policies of the United States Government, and has, further, involved the Federal Government in varied operations designed to save the value of the dollar. The emergency operations now even include large-scale export sales of heavy weapons—the high-technology instruments of sovereignty that have been forged at enormous cost by the United States Government.

At the same time that the gold reserve held by the United States Treasury declined over 35%, to $15 billion in 1964, this much bullion was not freely available for Treasury use because of Federal law establishing partial gold backing for American currency. The foreign commitments have been growing and by the middle of 1964 the total short-term claims against the United States amounted to $20.5 billion. Of these, $12 billion represented dollar claims on the United States held by official institutions of foreign countries, and about $8 billion represented individual holdings. These claims against the United States were net claims, what was left *after* subtraction of the claims by the United States against foreign banks and individuals.

Obviously, the sum of these short-term claims is far greater than the size of the U.S. gold reserve. This means that if some significant proportion of these chits held abroad should be presented for redemption, in gold, to the United States Treasury, there would be danger of an international crisis over the value of the dollar. This is the sort of international currency crisis that has plagued Great Britain repeatedly since the Second World War. British currency, and other claims for payment held abroad against Great Britain, exceeded the gold and other currency reserves which the British Treasury had at given times. The presentation of British pounds for redemption in large quantity resulted in a fall in the international value of the British pound. This is the sort of potential crisis in the value of the dollar that has been generated for the United States.

How did this happen? The United States has had a favorable balance of trade year by year since the Second World War. This means that the United States has received more foreign currency in payment for goods and services sold year by year than Americans spend abroad. How, then, was the favorable balance of trade converted into an unfavorable balance of payments?

Americans make sizable payments abroad by granting aid for economic development to various countries, by traveling, by investing, and finally, by military spending. American investments abroad result in income returned to the United States, as well as spending within the United States, for new machinery, and the like. Dollars granted by the United States Government for foreign economic development have, since 1960, been strongly tied to use for purchases within the United States. By 1964 as much as 80% to 90% of these funds were "tied" to spending within the United States and therefore not a source of a major accumulation of dollar claims abroad. American travel abroad has amounted to an outlay of about $1 billion a year. However, the largest single spending by the United States abroad, since World War II has been for military and allied purposes. About $3 billion a year has been spent, incidental to the presence of U.S. forces abroad. This $3 billion is apart from the budgeted cost to the United States Government of the troops and their equipment, and is also separate from military equipment shipped abroad.

In addition, a publicly unknown, but still considerable amount of dollars must pile up abroad owing to the various activities of the Central Intelligence Agency. The CIA and its sister agencies are reported to have staffs of 200,000 and annual budgets of $4 billion, the bulk of which surely is paid out abroad.

In 1962, the President's Council of Economic Advisors indicated that these military expenditures abroad have been the dominant factor in converting a favorable balance of trade into an unfavorable balance of payments for the United States, and thereby the prime cause of the accumulation of claims on U.S. dollars abroad. For example, since 1955, United States military spending abroad has been one and a quarter times as large as the total deficit in our balance of payments during this period. Looking at this another way—if the armed forces had not been spending dollars abroad, the balance of payments to the United States would have had an average surplus of $500 million a year, instead of the accumulating deficit.

What appears to be a problem in finance is in fact a political matter of wide importance. If foreign governments, by cashing in their proper claims on United States gold, are able to affect the international value of the dollar, then that is unspoken political pressure on a large scale. This is, of course, appreciated by the United States Government. The Joint Economic Committee of the Congress has declared: "American officials have allowed the fear that foreigners might convert their dollars into gold to become an all-pervasive stifling influence on United States initiative and action on a wide range of domestic and international problems."

If the international value of the dollar is threatened, a decline in the worth of the dollar at home cannot be excluded. Worry about the international balance of payments and the United States Treasury's gold reserve seriously restricts the United States Government in handling an important aspect of our domestic economic policy. One of the classic ways by which the Federal Government can either encourage or discourage new capital investment within the United States is by regulating the interest rate. Thus, if the Government would like to encourage capital investment, it can reduce the interest rate, thereby making money cheaper to borrow and to use.

On the other hand, if the Government felt that the pace of new investing and spending was too high, leading, for example, to the dangers of rapid price increases, then the Government could raise the interest rate, thereby helping to make money more expensive to get and to use. But flexibility for these purposes is now restricted: if the United States Government were to lower the interest rate for domestic reasons, then this interest rate would have to bear comparison with interest rates prevailing abroad. If the result were to encourage a flow of capital from the United States to places where higher interest rates could be earned, then that would be a highly unfavorable result for the United States balance of payments and for the accumulation of claims on United States gold, even though the domestic results were the desired ones. In sum: America's unfavorable balance of payments and the drain on the United States gold reserve has become a major source of economic and political pressure on the United States.

Experience with such difficulties in other countries suggests that the very existence of dollar-exchange problems could generate pressure to "reach for gold" in search of maximum security. In addition, the continued loss of gold—reflecting a net deficit of the American economy in relation to the rest of the world—could undermine the wide use of the dollar as a reserve currency, and thus the extensive world-banking function performed in the United States.

A modern industrial society, with elaborate division of labor, requires reliable instruments of exchange, both for domestic and foreign economic relations. These essential economic instruments will be placed in jeopardy if recent tendencies affecting the American dollar are sustained.

Specialists in international finance and banking can devise new monetary systems and methods, which affect the timing and the routines for settling the payment of international accounts. But there must be payment, unless it should be agreed that the United States may continually use up resources of other nations without compensation. Such agreement, however, is unlikely. Therefore, the root problem remains: How can the United States pay for the goods and services bought from other countries for United States military programs?

A large net gain in United States exports of merchandise during the next few years to countries holding major dollar claims is not likely. Prudence does not permit the forecast that United States military spending abroad may be cut in large proportion by the transfer of these obligations to other countries. West German industrialists do not acclaim the prospect of further depleting their fully employed labor force by adding to their country's divisions. Such depletion would also greatly strengthen the bargaining power of West German trade unions.

In the short run, the United States can try to apply a variety of measures to stem the gold outflow. These include: limiting duty-free imports by American tourists; allowing fewer families of servicemen to reside abroad; restricting to American sources some classes of military purchasing for overseas use; asking foreign governments to permit the United States to supply American tourists with their foreign currency by exchanging tourists' dollars for "counterpart funds" held by the United States; selling arms in order to recover some of the dollars held by various countries; and similar measures. But, also in the short run, the United States Government has been compelled to rely on the good will of European bankers who are asked to protect the United States currency by holding dollars rather than redeeming them for gold.

Another conceivable method would involve sharp curtailment of imports and concurrent reduction of America's current consumption in order to balance international payments. A policy of sharp United States import curtailment would be economically and politically damaging to many friendly countries. Such curtailment would also be extremely unpopular within the United States. Americans fear the major extension of government controls over many aspects of life that would be required by such programs. Besides, such a policy would probably reduce the level of living of the American people.

By the end of 1960 the Kennedy Administration decided that various steps should be taken quickly to reduce United States dollar spending abroad, especially by the armed forces. Secretary McNamara organized a very detailed program along these lines.

But the most important move toward improving United States balance of payments, and cutting down the hemorrhaging outflow of dollars and gold, was the program for selling weapons abroad. Charles J. Hitch, Assistant Secretary of Defense, on December 12, 1962, told a committee of Congress: "We believe that the most promising method by which we can reduce the net adverse balance is to raise the level of our receipts by encouraging increased procurement of United States military equipment by our Allies." And so the United States Government, through the Department of Defense, established an international operation for wholesaling American weapons under Henry Kuss, Deputy Assistant Secretary of Defense, the Office of International Logistics Negotiation.

Everyone knows that many sorts of weapons and firearms can be bought by civilians in retail shops that sell sporting goods and surplus military equipment. But these are light firearms and weapons. Heavy weapons, from mortars on up, are not traded among civilians. The exchange of these goods is usually reserved to exchanges among governments. These goods are a form of political currency. They are instruments of sovereignty—particularly the larger weapons such as tanks, artillery, rockets, military aircraft, and all sorts of munitions and military communications equipment.

The military materiel produced by the United States is the product of a costly research, development, and manufacturing program. It was produced for the United States Government under a mandate from the American population for the establishment of a defense organization that would insure the security and sovereignty of American society. Now the Government, indeed the Department of Defense itself, is busily engaged in selling these instruments of sovereignty in order to gather up, in payment, dollars held abroad, and thereby lift potential pressure from the international value of the American dollar.

How well are these programs working?

During the last decade, most of the military spending abroad that entered the international balance of payments was located in Western Europe. Let us see what happened, from 1961 to 1963, while this program of selling military goods to save the dollar was getting under way on a large scale. In 1961, total dollar expenditures in the NATO countries, by the Department of Defense, amounted to $2.7 billion. This included private expenditure by American soldiers and their dependents, salaries and wages to local citizens hired to work around American military bases, the cost of equipment, construction and materials, and payments to support and operate the far-flung NATO organization. Also, in 1961, the United States had received $375 million in payment from various NATO countries. Therefore, the net adverse dollar balance, owing to Department of Defense payments in Europe, was $2.3 billion. By 1963, the Defense Department's dollar expenditures in the NATO area totaled $2.6 billion, a reduction of $100 million, owing to the various steps taken by the Defense Department to cut down its purchases in Europe. At the same time, receipts to the Department of Defense from various European countries totaled $1.2 billion. The result was a net adverse dollar balance of about $1.4 billion. What were these receipts from NATO countries?

The Department of Defense's military sales program has encouraged purchase of U.S. military goods and services, and these receipts from NATO include shipments of military supplies purchased through the Department of Defense, and reimbursements to the United States for logistical support to the United Nations and other nations' defense forces.

Taking into account the activities of the Atomic Energy Commission, and other U.S. agencies involved in NATO affairs, the net adverse dollar balance in 1961 was $2.6 billion, in 1963, $1.6 billion, and the objective by 1966, according to the Department of Defense, is a balance of payments deficit in the NATO countries of $1 billion. A major element in achieving this goal, however, seems to be an expectation of a greatly increased volume of sales of military goods to NATO countries.

In November, 1964, Secretary of Defense McNamara announced with pride the conclusion of a treaty with the West German Government wherein that government agreed to purchase $700 million worth of military goods from the United States during the next two years.

All this, however, does not begin to plug the gap between

U.S. income and the expense of United States military operations in the NATO area alone.

Consider the case of U.S. armed forces in Germany, for whom the United States pays three times over. How is it done? First, the defense budget of the United States Government pays for the equipment, maintenance and operation of the troops actually in Germany. At the end of 1964, about 400,000 American servicemen were in that area. Assuming that these were divided between the services as, roughly, 85% Army and 15% Air Force, then, taking into account the average cost per soldier in each service, the cost of United States forces in Germany is $5.4 billion, each year.

A second payment for these forces is made by American society in the form of the civilian goods and services which these able-bodied men do not produce or provide in the United States, while they are in military service. The value of the goods and services foregone by American society is equal to the number of military men in Germany multiplied by the average personal income of a consumer unit in the United States. This was $7,500 in 1963. By this reckoning, American society deprived of the work of these men, failed to receive $3.0 billion worth of goods and services.

Since American servicemen abroad spend their dollars abroad, and since other dollar payments are made there in order to maintain these forces, the Government of the United States has become involved in the weapons-sales program in an attempt to get back those dollars, lest their continual accumulation result in further drain on U.S. gold reserves. This results in the third payment for the presence of U.S. troops in Germany, in the form of $700 million worth of military goods which are produced by American society and shipped abroad in order to get the dollars back.

Altogether, these three forms of payment by America for the presence of U.S. troops in Germany, amounts to $9.1 billion per year.

The $700 million worth of military goods to be sold to West Germany each year tells us that the cost to the United States, in the form of payments deficit and claims on U.S. gold, amounts to $1,750 per year for each American serviceman stationed in Germany.

The international sale of sovereignty in the form of heavy weapons, particularly to West Germany, by other NATO countries too, has become built into the operation of the whole NATO system. The London *Economist* reports (August 22, 1964): "It is estimated that since rearmament began seriously in 1956, military orders worth about DM [Deutschmark] 10,000 million have been placed in the United States, partly with the object of offsetting the cost of maintaining United States troops in Germany. France, which does not claim support costs, has received orders worth DM 2,500 million." In June, 1962, the British and West German governments signed an agreement whereby the Germans agreed to purchase £108 million worth of military and related materiel in the next two years. In connection with all these programs, West German soldiers are being trained in the operation of new weapons, and so the Associated Press reported from New Mexico on July 17, 1964, that "a West German Air Force missile group conducted a successful overland firing of a ballistic missile from near Blanding, Utah, into a White Sands target area today."

Co-operating with the Department of Defense's weapons selling effort is a group in the United States Treasury. In the eyes of the Treasury group, the weapons-sales program is a most commendable effort because it has helped to slow down the now-dangerous outflow of U.S. gold.

Treasury officials point out that the United States has the most modern military technique, missiles, and tanks, whose research and development costs have been charged off against the original orders placed by the United States Government. The United States is thereby able to sell to the Europeans ultramodern materiel at relatively low production costs. A medium tank, it is pointed out, would cost one and one-third times the United States price if produced in Europe. Also, buying from the United States means getting delivery right away, since the U.S. plants are already established and operating.

As Secretary Henry Kuss's staff listing shows, the most important buildup of military sales abroad was to the West German Government. The first agreement of this sort was made in 1961, for two years, to be renewed again in 1964.

A major new item in the 1964 agreement was the Bonn Government's order of three modern missile destroyers to be built in American shipyards. (One side effect of this program is its contribution toward freeing West German shipyards to participate in the world merchant-shipbuilding market, while U.S. shipbuilding capacity is focused on the military side.)

United States weapons salesmen come up against the problem of competition and pressure from possible European vendors and sometimes compromises are made in the form of co-production arrangements, whereby United States and European firms share in the production of planes, tanks, and similar heavy materiel. Of course, once the United States becomes a source of initial supply, there is the continuing spare-parts business, and it becomes economic for the Europeans to purchase the use of U.S. training grounds.

A five-man staff of the United States Treasury operates as a point of contact with the Department of Defense, servicing this effort by handling credits, accounting, negotiations with banks and finance departments in various countries.

But the hazard to American sovereignty, mirrored in the threat to the value of the dollar, cannot be reversed by undertaking the systematic sale of United States sovereignty in the form of heavy weapons.

One of the earliest diagnoses of the strategic role of the gold reserve and balance of payments issues was made by Mr. Terence McCarthy, consulting economist in New York City. In a paper he prepared in 1963, Mr. McCarthy concluded:

> . . . The decline in England's position as a great power dates, not from the end of World War II, but from the time the international financial community recognized that England could no longer meet her short-term obligations with assurance, and that sterling could no longer serve as the base of the international monetary order.

Once thoroughly weakened, world financial power cannot easily be regained. The U.S. has attained a world position through the integrity of her currency. She will lose this, together with the ability to shape much of the world's political future, if the flight of gold is not soon halted. This can be done only by curbing the extraordinary extravagance in the military area, and by strengthening the U.S. fiscal position so that short-term claims upon her gold reserves will be transformed into long-term foreign investments in the American industrial system.

8
Depletion for Export

If you were an official of one of the big governments of the world, and one day you decided it would be desirable to slow down the economic development of a less-developed country, how would you accomplish this without looking like a big bully pushing a little fellow around? Is there, in fact, a way in which you might do this that would even produce a political profit, leading you to be hailed by a considerable number of people as a stalwart friend of independent statehood among the developing countries?

The experience of the last fifteen years points the way to a straightforward and quite reliable solution to these apparently complex problems. The key formula is called "military aid." Such programs are operated by the principal countries, East and West. Here are some of the main ingredients of the recipe.

Identify some of the principal military men in the developing countries for a starter, and invite them to some sort of military briefing, or offer them guest status as observers of maneuvers or similar activity. The visit is, of course, at the expense of the host country, and the occasion obviously suggests the merit of visiting a number of military bases, inspecting materiel, old and new, and observing training programs in action.

During their stay in the host country, the visiting dignitaries are introduced to other military personnel from various newly developing countries, who, as students, are already participating

in various officer- and technician-training programs. This brings
the point home to the guest: They, too, could perhaps participate
in the valuable training programs they have observed, thereby
enhancing their own personal professional status while raising
the level of competence of their country's armed forces.

Our guests arrive home fully equipped with ideas to be presented to the senior politicians of their country as offering feasible steps to be taken in order to improve national military competence and thereby add to the stability of the government.

Since every government would like to think of itself as a stable
one, these ideas soon prove quite attractive. Thereafter, missions
of military advisors are dispatched from the host country while
selected cadres of local officers and technicians are dispatched
to the host country for training. In conjunction with the training
effort, agreements are reached regarding both gifts of arms and
/or the purchase of arms from the host country at nominal prices.
By such steps is the military-aid process put in motion.

What does all this mean to the newly developing country?

Military organization, in newly developing countries, plays a
key role in inhibiting economic development. The direct cost of
military activities to such countries involves the skilled manpower and materials used up by the operation of military organizations and their equipment, not to mention the money used to
buy them. In really poor countries, military-aid programs lead
to the diversion from technical civilian work to technical military
work of a considerable portion of those people who know how
to use a screwdriver. When the United States closed down several
missile installations in Turkey, early in 1963, the Turkish economy reaped an immediate bonus: 2,000 Turkish technicians suddenly were ready for employment. These men had been working
in and around the military installations. As a good-sized engineering school may turn out 200 graduates each year, it follows
that 2,000 technicians suddenly available represents the equivalent of the output of several major educational institutions over
a period of years, as well as the capital outlay which these institutions would require and the long period of time required
to build them up.

A few years ago, while visiting Argentina, I was staggered by a display of local naval forces—mostly castoff destroyers, cruisers, and aircraft carriers, of major powers. In Buenos Aires I tried to learn, from informed citizens, the possible identity of the enemy against whom these forces might be directed. My inquiries all proved unsuccessful. Still, the Argentine Navy continues to be a major item in that country's budget, and a consumer of thousands of trained men.

When my airplane landed in Santiago, Chile, I was startled at the display of United States-built jet fighter planes I saw at the local airport. I asked myself: Who is the enemy? Against whom would these planes be required to fight? Again, there is no ready answer. In both Chile and Argentina the value of goods and services produced per person averages about $450 per year. The economic development of Latin America is being braked by the manpower and money lavished on the military.

There are varied ways of adding to the armed forces of developing countries. Here is an example of how the sale of military equipment has been made part of a tie-in offer on the sale of commercial aircraft. The New York *Times* reported from Buenos Aires on March 25, 1964: "United States and a British concern are offering Argentina warplanes at bargain prices in hopes of selling her $30 million worth of commercial jetliners, reliable sources said today.

"According to diplomatic and business sources, Britain's Vickers Corporation has offered the Argentine Air Force 24 Canberra jet bombers at reduced prices provided the Government buys VC-10 jetliners for Argentine Airlines.

"The American Douglas Aircraft Company is said to be offering a similar deal in A-14A fighter-bombers if Argentina equips her national airline with DC-8's."

During a visit to Ghana, in 1962,* I learned that the first company of paratroops was being trained for the Ghanaian

---

* I was visiting in Ghana as guest of the Accra Assembly, an international meeting, mainly of representatives of nonaligned countries, to consider problems of the "world without the bomb." This meeting was underwritten by the Ghanaian Government whose chief, President Nkhrumah, was instrumental in assigning a part of his government's military budget to pay for this conference.

Army, and that mine sweepers were on order for the Ghanaian Navy. Ghana recently has had a per-capita Gross National Product of about $210 per year, a literacy rate of 25%, and is supplied with about one doctor per 18,000 inhabitants.

Egypt, with a literacy rate of 30%, and a Gross National Product per capita of about $125 per year, offers a notable example of the military-aid process. Some 60,000 to 100,000 members of the Egyptian armed forces are on regular active duty. The air force includes 250 to 400 fighter planes, bombers, and miscellaneous aircraft. Assuming a ratio of ten skilled men to each aircraft (airmen, ground maintenance, etc.) this means that 2,500 to 4,000 highly trained technicians are being used full time for the operation of such aircraft. Furthermore, the Egyptian Army is well supplied with tanks, field artillery, and smaller weapons, all of which require proper maintenance by men whose civilian skills are certainly comparable to those of an automobile mechanic or a semiskilled machine operater.

The second major cost of the military-aid program to the recipient country is in the form of goods and services which are not produced because their potential producers are the skilled workmen employed by the military. In countries already developed, and well stocked with all sorts of goods and large numbers of skilled people, these depletion effects can, for a time at least, be carried even though they cause a certain amount of stress. For the newly developing countries, however, where there is no accumulation of modern goods or stockpiles of retired specialists who can be brought back to work in a pinch. Concentration on military work produces an immediate crush. I discovered in Israel, during 1963, that there was a severe shortage of mathematics teachers in elementary and high schools. One reason for this shortage was that graduates trained to teach mathematics were simply not going into the school system; they were being attracted to employment in or around the armed forces. The military budget of Israel consumes 9% of her annual output of goods and services.

The African continent (apart from South Africa) is a major candidate for economic development. Nevertheless, in 1964, these nations developed national armed forces with military budgets totaling $978 million. (To this same group of nations, the United States Government in 1963 granted $285 million in economic assistance and $27 million in military aid.) For these impoverished populations nearly a billion dollars of military budgets is a serious brake on economic development. The relatively high skill of the manpower used up in these armed forces means that these military budgets don't begin to measure the true cost in enterprises that "could have been"—but for the money and organizing ability used up by the military. It is estimated that in Ghana, for example, an infantry battalion costs between $1.6 and $2.8 million a year for maintenance—the amount of capital required for financing medium-sized enterprises of many kinds.

A third form of the depletion effects of military programs lies in the strengthening of authoritarian traditions and organizations which quash democratic processes. Long before Fidel Castro emerged in Cuba, the United States Government had given $10 million of military assistance to the Batista regime, while the total effort for economic assistance from 1946 until Castro's advent to power amounted to less than $3 million.

A classic example of the political consequences of such military-aid programs is the case of Peru.

Senator Ernest Gruening (Dem., Alaska) has reported:

A military coup overthrew the existing government of Perú last July (1962) even as the Presidential election ballots were being counted. Army officers invaded the Pizarro Palace, seized and imprisoned President Manuel Prado and established themselves in power.

The tank which crashed through the palace gates was a Sherman tank made in the United States and supplied by us to Perú as a part of our military-aid program. The officer who carried out the capture of the palace, Colonel Gonzalo Briceño, was trained at Fort Benning, Georgia. Others of the junta and of its military cabinet likewise received their training in the

United States. Several had been only recently awarded the United States Legion of Merit, in their citations, services to the "objectives of democracy" were stressed.

Seven candidates had been vying for the Presidency in Perú; three were closely bunched far in the lead. They were General Manuel Ordia, a former President who had come into power in 1948 through a military coup; Fernando Belaunde, candidate of the Popular Action Party; and Raúl Haya de la Torre, long the head of the moderate left-wing anti-Communist APRA Party. None of these had secured quite the one-third of all the votes cast required by the Peruvian constitution, which provides that in such an event election shall be by the Congress. The military apparently feared that Haya de la Torre would be chosen and would institute what to them were objectionable social and economic reforms. To prevent this they took over.

The Kennedy Administration promptly announced that aid to Perú, under our foreign aid program, would be suspended, and withheld recognition of the new government.

Several weeks earlier, a similar sequence of events had taken place in Argentina. There the military, dissatisfied with the results of the general elections, seized President Frondizi, imprisoned him on an island, and installed a creature of their own, Jose Guido, in his place. The Kennedy Administration, however, recognized the new Argentine regime and continued its aid. Shortly thereafter, several hundred million dollars were pledged.

The United States military-aid program in African countries began with $3.9 million to Ethiopia in 1954. By 1963, in 14 countries, $27.2 million were being spent. In Latin America, the military grant program began in 1952, with $200,000 being spent in Peru and Ecuador. By 1963 this program was a $64 million a year operation with nineteen client governments. The Near East military-aid programs grew from $9.5 million being spent in two countries (Greece and Turkey) in 1950, to $361 million spent in 1963 in ten countries. Finally, Far Eastern military-aid operations (exclusive of the cost of United States armed forces), burgeoned from $1.9 million in 1950 (3 countries), to $763 million in 1963 (7 countries).

The published report on U.S. foreign-assistance programs shows that from 1946 to 1963, $32 billion were spent by the United States for various forms of military aid, and $36 billion for economic assistance of all sorts. During the period 1946 to 1963, $15 billion of military aid and economic aid were directed to Europe. Therefore, discounting the European expenditures, $20 billions were formally earmarked as economic assistance and $17 billions for military-aid programs in the rest of the world, programs whose effects include depletion of economic development in these countries.

We must now qualify the meaning of these numbers. We know, from a former administrator of the Agency for Industrial Development, that out of the total amount of economic assistance, only a part has been used for this purpose. The remainder had other purposes. According to Dr. D. A. Fitzgerald (former deputy director of the United States International Cooperation Administration): "A lot of the criticism of foreign aid is because the critic thought the objective was to get economic growth, and this wasn't the objective at all. . . . The objective may have been to buy a lease, or to get a favorable vote in the UN, or to keep a nation from falling apart, or to keep some country from giving the Russians airbase rights, or any one of many other reasons."

This assessment is seconded by Senator Wayne Morse, who wrote in 1964: "Sad to say, of the economic section of the program not more than half is devoted to bona fide economic development. Supporting assistance, the contingency fund, and nonproject loans from the development loan fund are but political props and payoff to foreign governments. They do not develop; they merely patch over and perpetuate lack of development. Even the technical assistance program is being used for transportation and communication projects against the day when they may be of use to American forces, and to train small-time police states in emerging countries."

The cost of training in the use of weapons, and the organiza-

tion of armed forces, does not measure the depletion effect of
these weapons and armed forces once used in local wars that
seem to have no end. The Government of the United States has
become a participant in military operations of unique quality;
they are considered, militarily, interminable. The war in South
Vietnam is the classic case in point.

By 1964 military operations in Vietnam were costing the
United States about $2 million a day or more. An assessment
of this war, prepared by Mr. Willard Matthias of the Central
Intelligence Agency's Board of National Estimates, stated, in
June, 1964:

> The guerrilla war in South Vietnam is in its fifth year and
> no end appears in sight. The Vietcong in the South, de-
> pendent largely on their own resources but under the direction
> and control of the Communist regime in the North, are press-
> ing their offensive more vigorously than ever.
>
> The political mistakes of the Diem regime inhibited the ef-
> fective prosecution of the war, which is really more of a polit-
> ical contest than a military operation, and led to the regime's
> destruction.
>
> The counter-guerrilla effort continues to flounder, partly be-
> cause of the inherent difficulty of the problem, and partly be-
> cause Diem's successors have not yet demonstrated the leader-
> ship and inspiration necessary.

The essential elements for sustained, successful guerrilla warfare are: (a) an organization of dedicated men prepared to take
high personal risks for their purposes; (b) the group must have
technical knowledge on how to operate secret military organizations; (c) the group must be substantially supported by the surrounding population.

Where these conditions are met, a group of determined men
can hold out successfully against large, well-equipped and even
ruthless military opponents. Nevertheless, the United States, after
1960 proceeded to mount "counterinsurgency" forces, on the assumption that guerrilla warfare might be successfully countered

by men whose principal training was in the knowledge of how to function under jungle conditions, and the like.

In 1957-58, while conducting an investigation into the problems of inspection for disarmament, I had occasion to study the feasible methods of evasion of disarmament agreements that had been used by underground military groups. The evidence available then led to the formulation I have summarized on the conditions for successful underground military (guerrilla) operations. This formulation spells the failure of the much-heralded counter-insurgency program of the United States Army, and it spells the failure of the application of such techniques to South Vietnam.

In November, 1964, the Vietcong carried out a raid, using 6 mortars, on a United States airbase at Bienhoa just north of Saigon. This military airfield is located in a populated area. Since 40 to 50 men would be required to carry the mortar parts and the ammunition used in this attack that destroyed 30 aircraft, it is reasonable to assume that they could not have entered the area, reconnoitered the ground, fired their weapons, and then disappeared with them as they did without being observed by people living in the area. Since the subsequent search operation disclosed no trace of these men and/or their equipment, it is only reasonable to infer that they had the support of the surrounding population, since without them this total dispersal would not have been possible. Under such conditions, the United States may expect to expend $2 million a day in Vietnam indefinitely, without attaining any military advantage at all.

This sort of fruitless military operation inevitably depletes the whole of the country in which it is conducted. Orderly economic activity of every sort is frustrated by the prospect of investments in zones of military operation, and havoc is introduced into every sort of civilian life by the sustained movement of armed forces, failure of communication, burning of villages and towns, and the exhausting effects of sustained uncertainty of personal safety.

Military exports constitute only one of the means by which a depletion process can be transferred abroad. In a way that is not immediately apparent, the existence of major sectors of depletion within the economy of the United States serves to transfer this weakness abroad.

Since the United States suffers from shortages of medical staffs at home, the country is unable to launch any major effort toward stepping up medical capability in most of the world.

The construction industry, especially in the area of building apartment dwellings on a large scale, is one of the technologically depleted industries of the United States. Our major construction companies do not operate research and development departments. Neither the industry associations nor various governmental bodies operate research institutes on the materials, techniques, and economics of construction. Apartment buildings in the United States are constructed by methods technologically analogous to the handicraft techniques used for the manufacture of automobiles in 1905.

As a derived effect of the technological backwardness of the American home-construction industry, there is American society's inability to help the newly developing countries with their remarkably complex problems in housing and urban development. In Africa the urban population is estimated as growing from 58 million in 1960 to 294 million by the year 2000. The city centers of Asia will grow from 559 million to 3,444 million during the same period, and in Latin America the growth in urban population will be from 144 million to 650 million. All told, during the next forty years, more dwellings will have to be built than hitherto in the entire history of man. Against such requirements, the limited United States efforts in the area of the development of building-construction techniques, and design and operation of urban centers, are very far from sufficient. Should newly developing countries take United States cities as a model, they would speedily acquire the array of problems that plague American cities.

Similar considerations apply to the whole array of depleted American industries. In each case, these underdeveloped industries contribute toward making the United States a less-competent model and source of innovation for the developing countries.

American concentration on military and related activities, in relation to the developing countries, is a reflection and an amplification of the emphasis these activities have been given within American society. But note that military-aid spending faithfully reflects the 50% share of such activity in the Federal Government's budgets. As late as 1960, I had calculated that if the then-unused production capability of the United States were marshaled in a great effort to facilitate the industrialization of the rest of the world, then the United States, by operating a "peace race," could change the nature of the political contest between the United States and the Soviet Union in the developing countries of the world. This calculation was based on the existence of about 30% unused capacity among American industries. These ideas were developed in my book *The Peace Race*. Soon afterward the rising military and space budgets of the United States made such policy initiatives unfeasible. There was a massive flow of technical talent and fresh productive capital into the areas of military and space operations. The unused industrial capacity that remained was marginal economically. Above all, the unemployed manpower that remained was no useful cross-section of the labor force, representing instead a heavy concentration of the unskilled and the educationally deprived. These developments made it unfeasible for the United States to mount great constructive efforts aimed at facilitating the industrialization of the rest of the world.

During the nineteenth century, it was the export of skilled manpower and capital from Western Europe that made rapid industrialization of the United States possible. Now, in the last third of the twentieth century, the United States has become incapable of performing this historic service for those nations of the world less developed than herself. The American economy has become depleted enough to restrict the quantity and quality of human and material resources that the United States might make available to newly developing areas of the world.

Finally, the export of depletion is encouraged by the example this country sets for the newly autonomous nations of the world. After all, any new government must find a model that will help to answer the question, "What does a fully developed society look like?" What main elements must the newly developing countries contain in order that they may one day provide a level of material well-being for their people, far and away better than what is now available to them? In the United States the developing countries see the world's most prosperous and efficient society with a government that uses more than half the nation's budget for military programs, atomic energy programs, and space programs. Therefore, let no one express righteous dismay if the governments of newly developing countries indulge themselves in armed forces, fancy airports, and all sorts of monumental projects that serve no productive purpose. In these respects, the new nations are only imitating the available model that shows how to be a big country.

9

The Depleted Society

Public Life Without Law
Private Life Without Purpose
The Politics of Depletion

Should the President or the generals decide about the use of nuclear weapons? This was a central issue during the Presidential election campaign of 1964. The Republican candidate urged that control of nuclear weapons should be in the hands of field commanders who would respond to military-political circumstances as they saw them close by. Editorial opinion of the American press and the opinions of the American public, as gauged by public opinion polls, showed a strong preference for having such control reside in the hands of the President. However, the essential fact, forgotten in this dispute, was that neither the President, as Commander-in-Chief, nor his subordinate officers, are empowered to apply military force without a formal declaration of war. That declaration, by Article 1, Section 8 of the Constitution, is reserved to the Congress—which alone has the "Power . . . to declare War. . . ." The very occurrence of this election campaign debate and the apparent victory of the civilian point of view involves a fundamental denial and evasion of lawful behavior as defined by the Constitution.

156

Unlike the economic depletion of industries and people as a result of long concentration on overkill, there are costs of depletion that defy measurement. These are the costs of the deterioration in the quality of public and private life.

One of the proudest features of Western tradition is the idea of government as a rule of law and not of men. The rule of law requires the formal operation of law-making bodies and the administration of these laws on an impartial basis according to a strict procedure (due process). In order to safeguard the independence and impartiality of law-making and the administration of laws, many principles were developed; an example is the separation between branches of government to help insure that the administration of law and the interpretation of law may be separate from the body that formulates the law. Further, where rule of law is administered by a representative government, law-making and due process must be incorporated in institutions that guarantee government by consent of the governed. Such procedures are designed to insure the performance of public officials as public servants rather than as autonomous managers of the public.

Americans, in common with most people of the West, have long accepted the notion that military power is ultimate power. Might may not be right, but most of us have agreed with Voltaire that God is on the side with the heaviest battalions. If it were true that the strongest military power always gets its way, then the United States, possessor of the greatest stock of nuclear military weapons in the world, should be able to exercise its will among other nations with substantial success. But this has not been the case; military power is becoming increasingly ineffective as an instrument of international policy. In some places where vital American interests are deemed imperiled—Vietnam and Cuba to name the most familiar—our vast military power has been virtually useless.

The repeated frustration of U.S. military power in enforcing United States Government policy has generated a mood of desperation among some Americans. Insofar as desperation informs a readiness to take extreme action, the extent of this desperation is defined by the agreed readiness to use nuclear military power to destroy entire societies—in wars that involve the anticipated destruction of one's own society. An acknowledged readiness to go to this extreme suggests that for these Americans, little remains of the common, formal restraints on behavior. The 1964 Presidential election returns indicated that they are not so few in number that their influence may be dismissed as inconsequential. A society equipped with nuclear weapons, and harboring a sizable number of citizens who are prepared to use nuclear weapons on a large scale has moved, by implication, toward the decision that the end justifies the means. One of the casualties of such a tendency is the rule of law itself.

Public Life Without Law

In many countries of the world, the Central Intelligence Agency practices an extraordinary entrepreneurship. Under Central Intelligence Agency "contracts," military operations have been carried out by private firms. For the ill-fated invasion of Cuba in 1961, the CIA "employed" private aircraft companies and private ship owners. In the South Vietnam war, an air-cargo company, Air America, has been "contracted" to airlift South Vietnamese special forces from secret air strips in South Vietnam and Thailand into Laos, Cambodia, and North Vietnam. The equipment operated by the Air America firm includes about 200 aircraft, ranging in size from 4-engine Boeing Stratoliners to helicopters and light planes. If an international law were broken and you asked the question, "Who is responsible?" one answer would be: "Air America, a private firm."

These tactics, of course, are a subterfuge used by the CIA to conduct military operations that are, at times, even contrary to the stated policies of the United States Government. Mr. Richard Starnes, correspondent for the Scripps-Howard newspapers, reported from Saigon on October 2, 1963, that the CIA "flatly refused to carry out instructions from Ambassador Henry Cabot Lodge."

Mr. Starnes continued:

> CIA "spooks" [a universal term for secret agents here] have
> penetrated every branch of the American community in Saigon.
> . . . Few people other than John Richardson [Chief of the
> CIA apparatus in Vietnam] and his close aides know the actual
> CIA strength here, but a widely used figure is 600.
>
> For every State Department aide here who will tell you—
> "Dammit, the CIA is supposed to gather information, not make
> policy, but policymaking is what they're doing here"—there
> are military officers who scream over the way the "spooks"
> dabble in military operations.
>
> One very high American official here, a man who has spent
> much of his life in the service of democracy, likened the CIA's
> growth to a malignancy, and added he was not sure even the
> White House could control it any longer.

The story of the CIA in South Vietnam, said Mr. Starnes, "is
a dismal chronicle of bureaucratic arrogance, obstinate disregard
of orders, and unrestrained thirst for power."

On December 27, 1964, Tad Szulc of The New York *Times*
broke the story of the unwillingness of Federal officials to prosecute several people on charges of allegedly smuggling war materials from the United States to other countries. The Central Intelligence Agency and the State Department, Mr. Szulc reported,
"have acted to hold back prosecution of . . . two pilots who
allegedly flew . . . fighter bomber trainers to Haiti illegally." This
refusal to prosecute occurred despite the fact that U.S. investi-
gatory agencies "had obtained what they considered reasonably
conclusive evidence of violation of the Neutrality Act and the
Munitions Export Act." Mr. Szulc reported that the CIA did not
wish one of its former operatives to be brought to trial lest there
be disclosure of some aspects of CIA operations.

Wire tapping is virtually the standard operating procedure for
the CIA, despite repeated refusal by the courts to admit such
materials in evidence.

There is more on the list of *illegal* CIA activities. For instance, part of the operation for the Bay of Pigs invasion was the arrest in Miami, just before the invasion, of Mr. Rolando Masferrer, a former police official of the Batista regime in Cuba. Evidently, the CIA wanted this man out of the way, so Federal agents arrested Mr. Masferrer and placed him under guard in Jackson Memorial Hospital. Messrs. Wise and Ross, in their informative book, *The Invisible Government,* report: "Ten days after the Bay of Pigs disaster, Federal Judge Emett C. Choate ordered Masferrer released and accused the Federal government of having shipped him off to a 'government concentration camp' in Texas. 'The President', said Judge Choate, 'has no authority to direct anyone to disobey the law.' Seven months later, on November 9, 1961, the Government quietly dropped the case against Masferrer without explanation." Apparently, Mr. Masferrer had been engaged in his own plans for running arms and men into Cuba for anti-Castro operations. For this he was charged and indicted by a Federal grand jury for conspiring to violate the United States neutrality laws. A short time later, 132 lawyers presented a brief to Attorney General Robert Kennedy, charging that the Federal Government, by organizing the Bay of Pigs invasion through the CIA, had acted in violation of the neutrality laws. This was denied by the Attorney General on the grounds that these laws were "not designed for the kind of situation which exists in the world today."

The case of Masferrer was one of illegal political arrest. Once this practice can be carried out by groups such as the CIA that act in secret, even inside the United States, then legality as a rule of private and public performance is seriously undermined.

In the field of international law, one of the important sets of constraints on the behavior of governments is the Geneva Convention, which sets limits to warlike behavior. The Geneva Convention on the treatment of prisoners of war was signed by the United States on August 12, 1949, and ratified July 6, 1955. Under these rules the torture of prisoners of war is expressly prohibited. After the end of the Second World War former Japanese officers who had been responsible for torture of prisoners were tried as war criminals for these acts. However, during 1963-

64 in the fighting in South Vietnam, the United States has been a party to the torture of Vietcong prisoners by Vietnamese soldiers and their American "advisors." The Vietnamese soldiers were paid for, equipped and "advised" by the United States Government. In this case, the breaking of international law, to which the United States Government has been a party, has been compounded by the announcement of these acts in the United States mass media, together with color photographs of prisoners undergoing forceable interrogation.

A Maryland physician on January 24, 1965, wrote to the editor of the Washington *Post*:

> . . .The American press has been far from guiltless thus far in the Vietnamese dilemma. When I returned this summer from a two-year tour in South Viet-Nam with MEDICO, the first thing that struck me was a pictorial article in *Life*, calling the treatment of Viet Cong prisoners "unnecessary and cruel."
>
> The "cruel torture" was harmless harassment such as minor electrical shocks from battery-powered field telephones and the pouring of water over cloth-covered faces giving the sensation of drowning. American advisers have told me that many Viet Cong youths reveal weapon and troop locations with this treatment. But the press apparently wanted "kid-gloves" for these Viet Cong, who were guilty of murder and treason, conspiracy and more of the same, and who by right should have been placed before a wall and shot.

The photographs referred to in the Washington *Post* letter appeared June 12, 1964, in *Life*, whose correspondent wrote:

> The Vietnamese commander whipped the captives with a bamboo cane and booted them as they lay trussed on the ground. The women and children watched the torture of their husbands and fathers with steady faces. The guerrillas were jackknifed into positions of agony. They were held under the river's surface and tortured with water that was forced into their noses. Rags were put over their faces and then water was

poured over the rags to give the impression of drowning. Pho-
tographer Okamura protested: this seemed needless and cruel.
A soldier replied, "But this is my duty." But the prisoners
would not talk.

As though writing a case study for a manual of instructions on
how to rationalize the breaking of international treaties, the U.S.
State Department, according to the New York *Times* (January
15, 1965),

> . . . declined today to state whether the United States still felt
> bound by the Geneva accord prohibiting foreign military inter-
> vention in Laos.
>
> The department's silence reflected the difficulty of the posi-
> tion in which the country finds itself as a signer of the 14-nation
> accord, which was reached in July, 1962.
>
> The principal objective of the agreement was to guarantee
> the neutrality and independence of Laos. . . .
>
> The Administration's dilemma, imposed by conflicting legal
> obligations and military objectives, has been heightened by the
> increasing activity of United States warplanes over Laos on
> reconnaissance and attack missions that have been going on
> quietly for about six months.
>
> On Wednesday a squadron of American fighter bombers
> wrecked a bridge on a Communist supply route near the cen-
> tral Laotian town of Ban Ban.
>
> Officials acknowledge privately that there is no legal basis
> under the 1962 accord for carrying out such missions in Laos.

At the same time there was no indication that the Department
of State had attempted to bring to bear the machinery of the
United Nations for handling what was presumably a treaty violation by pro-Communist forces.

Due process of law—the rules that govern the behavior of
public administration and the interpretation of laws—has been
circumvented for the handling of personnel problems of former
employees of the Central Intelligence Agency. Such people do not

have ordinary rights of appeal to the courts with respect to the decisions concerning their tenure by their employer, the CIA.

The Bay of Pigs invasion involved a host of illegalities by the Executive branch of the Federal Government, including a decision to wage war, to send unmarked U.S. Navy jets over the beaches of Cuba. Who gave the President the right to make decisions of this sort? By what law did he, independently of the Congress, order into action American armed forces without identification?

The tradition of governing by the consent of the governed has also been abridged by actions of the CIA, which has used private foundations as covert instruments for the administration of funds. By such means actions are taken, ostensibly by private groups, which actually represent decisions of government agencies. This manipulation of formally private bodies by government makes it extremely difficult to hold governmental bodies responsible for their actions. How is one to be sure when an action is that of a public body with public accountability, or a private body that need answer to no one?

In May, 1964, there came to light a remarkable example of actions undertaken by the United States Government, actions that were not authorized by any known consultation of the electorate, either directly or indirectly. The Atomic Energy Commission announced in April, 1964, the loss of 1,000 grams of highly toxic Plutonium-238; the radioactive element had been in an orbiting earth satellite that was subsequently lost. This dangerous material could very well have entered the atmosphere and drifted to the surface of the earth. The satellite bearing the plutonium was orbited, presumably, in the name of the people of the United States. But who knew of this before the Defense Department and the Atomic Energy Commission decided to reveal their technical failure? Indeed, it is pertinent to ask: What else have these agencies undertaken with public funds that they have not yet told us or our elected representatives?

The greatest part of action by government is conducted in accord with law. That is essential for orderly functioning of large organizations. However, government actions that depart from law need not be large in number to establish that, in fact, law-abidingness has been seriously abridged. We know that even in totalitarian societies there are laws, rules, and procedures which are generally followed. But only a limited number of arbitrary actions by leaders are needed to alter the quality of public life from rule of law to the feasibility and danger of arbitrary action on important issues and toward individuals by government administrators.

The idea that a public official is a public servant and not a manager of the public is an essential feature of lawfulness in the structure of a democratic society. But during the last few years public officials have repeatedly managed and manipulated, misled and misinformed the American public on many matters of obvious public importance.

The American public has been frightened into approving enormous military appropriations by announcements of a "missile gap," a "bomber gap," and a "conventional-forces gap." Not only have none of these materialized; even more alarming is the strong presumption, based on solid clues, that gap predictions never were more than fictions. During 1961 and 1962, as part of a campaign to "sell" civil defense to the American people, the Federal Government lent its prestige to absurd propositions published in *Life* magazine. We read that 97% of us would survive a nuclear war provided we were enclosed in the preposterous fall-out shelters that were proposed. Note the flat contradiction between the public-relations campaign for civil defense of a few short years ago and the more recent instruction to the American public, that, in an all-out nuclear exchange, 100 million Americans would die within the first hour.

News manipulation and outright deception, inspired and foisted on the press by government agencies, have been a sustaining feature of the reporting from the South Vietnam war. The use of the half-truth in public announcements, as discovered by Karl E. Meyer of the Washington *Post* in 1964, "is evidenced by the continued talk about North Vietnamese help for the Vietcong guerrillas. In fact, the chief source of supply for the guerrillas has been the U. S. itself; an informed guess is that 125,000 light weapons were lost to the Vietcong in the past two years. The present Communist offensive in Vietnam was made possible, according to the best informed sources, by the prodigious haul in weapons between February and October of last year." Half-truths have been the basis of repeated front-page announcements concerning impending attacks on the Vietcong supply line from the North.

Mr. David Halberstam, crack correspondent for the New York *Times* in South Vietnam during 1963-64, has described how President Kennedy reacted to his Pulitzer Prize-winning reporting on the administration-supported Vietnam Government:

> On October 22, Arthur Ochs Sulzberger, the new publisher of the *Times,* went by the White House to pay a courtesy call on the President of the United States. It was a time when, except for Vietnam, the administration was riding high and feeling very cocky: Kennedy was sure his 1964 opponent would be Goldwater and was confidently expecting a big victory. Almost the first question the President asked Mr. Sulzberger was what he thought of his young man in Saigon. Mr. Sulzberger answered that he thought I was doing fine. The President suggested that perhaps I was too close to the story, too involved (this is the most insidiously damaging thing that can be said about a reporter). No, Mr. Sulzberger answered, he did not think I was too involved. The President asked if perhaps Mr. Sulzberger had been thinking of transferring me to another assignment. No, said Mr. Sulzberger, the *Times* was quite satisfied with the present distribution of assignments. (At that particular point I was supposed to take a two-week breather, but the *Times* immediately cancelled my vacation.)

Manipulation of information to the public extends to sources of information and the creation of new knowledge. Thus, the Central Intelligence Agency has been revealed as a financial backer of the Center for International Studies at the Massachu-

setts Institute of Technology. In May, 1964, the United States
Information Agency was discovered to be using Federal funds
for the covert financing of "privately" published books that were
later given heavy advertising and promotion.

A volume on *The Strategy of Deception* was contracted for by
the USIA, which then arranged for publication by a private publisher and distribution by a book club—all without benefit of
disclosure in the book of its official sponsorship. In the USIA
budget for 1964 there was a $90,000 sum for "book develop-
ment" and the 1965 budget requested $195,000 for this purpose.

We are indebted to the authors of *The Invisible Government*
for compiling these examples of deliberately misleading public
statements by government officials.

In May, 1960, after the U-2 plane was downed in Russia:
"There was absolutely no—NO—no deliberate attempt to vio-
late Soviet airspace. There never has been."—LINCOLN
WHITE, State Department spokesman.

As the Bay of Pigs Operation was going into action in 1961:
"The American people are entitled to know whether we are
intervening in Cuba or intend to do so in the future. The answer to that question is no."—Secretary of State DEAN RUSK.

While the CIA was engineering the overthrow of a Guate-
malan government: "The situation is being cured by the
Guatemalans themselves."—Secretary of State JOHN FOSTER
DULLES.

I think that the readiness of government officials to act in a
desperate, even lawless way is bound up with our country's commitment and readiness to use even nuclear weapons to secure
political goals. The examples of lawlessness and arrogance by
officialdom that I have cited here do seem to be lesser violations
of humane, democratic values than the end-of-society extremism
of nuclear war. Nevertheless, the corrosive development of lawlessness in our public life, and its effects on the individual, are
an important reason for moving with urgency to find ways of

replacing the policies of the arms race with their fixation on an overkill and the motto that anything goes.

Private Life Without Purpose

During the two decades since the end of World War II, the quality of American life has been retuned in response to the demands of a unique phenomenon, World Cold War. This war demands constant vigilance, and a constant readiness to act with force of arms. It seems to me that it demands, too, a definition of some sort as to how it might be resolved. Although we have been engaged in this war for twenty years, no one has defined what might be its successful resolution.

The military vigilance and the pressure for uncritical support of government policies that has dominated American life during this period has given it a special tone, just as economic problems of the depression and the rise of totalitarianism in Europe gave a special cast to American life during the 1930's and 1940's. But while the consuming problems of that period had definable solutions to which we could set a purposeful course, the Cold War problems of the last two decades have had no defined resolution. Lacking understandable goals, our activities on the national level have acquired a quality of purposelessness.

On the individual level, too, the Cold War has generated a suffocating purposelessness. The nuclear arms race has created a condition without precedent in human experience. For the first time, the human race has had to face the prospect of extinction. Owing to the destructive capability of nuclear weapons, a few men in a few governments now hold the power of "no future" over all of us. The knowledge of this possibility erodes the foundation of purposeful living, which surely must include a plausible expectation of a future, opportunities for personal development and enough self-esteem to make use of opportunities. The assurance of these basic conditions for purposeful living has been seriously threatened. One result of this is the feeling of individual powerlessness and hopelessness, especially among the youth of our country.

I am not implying that there is uniformity either in the perception of the threat or in the intensity of response to it. There is, of course, a variety of ways of experiencing and responding to the "no future" condition. The range of personal response extends from indifference and neutrality to concern and involvement. Nevertheless, these variations in experience and response are all reactions to the frustration of a common want, the desire for human solidarity in a common constructive purpose, in a definable future.

Many Americans feel helpless to affect their destiny, and acting together in compliance to the demands of defense does not satisfy their desire to do so. Many Americans have even come to feel uncertain about the quality of their allegiance. They have tried to reassure themselves and their fellows by such rituals as daily ceremonial oaths of allegiance. Symbolic acts of patriotism can be, at best, an adjunct to, but not a competent substitute for solidarity of common purpose in the lives of individuals and especially in the lives of communities. The absence of a common constructive purpose to rally around on a national level coupled with the threat of "no future" for oneself and one's family have produced widespread feelings of powerlessness, of incompetence to affect one's destiny, of alienation.

What is alienation? The concept itself is not new. The psycho-analyst-philosopher Erich Fromm has described it in his book, *The Sane Society*:

By alienation is meant a mode of experience in which the person experiences himself as an alien. He has become, one might say, estranged from himself. He does not experience himself as the center of his world, as the creator of his own acts—but his acts and their consequences have become his masters, whom he obeys, or whom he may even worship. The alienated person is out of touch with himself as he is out of touch with any other person. He, like the others, is experienced as things are experienced; with the senses and with common sense, but at the same time without being related to himself and to the world outside productively. . . .

In idolatry, says Fromm, God is a thing. But:

If man is created in the likeness of God, he is created as the bearer of infinite qualities. In idolatory man bows down and submits to the projection of one partial quality in himself. He does not experience himself as the center from which living acts of love and reason radiate. He becomes a thing, his neighbor becomes a thing, just as his gods are things. "The idols of the heathen are silver and gold, the work of men's hands. They have mouths but they speak not; eyes have they, but they see not; they have ears but they hear not; neither is there any breath in their mouths. They that make them are like them; so is everyone that trusts in them." (Psalm 135) . . .

What is common to all these phenomena—the worship of idols, the idolatrous worship of God, the idolatrous love for a person, the worship of a political leader or the state, and the idolatrous worship of the externalizations of irrational passions—is the process of alienation. It is the fact that man does not experience himself as the active bearer of his own powers and richness, but as an impoverished "thing," dependent on powers outside of himself, unto whom he has projected his living substance. . . .

Man has created a world of man-made things as it never existed before. He has constructed a complicated social machine to administer the technical machine he built. Yet this whole creation of his stands over and above him. He does not feel himself as a creator and center, but as the servant of a Golem, which his hands have built. The more powerful and gigantic the forces are which he unleashes, the more powerless he feels himself as a human being. He confronts himself with his own forces embodied in things he has created, alienated from himself. He is owned by his own creation, and has lost ownership of himself. He has built a golden calf, and says "these are your gods who have brought you out of Egypt."

These ideas are important in many societies and at many points in history. What is new, however, is the extent and intensity of alienation in our society today. I think it can be said that never before has a society so intimately interdependent as ours been beset by the disintegrating influence of so many alienated citizens. I do not mean to suggest that we, as a nation, are about to fly apart. But we are in trouble; alienation and its accompanying evil, sustained, widespread anxiety, are symptoms of a national sickness. The sickness is being caused by our trying to solve the political problems of the Cold War with a program of overkill that has become politically ineffectual and has resulted in the depletion of materials and men, and of the meaning of ideals that we have been taught to value.

The tone of a period is often expressed in clearest form by the young people. They respond to the current condition without long years of habituation to other circumstances. Dr. Benjamin Spock, the eminent doctor, has diagnosed major effects of Cold War as conditioning on our children:

American children, recent studies show, are being made increasingly anxious by the cold war. Between 25 and 50 per cent of our children in U.S. schools today expect nuclear attack. The young ones worry most about being poisoned by fallout, about being separated from their parents in a disaster, about the maiming or death of their families and themselves. Adolescents speak with some bitterness about the uncertainty of their future, about the possibility of their giving birth to deformed children, about the futility of working hard at school.

Children have also been infected with an unhealthy suspiciousness. When a fifth-grade class, for example, was looking at a picture of the Russian countryside showing a tree-lined road and one child asked what the trees were for, others quickly suggested, "So the people won't know what's going on beyond the road" and "It's to make work for the prisoners."

Until very recent times America has been an outstandingly buoyant nation. We have imbued our children with optimism. We have brought them up believing that they would be able

to cope with whatever life offered, and so they've usually succeeded. We've never restricted their vision with narrow traditions or cautions, so they have been extraordinarily creative.
We have given them a natural trust in people and a trust in
their own ability to deal wtih people. As a result, they've impressed the world with their self-assured friendliness.

Up to a few years ago, America's influence in the world was
always on the ascendant. Whatever we've set our minds to—
whether it was expanding our exports, helping to win wars,
developing the atomic bomb, rehabilitating Europe with the
Marshall plan—we've succeeded. But in recent years, we've
run into repeated conflicts with the Communists and we have
had to be satisfied with stalemates. In certain psychological
aspects, we have reacted neurotically to these setbacks. Instead
of calmly pursuing the course which would serve our long-
time aims, we have often seemed obsessed with the fear of
what the Communists would do to us.

To the degree that we adults become fearful and suspicious,
we pass such attitudes on to our children. . . .

The exaggerated fear of Communist nations that will be carried into adulthood by an increasing number of today's children
will lower their optimism, their self-reliance, and their total
effectiveness. Furthermore, this fear and its consequences could
be played upon by an unstable leader, just as fear in Germany
was exploited by Hitler, to push this country into war. The
repercussions of fear of outside aggression could be extended
disastrously into a wholesale mistrust of all one's fellow men,
including one's neighbors.

Adolescents have been taught not to challenge the Cold War
society. It is disloyal to criticize and besides you might be called
a Communist. Such strictures close off many channels for expression of the ordinary normal questioning of adult standards that
has been part of adolescence. They are taught, instead, that it is
dangerous to challenge any important part of the *status quo*.

Probably the most common response to the restraints on challenge is a degree of adaptive resignation. Adjust to things as they

are. Develop a "cool," detached, don't-get-involved attitude. Be "objective," don't let your feelings interfere. The reverse of the coin reads: Don't be human; be a machine; be a robot; function without feeling; be daring—experiment with alcohol, fast cars, sex, marijuana.

Narcotic addiction among teen-agers has reached epidemic proportions in numbers of upper-middle-class neighborhoods, to the surprise and distress of parents who have not understood the strength of the feelings of alienation produced among their children by the sense of having no future. The rising incidence of venereal disease, especially among teen-agers, reached such proportions that President Kennedy included a specific reference to it in a message on health to the Congress.

One of the most distressing responses to powerlessness is the helpless rage of people who feel crushed and terrified. This is revealed in extremist and violent acts, personal and social, by young people. Since 1952, both the number and rate of law-breaking cases classified as juvenile delinquency have gone up. Our newspapers have reported in ample detail that feature of juvenile violence that has especially shocked the adult community: the apparent absence of cause or purpose in acts of violence against strangers.

In American political life, such helpless rage has been given expression in proposals for a nuclear confrontation that will settle the unbearable tension of the Cold War once and for all. In June, 1964, a student's letter to the editor of the New York *Times* supported a political candidate with the following reasoning:

... Have the critics paused to consider, even momentarily, the possibility that a few solutions in an era of indecisiveness might be a good thing for the country? Perhaps the man whose mind is least cluttered with conflicting positions, each containing its modicum of truth, will also be the man whose outlook, over-simplified as it may be, is most positive, hence most efficacious. ...

If intellectualism must be equated with relativism, then the national interest may well dictate a decrease in the power of intellectualism in the Federal Government. Better to have in the Presidency a man who might push the nuclear button too quickly than one whose conscience would restrain him from pushing it at all.

During the Cuban missile crisis in October, 1962, adults, adolescents and children, too, felt powerless to dissipate the gathering storm of nuclear war with its threat of no future for all of us. Several colleagues reported instances of school children bidding tearful good-byes to each other. In some schools there was wholesale breakdown of discipline: children wandered about. Large numbers of college students went home—to spend their last hours with their families. There was an overriding sense of powerlessness and of the imminent end of the world.

Quiet, careful compliance with the *status quo* has not been an attitude restricted to the ordinary citizen. These views have shaped the behavior of our experts on the understanding of society itself.

The social sciences of the Cold War period have been oriented heavily toward concentration on methodologies and techniques, to the neglect of defining cause and effect in areas of behavior that facilitate the solution of social problems. "Value-free" social science and concentration on technique as against problem-solving have been new themes that have shaped the choice of studies of many university graduate students during the last years. The issue here is not clear-cut, not black or white. It is rather one of emphasis. When methodology dominates the social sciences while "problem-oriented" inquiry is declared unfashionable, intellectuals cast themselves in the role of skilled mechanics, ready and waiting to solve the problems which others may bring to them. This is the posture of the depleted intellectual in the depleted society.

More broadly, America's intellectuals, scientists, engineers, and professional men have developed a fascination for technique and methodology, with lesser attention to the end result of the work in hand. The assumption, often justified, is that the individual, even with his close colleagues cannot influence the end use of their product—whether a bar of soap or a computer.

Our literary critics should be able to teach us quite a bit about the special temper of our times. In mass-circulation paperbacks and films of the Cold War society who is the outstanding hero? He is the man of action who can do something about his fate. He is James Bond who does this by supercompetent deception and skillful violence. He is Humphrey Bogart who manages with great personal "toughness" and cynicism.

There are Americans whose response to the depleted society has been criticism combined with a search for constructive alternatives. It is significant, however, as a measure of strength of Cold War pressures, that the several organizations, like the National Committee for a Sane Nuclear Policy (SANE), which have favored nonmilitary alternatives to the Cold War, did not come into being until 1958. Except for long-established pacifist societies, like the Quakers, it took from 1945 until 1958 to bring into being American organizations devoted to independent criticism of government actions and a search for major alternative policy to the Cold War and its depletion process.

During December, 1964, Americans read with amazement of the student rebellion at the Berkeley campus of the University of California. Adult amazement stemmed from ignorance of the depth of resentment among students against many features of Cold War society. The sensational newspaper accounts of mass student rebellion at Berkeley did not report that, underlying the issue of free speech that was publicly debated, there was long-standing resentment, especially among graduate students and teaching assistants, of the changed character of the University. "Scholarship has become secondary to the interests of the military-industrial complex," said a student spokesman. "Does this type of University serve society?" But rebellion has been the choice of a limited minority of Americans. Most people have held to an uneasy confidence or acquiescence in policies that have promised national security based primarily on ever-larger military forces.

Confidence in official policies, however, has not allayed anxieties. They are aroused and reinforced by the appearance of contradictions between theory and practice, between what we are supposed to believe and the way things are. The Constitution, we have all been taught, is the basic law of the land. But Constitutional constraint has been violated under pressure of fast-moving Cold War tactics. We have become a churchgoing people in enormous numbers, but the precepts of every faith have been undercut and violated by warlike preparations and warlike behavior. No religious faith condones torturing war prisoners. But with and through our allies in South Vietnam we have done it. No American church condones genocide or suicide, but we have been preparing for it

The ideology of the Cold War has taught that political superiority was attainable provided the United States accumulated enough military power. The reality has been a military-nuclear stalemate and an array of political struggles in which America's numerical military power has not been decisive. Rising productivity in our industries, we have long believed, carried the promise of a rising level of living for all. This does not square with 35 million of our countrymen numbered as impoverished. One of the proud beliefs of Americans has been that the United States is industrially and technologically pre-eminent. But this is abridged by the development of industrial depletion on a large scale. The principle of government by the consent of the governed is contradicted by "news management" and public misinformation on vital issues.

Presidents Eisenhower, Kennedy, and Johnson all have acknowledged that the only way to win nuclear war is to prevent it. In 1961, therefore, our Government set up the Arms Control and Disarmament Agency to devise orderly, inspected schemes for arms limitation and disarmament. This agency, under the State Department, was endowed by 1964 with a total of 166 employees. A staff of 413 was employed by the American Battle Monuments Commission in 1964.

The Cold War is supposed to be a contest between authoritarian Communist forms of society and democratic forms. We have urged that the Soviets permit self-determination of form of governments in areas under their rule. But the United States has been supporting dictators who permit no self-determination whatever. Our espousal of rule of law as a basis of behavior within and among societies is contradicted by lawlessness practiced by our own Government. High value to human life is an oft-repeated principle in the West, but there is dramatic evidence of the denial of this principle by the plans and proposals for destroying whole enemy societies (subhumans, that is) in nuclear war.

Knowledge of major contradictions between theory and reality produces distrust, disorientation, and a feeling of alienation. Whom should a person believe? Whom should he trust with respect to issues and policies that literally mean life or death for all of us?

The Politics of Depletion

Words like "powerlessness" are inexact. There are degrees of powerfulness and powerlessness, and such capabilities are in one continuum. Still, with respect to these qualities, there is a recognizable qualitative difference between the political tone of the United States during the 1950's and the 1960's, as contrasted to the two previous decades. One way of seeing this is to contrast the responses of Americans to two military-political crises: the attack on Pearl Harbor in 1941 and the Cuban missile crisis of 1962.

In response to the Pearl Harbor attack there was general confidence of achieving victory. During the Cuban missile crisis, however, the American people were doubtful about the results and there was real helplessness about what to do. If nuclear war did break out, it meant no future. Following the Pearl Harbor attack, there was a strong sense of solidarity in the American population which responded quickly to all sorts of mobilization efforts. There was a general sense of meaningful individual responsibility; Americans felt that what they did individually could affect the outcome. But during the Cuban missile crisis there was a sense of atomization and alienation among many Americans. There was panic and disorientation in parts of the population.

We were onlookers at the gathering storm. The Pearl Harbor attack was followed by substantial development of common purpose among Americans. During the Cuban crisis there was much evidence of individual helplessness, and panicky discussion of leaving the cities, and even leaving the United States.

The loss of confidence and sense of powerlessness during the Cuban missile crisis reflected the fact that there really was nothing that individuals could do to affect the outcome of a military-political pressure game that was directed by the top leaders of the United States and the Soviet Union. In this scenario, once described as an "eyeball-to-eyeball" confrontation, there was no clear way for individual citizens to act meaningfully with respect to decisions that chose life or death for all of us. This was the meaning of powerlessness during the Cuban missile crisis.

Limited ability to affect one's destiny has involved more than the basic issue of life or death or our country. A major part of the Cold War political climate has included the frustration of discussion and debate concerning policy alternatives. The implication has been repeatedly developed during the Cold War period that the Government knows best about matters of international politics, that the very nature of the East-West confrontation requires national unanimity in support of Government positions; therefore critical dissent with respect to Government policies can be disloyalty to the society itself. Under the impact of such reasoning, enforced by private and public committees which could ruin a person's reputation, traditions of loyal opposition were shattered. Critics could find little place within the framework of community institutions.

One of the most important types of powerlessness developed during the Cold War has been the self-imposed reduction of decision-power by the Congress of the United States with respect to "the common defense and the general welfare." This is an area of decision-power specifically assigned to the Congress by Article I, Section 8, of the Constitution of the United States. During the Cold War period, power of decision by Congress involving international politics and military affairs has been left, increasingly, to the Cold War institutional machine. This is a network

of organizations, public and nominally private, which was established to develop theories and techniques for military and
political Cold War policy. For example, the decision by the Government of the United States to launch a military invasion of
Cuba was a major policy decision, formulated and implemented
by the Executive branch with the participation of the various
Cold War organizations, but without any participation whatever
of the Congress. This was a violation of the Constitution.

The reduced political competence of the Congress has weakened one of the ways that American citizens have had for ex-
pressing responsibility for public policy. Members of the House
of Representatives, for example, must stand for election every
two years. If these Members were indeed involved in deciding
on Cold War policies, this could evoke participation by interested
citizens. However, once the Congress plays the part of mainly
rubber-stamping Executive branch decisions, then there is virtually no direct, orderly way by which many citizens can have
credible participation in selecting security and allied policies for
our country. The President, after all, is elected once in four years
and is not beholden, as are the Members of the House of Representatives in particular, to the several thousand citizens that each
Member represents.

These conditions have contributed to a widespread sense of
powerlessness among Americans, to frustration and cynicism with
respect to public life and "politicians."

Society-wide pressure for political conformity, together with
general approval for preparing and committing acts of great violence, have contributed mightily toward shaping the quality of
life of our youth. Psychologists like the late Dr. Robert Lindner
have defined a transformation in the quality of adolescence. Responsive to the social and political climate of the Cold War,
American adolescents have been shifting from privacy and introspection to pack-running as a feature of the transition to adulthood. In place of introspection and restraint on overt expression
of emotionality as dominating features of adolescents, our young
people have taken to "acting out" their feelings, including violent
feelings. These have been important features of a shift from "rebellion" to "mutiny" as the locus of adolescent behavior.

For our children and adolescents the awareness of contradiction between textbook teachings and our country's political behavior produces a crisis of identity: Who am I? To which of these should I be loyal? The textbooks in our schools teach our young people, among other values, about the worth of self-determination in politics (no taxation without representation); the desirability of rule of law to make available justice for all; and the worth of individual liberty and human life. The manifest contradiction between such ideals and the reality of so much of Cold War behavior has made many Americans, young and old, ashamed of our Government's actions. Recently, I received a note from a housewife who had attended a public meeting that I had addressed on some problems of public policy. She wrote:

> . . . The great difficulty about our being a Democracy is how do we speak to authority or protest about actions like our behavior in South Viet Nam. What are our reasons? How did we ever land there in the first place? Many people I know are horrified at this breach of international relations. It seems just the wrong thing to do if we pretend to be noble and interested in peace and arms cutbacks and the respect of small nations and their independence. I don't understand why the United Nations does not protest *our* imperialism.
>
> There are many inhibited people like me here.
>
> What can we do to feel like a citizen of a proud Democracy and not ashamed of being an American?
>
> I've written our Senators Javits and Kennedy: I'm sure I'll get copies of the *Congressional Record* to read! It happened once before. It seems to me that we as taxpayers ought to be able to protest about where our money goes to. The poverty program gets a paltry sum compared to the military.
>
> Can you find time to write what effective thing can be sent and to whom? Mr. Humphrey is a sound thinking person. Sorry this is so long a note.
>
> Sincerely yours,
>
> (signed) G. S.
>
> P.S. I have felt so inhibited that I almost wrote that my folks were in America before the Civil War (to explain my right to

complain about our government's actions). This is what the McCarthy years have done.

Most Americans have responded to a sense of powerlessness during the Cold War period by an attitude of "neutrality": The issues are so complicated that they can only be understood by experts; therefore, leave these big decisions on public affairs to the authorities who know about these complicated matters. The most characteristic style of support for Cold War official policies has been by a process of identifying with the authorities, repeating official policy views and often supporting them with fearful insistence. Most of the "liberals" of American society have been in this latter group. The implication among many of them has been that if the Government does it, it must be good for the people.

On the other side: I think the main form of opposition to Cold War policies has been a sort of moral withdrawal from association with government. This view of the matter draws upon the folk tradition of the "politician" as a man of devious and probably tainted ethics. (As part of the Reform Movement within the Democratic Party in New York City, young women have volunteered to serve as poll-watchers on Election Day. At one polling place on New York's fashionable East Side a Democratic party "regular" spotted one of the "reform" watchers and asked with genuine surprise: "What's a nice girl like you doing in a place like this?")

For many people, feeling powerless serves to amplify the estimated competence of whatever it is they fear or oppose. Thus, if government policy is opposed, then the powerless are prone to see government as an enormously competent, overpowering machine. That view of the government lends credence to the individual's feeling of powerlessness. Moreover, from the standpoint of those who are convinced of their political enfeeblement, acting in a lawful way means playing the game within the constraints set by the power-holders. That means sure frustration. This reasoning, in turn, justifies extremist evaluations and actions.

The new right wing in American politics is composed, in good measure, of frightened people who are reacting, even more than they themselves know, to the powerlessness engendered by the depletion process within American society. The reality of depletion is the kernel of truth which has shocked so many Americans toward the estimate that "this can't be happening to us." Overly fearful response to manifestations of Soviet technical competence, like the launching of the sputniks, has led many Americans to look for ways of adding to the strength of the United States under the guidance of Cold War policies. But this response, with its enlarged military budgets and costly space race, only weakens the country further by depletion of many aspects of life. Frustration and feelings of powerlessness are, in turn, amplified by the contrast between promises of Cold War policy and reality, dominated by a combination of military stalemate and domestic depletion.

In this sense, I believe that as a nation we have been more aware of a depletion process than we have conceded to ourselves. There is a growing sense, however unformulated, that there is something fundamentally wrong with the bearers of conventional wisdom who try to use ever more military power even though that results in no solution internationally and rapid depletion at home.

It is entirely possible that the men of the far right in American politics have been more responsive to the contradiction between ideals and behavior than the liberals of American society. The far right perceives among many Americans the strength of allegiance to traditional ideals and values of individual worth and human liberty. They proclaim these ideals and then use the contradiction between them and reality to justify extremist methods.

The use of traditional ideals by the far right in American politics is, in good part, a reflection of the fact that the sort of depletion process which I have been defining in this book has no recognizable place in the "ideal culture" that comes out of the elementary and high-school textbooks of our country. Since this *couldn't* be happening to us, it must be caused by some alien force powerful enough to seize control of important parts of the United States Government, which, in turn, has been made into the instrument for subverting classical American virtues. Therefore the condition is desperate, calling for desperate measures. That is the meaning of the famous phrase that "extremism in the pursuit of liberty is no vice."

The ideological appeal of the far right to the powerless includes many formulations that do not stand up very well under scrutiny. For example, there is a generalized idea that if government would only leave us alone, then the play of normal competition with American society would produce good solutions for our economic and allied problems. This view of the matter ducks the fact that the most important area of government intervention in American life is the military system whose cost takes up more than half of the Federal budget and whose activity has done very much to inhibit managerial and economic initiative in many industries.

On the other hand there is evidence that certain government policies can be powerful stimuli for promoting industrial and technical efficiency, without impairing in the least the political liberty of individuals. For example, in the electric utility industry, regulation by government has required public-utility firms to justify the levels of cost upon which rates to customers are based. At the same time this industry, serviced by an efficient group of machinery suppliers, and by a steady flow of engineers from universities and technical institutes, has been well equipped to respond to these pressures on costs by improving productivity of labor and capital. One result is that the price of electricity in the United States has been *declining* for nearly two thirds of a century. Obviously, this sort of enviable performance does not square with the unqualified proposition that "the government" should just leave us all alone.

The anxieties and the powerlessness felt by so many Americans reflect real conditions of depletion in our country, real problems which can and must be solved. Failing the availability of solutions these anxieties can be demagogically exploited by the far right. In the absence of actual solutions to fear-producing problems, "extremism"—to many people—looks like a positive, courageous attitude, and "moderation" means approval of anxiety-producing conditions as they are.

For many people, the contradiction between American ideals and American actions threatens self-identity: If the world is not the sort of place that I have been taught it is supposed to be, then who am I? What is the real source of order in this world? And why is there a contradiction between ideals and the world as seen in the daily paper?

This threat to self-identity is especially meaningful to Americans whose occupations are vulnerable and insecure. Here are included the middle-management men of the great corporate hierarchies, small businessmen, many independent professionals, and notably, the management men and technicians in industries whose future would be problematic if the Cold War were to end.

In sum: the politics of the far right is the politics of accommodation to depletion and powerlessness. Increasingly vigorous implementation of Cold War policies can only intensify the depletion of our country.

In order to make the turn away from depletion and powerlessness, and toward a productive society, it is essential to diagnose the causes of the depletion process. I hope that the analyses given here have made a contribution in that direction. Beyond having such knowledge, it is necessary to open up a discussion of alternatives for public policies extending from firms and communities on to the Federal Government.

A creative discussion of alternatives to depletion policies is surely served by the free functioning of critical, creative intelligence in our country. This has been discouraged during the Cold War period. If foreign policy, for example, must be bipartisan and hence unanimous, then criticism, opposition, is taken to be the stance of a fringe that is possibly disloyal and, at worst, subversive. The Cold War pressures toward monolithic political thought and expression must be halted in favor of affirming the constructive function that a loyal opposition serves. The very act of creating a climate that explicitly welcomes criticism of every sort will contribute something toward lessening the powerlessness which so many Americans have felt. Such discussion, by encouraging the decision-making competence of people in many walks of life, will encourage mutual responsibility.

Some people think that Cold War policies have caused such extreme deterioration in many domestic and world conditions that it is virtually impossible to formulate constructive policies that might replace Cold War patterns. One variation of this view is that the formulation of alternative policies for American society is unnecessary anyhow, since "the system" will crumble of its own depletion. The function of a critic, in this view, is simply to act in ways that speed the process of decay; no constructive alternatives are either needed or conceivable.

I find such formulations unacceptable on either moral or scientific grounds. In my judgment the depletion process is definable and is not a mystery, and I know of no automatic way, apart from the creative intervention of men, whereby the depletion process can be turned into constructive rebuilding of our country. Finally, I see in all the defeatist reasoning, whether of the right or of the left, an admonition and promotion of powerlessness—which is anathema to me. That is why I regard these analyses of depletion in American society as being finally useful only insofar as they are helpful guideposts to policies of reconstruction.

10

Beyond Automation: New Markets, New Jobs for Americans

A spectre of automation haunts many Americans. The classic forms of mechanization of work have been supplemented by automatic control of work operations—like the thermostat in the refrigerator that turns the compressor on and off in order to keep the interior temperature within desired levels. Several industries and services offer spectacular examples of the transformation effected by the introduction of older and newer forms of mechanization.

Car and truck production increased from 4.8 million units in 1947 to 9.1 million in 1963. At the same time, the number of production workers of the auto industry declined from 626,000 to 572,000.

The tonnage of steel produced was similar in 1950 and in 1960; but by 1960 production-worker employment in steel averaged 461,800 compared with 540,000 in 1950—a drop of almost 80,000.

There are fewer elevator operators employed today and routine clerical work of sorts can be carried out much more swiftly by accounting machines and computers than by office workers.

185

All told, according to the knowledgeable estimates of Mr. Ewan Clague and Mr. Leon Greenburg of the United States Bureau of Labor Statistics, America will witness during the 1960's the permanent loss of at least 200,000 nonagriculture jobs per year owing to mechanization and automation.

Many Americans are persuaded that automation is a job-devouring Frankenstein, a monster wrought by man in the effort to lower the cost of production by using more and more machines and fewer and fewer manual operations. Many Americans blame automation for the fact that new job opportunities are drastically reduced and hundreds of thousands of people face the prospect of finding their skills made obsolete and their opportunity to retrain for new work narrowly limited.

The countries of the European Common Market also have undergone a rapid process of automation and mechanization of work. The rate of productivity growth in these countries has been at least the equal of that in the United States. Indeed, from 1951 to 1960, the average growth in output of goods and services in these countries of Western Europe was 5.5% per year, contrasted to the rate of 2.7% in the United States. At the same time, the countries of the Common Market area in Western Europe have enjoyed full employment for a long period, except for southern Italy, which had a profoundly lower base to build on but which, nevertheless, has been undergoing rapid economic development.

Why is there a high rate of mechanization of work, together with full employment, in these countries of Western Europe, and automation with sustained unemployment in the United States? There is this crucial difference between these two areas: In the countries of the Common Market, expenditures for military and allied purposes has been about 4 to 5% of Gross National Product compared with 8 to 10% that the United States has spent. More critically: Of the available technological talent in Western Europe a much higher proportion than in the United States is devoted to research and development and production of civilian goods. The result is plain for all to see.

Automation, in combination with a depleting defense-intensive industry and a defense-oriented use of technology, is responsible for only a modest rate of over-all economic growth and for sustained unemployment. Automation, in combination with a civilian-oriented use of technical and other production resources, produces a high rate of general economic growth and high employment levels. The factor controlling the impact of automation in the United States is not the automation itself, but rather the orientation of the economy in which automation is introduced.

In discussing Cold War science and technology I pointed out the connection between availability of technical competence and the ability of industries to grow. Once many American industries become unattractive as investments, compared with counterpart industries abroad, then U.S. capital is moved abroad for investing.

During 1964, U.S. capital to the amount of $6 billion was invested abroad. At an estimated cost of $8,000 per average job-year in the United States, this means that the equivalent of 750,000 job years were exported. Let us assume that there was conceivable alternative U.S. investment for only half of this money, even under altered U.S. conditions. That is still 325,000 job-years, and exceeds the estimated 200,000 annual job losses owing to mechanization within our country.

Mechanization of work is an irreversible and, in many ways, an irresistible process. The desire of management to replace manual work by machine work has its roots in two factors: First, the availability of technological alternatives; second and critically, as the wages of workers rise more rapidly than the prices of machinery, there is a gradual pressure that favors the use of machinery. This is the underlying dynamics of the mechanization process that is operative in all industries where cost minimization plays an important part in calculating the success of management.

The national discussion about automation and its prospects, carried on by spokesmen for labor, management, and government, has proceeded on the assumption that there are virtually no boundaries to the sphere of work that could be automated and mechanized. Actually, a very large and vital sector of useful work is by its very nature excluded from automation—the human care of human beings. This work includes the care of all people, even the able-bodied adults, but especially the young, the old, and the infirm. Human care work includes education of every sort, medical services, and very much of desirable leisure-time activity. All of these services have this common feature: Interchange between human beings is the essence of the work. It is of great importance to note that the human care of human beings has become one of the major areas of depletion in American life.

In the next pages I give the size of some of the major markets and new areas of job opportunities that could open for Americans when we decide to put the brakes on spending that depletes our country and our lives, and to encourage, instead, productive investments of every sort. These productive investments can be undertaken by individuals, by firms, by corporations, by towns and counties, by state and Federal governments. For example, the initiative for new jobs and markets in water supply is generally accepted as the responsibility of government—local, state, and Federal. In the case of housing, on the other hand, American practice has emphasized private investment. However, it is now appreciated that for millions of Americans, there will be no opportunity for living in decent housing until the community, using the instrument of government, helps to make this possible.

New Markets, New Jobs

Housing: An informed estimate by Federal housing experts counts 9,225,000 substandard housing units in the United States as of 1963-64. It is hoped that the private sector will renew or replace 2,225,000 of the present substandard units over the next 5 years. This leaves 7 million housing units, each "unit" a family dwelling, to be replaced by the initiative of the community. Of these 7 million units, 4 million could be upgraded at an average cost of $3,000 per unit. The $12 billion required for this purpose, spent over 5 years, would lead to an expenditure of $2.4 billion per year. The remaining 3 million housing units would have to be replaced completely. Assuming that this could be done at an average cost of $10,000 per unit, the total expenditure of $30 billion would amount to $6 billion per year over 5 years. By this reckoning the total outlay needed to improve or replace present substandard housing would be $8.4 billion per year. On the assumption that this much money would have to be used to buy all sorts of production services to get the work done, $8.4 billion per year would generate the annual employment of 950,000 men at an average rate of cost of $8,000 per man year.

Health Care: From 1950 to 1963, physicians in practice in the United States dropped from 109 doctors per 100,000 population in 1950 to 97 per 100,000 in 1963. The availability of physicians per 100,000 of the population varied considerably. In the state of California, one of the states best served with physicians in practice, there were 128 physicians per 100,000 population in 1963. The nation's requirement for new physicians in practice can be plausibly based on the following: Estimated growth in the population up to 1975, the desirability of bringing the national average at least up to the California level; producing enough trained medical men to staff medical schools and research laboratories; and finally, it would be highly desirable for many reasons if the United States were to produce a modest surplus of medical men who would be available to extend medical education and medical services to the one half of the human race that has very little of them.

To achieve these goals, the United States will have to build up medical education to a level of 200 physicians for every 100,000 of its population. This rate of medical training would allow for the usual number changing their career plans, an adequate number for research and teaching purposes, and a number sufficient to raise the U.S. level to the 1963 California standard. It would also provide a certain number to work abroad. Currently our medical schools graduate about 7,700 physicians each year. The new requirement, taking into account the expected growth in population, is about 22,000 physicians graduating each year. Preparation must be made for graduating about 15,000 additional physicians per year.

The cost of training a medical student is about $3,000 per year. Direct costs for training an additional student body of 60,000 medical students (to get 15,000 added graduates per year) would require an annual outlay of $180 million. The increased number of students would require the construction of about 150 new medical schools at an estimated average capital investment of $15 million per school, or a total outlay of $2,250,000,000. Because new buildings and new equipment can be produced far more rapidly than the teaching and related staffs required to staff them, it should be assumed that a program to increase the number of medical schools needs at least 10 years of effort. On this assumption, the capital outlay would be about $225 million per year for new construction of medical schools. Again, reckoning the man-years involved for this work at $8,000 per man-year, the new medical construction program would involve 280,000 man-years of work each year for the duration of the program.

Education: Public schools, secondary schools, and colleges of the United States currently educate 44 million students. The operation of these institutions in 1964 cost the people of the United States $26.8 billion, i.e., 4.3% of the value of all goods and services produced in the United States during 1964. For all that, this is a modest sum, amounting, for the elementary and high schools, to an annual expense of about $455 per student.

In order to do an acceptable job of training our young, and to make educational opportunities available to as many adults as desire them, our educational systems are badly in need of major beefing up.

During the last decade, the true cost of cheap education has begun to come to our attention in vivid fashion. We know that there is human damage caused by segregated or inadequate facilities, by understaffing and other skimping and deprivations. There is no assurance that it is possible to make up for such experience once endured for a sustained period. Nevertheless, we owe it to our children to make an effort, with a program of remedial education, to make up for some of the deprivation. Allowing for the extent of segregated and grossly inadequate educational facilities, I estimate that a remedial education program will require an annual outlay of $2 to $4 billion over a five-year period. This includes all teaching staffs and materials required.

Improving the educational system as a whole is essential if we are to provide education of a reasonably good quality for all the youth of our nation. A first step in this direction should be an increase in the salary of teachers by 50%. In 1964, the average annual salary of classroom teachers in primary and secondary public schools was $5,963. Whatever else may be said about it, this is not a salary level that will attract hundreds of thousands of high-caliber men and women to careers in teaching. By way of contrast: Early in January, 1965, the Atomic Energy Commission announced a program of one-year internship for college graduates. The salary offered to men with a master's degree in engineering or science was $7,950 to start and as much as $8,935 by the end of the first year. It is perfectly clear that we have no trouble attracting able people to activities that have financial priority. We now have to give such priority to our educational system. An increase of 50% in instructional salaries will cost, over a 5-year period, $17.85 billion.

The construction of new classrooms urgently needed to replace outmoded equipment and to be ready for a growing school population will require $20.36 billion over 5 years. At the same time, it is prudent to provide for improvement in the art and science of teaching, including the training of teachers and research in educational methods. I estimate that this would cost, over a 5-year period, $3.49 billion.

Finally, colleges and universities urgently need funds to build up teaching staffs and expand laboratories, allied teaching facilities, and dormitory space. The universities must be relieved of pressures to look for scraps from the Defense Department table to meet their needs. Over a 5-year period the universities will require $14 billion.

These 5-year programs of improvement of the educational system will require $55.8 billion, an annual outlay averaging $11.16 billion.

A third category of new education effort is required in job training and retraining. Here the purpose must be to provide for the nation's working population the skills necessary for their continued employment, and thereby the continued productive growth and prosperity of the nation. To begin, it is important to provide a high-school diploma for 2,500,000 among the unemployed. This will cost us in facilities, teachers' salaries, and the like, $1.25 billion over 5 years. In parallel, we should provide job training for 4 million of the unemployed, many of them unemployable because of a deficit in their work capabilities. The job-training aspect of education improvement would cost us $5.25 billion over 5 years.

Altogether, the 5-year programs for bringing our education system up to a reasonable standard will cost between $14.2 and $16.2 billion per year. Assuming an annual outlay of $14 billion per year, at an average man-year cost of $8,000, the new educational effort will generate directly 1,750,000 jobs.

The total education program outlined above is by no means a complete tally of our requirement. In 1963, 83,200 teachers in the elementary and secondary schools of the United States had substandard credentials, and 1.5 million students in the elementary and secondary schools were taught in grossly overcrowded conditions. In October, 1964, for example, the Board of Education of the City of New York devised a 5-year "crash program" to provide quality education for all the children in America's largest city. The Board estimated the total cost of the program at $8.1 billion over a 5-year period. Of this amount it proposed that $4.7 billion come from the city budget, $1.9 billion from the state, and $1.5 billion from the Federal Government. The program called for the construction of 300 new schools to eliminate overcrowding, short-time class sessions, and obsolete facilities, and for the expansion for school programs in accordance with modern standards.

The programs for improvement in education outlined here are not based upon "gold-plated" conditions. Rather, the idea has been to reach a reasonable standard of educational competence that will wipe out the block of massive functional illiteracy in our country and give our children the opportunity, which they can only get through education, to find their personal fulfillment to the limits of their capability in a productive society.

A fourth and final category of education is nursery schools. Educators and psychologists have come to place great value on nursery schools, which care for children 3 to 6 years old. Of the

12.3 million children aged 3 to 6 in America today, 2.1 million are now accommodated in public school (mainly 5-year-olds). This leaves a 1963 nursery-school population potential of 10.2 million. Nursery schools are good for the children and good for their parents.

For the 3-year-olds, a pupil-teacher ratio of 7 to 1 is desired. For the 4-year-olds, 10 to 1, and for the 5-year-olds, there may be 18 pupils to each teacher. For each class group of the 3- and 4-year-olds an assistant is needed for the teacher. The assistant should be an adult who has a good feeling for taking care of small children. That is the main formal requirement for this job.

The establishment of nursery schools in the United States would require 600,900 teachers at an estimated salary of $7,000 per year, and 498,000 teacher's assistants at $5,000 per year, a full-salary load cost of $6.7 billion per year. In order to accommodate this work, 568,000 classrooms would have to be constructed and equipped at a total capital outlay of $14.2 billion. Buses would have to be provided to bring these young children to and from their schools. This would require an outlay of about $1 billion. If this construction were carried out over a 5-year period, the average annual construction cost during the first 5-year period would be $3.04 billion.

The jobs that would be generated by the nursery-school market would include 1,098,900 teaching and teaching assistant jobs and 380,000 additional man-years for each year of the 5-year buildup period, assuming an average annual man-year cost of $8,000.

Clean Water: Drinking water of acceptable purity is absolutely essential for the maintenance of life, and we are running short of water in the United States. In December, 1964, Dr. Hollis S. Ingraham, Commissioner of Health for New York State, warned that the water shortage being experienced during the winter of 1964-65 will become a normal condition by 1985 owing to the growth of population and the increased demand for water by industry. The total available water supply is being severely diminished in New York State because of years of unrestrained pollution of lakes, streams, and rivers. Cities, large and small, and many industrial plants have proceeded on the assumption that their increment of waste to the total water supply was sufficiently small to make little difference. Over the years, the growth of population, and the size and diversity of industrial activity, have resulted in an emission of waste that now blights a substantial part of the natural waterways of the State of New York. On the basis of a close analysis of the sources of pollution and the requirements for municipal and industrial sewage-control plants, Governor Rockefeller has proposed a $1.7 billion program of capital outlay extending over 5 years to halt the pollution of waterways from 2,100 identified sources. These sources include 1,167 communities throwing poorly treated and even raw sewage into the state's waterways.

The condition in New York State is not unique; the same sorts of causal factors are at work throughout the nation. Therefore, the New York State plan can be used as a basis for an estimate of the national requirement. The population of New York State is 9.4% of the nation. Accordingly, we may estimate that the national requirement to insure a fresh-water supply by the minimal act of curtailing pollution of natural sources will require an investment in the order of magnitude of $17 billion. Again, using our previous mode of reckoning of $8,000 as the worth of an average man-year of activity required in this program, a national effort to control waterways pollution would generate 425,000 man-years of work each year over a 5-year period.

Once the massive pollution of the nation's sweet-water sources has been stopped, it will be necessary to undertake a nationwide effort to expand the availability of sweet water for human and industrial uses. Mr. Terence McCarthy, consulting economist in New York City, estimates that annual capital outlays of not less than $4 to $5 billion per year will be required thereafter. For further development and expansion of our potable water supplies, these investments do not begin to take into account the possible large-scale use of nuclear reactors for desalting ocean water on a large scale.

Railroads: The technological and economic decline of American railroads since the Second World War is one of the grim chapters in a national depletion process. Under the impact of heavily subsidized competition from trucks, airplanes, buses, and private cars that use government-built roadways, airports, and traffic control, the railroad network of the country, long pre-eminent as a means of transportation, has been decaying.

By 1963, there were 214,500 miles of railroad routes, and the railroads represented asset values of $25.7 billion, after allowance for depreciation. From a low point in annual capital expenditures of $646 million in 1961, the railroads began to refurbish their equipment and roadways. By 1963, annual outlays had risen to the level of $1 billion. This is far short of what is required to bring American railroads up to economic and technically feasible transportation standards.

It is reasonable to assume that not less than 50% of the principal equipment and roadways of American railways require replacement or major renewal. A 5-year capital investment program with this goal would require an average expenditure of $2.58 billion per year. Since American railroads are investing at a rate of $1 billion per year, the increment required to accelerate this renewal process is an added $1.58 billion per year. With 214,500 miles of railroad routes, this total capital outlay amounts to $12,-000 per mile per year. This compares to the current outlay for maintenance per mile of about $5,500. All this new capital outlay would mean that in 5 years there would be an average expenditure of $60,000 per route-mile. This becomes the obvious best buy in transportation right-of-way, compared with the cost of superhighway construction, which runs at $1 million per mile and more. The proposed increment to present capital outlays in railroads would generate a requirement for 197,000 man-years of work, annually.

It is altogether possible that this desired increase in the rate of capital investment in American railroads could be generated entirely from the private market, especially if the railroads were given some form of tax incentive to accelerate this process during the desired period.

(It may occur to some readers that it doesn't seem reasonable to assume the possibility of replacing heavy equipment bought

many years ago with currently produced equipment on the basis
of depreciated value of the original purchase. Prices have risen
so much during the last decade that there is a real gap between
the original and the replacement price. While that is so, it also
remains that the use of modern production techniques for manufacturing railroad equipment yields many economies. Furthermore, depreciation funds, if accumulated and compounded over a
long period, have grown in magnitude as much as or more than
price increases of the last decades.)

A new chapter in rail transport remains to be written. In 1964
San Francisco was the scene of a ground-breaking ceremony for
a billion-dollar rapid-transit system in the Bay area. The planned
75-mile rapid-transit network will be the first new rail rapid-
transit system constructed in the United States in half a century.
A superhighway system with the same capacity would have cost
at least five times as much to build and would have required four
times as much land.

Furthermore, a simple human factor argues powerfully for extended use of railroad systems. The National Safety Council
announced in January, 1965, that during the previous year 48,-
000 persons were killed in traffic accidents on American highways. In addition, more than 2 million persons were injured in
auto accidents and the cost of damages has been estimated at
about $8 billion during 1964. A modernized rail system for short
and intermediate distance will prove to be attractive to many
people as an alternative to crowded roads.

Natural Resources: Stewart L. Udall, Secretary of the Interior,
informed us in 1964 that a prudent Federal effort for natural resources development and conservation should amount to $4 bil-
lion per year, over a period of ten years. This would be twice the
current rate of expenditure for conservation and development of
natural resources. The additional $2 billion for development of
resources would generate a quarter of a million new jobs. The
new money would be expended in parks and recreational areas
that have been used increasingly, in fish and wild-life conservation, and in restoration of the great public grasslands domain
(130 million acres). These lands have become badly eroded and

an erosion-control program would produce a massive return in increased output of forage. In addition, public forest lands are in need of extensive work, says the Secretary, if they are to produce their fair share of timber needed during the coming decade. Several million acres require reforestation. Finally, soil- and water-shed-conversion projects would show quick results on millions of acres of eroded or strip-mined land. Contour terracing, strip-planting, and gulley control would restore these areas for the protection of watersheds and would improve the quality of their water yield.

These eminently plausible investments for conserving the very soil of our country take on critical importance in view of the role we are destined to play as the breadbasket of the world.

An analysis by the Department of Agriculture underscores the point that, before the Second World War, American grain exports of 5 million tons were 22% of the total movement of grain among major regions of the world. By 1960-61, North American exports of grain were 39 million tons, 86% of the world's total interregional grain shipments. By 1980, these could amount to 58 million tons of grain on the basis of world requirements and North American production capability.

New Water and Hydro-power: A highly imaginative scheme has been devised for a North American Water and Power Alliance. Using streams in Alaska, Canada and the continental United States as a source of supply, a vast interlocked network of canals, dams, and lakes would use for power, drinking water, and irrigation water that now goes to sea. The Ralph M. Parsons engineering firm, which authored this plan, estimates that vast quantities of water could thereby be supplied to water-short areas of the United States and Mexico.

Using established engineering methods, the network would require a capital investment of about $100 billion over 20 years of construction, and would pay for itself with estimated sustaining revenues from sale of water and power of some $4 billion per year, as against annual operating costs of about $500 million per year.

The work would require treaties between the United States,

Canada, and Mexico, planning time of 10 years and large quantities of steel, cement, earth-moving equipment, pumps, generators,
and the like. Various by-product effects of this enterprise would
include increases in land values, because of productivization, by
some $48 billion.

Annual construction spending of $5 billion means (at $8,000
per job year) 625,000 job-years.

Renewal of Depleted Industries: How much fresh capital investment would be required to reconstitute the depleted industries
of the American economy? A reliable reckoning of this sort is
preferably based upon detailed studies, industry by industry.
These do not exist. In their place I will attempt a rough estimate,
starting with the shipbuilding industry as a base.

An American version of one of the most mechanized yards in
the world would cost an estimated $70 million. Assuming com-
petitive costs and pricing, and a merchant shipbuilding market
for the United States alone of about ten times recent levels, rising
efficiency in the use of ships, and ten years' amortization of vessels, a capital investment of about $5 billion would be required
for shipbuilding alone.

For the whole set of depleted industries the necessary capital
investment for renewal could not be less than five or ten times
that amount, or $25-50 billion. (This would include, for example,
the construction industry which, with its largely archaic methods
in dwelling construction, accounts for about 5% of America's
Gross National Product.)

Annual investment for industrial renewal of $5-10 billion over
a 5-year period would generate 625,000 to 1,250,000 job-years
of work requirement.

Recreation: Let us examine one part of the lighter side of life
before concluding this sample agenda of new markets and new
job opportunities for Americans. Many of us enjoy swimming
pools in and around our communities. In 1960, there were 132
cities of 100,000 population or more with a total of 50 million
residents. What would it cost to construct large swimming pools

and allied facilities for public use on the basis of one pool for every 10,000 city dwellers?

New York City, with a population of 7.7 million, now has 17 public pools or one per 450,000 residents. San Francisco has one for each 350,000 and the District of Columbia has one public swimming pool for every 250,000 people.

A large community-size pool with related buildings and equipment can be built for $100,000. This does not include the cost of land, which varies considerably around the country. For a total price of $500,000,000 we could build one pool, fully equipped, for each 10,000 city dwellers in cities of 100,000 people or more. Again, suppose we spread this capital investment over a period of 5 years. With an outlay of $100 million per year this would involve an assortment of equipment purchases and construction work. Calculating the man-years that would be purchased with this outlay on the basis of $8,000 per man-year, the public-swimming-pool program would generate 12,500 man-years of work each year—and obviously would add to the enjoyment of our people's lives.

What is outlined in this chapter is only a very partial agenda of things that need to be done in our country in order to bring economic competence and the level of living up to a reasonable standard. Furthermore, every one of these activities involves capital outlays and continuing efforts that generate a market for equipment and services of every kind—and jobs for millions of Americans. All together, the new jobs directly accounted for by opening up the new markets that we have discussed total 7,200,000. Since each one of these involves productive work, there are indirect results that ramify widely. I suggest that these estimates be understood as giving us the order of magnitude of what is plausible in terms of new markets and new job opportunities for Americans—within the framework of available institutions and accepted methods.

The meaning of 7.2 million new jobs from this group of activities alone becomes clearer as we take into account all the things that I have not even begun to detail. Hospitals and nursing homes are now short of meeting present requirements by as much as a million beds. Most of the country has deplorable ambulance services. In New York City it is not uncommon to have to wait 20 minutes and longer for an ambulance to arrive at the scene of a street accident. Fire engines get to a fire a lot faster. It is entirely plausible to establish networks of emergency ambulances stationed on the streets to reach medical emergencies as quickly as one can now dispatch a police car by radio.

Urban renewal that extends to major rebuilding of our cities has been estimated as requiring capital investments of $10-15 billion per year. Of this sum, my housing-renewal estimate accounted for $8 billion. Assuming the need to invest an additional $4 billion for the wider functions of urban renewal, this means a further requirement for 500,000 job years.

In my lengthly agenda on education no mention was made of the retraining of military industrial technicians, workers, and managers that will be required on a large scale in order to equip them for civilian vocation. Air-pollution control is just as important as water-pollution control and we have only begun to try to take this set of problems in hand. Transportation to our airports is now a national inconvenience, with many of the journeys from airport to city center taking more time than the air journey from city to city. Professor John E. Ullmann of Hofstra University has suggested that Pennsylvania Station is the natural airport terminal for New York City since rail lines from that point could reach LaGuardia Airport, Newark Airport, and Kennedy International Airport. The modest development of rail transportation to make this possible has not, to my knowledge, ever been planned. We spend 10% of our Gross National Product on automobile transportation, but very little effort seems to be invested in designing and manufacturing a safer automobile or a safer airplane. One would think that these projects are worth major investment, in view of the human lives now taken by accidents.

Scientific work which improves our knowledge of nature could be substantially expanded in the interest of eradicating disease, lengthening and improving human life.

None of these estimates includes the capital investments that must be made for economic development of depleted and under-developed regions of the U.S., and for city building.

Two other calculations of potential investments and jobs for Americans during the next decade have been prepared. In *The Economic and Social Consequences of Disarmament* prepared by the U.S. Arms Control and Disarmament Agency, there is an impressive agenda of ways to use the resources freed from military work.

Professor Emile Benoit has compiled a further set of estimates, by amending the U.S. ACDA study, which total $65.0 to 67.4 billion annual outlays equivalent to over 8 million job-years.

If we add to my previous estimates the Benoit figure for new health-care facilities ($7.8 billion), urban water, sewage, and waste disposal ($4.5 billion), then the estimated job effects move up from 7.2 million to 9.2 million.

This gives us a measure of the extent of depletion caused in American society by the failure to invest capital and talent in our civilian economy. At the same time, these estimates tell us that there is no problem of job openings for the 6.7 millions now in the armed forces and in military industry.

All of these estimates refer to direct employment effects only. No effort is made to estimate the possible multiplier effect of a major turn to civilian, productive investment and operation, and away from military work and products. The military goods and services enter into no further production, once created. The alternative civilian investment and work is self-multiplying. All the new civilian investments are productive and their sustained use creates fresh value and work requirements.

High-school graduates are more productive and earn greater income than the men without this investment in their capability. Civilian investments of every sort add to the useful life span of our people. Civilian investments are used over and over again, thereby "turning over" the capital many times. The whole society reaps increased social return from productive capital that is kept in motion: There is more (real) income and spending; the tax base is enlarged; and tax returns grow.

Consider the effect of one factor, adding to the working life of men. If we add two years to the working life of 40 million males, then, at average earner income of $7,300, that means added value of products produced in the amount of $292 billion. This illustrates the massive return to the whole society from investment in health care and education.

Once the depletion process is reversed by a turn to productive investment, it is altogether likely that a major shortage of manpower will speedily develop, especially in the skilled occupations.

Against these perspectives it is interesting to examine the judgment that areas of neglect in American society could be repaired from the additional wealth created by general economic growth. From 1963 to 1964 the Gross National Product increased by about $40 billion. Let us assume that 25% of this, $10 billion, becomes available, through taxes, for allocation by government. Compare this total of $10 billion with the requirement in the sphere of education alone. The need is for new annual investment in education of about $16 billion.

How do the new investments get organized? Who is to be responsible for these classes of capital investment? And how can we see to it that the depleted industries of the United States are made competent once again?

11

Reconstruction Without Bureaucracy

The Senator, a veteran Republican, was late for our appointment. He was delayed by a television taping that was hurriedly arranged after the Secretary of Defense had announced, that same morning, that a large number of military bases in the United States were to be closed during the next two years. The Senator, full of indignation had denounced the proposed closings within his state as unjustified on military or economic grounds.

"What do you plan to do?", I asked the Senator. He replied, "I am thinking of proposing legislation that will require the Federal Government to take responsibility for the communities whose bases they close." I pointed out to him that there were about 500 military bases in the United States, that the Defense Department employed 1,000,000 civilians, and that his proposal would give a group of administrators in Washington offices power of decision over the lives of millions of people in hundreds of communities.

A few days later a Democratic member of the Senate was commenting to me on the difficulties that military industrial firms were having in the face of a reduction of defense orders from Washington. "We should do something for these firms," said the Senator. "After all, these people responded quickly enough when the Federal Government needed them and now it is only fair that the Federal Government find a way to help these firms carry on now that their facilities are not needed so extensively by the Defense Department. Why don't we set up an industrial consulting service in the Commerce Department? In that way the Federal Government could fulfill an obligation to help these firms adjust to working in the civilian field."

I responded to the Senator by noting that several thousand firms do work for the Department of Defense, and that the larger of them have many divisions and separate factories doing this work. In 1963 alone the Defense Department placed orders for about $30 billion worth of goods, of which $16 billion are concentrated in the major defense industries: ordnance, aerospace, military electronics, and shipbuilding. A consulting service that would be competent to give responsible analysis and guidance to this industrial network would have to include not fewer than 5,000 to 10,000 professional employees. Any effort to recruit this many specialized men would soon falter because there are only a few thousand men in the United States in the field of industrial engineering and management whose experience would qualify them for such responsibilities. Furthermore, taking responsibility for the operation of such a consulting unit would be an unworkable assignment. It would mean being responsible for an indefinitely large number of detailed decisions and recommendations in thousands of diverse situations.

The two Senators, one Republican and one Democratic, had this in common: Both felt that the way to handle a problem that includes a measure of public responsibility is to set up a Federal administrative organization to do the job. However, restoring our depleted industries and public services and converting the military industry to civilian work cannot be managed by a centralized administration—regardless of the amount of money one may be willing to spend. The crucial fact is that these activities all involve operations so far-flung that no conceivable central administration would be competent to cope with the millions of details.

Even with the most lavish use of modern communications and data-handling equipment there is no technically feasible way to administer the detailed affairs of thousands of enterprises from a single central office. This does not imply, however, that there are no steps the Federal Government can take to aid in the recovery of our depleted society. Quite the contrary. The essential policy issue to be resolved is this: How is it possible to organize efficient application of large resources without a centralized control bearing the twin penalties of bureaucratic waste and infringement of individuals' freedom? This issue is important to our country as a whole, and especially for the 3 million direct employees of defense industries, the million civilians employed by the Defense Department, and the 2.7 million men of the armed forces.

The shipbuilding industry is a good example of an industry beset by a depletion process *and* by the problems of converting from military to civilian work. About 60% of U.S. shipbuilding consists of naval orders. Here are some of the actions that the Federal Government could initiate to encourage the establishment of an economically viable civilian commercial shipbuilding industry: First, this industry lacks the research and development resources necessary to the technology of modern design, construction, and operation. The Federal Government should initiate the organization of Maritime Industry Research Institute, paying for one half its capital investment and one half its first year's operating budget. These amounts can taper off to zero over five years while firms in the industry gradually take up the full cost. Second, shipbuilding firms (and other industries slated for major technological renewal) should be encouraged, by tax incentives, to invest in research and development for new *civilian* products and new production methods. Over a three-year period these costs can be counted at one and one-half times their value when calculating taxable income. Third, the Federal Government, the major purchaser of ships, could announce a policy of systematic preference for purchases in the low-cost shipyards, with priority to those producing ships without production subsidies. Finally, the Federal Government should encourage the formation of new enterprises to undertake the design and construction of merchant vessels and fishery ships of all kinds on a competitive, nonsubsidized basis. This sort of system of "carrot and stick" incentives could be applied to the whole range of depleted industries.

The reason for suggesting government initiative is twofold.

First, the managements of these industries have not taken such steps on their own. Shipbuilders, in common with many other depleted industries managements, cannot return to economic viability unless they discard traditional methods and develop alternative technologies. Only then will they be able to offset the high cost of American wages per hour with a high level of productivity in the use of labor and capital.

Second, once new technical alternatives have been devised, it is necessary to create a corps of technical and managerial professionals trained in evaluating alternative technologies and modes of organization on the basis of cost-minimizing criteria. One of the characteristic features of depleted industries is the absence of such a corps of technically competent men. The rising cost of labor relative to machinery in the shipbuilding and ship-operating industries favors the mechanization of work in both spheres. Yet our marine engineering schools have not been training men in the functional integrated design of merchant ships. Marine engineers and naval architects scarcely nod at the all-important technology of modern materials handling, even though this technology dominates the cost of operation of modern merchant ships. (By contrast, a series of graduate courses at the Massachusetts Institute of Technology gives detailed instruction in the integrated functional design of modern naval vessels. For this technology, however, there are no economic, cost-minimizing criteria.)

As now structured, with heavy subsidies for both construction and operation, the shipbuilding and ship-operating industries contain no well-defined group with a major stake in technological improvement for cost reduction, for improved productivity of labor and capital. If, in this vacuum of industry leadership, the Government representing the whole society wishes to end the system of subsidies, impartial studies of the technical, economic, and organizational alternatives for its operation will be in order. Such studies must define efficient design for a shipbuilding and ship-operating industry which is integrated with allied methods of land transportation. The studies could be performed by people recruited from universities and technical institutes. One worthwhile by-product of centering such investigations in these institutions will be the training of a group of professors and graduate students in the problems of technological renewal of the industry.

I have read reports of discussions in private and public bodies whose conclusion is that the United States cannot have an economically viable shipbuilding industry. The inference is that U.S. ship operators should buy merchant vessels abroad and operate them under the American flag—with government subsidy for operation, of course. In other words, the possibility now exists that the deterioration of technical and managerial competence has proceeded beyond the point where it is feasible to reconstruct these industries within a predictable period of time. Whether or not this possibility is an actuality will be discovered when the redesign of the operation of these industries is undertaken.

This much is clear: From studies performed at Columbia University it appears that, with current ship designs and shipyard methods, cost reductions of about 30% are feasible provided certain improvements are made in the management of operations. If standardization of components and modular construction of ships on a programmed basis were introduced, together with major changes in design and production techniques, the cost of shipbuilding in the United States could be reduced by about 50% or more, thereby making this industry economically competitive world-wide—without the government subsidy.

Studies of the apartment-house construction industry disclose similar results. This industry, like shipbuilding, has virtually no organized research and development activities. By taking into account, however, even the present array of technological alternatives, costs per square foot of apartment housing construction could be reduced by as much as 50%. This slash of costs could make a considerable difference in moving ahead with large-scale city-housing and renewal programs.

Each one of the depleted industries has special characteristics requiring especially formulated redevelopment programs. For the machine-tool industry, for example, the absence of a stable production system has paramount importance. Owing to the sharp and unpredictable fluctuation of market demands, it has become impracticable for management in this industry to plan production operations so as to make use of modern production engineering techniques. The result is that productivity has been relatively low and prices have been high, compared with what is possible using presently available technologies. It is economically feasible to use much costly equipment only when one can make a reliable forecast of future utilization. This is precisely what cannot be done now in this industry.

Effective stabilization of demand in the machine-tool industry could be undertaken by various methods. In Sweden, for example, machinery-using firms are encouraged to put aside part of their profits during years of boom activity, so that these funds can be spent for new machinery during periods when general business activity begins to decline. This practice is encouraged by the Government, which excludes these set-aside funds from normal taxes. Thus the Swedish Government effectively encourages industrial firms to participate jointly in capital-spending planning that, in turn, operates to cushion or reverse decline in business activity. At the same time this pacing of new-machinery purchasing reduces market fluctuation of machinery sales and thereby facilitates more stable production operations in Swedish machine-producing industries.

Another approach to the stabilization of machine-tool production could take the form of a machinery-inventory bank, which could undertake the financing of inventories of machine tools during periods when the market falls below a given level of predicted demand. I first laid out the design of the machinery-inventory-bank idea in 1959. Here is the essence of the plan.

It should be possible to establish financial institutions, such as machinery-inventory banks, to stabilize factory operations by financing inventory holdings during market declines. Members of the bank would be individual firms. The bank would guarantee to finance the total production expense for the output of member firms up to, say, 10% under the bank's market forecast for the industry. The amount of inventory financing for which each firm is eligible would be controlled by its share of sales during the previous three years—a payoff for being successful. Membership in the bank would be voluntary. The capital would be drawn from the members, the private investment market, investments from pensions and other reserve funds of trade unions (which have a major stake in stable employment), and possibly (though not necessarily) the Government.

The directors of the bank would include representatives of management, trade unions, major customer firms, and possibly the Government. Giving customer firms a majority on the board of directors would guarantee against the use of the bank as a self-serving device for the firms or the unions in the industry.

The bank would prepare a long-range forecast of machine-tool requirements and would also define a stable production system. When market demand falls more than 10% below the line of average development, the bank would be prepared to finance the holding of inventory. This would enable the firms to operate a stable production system, thus utilizing the advantages of quantity production technology, and the productivity gains that come, virtually automatically, from such stability. The member firms could produce as much as they want. The bank would merely regulate the quantity it would be prepared to finance for inventory purposes.

Under this bank system, the member firms could operate highly efficient production plants at maximum potential. Low costs and relatively low prices would result. At the same time there would be nothing to stop nonmember firms from discovering ways of improving on this performance if they could.

The member firms would be assured the ability to operate a stable, hence low-cost, production system—with financial cushioning. In return for this privilege they should be required to comply with a program of price reduction over a period of years, to utilize standard components and modular principles of construction, and to spend some minimum percentage of sales on industrial research and allied activities. Other requirements might be added to these.

Items financed for inventory by the bank should not necessarily be completed machines, but rather standardized components and modular units. This means the bank could encourage rapid change in design and scrapping of obsolete units. Even more encouragement could be provided by including an obsolescence scrapping allowance within the financing system of the bank. The bank would encourage price reductions on machine tools during recessions.

During economic upswings, the bank would encourage the disposal of the goods held in inventory by levying a gradually rising interest charge on the value of the inventory. At the same time the machine-tool firms would have a major stake in selling these machines since only then could they recoup their administrative costs—which were not covered by the inventory financing—and gain a profit on sales.

Such proposals need to be discussed publicly. A full-scale inquiry should be made by a competent body, like the Joint Economic Committee of the Congress. The American public must be taught that strategic American manufacturing industries are, technologically speaking, an underdeveloped area. This may come as a shock to many Americans who are accustomed to thinking of the United States as the country *par excellence* of mass-production techniques.

The machine-tool industry is an excellent example of a depleted industry whose major firms make a very acceptable financial showing. However, to reverse the trend toward an aging stock of metal-working machines, and a productivity too low to offset American wage levels, the machine-tool industry will have to operate at a much higher level of internal productivity—a feasible task with presently available production technologies.

The goal of technological renewal of various depleted industries may require a fresh appraisal of certain cherished laws and administrative practices. For example, many industrial managers are genuinely fearful of initiating industry-wide negotiations on problems of limiting variety (standardizing) of their industry's products. They fear possible prosecution under the antitrust laws. Yet standardization is important to industrial systems; its practice should not be hamstrung unnecessarily by arbitrary legal issues. Industrial management needs clear guide-lines for pursuing standardization which is essential for cost and price reduction in many industries.

Public discussion can contribute to a constructive solution of the problem of America's depleted industries. Every major aspect of the issues—management, engineering, research and development, the provision of capital for investment, and necessary job retraining—deserve public consideration. The discussion can proceed with this major premise: For every sort of work there are technological alternatives for improving productivity and lowering cost. Moreover, the array of available alternatives is flexible enough to permit American firms to offset the relatively high level of American wages and thereby be competitive in the United States, and in the world marketplace. This conclusion is strongly supported by many independent studies carried out during the last fifteen years by graduate students in the Department of Industrial and Management Engineering at Columbia University as an adjunct to one of my graduate courses in industrial economics. The students have diagnosed the cost and productivity alternatives in hundreds of work operations. Separately, the National Industrial Conference Board discovered a few years ago that among American firms that produced the same products in the United States and abroad, product cost was lower in their U.S. factories than in their foreign plants, in direct proportion to the size of the investment per worker in the American plant. Briefly, the greater the degree of mechanization of work in the United States, the more these plants were economically competitive with those producing similar products abroad.

Throughout the discussion of industrial renewal and of industrial conversion from military to civilian work there is the recurring policy issue of how to preserve personal and political freedom in the presence of large public and private organizations. I believe that we can have confidence in the feasibility of extracting the benefits of large-scale organizations, while safeguarding personal liberties, if the following three conditions are satisfied: First, there must be multiple sources of decision-making in any industry, and in society generally; second, the right of independent organization must be preserved; third, decision-making should be located close to the point of performance of work.

The preservation of multiple sources of decision-making means the avoidance of monopoly. For example, as production workers or engineers or teachers organize to have a voice in the conditions of their work, the managers or administrators no longer have a monopoly of decision-power with respect to the work being done. This is assured by guarding the right of independent organization. This means that any person can initiate fresh organization and compete for decision-power where that is at issue. No group, governmental or private, can gain final monopoly in the organization of people in any sphere of work. Finally, I underscore the importance of attempting to locate decision-making close enough to the performance of work, ideally—so that those who participate in decision-making can literally *see* the outcome. This also makes possible direct checks on the performance of administrators of organizations of every sort.

The existence of these three conditions is the reason why the 5,000 defense installations and activities of all sorts within the United States cannot be converted to civilian uses under the direction of a central bureaucracy. The task is not only technically unfeasible; any attempt to administer such an operation on a centralized basis would be politically disastrous. The Department of Defense engages in about 6 million procurement transactions each year, involving tens of thousands of contractors. Any attempt to control, from a central point, a conversion process to civilian work among these contractors would generate an incredibly costly, unworkable, and politically dangerous centralized bureaucracy. The requirements of economy in public affairs, efficiency in administration, and concern for the preservation of individual liberty all dictate against centralized control, even of conversion.

The case of the New York Naval Shipyard is a classic example of what should not happen when a military base is closed. From 1962 to 1964 there were repeated official reports concerning the intention of the Department of Defense to close this naval shipbuilding base. The reports were disregarded except as signals for political lobbying. There is no evidence that during the period 1962 to 1964 any formal planning whatever was carried out for alternative use of the naval shipyard facilities and its payroll of

10,000 men. The failure in planning involved the Department of Defense, the Maritime Administration, the Government of the City of New York, and the trade unions representing the men employed at the base. Among the latter there was not only a failure to plan, there was also explicit denial of the desirability of such planning, even on a contingency basis. By the end of 1964, when the closing of the base was finally announced, the only inquiry into alternative use of these facilities and the work-force had been carried out by two of my graduate students. Their study was an exercise for our seminar on problems of conversion to civilian economy. Edited by Mr. Glen Scheiber, in the 1964 Manpower Studies, it was published by Senator Clark's committee. The same sort of planning failure has been enacted over and over again when military bases have been closed. Americans have yet to become accustomed to the idea that a massive and growing military establishment is not an ordained part of the universe.

The most important single measure that communities throughout the country could undertake is the formation of an agenda of community needs and resources, with special attention to alternative uses of military bases and military industries.

The character and the size of new markets and new job opportunities that should be open for Americans during the next decade was sketched in an earlier chapter. Such global estimates are useful because they inspire confidence to proceed with the detailed preparation that has to be done to make these opportunities real. Every community, however, has the final responsibility for preparing a detailed agenda of what it needs in the way of fresh capital investment in both the public and in the private sectors of its economy. These detailed plans and budgets, community by community, will form the basis for the bricks and mortar work and for investment in industrial and other spheres. Each community must ask the critical questions: What schools are required? What is needed to insure a reliable water supply? What is required to insure a clear air supply? How many hospital beds will be needed during the next two decades? What park and other recreational facilities must be provided for the population? What plans do the industrial and other firms of the area have for expansion

during the next period? What assets of manpower or other resources does the community have that could attract particular
classes of work? What public transportation and allied facilities
need to be developed in order to make the area attractive for many
sorts of industrial investment and for investments in new dwellings?

When the community has answers to these and similar questions, it can proceed to use all the public and private means at its
command to fulfill its plans. Thereby, the limits of local capability
will be defined, as will be the need for participation by state and
Federal governments. The preparation of detailed plans of this
sort, community by community, is the best way to insure constructive utilization of facilities now used by the military, and to
encourage the renewal of industries that need a helping hand in
order to flourish once again.

Perhaps the most important prerequisite for conversion planning is the understanding of a simple fact: Defense is not,
inevitably, a growth industry. Real limits exist to meaningful
additions to defense hardware and to defense research. The contrasts between the overkill era and the pre-nuclear condition
outlined in Chapter 2 are important understandings for military
industrial management, because they afford a confident basis for
the decision that vigorous planning for conversion to civilian
work is a plausible and essential activity. Competing for contracts in a declining market is no high road to success.

The problem of "lead-time" is present in every sort of capital
investment situation, public and private. Lead-time is the time
span between a decision to do some work and the actual beginning of it; it is the time needed for planning and budgeting. The
budget of community needs just described will surely require not
less than one to two years to complete. In sizable industrial factories the lead-time requirement for nuts-and-bolts planning of
the detailed conversion from military to civilian work calls for
a two-year span if the product is already reasonably defined. If
new-product research must be conducted, the planning period
will be longer.

Failure to use available lead-time constructively is an invitation to industrial and personal disaster. The Republic Aviation Corporation located on Long Island is a case in point. Republic had about two years' notice concerning the termination of its contract to produce fighter-aircraft for the Air Force. The management, however, did not use this time for an aggressive program of conversion planning. The result was that within a few weeks of contract termination, a firm with a work force of 18,000 men was reduced to a skeleton staff of under 3,000. Before 1965 the assets of the firm were taken over by another firm and the original top management of the Republic Aviation Corporation disappeared from the scene.

In industrial firms engaged primarily in military work the crucial capability for conversion is the establishment of strong departments for new-product research and market planning, and the preparation of detailed plans for review and renewal of the organization's structure and practices. There is no question that the task of internal managerial evaluation and renewal is one of the most difficult in the operation of an industrial enterprise. It is far easier to speak about this topic in abstraction than to do the job itself. What is involved is the detailed evaluation of occupations and people.

The conversion process requires that the nature and the distribution of professional work within the firm be evaluated continuously with an eye toward eliminating some functions, strengthening others, and introducing capabilities that may be absent in the military-oriented enterprise. Doing all of this often means changing the jobs of men. It means teaching them new occupational performance, a difficult and costly operation. After all, such conversion means telling a man that his work, however useful until now, is no longer necessary or must be modified. Even under the best conditions of individual and enterprise confidence, this generates a lot of malaise; anxiety about one's occupational future is not a happy thing to live with. But detailed evaluation and planning is the essential way of shortening the change-over period from military to civilian work and insuring reliable performance.

Some managers of defense industries have held that market

factors alone are quite sufficient to handle whatever conversion
may be required. If the conversion problem were confined to
financial resources alone, then this view might have merit. If, for
instance, the products of a given capital investment are no longer
required, the straightforward thing to do is to shut down the
facility and sell it at the best available market price. However,
this limited view of the matter does not take into account three
other forms of assets: a management, a research and production
organization, and the cumulative experience of these groups. To
make alternative use of these assets, detailed conversion planning
is required. Indeed, everything we know about the characteristics
of military-industrial management underscores the importance
of making the planning effort into an important, well-financed
operation in the firm.

Some of the principal military-industrial firms have been able
to produce a variety of minor products. These have included
aluminum sport boats, stainless steel caskets, heavy-duty land
vehicles, adhesives, wall panels, welding equipment, gas turbine
engines and cargo-handling systems. Even if we add to the list
the substantial market in jet transport, it hardly begins to suggest
the products and market area that would be required to engage
3 million men. The paucity of ideas for diversification of products
is a reflection of another characteristic of military-industrial
firms: They have generated a corps of managers with limited capability in entrepreneurship as classically understood. John
Gilmore of the Denver Research Institute described what one
airspace firm had to do to become competent to manufacture and
sell an industrial instrument to the civilian market:

> An aerospace instrumentation firm, considered by *the* cus-
> tomer to be very well managed, decided to enter the commer-
> cial market. . . . What sort of problems did they run into? They
> had trouble with cost control; they found that they were fa-
> miliar with basic technology involved, but not with the con-
> temporary applications; they had pricing trouble; and they had
> marketing trouble.
>
> To solve these problems, they hired some non-aerospace en-

gineers. They got a man from Bell Labs who was quite acquainted with commercial cost controls. They got another man from a firm which was a user of the sort of device they proposed to build. They hired a marketing man with industrial experience and gave him a great deal of authority. They finally got their $13.00 transistors replaced with some that cost $.90 and they finally got the new instrument on the market.

They now feel that they may have a whole new product line. They are successfully communicating with the commercial sector of the economy and selling into it.

Not long ago I presented a paper on civilian markets and conversion opportunities for aerospace and military electronics firms to an elite group of senior planning officers for major military contracting firms. I outlined the condition of our depleted civilian industries and diagnosed them as market opportunities because of the major capital investments they require; the condition of many activities in the public sector of the community that will require major capital investment was similarly described. The extensive discussion that followed my presentation included an altogether unexpected outburst, which seemed to represent the thinking of most of the men present. "All of this is very well," they said. "Much of what you are saying is plausible and reasonable, but what are we to do about our senior officers? What can we do to get our company presidents and vice presidents to take the conversion problem seriously?"

The senior management and technical officers of military-industrial firms have spent their careers becoming specialists in military industries. For many men that is their entire competence; they do not know how to operate in the civilian sphere. As they survey civilian markets they see no prospects of billion-dollar sales under anything that remotely resembles the insured conditions of doing business with the Department of Defense. These are the chiefs of firms without enterprise of Chapter 5. These men are unsure of the occupational position and, to allay their doubts, they have devoted themselves to seeking ways to extend the military markets. In the main, this means working out elegant technical improvements. That gambit has been fairly successful until rather recently.

Now, because of growing recognition of the overkill condition, these men have turned their talents to the generation of markets where the biggest customer is still the Government—space, supersonic aircraft, and other systems marginally relevant to a society depleted in essentials. Creating new markets in these spheres would continue the advantages to them (and the disadvantages to society) of the military markets. The proposed markets have these characteristics in common: selling to the Government; huge contracts for expensive goods and services; products that are justified in terms of national prestige; selling to Government agencies that are accustomed to the style of operation of the aerospace companies and the necessarily high costs accompanying their version of a "systems approach."

Insofar as such efforts have the effect of maintaining employment levels in the aerospace and related industries, while engaged in work essentially parasitic from an economic standpoint, the continued prosperity of these firms will be a drain on the society as a whole. Moreover, the sustained concentration of technical employment in these spheres will continue to block the application of technological talent to the depleted sections of American life.

For many military contractors, conversion to civilian work should be facilitated by the mainly civilian nature of the firm. Thus, the General Electric Company which does about one fourth of its business in the defense field, has a priceless store of managerial and technical talent, long trained in civilian operations, which it can deploy for effecting a conversion process. (It is instructive to examine the appendix list of 100 largest industrial defense contractors for the number of largely civilian firms in this roster.) Even in these firms, however, conversion capability will require deliberate handling, for the defense work is usually separated off in "defense divisions" or departments which share many of the defense industry characteristics that we have described.

It is useful to see the conversion problem through the eyes of a knowledgeable trade-union official. Mr. Ben Segal is director of education of the International Union of Electrical Workers (AFL-CIO). In 1964 he wrote the following:

> General Electric, Sperry Rand, General Motors, R.C.A., Westinghouse and International Telephone and Telegraph are among the large defense contractors we deal with. The result is that a good percentage of our members have been directly affected by the defense changes and cutbacks. The electrical manufacturing and electronics industry as a whole has shown a singular disinterest in conversion, and it has not been willing to co-operate with the union in any discussions dealing with conversion. Too many firms have been satisfied to make huge profits, engage in widespread subcontracting in order to pyramid their profits, and then proceed to lay off in ruthless fashion their employees who have rendered faithful service to the company. . . .
>
> To understand our concern, it is necessary to remember that we have been hard hit by the impact of automation and technological change. For example, by mid-January, 1964, there were 116,000 unemployed whose last job was in our industry. This represented a sharp jump of 32,000 over the 84,000 figure for December, 1963.
>
> What we are saying is that while we recognize the need for disarmament and recognize the need for reducing our defense expenditures, at the same time we are obligated to protect the jobs of our members. '
>
> Let me cite some specific current examples from our industry: International Telephone and Telegraph in the Nutley-Clifton [N.J.] area, is almost exclusively geared to defense operations. Our production and maintenance local in December, 1963, had 1,950 in the unit, today it is down to 1,600. . . . Still another of our locals that consists of technical engineers and production and maintenance workers, also in the same area, had 1,500 employees in December, 1963, and today it is down to 1,200 or less. In addition, it is estimated that in these same plants there have been large layoffs and downgrading of supervisory and management personnel.

The whole future of this local union in the Nutley-Clifton area seems to depend on getting additional defense contracts. I.T.T. has now bid, for example, on a contract to build some military radio equipment. If I.T.T. doesn't get this contract, it is estimated that 700 more workers will lose their jobs. So the officers of the local union have been to Washington innumerable times to lobby for this contract for I.T.T. I can't resist adding the ironic note that I.T.T. reported the highest profits in its history for the year 1963.

To cite still another case, at American Bosch Arma, reliance on a single contract—the inertial guidance system for a projected Titan III—resulted in disaster when the Pentagon did an about-face, decided not to proceed with a guidance system, and awarded a contract for revisions of the old one to another company. In January, 1963, there were 2,000 I.U.E. members —engineers, scientists, technicians production and maintenance and clerical employees. Today, 1,500, some with more than 30 years' service, are jobless.

When you add to this a large number of layoffs resulting from defense cutbacks and changes at the R.C.A. plant in Camden, N.J. and the Sperry Rand, Reeves Instrument and Ford Instrument plants in Long Island, then you can see the serious nature of the problem we face just in these two states.

Mr. Segal and his colleagues have been profoundly discouraged by the unwillingness of management in various industries to plan for conversion to civilian work. Accordingly, their main orientation in seeking jobs for their members is to the Federal Government. Mr. Segal's thinking is revealed by the following proposal for Federal action, which is in addition to his request for establishment of a National Economic Conversion Commission.

1. Establishment of Civilian Conversion Corporations where private corporations balk at planning for conversion from defense production to new products to meet civilian needs.

2. Release of government-held inventions that would serve civilian needs to Civilian Conversion Corporations.

3. Establishment of a Civilian Research and Development Commission that would employ engineers at the local level to carry out research into new community needs and production possibilities.

4. Creation of a Commission on Conversion Compensation and Training to provide for decent maintenance of the families of laid-off workers during a conversion-training period.

5. Establishment of Readjustment Fund for workers displaced by defense cutbacks. This fund could be set up by adding 1 percent to each government contract. It could then be used to supplement unemployment compensation to bring the worker up to the point where he would receive two-thirds of his regular pay for a two-year period. Proceeds from the fund could also be used to increase earlier retirements (*e.g.*, at the age of 55) and to set up retraining programs. About $35 billion is now spent on government contracts annually; a 1 percent collection would provide about $350,000,000 a year.

The most significant feature of these proposals is that they rely primarily on the Federal Government for enterprise initiative that is job-creating. Mr. Segal and his associates are reacting to the military-industry managers whose only response to the end of government contracts is to discharge employees.

State governments have a special stake in the conversion issue on two counts: First, military-industrial work is highly concentrated. California, New York, Texas, New Jersey, and Massachusetts—five states in all—account for more than half of defense industrial work. Second, state governments bear the primary burden of responsibility for financing and administering unemployment insurance and similar programs.

In January, 1965, the state government of California made an important token move toward utilizing the powers and the problems of the state government as an instrument for facilitating conversion from military to civilian economy. The state government signed contracts with four major military-industrial firms to prepare preliminary studies on waste management, data collection, care of the mentally and criminally ill, and transportation systems. These problems are far removed from the conventional expertise of California's major military contractors. But parts of the management of these firms are convinced that it is prudent to develop civilian capabilities. The state government, for its part, is persuaded that these problem areas will require major outlays of state funds during the next decade and that the large capital investment should be made in the light of a systematic analysis of technological alternatives.

By this means, with a modest outlay of half a million dollars, the state government will at once secure valuable information and, not less important, set in motion the development of civilian technological competence among their military-industrial firms. Edmund G. ("Pat") Brown, the knowledgeable Governor of California, has made concrete proposals designed to improve the competence of state governments in coping with local, interstate, and Federal issues in which the state government has a vital stake. Governor Brown suggests:

> First, we need a Council of Governors, operating much as the President's Council of Economic Advisors. The Council would provide a sort of domestic hot line over which Governors could send and receive suggestions and criticisms on a wide range of subjects—before, rather than after, federal executive policy had been established.
>
> Second, we need federal legislation creating formal regional structures within which states may take joint action on air and water pollution, park development, and other projects which are less than national but more than local in range. . . .
>
> One problem we can all hope will become *more* intense with time is conversion to a peacetime economy. The Council would be an ideal source of information for the federal government on public works that could take up the slack immediately after a defense shutdown, and on civilian industry that could move to an area to start building a new economic base. I believe the Council I propose would regularly put people's needs ahead of states' rights.

Governor Brown's proposal suggests that the classic either-or of central planning versus none at all is a trap. Instead, what is needed is planning between individual enterprises, groups of cities, groups of counties, groups of states: these are the relevant categories for coping with many issues whose solution requires crossing traditional political and enterprise boundaries. Thus, the transportation and air-pollution problems of major cities in the United States can be dealt with only on a regional basis, in combination with standards that should apply to the entire country. Control of automobile-exhaust fumes can best be handled by standardized requirements for the entire country, while the detailed measurement and day-to-day response to air pollution frequently require organization across county, city, and state lines.

One of the greatest regional planning achievements in the world is the Tennessee Valley Authority. Here is a combination of public capital investment in natural resources (including power generation, flood control, and watershed conservation), local organization for power distribution, growth of agricultural productivity and industrial investment—together with rising levels of living for the people of the area. The $2 billion capital investment of the TVA repays itself many times over in economic terms, and there is no measure of the improved quality of life represented by elimination of malaria and the end of danger to life from periodic flooding. (When I visited the TVA region in 1948, I found that there were many more foreign than American visitors. The well-publicized hostility of the private electric utility companies to public investment of this sort had made TVA "controversial," so that our public schools weren't even giving the children information about a great American achievement.)

The TVA experience gives us a model which could be applied for regional economic development. The development of Appalachia, for example, cannot be dealt with by a series of legislatively specified increments like new road construction. Such a region needs many-sided development of both natural and human resources. The TVA example of capital investment by government, in combination with local organization and initiative in education,

farm and industrial employment, is a way of organizing a population for productive work that gets desirable economic results
while avoiding the political penalties of centralized bureaucracies.

Harry Caudill of Kentucky, author of *Night Comes to the
Cumberland,* stated before the Congressional Public Works Committees, June, 1964:

> In June and again in September, 1963, representatives of the
> Eastern Kentucky Redevelopment Administration sent resolu-
> tions to the President's Appalachian Commission calling for a
> Federal agency patterned after TVA to develop the electric
> power potential of the area and to undertake its general social
> and economic rehabilitation.
>
> The Edison Electric Institute has estimated that the colossal
> sum of $175 billion will have to be invested in new electric-
> power generating facilities in the next 20 years. Steps must be
> taken to insure that the huge coal resources of Appalachia are
> utilized in meeting this goal. Dams at strategic locations in the
> Kentucky highlands could provide storage for cooling water to
> be used by huge mine-mouth generating plants. Extra-high-
> voltage transmission lines and the expanding grid system would
> make it possible to send low-cost power into New England, a
> region of high power costs. The [proposal] of Consolidated
> Edison of New York to go some 1,100 miles to Labrador for
> hydropower points up the possibilities of using Appalachian
> coal for electric power in the Northeast.
>
> The hydro- and thermal-power potential of eastern Ken-
> tucky could be developed for a billion dollars. And this could
> be made entirely self-liquidating [within 35 years]. However,
> such a self-financing corporation should be given a stern man-
> date to plow back into the impoverished counties in which it
> would operate a substantial portion of the money from power
> sales. At least 1 mill per kwh should be added to the price and
> invested in schools, roads, airports, flood-control, reforestation
> and reclamation and perhaps the building of entirely new
> towns. Sustained capital investment over a generation would

bring this deprived corner of the American hinterland abreast of the rest of the nation.

After all reasonable types of conversion planning for military-industrial firms and for military bases have been checked out, there will still be a substantial number of people whose work is no longer needed in these places. Occupational conversion and transfers among industries will therefore be a major aspect of conversion from military to civilian work. A study at Columbia University of the airframe industry disclosed that conversion to alternative civilian markets would account for about 58% of the employees in that industry. Similarly, an investigation of the military-electronics industry by Professor John Ullmann of Hofstra University, indicates that about one third of that industry's staffs would not be employable even with the full development of the whole array of major civilian markets. The most important occupational group that would be surplus, proportionately speaking, are the engineers and scientists in military electronics, 75% of whom would not be needed in an all-civilian electronics industry. The reason is that there is hardly any civilian operation that requires as high a proportion of technical talent as does military work.

The industrial concentration of defense work is shown by the following 1960 figures on the proportion of employees in each industry that serve the military:

Ordnance	100%
Aircraft and Missile	93%
Shipbuilding	60%
Communications Equipment	38%

The men long employed in military industry confront a genuine problem of major occupational change. One of the most important opportunities open to them may be in the teaching profession. The teaching of science and mathematics is of great importance in our secondary schools and junior colleges, and they have long been short of staff. Officials of Teachers College at Columbia University tell me that within one year a man with a bachelor's degree in science or engineering should be able to complete the necessary courses and the supervised practice teaching that are needed for secondary-school teacher training. The work would cover both teaching methods and updating in substantive fields of specialization. The master's degree in education earned at the end of a year could qualify a man for a teaching post in most of the education systems of the United States. I have told several groups of engineers in military industries about this professional possibility. In one group of 55, there were 26 who said that they were prepared to examine such professional alternatives very seriously. In other groups of 25 and 30, there were 6 in each case who indicated special interest in opportunities in the teaching profession. These are important proportions of highly trained engineering professionals. A profession that includes job tenure and summer recesses looks very good to veterans of military-industry job-hopping.

What is needed to make this a real opportunity both for these men and for the school systems that need their work? The main requirement is a system of forgivable loans that would enable the trainees to attend a university full time while sustaining their families at a minimally acceptable level. For example, a man may calculate that in order to maintain his family he wishes to borrow $8,000 from the loan fund. He gets this sum in monthly payments and the loan is forgiven at the rate of $1,000 for each year that he thereafter spends as a teacher. The Ford Foundation has operated such a system of loans to encourage preparation for teaching in engineering and the sciences. The same technique can be used more widely for encouraging transfer to the teaching profession.

For many engineers and management men a continuation of professional industrial work will be the desirable course. Coming from military industry, however, these men will require technical updating and retraining. Schools of engineering can contribute special courses that emphasize the economic aspects of engineering design. The military-industry technologists must be rigorously trained in the understanding that, in civilian industry, cost minimization has controlling importance for technological practice. On the management side, schools of business can make a major contribution by developing curricula oriented to military-industry managers who need training in the characteristics of civilian markets and civilian-firm managing. The instruction should encompass the essential requirements of managing with cost minimization, and unlearning the uneconomic management practices that have been desirable for servicing the Department of Defense.

Industrial workers in military industry have special problems of making a change-over to civilian work. Trade union officers have begun to consider these issues. Mr. Irving Bluestone, Assistant to the President of the United Automobile Workers, has formulated some of the key problems confronting industrial workers:

> For many, the need for new skills will act as a "Berlin wall" in keeping them from finding new employment. Retraining will be necessary—not so much to enhance promotional opportunity—but to insure simple eligibility in periods of job recruitment. We must not overlook either the fact that large numbers of workers whose jobs will disappear may not even own the rudiments of education prerequisite to being eligible for retraining.
>
> Even a retrained worker, however, cannot be certain of immediate job opportunity; for, in effecting necessary economic adjustments in the nation, jobs may not be available in his community. Mobility of the labor force cannot be made to mean that the worker and his family bear the full financial responsibility of picking up stakes and moving about until he finds a job elsewhere. He must be given information on the availability of jobs, where they are, what kinds of skills are required, what income may be derived. He must be given information about housing availability and costs in the new location, about schools, hospitals and all the other necessary community services as he contemplates picking up roots and settling anew. And, then, what about his moving costs when once he has found a new job? What about any losses he might

sustain in the sale of one house and the purchase of another in a different community? How about the burden of separate maintenance costs until relocation is completed? Family dislocation and relocation costs are rightfully part of the national burden of economic conversion and should be so recognized and accepted.

During the period of unemployment, retraining and relocation, the workers must still pay rent, buy food and clothing and provide the necessities and comforts of family life. This income must be sustained as well to provide needed purchasing power for the nation. A full review of the unemployment compensation system looking toward the establishment of adequate federal standards will be necessary.

Problems of occupational conversion of every sort will be vastly facilitated as trade unions, professional societies, and trade associations turn their attention to these issues. In each instance a constructive contribution will be made by considering the problem of conversion from military to civilian work and the allied issues of occupational change occasioned by technological renewal of the depleted industries. Once a many-sided, decentralized effort is widely set in motion, the problem of industrial renewal and occupational conversion will become many separate, workable problems.

The alternative is fantastic waste of human talents and industrial assets. On September 12, 1964, *The Saturday Evening Post* reported that on Long Island, owing to large layoffs in military-industrial firms, electronics technicians and engineers were found working as toupe consultants, ice-cream vendors, estate gardeners, firemen, short-order cooks, floor waxers and clean-up crews at the World's Fair. All of this is useful work—but gross underutilization of occupational capability.

Because of the lead that the Federal Government has taken in the concentration of talent and resources for the defense-space complex, it will be essential that the Government lead in signaling the reconstruction process. Analysis of economic fluctuation during the period 1953 to 1962 shows that the rate of growth in government (mainly defense) spending has increased, in parallel with a declining rate of growth in private spending. From early 1953 to early 1957, government spending grew 1% and private spending 6%. For the period of early 1960 to mid 1962, government spending showed 8% rate of growth and private spending fell 4%. The Federal Government has become the employer or the customer for an enormous block of industrial resources and technical talent. It is therefore appropriate that Government should lead in the reconstruction process by establishing a National Economic Conversion Commission whose primary duty is to invite and encourage local action by all levels of government, by firms, industries, and occupational groups of every sort. (See Appendix C list of military-industrial firms.)

There are many ways for organizing constructive relations between Federal, state, and local governments that also minimize bureaucratic problems. For example, the country needs a method for allocating Federal funds for many sorts of productive work. The method should be at once economically sensible and politically uncomplicated. Let us suppose that Federal funds are transferred from military and space budgets to be used for reconstructing depleted education systems. How is the money to be allocated? I suggest that we consider a method whereby the Federal share of funds for a local education system be decided by the income per person in the state during the preceding year. Thus, the cities, counties, or states in the lowest income bracket would get as much as 90% Federal funds while the most affluent communities would get as little as 20%. Thereby, Federal funds would be allocated so as to favor the growth process in the most economically underdeveloped states and communities. The same principle could be used for allocating funds for an array of constructive uses.

It is significant that reconstruction by renewal of depleted industries and by conversion from military to civilian work will not require any additional taxes. Rather, the productive work, newly performed, will multiply the wealth of the people and generate ever-larger tax revenues, which may make tax reductions possible. This could never be expected as a result of military spending, but it is a reasonable expectation from the expansion of productive work with its self-multiplying effects.

In the reconstruction process, money alone will not get results in many spheres. For example, investing money in certain depleted industries or voting funds for establishing medical centers will not, by itself, produce viable industries or competent medical centers. The supply of money will finally come against the constraint of the limited number of trained people available to do the added work. Thus, medical staffs for new institutions might be drawn from some of the men now doing medical research or working for the military, or by importing more doctors from abroad. But the only durable way to augment the supply of physicians and nurses is by increasing the numbers of our people trained in the professions. The same principle applies to the renewal of depleted industries. Making money available for capital investment will not, of itself, do the job. It will be necessary in many spheres to encourage the creation of a corps of technically trained men competent to solve the problems and insure the economic viability of these industries.

The creation of new markets and new jobs through a reconstruction process will make a major transfer of manpower and capital from military to productive uses an imperative for America. If we cherish both efficiency and freedom, this transfer of manpower will best be carried out by the methods of decentralized planning discussed in this chapter. If we fail to make the necessary transfer to productive work, whole sections of American society will be progressively undermined by the depletion process and eventually go beyond the point of repair.

On the other hand, competent performance of a many-sided reconstruction process over the next decade will open up for the people of America opportunities for material and cultural prosperity hitherto unknown. The perspective does not exclude difficulties. It does include significant enlargements of our productive capability for coping with the problems of a great productive society.

12

Dismantling the Cold War Institutional Machine

During the years since the end of the Second World War, a network of remarkable idea-men has spread root and flourished in our society. These men produce the theories and methods of military power, and devise ways for using military power for political ends. They and their organizations are now a full-blown institution of our society; we can describe them collectively as the Cold War Institutional Machine.

How many are there? Where are they? To begin, the machine does *not* include the uniformed armed forces or the labor force that is engaged in producing military goods. It does count as operants some 830,000 experienced and well-paid American professionals and their helpers. Idea-men of the Cold War form a significant portion of the civilian staffs of the Department of Defense, the Atomic Energy Commission, and the National Aeronautics and Space Administration. They are the employees of the so-called nonprofit corporations supported mainly by the Department of Defense. They are found on the military-research staffs of industrial firms and in military-related research groups in universities. Finally, the Central Intelligence Agency contributes a major group to this institutional network.

The civilian staffs of the Department of Defense include more than 1 million employees. The Atomic Energy Commission has about 7,000 on its own payroll (apart from the 35,000 on the payroll of AEC contractors), and the space agency employs about 30,000 people. I estimate that about 500,000 of these men are engaged in performing and supporting the functions of the Cold War Institutional Machine.

A smaller number of men, very important politically, are the 12,000 professional and supporting employees in the major non-profit corporations supported primarily by the Department of Defense. These are the various "think factories" set up around the country to develop political, military-strategic, and technical designs for implementing military-based strategies. Here is a list of principal organizations of this sort and the number of employees that each had in 1964:

Research Analysis Corporation	502
Human Resources Research Office	288
Center of Analysis (Franklin Institute)	286
Aerospace Corporation	4,931
Lincoln Laboratory	1,917
RAND Corporation	1,165
Analytical Services Corporation	88
Electromagnetic Compatability Analysis Center	182
Mitre Corporation	2,105
Institute of Defense Analyses	519
Logistics Management Institute	33
Hudson Institute	110
	12,126

The largest of these organizations, the Aerospace Corporation, was established by the Air Force to manage the conception and design of the Air Force missile program. The Lincoln Laboratory has been operated by the Massachusetts Institute of Technology and has specialized in a wide array of technical and strategic problems. The RAND Corporation, one of the oldest and most important of this group, has been the home for developing major nuclear military strategies and a great many studies in theoretical and applied subjects for servicing the design and employment of overkill forces.

The research staffs within industry devoted to military designs include about 200,000 men. These are the designers of mechanisms for implementing the nuclear military and political strategies. Military-related research in the universities includes about 20,000 men. The university groups and a part of the industrial-research group includes the staffs of international affairs departments and institutes of various sorts that are wholly or partially devoted to the solution of military and political problems involved in nuclear strategies.

Lastly, a principal establishment of the Cold War Institutional Machine is the Central Intelligence Agency. This organization, with its sister agencies, is said to have about 200,000 employees. I am guessing that about one half are in the business of information and ideas for cold-war military-political strategies.

These are the men and the organizations responsible for the bomber and missile-gap fictions. These are the groups that invented the military science fiction of counterinsurgency. The various theories for conducting nuclear war are the work of these men. So, too, are the detailed plans for trying to wield U.S. military power as the decisive instrument of political persuasion. These men are the architects of the Bay of the Pigs disaster in Cuba, and of the costly American commitment to Vietnam. It was their idea, under the guidance of one or another of their nuclear strategy theories, to devote hundreds of billions of dollars to nuclear-weapon military systems which, now constructed, are impotent to defend the United States. They developed the line of reasoning of how we can "win" a nuclear war while losing "only" 100 million Americans.

Secretary of Defense McNamara has made it abundantly clear that even our large advantage in numbers of nuclear-tipped missiles is no guarantee that the shores of this country can be defended. The American experience with Cuba, Laos, Korea, and Vietnam supply abundant evidence for the judgment that technical military strategies cannot solve political problems. The political judgments of the Cold War Institutional Machine have been notably defective in each of these three crises areas. Even among friendly governments in Western Europe the American military-political planners have failed: the ill-conceived plan for a multilateral nuclear force has been the latest and most disastrous invention of the Cold War planners. This international nuclear force would allow the proliferation of nuclear weapons, notably to West German control, while aggravating and inciting political differences among the nations of the Western world.

The Cold War planners have been left with one essential scheme: use military force of every intensity as a threat or destruction system to compel compliance with U.S. policy demands. The Cuba experience showed that the USSR was not deterred from attempting a major military gambit. U.S. nuclear power does not prevent new nuclear powers from developing. Neither does massive U.S. military power of every sort prevent Filipino or Vietnamese peasants from challenging U.S. supported governments with crude weapons and guerrilla organization that leads to interminable warring.

The military methods of the Cold War Institutional Machine have evolved into no-win strategies, both in nuclear and "conventional" war.

In the frenzied and costly search for "power," the idea-men of the Cold War Institutional Machine have lost the crucial connection between means and ends. Power has no autonomous existence: there is only power to do something; power applied in particular ways. In response to military stalemates, the ideologists of Cold War power counsel the dropping of restraint: prisoners are tortured, gas is used in military and quasi-military operations, the press is censored. Where does this go? Where does it end? It goes to the dehumanization of our people, to the sort of methods that identify the ruthless, totalitarian state machine. Somewhere in the quest for power wielding, the Cold War planners have forgotten about the idea that all this started in the name of shielding personal and political freedom and the dignity of man.

The failure of the Cold War planners in foreign affairs should be reason enough to dismiss them and their tactics as ineffective, and to seek alternatives. Yet there is another equally justifiable cause for dismissal.

Within the United States itself the Cold War Institutional Ma-

chine has been a major force in the economic and political depletion of American society. Although the money-cost of these institutions and the salaries of the men engaged in them is only a
small part of the military and allied budgets, their real cost to
society is many times greater. These organizations include a high
concentration of educated men. This fact has profound political
importance for our country, for it suggests that an overwhelming
proportion of the professional man-hours that have been available to the Federal Government have been squandered on a dead-
end effort. Worse, this considerable pool of brains and talent so
shamefully misused, has contributed to damaging the quality of
American life—the loss of respect for the rule of law, the creation
of a pall of no future, the political powerlessness generated in a
society once used to a joyous optimism based on real competence.

The considerable literature produced by our Cold War planners supplies no clear plan or a definition for terminating that war.
How is it supposed to end? Rather the pattern has been a vision
of continuing nuclear confrontation with primary reliance on
ever-growing nuclear stockpiles for backstopping periodic political crises that wind up as nuclear confrontations. Cold War planners claim, in fact, that there *are* no major alternatives for American policy apart from reliance on military systems of power.

As a contribution toward the discussion of alternative systems
of security policies for the United States, I have prepared a chart
displaying alternative security policies and budgets for the United
States. This chart is included in the Appendix.

The evidence developed in this book supports the proposition
that continuing the operation of the Cold War institutional network means continuing the depletion of the security of the United
States both internally and abroad. On the other hand, dismantling this network means shutting off the primary source of policies that have proven ineffective for advancing the general welfare of American society. Some positive good will come of the
dismantling, too; that will be discussed later. Dismantling this
generating machine for military and political disasters would
leave unaffected the armed forces themselves and the long-term
Executive branch institutions, like the State Department.

The nature of the Cold War Institutional Machine suggests there is little hope in trying to convert it to other purposes. For the body of ideology and techniques that differentiates the staffs of these institutions is highly specific to a military power-based orientation. That is why the problem is one of dismantling, which means folding up the organization and, at the same time, seeking constructive opportunities for the able men and women engaged in these units. Many of the military technologists will want to try for a job in civilian technology, research, and development. Some considerable number of them will be interested in teaching careers. For part of these people it will be important to provide opportunities to finance retraining. This can be done effectively by means of the forgivable loan system discussed in Chapter 11. The loans would help support a person and his family through as much as two years of advanced training needed to take a position of responsibility in community activities earmarked for major rejuvenation.

It is possible that some of the research and development establishments of the Cold War Institutional Machine could be converted to work on civilian productive problems. The conversion of such units would immediately raise the problem of how to insure their viable operation without continued dependence on a single government agency. Multiple sources for support of research would be far better than reliance on a single source. A research institute in the building construction field, for example (we don't have one in the United States, now) could be supported by a combination of private firms, foundation funds, and industrial trade association grants.

The Federal Government, for its part, will have to learn new ways to support civilian research that will fall in its domain. Here it will be useful to examine experience in Great Britain and other countries in which systems of research grants to individuals and small groups of investigators have been supplemented by "block" grants to departments and institutions. The latter grants are given without restriction on how the money is to be spent. Not only does this method give the institutions considerable flexibility; it also has the desirable effect of restraining the growth of central government bureaucracies because block grants can be administered and audited by staffs of modest size.

The method for dismantling is uncomplicated. Since all these institutions are financed from the public purse, the Congress has only to cut off new appropriations.

The dismantling of the Cold War Institutional Machine will very likely have a major beneficial effect on the operation of two important American bodies: the Congress of the United States and the Department of State.

The political power of the Congress and of the nonmilitary Executive departments has been eroded, partly by the enormous financial demands of the defense establishments and partly by the fallacious idea that security is basically a military issue rather than a political one. A first step toward revitalizing the decision-making capacities of Congress is being made through the recognition that power in international affairs is a blend of economic, political, and military components, and that the current blend of surplus power for destruction with political and economic weakness is poor policy indeed.

During 1964, as a result of conversations with Members of Congress, I became aware of the degree to which the security issue has been perceived by Members of Congress and the Executive branch as being primarily a military-technical problem. This is a misperception. Military technology is one among many instrumental devices for implementation of policies. This is clear from the chart on alternative security policies in the Appendix. Also, Members of Congress have felt that the military aspect has become so complex (and so essentially a technical problem) that the main decisions on the forces required (and therefore the budget size) must be left to military officers, military technologists, and the Secretary of Defense.

Accordingly, one of the root security problems for the United States is the development of confident understanding in the Congress and in the Executive branch that the essential decisions on allocation of resources among the economic, political, and military facets of security policy are political decisions, and that the Congress is competent to make them.

Members of Congress are sometimes inhibited in their ability to reconsider the security issue of American society in a fundamental way. Only a few Members see themselves as political prime movers, as initiators of discussion or action on fundamental policy issues, especially in the field of security policy. This may be due to the enormous prestige that the military has enjoyed, coupled with the fact that there has been little public discussion about alternative political and economic policies for the United States.

A second limitation on the Congress is the system of organization whereby Congressmen specialize in the problems that are within the responsibility of their committees. The committee is, in a sense, comparable to a department in a college that includes the specialists in a particular field. Most Congressmen feel restrained from discussing security issues insofar as these are defined as primarily military-technical issues and are, therefore, the special province of the Armed Services Committees of the House and the Senate.

A third restraint on reconsideration of security policy in the Congress is the quiet but widespread fear that conversion from military to civilian economy could not be carried out without serious economic dislocation. This is not a long-range economic estimate. The judgment reflects the fact that the detailed blueprints for smoothing conversion and minimizing disruption have yet to be developed. In the absence of practical plans for conversion, Members of Congress see the curtailment of specific defense spending as a threat to employment in their districts and states. Many Congressmen, involved in helping to secure contracts for their areas, see their own political prestige as tied to that function. But the prospect of major new productive investments, private and public, will alter local economic and political dependence on military contracts.

There was once a time when the senior staff members of the Department of State were primarily versed in politics, law, diplomacy, and economics. Under the pressure of operation of the Cold War Institutional Machine, State Department specialists have been increasingly oriented to political strategies and plans based primarily on military power. To the degree that this has taken root among the staff of the Department of State there will have to be a reorientation, favoring innovation in the political and economic field. Such innovations are needed to enable the United States to wield constructive economic and political capability as an instrument of international political power. This reorientation will be especially important against the background of growing realization of a nuclear military stalemate.

It is important to recall that the Defense Department has been asked repeatedly to handle crisis situations (Laos, Vietnam, Cuba) that were generated by failures of political and economic policy. Such requests to our Defense Department have been an important part of the justification for a program of ever-more-elaborate military forces. Accordingly, it is not surprising that senior military men view themselves as basically responsible for American security.

But such demands on the Pentagon are unreasonable. For it is not within the competence of the military art to fill every gap generated by poor political and economic policies. Plainly, it is the responsibility of civilian authority, mainly the Congress and the Department of State, to develop appropriate political and economic capability and so relieve the military of this burden. As the foreign relations of the United States are put on a more competent basis, relying increasingly on political and economic methods, Americans will be able to turn greater attention to the neglected business of our society.

13
Useful Work
for All

The single most devastating consequence of the depletion process within American society is the reduction of the amount of useful work available for Americans. Here is why. First: many American industries have been so depleted technologically and economically that employment within them has declined absolutely, or has failed to grow—taking into account both the growth of markets and of internal mechanization. Second: high-technology resources and fresh capital have been concentrated in the military-related industries whose output lacks the multiplying effect characteristic of civilian production and products. Third: no major capital fund has been organized for making productive 35,000,-000 Americans who live in poverty. Fourth: no major capital fund has been organized for economic development of the under-developed regions of the United States. Finally: capital that could be invested in the United States has been sent abroad where more rapidly expanding markets, and a higher general level of productive economic growth, have given promise of superior investment opportunities. The result of all this is that about one fifth of the citizens of the richest nation of the earth live in poverty, a significant portion of its industry is in varying states of depletion, and more than 5% of its able workers cannot find employment.

These results contradict the conventional wisdom of our time, which views the defense industry as a support for the economy. Individuals in defense work are seen to be prospering; so too are the firms or other organizations that employ them. Groups of firms in defense business have prospered, and so have the towns and the regions in which such work is concentrated. Prosperity is measured here by the salaries, wages, and profits received, and by the goods and services purchased with this money.

Unseen in such a calculation is the fact that all of the goods and services requiring the use of these men, as well as the capital used for military work, have been provided at the expense of the rest of the society. The rest of us have also failed to receive from all of those engaged in military work the average output of civilian goods which they, of course, cannot produce since they are other-wise engaged. These forms of payment for the military work represent parasitic growth which depletes many aspects of our life. This is the way we have finally paid for the operation of the defense-space complex.

In the conventional wisdom, however, the military-oriented activity is seen only as support for the economy by the test of money put into circulation. Thereby, if there is sustained or growing unemployment within the United States, it must be owing to some other cause, namely, automation. From this diagnosis it has been inferred that since automation is bound to continue, then so will the level and the growth of unemployment. Accordingly, on both humane and economic grounds, it is only reasonable for a highly efficient society to keep alive those of its citizens who are no longer needed in employment, and whose further failure to perform as active consumers stymies the operation of the distribution mechanism for goods. The suggestion has been made, therefore, that the Federal Government provide every jobless American with a minimum annual income of $3,000. It is further suggested that those American families with less than $3,000 a year income receive cash grants to bring each of them up to that basic level. Based on the 1962 census, this would cost the Federal Government only $11 billion a year.

The argumentation around this proposal is many-sided. The essential reasoning that underlies it, however, is that by this means American society would regularize the handling of a problem that we are stuck with anyhow. From now on, the thinking goes, the big new problem is leisure because the machine is more efficient than man and will become increasingly so.

I find such reasoning defective on scientific grounds: The hypothesis of a depletion process explains much more about sustained unemployment and economic underdevelopment in the United States than does the hypothesis of automation undermining the economic usefulness of man. Furthermore, I regard the proposal for massive programs of doles to able-bodied men and women as a reprehensible abdication of community responsibility, a moral and intellectual failure to make productive use of human capability by providing useful work for all.

Some people believe that the useful work for all idea is utopian while the Congress could readily support a $3,000-a-year minimum-income scheme. There are, in fact, many considerations that would enter a debate—pro and con—on the minimum-income idea. However, the $3,000-a-year-dole idea is part and parcel of depleted society. It rests upon the restraints created by the large parasitic economic growth since 1945, with its resulting limitations on useful work. These limitations would be terminated by conversion from overkill industry and by a competent reconstruction process.

There are alternatives to the depleted society. They involve a halt to the depletion process, a beginning in the task of reconstruction in American society, and the elimination of poverty by implementing the principle of useful work for all who are capable. Here are five guideposts for the planning and implementation of such alternatives:

First: *The pre-eminent requirement is the provision of useful work for all in our society.* Man needs to do productive work not only to exist, but also because productive work with and for other people fulfills man's need to be and to feel useful and wanted. Only the provision of useful work for all who are capable of it, with concomitant income, can erase the degrading effects of long-term withdrawal from, or denial of, such work. By contrast, programs for enlarged, continued charity to the poor who are capable of work is a form of sustained degradation. Provision of new useful work on a large scale requires the co-operation of private and public bodies toward enlarging productive opportunities.

Second: *Constructive private and government planning, in concert, is needed to generate useful work for all.* Private planning is traditionally acceptable as a method. During the last thirty years the American consensus has developed toward acceptance of use of government, too, as a planning instrument. With respect to government there are new issues: Planning for what? Government military planning is widely appreciated. The principle of using government as an instrument for planning useful work for all is partly accepted.

The preamble to the Full Employment Act of 1946 laid down the principle of Federal Government responsibility for affording "useful employment opportunities":

> The Congress declares that it is the continuing policy and responsibility of the Federal government to use all practicable means consistent with its needs and obligations and other essential considerations of national policy, with the assistance and cooperation of industry, agriculture, labor, and State and local governments, to coordinate and utilize all its plans, functions, and resources for the purpose of creating and maintaining, in a manner calculated to foster and promote free competitive enterprise and the general welfare, conditions under which there will be afforded useful employment opportunities, including self-employment, for those able, willing and seeking to work, and to promote maximum employment, production, and purchasing power.

Third: *Private and public bodies, including town, county, city, state, and Federal governments, should be encouraged to formulate concrete plans for investing in new productive activity.* These plans should include detailed estimates of cost effects, employment, income to be generated, and "lead-time" (the time required to set new work in motion). Specifying "lead-time" is crucial, for it enables one to know how long it takes to set new investments in motion once a decision to do so has been taken.

Fourth: *Conversion from military to civilian economy can be*

made a major opportunity to find the people and develop the skills
needed for new productive undertakings. The role of conversion
has been outlined in Chapter 11.

Fifth: *The pace of a war against poverty must be rapid enough*
in demonstrating the reality of new opportunity for useful work
to prevent further mass deterioration of morale and work capa-
bility, especially among American youth. So long as our deprived
fellow Americans feel useless and unwanted we may expect some
portion of them to express their desperation, sometimes in violent
ways that shock the larger community. From the data in Chapter
10 on new markets and new jobs for Americans, it is quite clear
that there is no shortage of useful work to be done in our country. Nevertheless, many Americans may feel grave doubt about
the feasibility of useful work for all as a general condition of
American life.

There is a lingering fear that the increasing pace of mechanization of work will frustrate every effort in this direction. Therefore
I think it is most important to stress the fact that a major part of
the work to be done in the United States is of a sort that can never
be mechanized. It will be worth while to review briefly some of
the observations made earlier.

The human care of human beings describes a class of work
that has been heavily depleted during the last years. Here are
included the major functions of education, medical care, community services of every sort, the care of the young, the convales-
cent, the aged, and the supervision of play and recreation for
children and adults. Human care of human beings also includes
every sort of institution for the correction of undesirable human
behavior.

The crucial fact about the human care of human beings is that
the very nature of work to be done excludes the possibility of
mechanization. This whole class of activity represents, in a sense,
a limit that mechanization cannot penetrate. No computer, however ornate, will ever be able to take a child by the hand and
answer the question, "What is the sky?"

It would make an enormous difference to the lives of millions
of city children if they could have the experience, many times

over, of going to summer camp. Widespread efforts in many communities for establishing this feasibility would automatically generate an enormous demand for teachers and older teen-agers to take responsibility for the conduct of such camps. The parks in our large cities could be made much more inviting by increased planning and supervision of the playgrounds and parks. On a visit to Sweden in 1962 I discovered that pensioners with disabilities had the privilege of calling upon home-making services provided by the Government. A housekeeper, government-paid, would come twice a week to put the house in order and perform all manner of helpful service to help keep the household going. Similar services could be provided for convalescents and the aged in our own country.

"Unemployment: Benefit not Burden" is the title of a highly imaginative paper by Mr. William B. Shore, Information Director of the Regional Plan Association of New York. Mr. Shore calls our attention to an array of jobs that could be filled by men and women now unemployed. Kindly adults could work in large numbers supervising the play of small children in playgrounds. City-owned buses could be substantially speeded along their way by the availability of a fare-collecting conductor. Lots of people are available in New York City—and our other major cities—who would be perfectly competent to keep the streets cleaner.

None of this argument about the importance of useful work for all lessens the obligation to provide a minimum income for every citizen who, in the last analysis, is incapable of useful work that also pays a wage. From this standpoint it will be necessary to examine the levels of Social Security payments. For a retired couple, recent monthly Social Security payments have averaged just under $130 per month. This adds up to $1,560 per year, well under the $3,000 a year poverty margin.

These analyses invite examination of the War on Poverty program as undertaken by the Federal Government since 1964. The first stage of the War on Poverty was to be operated through the Economic Opportunity Act with a proposed budget of $945 million. For 35,000,000 Americans in poverty, this averages $27 per person. This sum compares favorably with spending for such purposes by the Government of India, recently amounting to about $11 per person per year under the Third Indian Development Plan. However, the United States rate of spending for our underdeveloped population compares unfavorably with the activity of the Government of Ghana, which, in its second development plan, marshaled $38 per person per year for economic development. Also, in the United States, investment in manufacturing firms averages more than $16,000 per employee.

It is altogether reasonable to expect that there will be no major diminution of poverty in the United States until there is appropriate reduction in the size of the defense-space complex, together with the transfer of money and manpower from these areas of parasitic growth to productive use. So long as defense and space budgets are maintained at the level of one half and more of the Federal budget, an automatic veto will be cast on the effectiveness of antipoverty efforts. This veto effect resulting from parasitic economic growth has not been understood by politicians or economists.

In Charleston, West Virginia, on September 19, 1960, the Democratic Presidential candidate John F. Kennedy declared: "Economists tell us that an unemployment rate of 6 percent is the danger signal. When a community passes that point it is officially regarded as an area of 'substantial labor surplus.' If it remains there it is entitled to special Government help through defense procurement and other programs."

In a similar vein, economist Leon H. Keyserling in a report on "Progress or Poverty" has suggested that Federal taxation be increased by $195 per person per year from 1965 to 1975. Keyserling suggests that by 1975 "national defense, space technology, and all international" items could take up $421 per person or about two thirds of $677 per-capita taxes to the Federal budget. Furthermore, of that suggested $195 increase in taxes per person, Keyserling's proposal is that $120 per person be added to the defense and related budget by 1975. Keyserling writes, carefully, that such a recommendation is not based on the findings of his study, but that ". . . if these increases should prove necessary, there would still be plenty of room for serving the great priorities of our domestic needs."

The essential point that needs to be reckoned with by statesmen and economists is that defense activity, defense procurement, does not "bolster the economy." If defense and allied spending were raised $120 per capita by 1975, this would result in defense and allied budgets of $96 billion per year. Under these conditions there would most certainly not be "plenty of room" for coping with the urgent domestic needs of our people. Such increases would only aggravate the present condition of depletion.

Some American economists diagnose America's essential economic weakness as one of distribution of income: Too small a proportion of income is in the hands of America's poorly paid workers. Therefore, more equitably distributed income would have the automatic effect of increasing demand for the product of many industries, which, in turn, would employ all workers, thus solving the problem of underemployment. Such analyses have this attractive quality: Obviously, if poor people had more money, they would probably spend it very quickly for more goods and services and that would certainly put a lot of money into circulation and would generate additional jobs. But would the job-creation from this source solve the problem of underemployment in America?

What is the main cause of underactivity in the principal fields that have had low level of employment during the last two decades?

In the sphere of public expenditures, education, medical care institutions, water supply and natural resources have all been areas of underexpenditure and therefore underemployment for thirty years and more. However, a low level of performance in these fields is not caused by low consumer demand for these goods and services, but rather by a failure to invest. The governmental bodies that are competent in each of these fields have refused to allocate the money and the manpower that would be necessary to do a better job. Nondefense spending by the Government, as I showed in Chapter 6, has been declining. The feeling has been that tax rates are high enough, and that military and related spending deserves priority.

In the case of the capital goods industries that have either failed to grow or have declined, here again the problem is primarily one of investment decisions, mainly by the managements of capital-goods industries. In this case the failure has been a failure to invest in research and development and in fresh capital outlays in the machinery producing industries themselves. Collateral defects in industrial organization have not been repaired. In response to high machinery prices caused by these deficiencies, customers have not found it economic to invest heavily in replacement equipment on a sustained basis. The result has been a low level of activity in many of the machinery-producing industries. The determining element has been in the area of investment decisions within the capital goods and allied industries themselves. The problem has not been one of final consumer spending as a generator of activity in capital goods.

Finally, there are the durable consumer goods industries that have become incompetent to supply potential markets. The building-construction industry is a case in point. Because of technological and organizational incapacities this industry has been unable to reach a very large potential low-rental paying market. Moreover, a remedy for this condition is not feasible in the absence of major reorganization of the industry, and as long as technical talent is not available in considerable quantity to do the research, development, and applications work that is needed to make the housing-construction industry a competent supplier of potential markets. The result of these restrictions is a limitation on employment.

In sum, the crucial decisions in major industrial sectors have been investment decisions, public and private: These would not be altered significantly by increases in final consumer demands for consumer soft and hard goods. Present plant capacity in these industries is capable of significant increments to output with modest increases in employment. Also, in many classes of goods more purchasing power would generate increased demand for goods manufactured abroad.

A depleted society is hard put to initiate the crucial changes in investment decisions, public and private, that are essential for raising the level of activity in the main spheres of underemployment. That is because of the high proportionate use of tax money for military and related purposes, the high proportion of technical talent that is being used up in the military-space industry. Finally there is the effect of the political consensus which sustains priority to these uses of our money and manpower. This combination of factors restrains the investment decisions essential for raising the activity and thereby the employment levels of depleted sectors of the American economy.

There is no escaping the fact that, apart from intention, efforts to initiate a meaningful war on poverty are contradicted and checkmated by massive military spending. It is like trying to operate an automobile with one foot on the accelerator and one foot on the brake.

These analyses define the requirements and the limits of American capability for carrying out every sort of major constructive effort within our country. These are major constraints on the ability of American society to respond to the growing hopes, aspirations and demands of American Negroes and others who have been long underprivileged. On June 9, 1963, the Board of Trustees of the National Urban League made public a brief statement "urging a crash program of special effort to close the gap between the conditions of Negro and white citizens." The depleted condition of the American Negro cannot, and therefore will not, be corrected so long as the general depletion process described here continues to operate within American society.

The education, the new housing, the medical care, the job retraining, and the investments needed to create new jobs for all of the impoverished in America will become available once we turn our attention to reconstruction of American society and the provision of useful work for all who are willing and able.

14

Our Stake in

World Development

Almost everyone thinks that the condition of life in the developing countries of the world is deplorable and that serious improvement will surely take a very long time and will require the export of masses of equipment and manpower from the industrialized countries in order to help the developing countries get going. There is no question but that capital and knowledge will have to be brought in from the industrialized areas of the world. But that will not be decisive.

The grim fact is that the developing countries have been squandering the entire capital fund sufficient for their economic development. They have been using this money for building their own armed forces.

Based upon the economic data of 1959, computed by Professor Wassily Leontief at Harvard, the industrialized countries of the world were adding to their Gross National Products at an average rate of about 4% each year. The developing countries were growing at about 2.1% each year, while receiving about $4 billion a year in capital for economic development from the industrialized countries of the world. At the same time, however, the developing countries were spending for military purposes $18 billion a year, compared with the total military expenditures by the industrialized countries of $102 billion per year.

Professor Leontief came to this conclusion with respect to the impact of possible capital transfer on growth rates in the developing countries: ". . . the break-even point between the rates of growth of economic expansion for the two groups of countries would not occur until the underdeveloped countries had raised their annual growth rate to about 4.3% at the minimum. . . . If foreign aid from developed countries was to provide the substance of [the necessary] rise in investment, it would require an increase of capital transfers during the first year of at least 500% under the most favorable of conditions." This would mean that capital transfers to the underdeveloped countries would have to reach a level of $20 billion a year or more in order to cause their growth rate at least to equal that of the industrialized countries of the world.

At this point, we confront a decisive fact. The developing nations, in 1959, were spending $18 billion for military purposes. If this sum were transferred to productive investment by these nations, it would cause them to exceed the break-even rate of growth. Spending $22 billion for development would start the process of catching-up with the industrialized nations.

The meaning of this calculation is straightforward: The single most important move the United States could make to facilitate economic development for the impoverished two thirds of humanity would be to encourage the reduction of armed forces and military spending everywhere. This could be done only if the major powers set an example by carrying out, on their own account, a major change in the use of their own resources accompanied by internationally agreed upon and controlled disarmament treaties.

The second primary requirement for economic development in Asia, Africa, and Latin America would be the provision of technological capital, particularly in the form of knowledge carried by trained men from the industrialized areas of the earth. Neither of these two principal requirements for economic development are readily forthcoming from a society in the grip of the sort of depletion process we have been diagnosing. Conversely, both these principal requirements can be met by a society involved on its own account in the transfer of resources from parasitic to productive uses.

Since the Second World War, the rate of economic growth in the industrialized countries has proceeded at a speed that far outstrips the development efforts in Asia, Africa, and Latin America. This can be illustrated for the United States and Latin America in terms of the electricity produced per person each year, which is a sensitive measure of the degree of industrialization achieved in a society.

From 1950 to 1962, the kilowatt-hours used per person per year in all the countries of Latin America grew from 128 to 352, an increase of 224 kilowatt-hours. At the same time, in the United States, the use of electric power increased, per person, from 2,562 kw-h to 5,050 kw-h, an increase of 2,488 kw-h. As a result of this markedly different rate of growth, the 1950 gap between the United States and Latin America was 2,434 kw-h per person, and by 1962 this gap had enlarged to 4,698 kw-h per person per year.

I have compiled a set of data that reveals, in vivid form, the present condition of the countries of Asia, Africa, and Latin America, as compared to the United States, in terms of economic development. The table requires no further explanation; it is a portrait of world poverty.

Economic development for Asia, Africa, and Latin America involves issues of the organization of the economy and of priorities to classes of economic development; it means, too, that these issues must be resolved in ways consistent with desired self-determination for newly independent countries.

In my book, *The Peace Race* (Braziller and Ballantine Books, 1961), I noted that many political leaders in the United States have proclaimed the doctrine that freedom in society is obtainable only under competitive private business. This is the "ideal culture" of the American business class. But the large middle class and accumulations of capital necessary for such a regime are not usually present in underdeveloped countries. Against this, the Soviet ideology for economic development at home and abroad is equally straightforward. The main feature is organization of the entire society as one "firm" of many subsidiaries with its management in the government. No independent organizations, either

MEASURES OF WORLD POVERTY, 1962–1963

Country	KW-H Per Person Per Year	Infant Mortality Rate Per 1,000 Births	Daily Caloric Intake	Literacy (%)	Life Expectancy in Years	People Per Physician
United States	5,050	25.4	3220	96	70	1,000
FAR EAST						
Burma	22	148.6	1990	60	35	15,900
Cambodia	14			55	44	49,600
Indonesia	20	84.1		45	32	48,600
Japan	1,450	28.6	2240	95	68	900
South Korea	79	9.3		85	47	3,000
Laos	4			15	30	45,000
Malaysia	220			50	58	5,100
Philippines	110	73.1	1950	75	55	1,700
Taiwan	410	30.7	2360	90	63	1,600
Thailand	25	53.3		70	50	7,900
Vietnam, South	33			20–40	35	28,800
NEAR EAST & SOUTH ASIA						
Cyprus	431			82	67	1,400
Greece	321	39.8	2930	82	68	800
Iran	50			15		3,900
Iraq	139	27.2		20		5,200
Israel	1,277	31.4	2800	90	70	400
Jordan				30		5,700
Kuwait	1,274			30		1,000
Lebanon	279	13.6		80		1,200
Saudi Arabia				5–15	30–40	12,600
Syrian Arab Rep.	60	53.6	2330	30–35	30–40	5,000
Turkey	127	165.0	2830	35	48	2,000
United Arab Rep.	140			30	53	2,600
Yemen				25	30–40	160,000
Afghanistan	9			5–10		34,400
Ceylon	32	56.8	2060	70	60	4,500
India	47	86.5	1990	24	47	5,200
Nepal				5	25–40	71,700
Pakistan	24	96.6	1970	20	35–40	8,700
AFRICA						
Algeria	100		2230	10		6,670
Angola	31			5		14,400

MEASURES OF WORLD POVERTY, 1962–1963 *(Continued)*

Country	KW-H Per Person Per Year	Infant Mortality Rate Per 1,000 Births	Daily Caloric Intake	Literacy (%)	Life Expectancy in Years	People Per Physician
AFRICA *(Continued)*						
Basutoland				60		17,700
Bechuanaland						12,600
Burundi	5					58,700
Camaroon	235		2470	5–10		37,600
Central African Rep.	8			5–10		39,700
Chad	4			5		70,000
Congo (Brazzaville)	38		2470	20		13,600
Congo (Leopoldville)	357			50		63,400
Dahomey	5			5–10		18,100
Ethiopia	8		2295	5		93,900
Gabon	50			5–10		7,700
Gambia	21					18,700
Ghana	61		2605	25		17,900
Guinea	45		2400	10		28,700
Ivory Coast	36			20		22,700
Kenya	51		2240	20–25		11,300
Liberia	186		2540	5–10		12,550
Libya	93		2180	30		4,500
Malagasy Republic	20			30–35		27,500
Mali	5			5		45,600
Mauritania				1–5		34,000
Mauritius	96		2270	50		4,500
Morocco	94		2480	15		10,700
Mozambique	23			2		20,200
Niger	3			5		65,700
Nigeria	14		2680	20		38,600
Nyasaland	10			5–10		44,200
Rhodesia, Northern	705			20–25		9,800
Rhodesia, Southern	454			20–25		5,100
Rwanda	4					189,300
Senegal	55		2600	10–20		52,500
Sierra Leone	21		2200	10		22,600
Somali Republic	5			5		27,800
Rep. of South Africa	1,512		2630	40–45		2,000
Sudan	11		2295	10		32,000
Swaziland						10,400
Tanganyika	19		1800	5–10		16,800

MEASURES OF WORLD POVERTY, 1962–1963 (Continued)

Country	KW-H Per Person Per Year	Infant Mortality Rate Per 1,000 Births	Daily Caloric Intake	Literacy (%)	Life Expectancy in Years	People Per Physician
AFRICA (Continued)						
Togo	5		2645	5–10		47,800
Tunisia	67		2170	25–35		8,900
Uganda	65			25		13,600
Upper Volta	2			5–10		68,700
Zanzibar	38			5–10		7,100
LATIN AMERICA						
Argentina	543	61.2	2950	86	59	780
Bolivia	119	90.7		31	50	4,000
Brazil	363	170.0	2680	50	53	2,100
Chile	642	116.2	2570	80	52	2,000
Colombia	275	89.6	2200	62	46	2,900
Costa Rica	372	71.9		88	60	2,830
Dominican Republic	147	113.2		64		5,200
Ecuador	97	104.0	2230	60	52	2,900
El Salvador	160	71.5		43	51	6,150
Guatemala	106	84.8		30	37	6,460
Haiti	22			10	33	11,000
Honduras	67	49.9	2200	35		4,800
Mexico	337	70.3	2440	56	60	2,050
Nicaragua	136	65.1		40	50	2,820
Panama	293	54.4		83	62	2,630
Paraguay	64	52.1	2500	68	45	1,820
Peru	275	97.2	2050	50	46	2,300
Uruguay	489	49.1	2960	88		860
Venezuela	715	51.4	2490	51		1,300
OTHER						
British Guiana	211			80	52	3,130
British Honduras	44			89		4,300
Jamaica	373			80		2,500
Surinam	293			80		2,170
Trinidad and Tobago	625			80	61	2,870

SOURCES: *Statistical Abstract of the United States, 1963* (pp. 910–11); *Selected Economic Data for the Less Developed Countries* (Statistics and Reports Division, Agency for International Development, May, 1964).

inside or outside the "firm" are permitted. In this scheme, the absence of personal and political freedoms is considered a fair price for economic efficiency.

While conditions of American life, especially in material wealth, are envied around the world, they often tend to be regarded as unattainable by others, and the Soviet pattern for economic development is viewed as more realistic. This accounts for a major part of the attractiveness of the Soviet system, despite its history of authoritarianism, to so many people in the less industrialized countries.

Can a method that combines economic planning with personal freedom be offered to the industrializing countries in place of the Soviet system? Yes, but the United States has not offered it because of its own internal political conflict.

This conflict lies between what we say we believe and what we actually do in our industrial society. There are the more conservative Americans whose views dominate the press and other public media. They believe that economic efficiency and freedom in society are obtainable only when private business management is dominant, and preferably competitive. These ideas have permeated American thinking and have formed the main basis for America's proposals for economic development abroad. However, the majority of Americans who support the export of these views are, in their own economic lives, in conflict with them.

American industrial society actually includes ways of combining the efficiences of large organizations, government or private, with individual liberty. The crucial requirement for this combination is freedom of association as a part of the general right of independent organization. This includes the right of anyone to form new organizations in any field. It means that no organization or enterprise can prevent the formation of others. And further, it means that organizations can be formed to express the collective will of members, subject to their own decisions. When this right of independent organizations is general—extending from trade associations and trade unions to poetry circles—it results in many sources of power in economic and social life. This right restrains monopoly of decision power in society. Thus, the presence of autonomous trade unions in industry restrains the use of managerial position for dictatorial power. *The widespread application of this right of independent organization in many aspects of life is an essential condition for freedom in modern industrial societies.*

That is what we say we believe. What, in fact, do we believe?

The conventional managerial attitude in the United States views independent organization by workers, and the resulting multilateral decision-making in economic life, as a threat to the decision-power of management.*

Thus the men of power in major American industrial firms are unable to make a political case for the principle of independent organization to the extent that they themselves would prefer to withhold this right from their opposites. These attitudes prevent the proposal of the principle of independent organization as a desirable alternative to the Soviet system, in which every town is a company town and every union is a company union.

The multilateral character of decision-making in American industrial life has had a crucial effect on the rapid pace of growth in industrial productivity. The very success of worker groups, whether in or out of unions, in pressing the employers for higher wages has compelled American employers to conserve increasingly expensive manpower by mechanizing work. The result of the growth of bilateral decision-making in American industry has been the highest level of labor productivity in the world.

So long as what we believe—and not what we say we believe —continues to dominate United States policy, the energetic leaders of industrializing countries will turn to the Soviets as a model for their own policies. Since we refuse to show them how, they resign themselves to the idea that there is no practical way for combining rapid economic development with individual freedom, especially in a poor country. They must conclude that, if this combination could be achieved in their own countries, then the

---

* During a visit to Moscow an American businessman said to me, "Now that things are getting better between Russia and the United States, maybe we can learn something from them." "What is that?" I asked. He replied, "Perhaps they can teach us how to take care of the unions."

United States would surely be telling them how, since the United States does, indeed, contain this combination.

Let us examine the ideas that underlie the conservative business viewpoint toward economic development. If any of the following points are valid, then there *may* be no alternatives, and competition with the Soviets could only take military forms.

A monopoly of managerial control is absolutely necessary for planning and operating large industrial and technological undertakings. Managerial ideology includes a fiction: Management must have the monopoly on decision-making if an enterprise is to be efficient. From this assumption, it follows that an independent union is not only a sort of general nuisance, but also a most annoying challenger to operating efficiency. Several studies have shown that, on the contrary, bilateral decision-making can contribute to rapid growth in industrial productivity. The operation of worker decision-making compels management to improve efficiency in production. The envied productiveness of American industry is not the result of higher levels of technical competence than, say, in Western Europe. Rather, American management has been more sharply pressed to make use of mechanization and automation by the greater decision-power of American workers. Workers often have a decisive say in certain questions of production. The workers' decision-making powers are usually centered in the local union at the plant level. These powers have evolved to the point where workers now have rules, criteria, codes, and organizations quite different from, but parallel to, those of management.

In large industrial organizations planning is important. Planning is a technique of harmonizing the various units, *i.e.,* workers, machines, raw materials, and the like, of a complicated structure. It requires well-defined goals and rules to enable technicians to choose methods of operation. Desired results (such as quality of product, safety of operation, minimization of cost) can be managerially dictated, or can be democratically decided with the participation of large numbers of people. Once the general standards have been set, the follow-through becomes a technical process.

Managerial rule is absolutely necessary to industrialize under-developed countries rapidly. Israel industrialized rapidly with wide use of agricultural and industrial co-operatives. Co-operatives are democratic rather than managerial.

In the less-industrialized countries, unilateral managerial control over an entire society is justified with the claim that material progress can be achieved only by forced deprivation of the population (for example, the taxing of a peasant, who earns only $60 a year, to build a new factory). Under these conditions, unions and other independent organizations are a luxury that cannot be tolerated by management. The claim may be true under certain conditions: when material progress must be produced out of the meager savings of a population, or when additional revenue is needed to support large military organizations. I believe that industrialization and economic development can always be democratically achieved. Creative energy and imagination of large populations can be harnessed for the common good. When the tribal family is abandoned for the town and factory, people need organizations like trade unions to give them a voice in their new lives. Managerial control, as the only method for economic organization in the developing countries, does not meet the test of either theoretical or factual analysis.

Political freedom can flourish only where free, private business exists widely. The free-market idea of small business does not appear to be spreading to the rest of the world. Neither, then, is freedom. Is this true—or do we have our definitions crossed?

In point of fact, the dominating economic organizations (in industry, in trade, and in banking) in the United States are not small enterprises competing in uncontrolled free markets. Large organizations are dominant. Is there anything in their operation that supports and gives strength to personal and political freedom? Mainly, I submit, the absence of monopoly in decision-power. The presence of trade unions is not the only curb on managerial powers: Various governmental and other autonomous bodies which affect the operation of industrial firms are also important. When the managements of large firms are not the sole decision-makers, they are restrained in the political extensions of their managerial control.

At one time, in the United States, political monopoly power was automatically checked by the large numbers of small firms with freedom to buy and sell in the marketplace. There was no bully on the block; everyone was about the same size.

In a society with large industrial firms, markets become increasingly subject to managerial decision, and the main economic relationship changes from buyer and seller to that of employer and employee. Under the employment relationship, the right to organize independent unions, rather than the relation of independent buyers and sellers, became the more significant device for insuring the rights of individuals.

Antitrust laws in the United States were based on the proposition that small firms and their free, competitive behavior in the marketplace were essential for economic efficiency and freedom in society. It was assumed that the competitive bidding of free markets determined what would be manufactured. Such understanding was part of the deep-rooted tradition that surrounded much government antimonopoly regulations. *Today it is multilateral decision-making in production, rather than competition in the marketplace, that restrains monopoly of economic power by big business.*

The idealized image of the United States as a land of free private business does not take into consideration the regulated industries (public utilities, airlines), the subsidized industries (agriculture, shipping), the Government suppliers who have only one customer, and the variety of economic organizations which includes the New York Port Authority, Tennessee Valley Authority, electricity co-operatives, the Atomic Energy Commission, and the Federal Government—the largest employer in the land.

Once former colonial countries obtain independence, the overriding problem that confronts their governments is how best to carry out a speedy and effective process of economic development. We should note that, since 1955, Cuba, Zanzibar, part of Laos, and much of South Vietnam have come under Communist or pro-Communist rule despite the fact that in the East-West power conflict the West has spent almost twice as much as the East on military budgets. The political-economic strategy for industrial development proposed by the United States for Asia, Africa, and Latin America has not been persuasive and, in action, the allied economic and military-aid programs have been less than effective.

Senator Wayne Morse has long been a strong protagonist of world economic development. In fact, precisely this concern has made him a severe critic of the U. S. economic-aid programs. In an extensive evaluation of the Foreign Assistance Act of 1964, Senator Morse had this to say:

. . . sad to say, of the economic section of the program, not more than half is devoted to bona fide economic development. Supporting assistance, the contingency fund, and nonproject loans from the Development Loan Fund are but political props and payoffs to foreign governments. They do not develop; they merely patch over and perpetuate the lack of development.

Even the technical assistance program is being used for transportation and communication projects against the day when they may be of use to American forces, and to train small-time police states in emerging countries.

In the words "economic freedom of choice" without which the security of this country will never be strengthened in this world, are being relegated to whatever is left over in the foreign aid pot. Education, sanitation, vocational training, capital projects, agricultural extension—the activities that our officials trot out to gain support for aid among the unknowing American people—these constitute at most only about 40 per cent of the $3.5 billion being requested.

Cutting the $1 billion-plus military aid expenditure in half and applying the unproductive economic aid to genuine economic development projects would do more to strengthen the

long-run security of the United States than any other changes
that could be made in the foreign aid program. . . ."

One of the noteworthy limitations of both the Western and the
Soviet blueprints for economic development is the inattention to
agricultural development. In the United States, even though this is
the land of the highest agricultural productivity in the world, the
emphasis in economic-development theory has been on industrial
development. On the Soviet side, too, economic-development
theory has emphasized basic industry—steel mills and other heavy
industry; in brief, the industrial base of major military forces,
which requires undefinably large capital investment. For the
Soviet Union the consequences of such economic planning have
been catastrophic: Forty-eight years after the October Revolution the Soviet Union finds itself without a reliable food supply.
Agriculture has been grossly neglected while steel mills, military
industry, and Sputniks got the cream of technical talent and the
priority use of available capital. But the important point for this
discussion is that neither the American nor the Soviet designs for
economic development of underdeveloped areas has promised
fulfillment of the fundamental human need of ending hunger, so
that a life span of thirty-five years need not be man's fate.

At the 1963 meeting of the World Food Congress in Washington, we learned that every day now about 10,000 people die of
malnutrition or starvation; that in India alone about 50 million
children will die of malnutrition during this decade; and that more
than half of the world's inhabitants experience hunger as a regular
condition of their lives.

This world-wide disaster has been generated by a two-sided
failure: First, elementary public health methods have reduced
infant-mortality rates, but population growth has not been regulated; second, at the same time, agricultural productivity has not
been sufficiently advanced to offset existing hunger, let alone
support a larger number of human beings. Around the world the
acres of cultivated land per person have declined, and the crops
available per person have advanced *only where capital investment*

and modern agricultural technique have boosted yields per acre fast enough to offset population growth. This has been done, with the greatest effect, of course, in the most industrialized countries. In September, 1964, the American Chemical Society heard a paper by Dr. Raymond Ewell of the State University of New York. He estimated that during the next decade famine will threaten the lives of hundreds of millions of people in Asia, the Middle East, and South America.

Authoritative researches by the U. S. Department of Agriculture find that:

. . . Per capita grain production in the less developed world is now lower than it was before World War II. . . .

North America is emerging as the breadbasket of the world. Prewar net grain exports were 5 million tons or 22 percent of the world total of net regional exports. In 1960/61, net regional exports were 39 million tons or 86 percent of the world total. Present trends indicate net exports of 58 million tons in 1980 and 94 million tons by 2000. . . .

Densely populated, low-income countries face the possibility of being trapped permanently at low-income levels. Historically, population was in equilibrium, but with the widespread improvements in health, sanitation and disease eradication occurring in recent decades, population began to grow in a rapid, uninterrupted fashion. The cultivated area has traditionally expanded apace with population but the supply of readily reclaimable land is now nearly exhausted. This diminution of the easily reclaimable land supply while still at the subsistence level, has created a low-income trap. With the amount of land which can be brought into cultivation restricted by the increasing costs of making new land productive and the limited capital available, yields must be raised to meet the needs of population growth. Raising yields requires capital. If incomes are still at the subsistence level, the needed capital is not forthcoming and countries become dependent on external sources of food, capital or both. . . .

Two-thirds of the world's people live in countries with nutritionally inadequate national average diets. The diet-deficit areas include all of Asia except Japan and Israel, all but the southern tip of Africa, the northern part of South America, and almost all of Central America and the Caribbean.

The diet of people in these areas averaged 900 calories per day below the level of the one-third of the world living in countries with adequate national average diets in 1959/61, and 300 calories below the average nutritional standard for the diet-deficit areas. The daily consumption of protein was less than two-thirds of the level in the diet-adequate countries; the fat-consumption rate was less than one-third. . . .

The diet-deficit countries are poor and food deficiencies merely reflect the low level of living in general. Per capita income in the base period was only $97 compared to $1,074 in the diet-adequate countries. Although economic development is taking place, it is to a large extent offset by increases in population. These countries are already densely populated—53 persons per 100 acres of agricultural land compared to 17 persons per 100 acres in the diet-adequate countries. And the population is increasing at a rapid rate of 2.1 percent annually, compared to 1.3 percent in the adequate areas. . . .

The basic problem of the diet-deficit countries is one of productivity. The people cannot produce enough food to feed themselves or produce enough other products to afford to buy the food they require. Food production has barely been able to keep ahead of population growth, much less provide for the expanded demand resulting from some improvement in per capita income, most of which goes for food. . . .

Under present conditions, the major capability for expanding agricultural production is concentrated in the industrialized countries where populations are already well supplied with food. But capability for expansion of agricultural output is at a woefully low level precisely in those areas of the earth that are already centers of malnutrition and are also bearing the burden of rapid population growth.

At the conclusion of his excellent study on "Man, Land and Food," Lester R. Brown of the U. S. Department of Agriculture wrote:

Agricultural production potential is now concentrated in North America. Production potential is determined largely by the availability of land and capital, the level of agricultural technology and the nature of institutions. Institutions must be such as to closely link effort and reward. To the extent that they fail to do this production potential is reduced. All the less developed regions lack capital, an advanced agricultural technology, and the requisite institutions. . . .

This summary statement defines the essential conditions that must be satisfied if agricultural productivity is to be advanced rapidly in Asia, Africa, and Latin America. Yet the fact is that neither the industrialized countries nor the international organizations concerned with economic development in these areas now has programs in motion to fulfill this condition. In the United States, however, private persons have produced an ingenious plan for filling this gap.

Mr. Morris Forgash, President of the United States Freight Company, has prepared a detailed plan for establishing A Bank for Economic Acceleration of Backward Countries. The bank is to be an international financial institution based upon governmental and private capital subscription. Its program is designed to facilitate land reform and the creation of large populations of farm owner-operators. At the same time the bank will sponsor technological development of agricultural methods to increase the yield from the soil, thereby enlarging the income of the farmer-cultivator and insuring the repayment of bank loans. Included in the Appendix to this book is a statement of the prospectus of the Bank.

At the outset, 50% of the capital of the bank would come from the private capital market and 50% from the governments of subscribing countries. The initial authorized capital would be $10 billion, enough to generate $70 billion in credit. The value of the bonds issued by the bank are to be guaranteed by the governments participating in its formation. The redemption value of the bonds will be adjusted to account for change in the purchasing power of the currency in question; the bonds will thus have firmer value than the currency of any one of these countries. The income on these bonds, at the rate of 4%, is to be exempt from taxation in all countries signatory to the treaty that establishes the bank. This automatically would make the securities of the bank a "best buy" in the international financial market; so much so that these securities would corral large sums of capital nervously held by deposed dictators and their like.

The principal business of the bank would be low-interest financing of farm improvement in the interest of raising the productivity of the soil, thereby guaranteeing the farmer direct, substantial, and personal benefit from any improvement in his farming methods. The principal capital of the bank would be applied for land acquisition and resale on time payment to individual farmers or to co-operative groups of farmers. The bonds issued by the bank would be, in turn, a most attractive form of payment to large land holders, for these securities would have unparalleled guarantees throughout the world.

The bank and its branches in various countries also would assist in the establishment of central buying agencies for farm produce, in order to facilitate efficient marketing arrangements. Other agencies of the bank would finance the purchase and use of modern farm equipment, seed, fertilizer, and the like, all designed to improve farm productivity, and so guarantee repayment of loans made by the bank. The same institution would be prepared to finance through long-term loans the construction of roads, highways, port and rail facilities, and other transportation linkages that would give the farmers access to markets.

The underlying strategy of the bank is that the creation of an increasingly productive agricultural population has multiple accelerating effects in economic development. The farmers earning an increasing cash income become a local assured market for manufacturing industries. As the productivity of the farmers grows, food requirements of the given country are met by the work of fewer people, and manpower is released from agricultural work to be used in industrial and urban occupations. Further, an efficient agricultural population assures a country its food supply; this, in turn, is a basis for stable economic growth insofar as the economy will not be disrupted by periodic food shortages that can be remedied only by costly importation of large quantities of foodstuff.

In my opinion the design of the Bank for Economic Acceleration of Backward Countries is a major contribution, in its own right, to the problem of world economic development. The plan deserves the most careful analysis and implementation by the Government of the United States. The design of the bank and its suggested mode of operation avoid many of the political pitfalls that have hampered the efforts of the United States over the past years in the field of foreign aid. The bank is to be an international institution governed by an international board, including subscriber and client country representatives. The loans extended by the bank are to be based upon proper economic evaluation of the investment opportunities and plausible estimates of reliability of repayment of loans.

It should be understood that ordinary banking operations in this sense are no deterrent to economic development. On the contrary, in most of the developing countries capital is available for loan purposes at very high rates of interest. Payments of 20 and 30% interest rates on loans for productive purposes are not at all uncommon. An international bank whose charges for the use of money were just above 4% would make available large blocks of capital at dramatically advantageous rates compared to present conditions. Also, a major factor insuring repayment of loans would be the skill with which investment areas were selected, and the auxiliary support that is given to the borrowers of capital. For example, proper conduct of land-reform operations and improvement in agricultural productivity have the effect of sharply raising the productivity of the soil. The value of this would be proportionally far greater than the payment made for borrowing the use of bank funds. After the Second World War, the American Occupation authorities ordered a land reform in Japan, which was dramatically successful. For the first time in its history Japan became an exporter of rice.

The essential strategy of the bank, then, is to help establish incentive agriculture so that the rational application of productive capital and talent to agricultural development by land reform and technological follow-through will raise the productivity of the farming population.

Apart from initiative toward establishing the Bank for Economic Acceleration, the United States might in other ways encourage economic development in Asia, Africa, and Latin America. The most important such action, by far, would be for the United States to move toward reducing and eliminating the military budgets of the developing countries. This would surely be feasible only as part of a general scheme for disarmament among the big powers as well. Nevertheless, the importance of the military expenditures made by developing countries is so crucial that even the beginning of action toward reducing these burdens would have an exhilarating effect on the pace of economic growth in these areas.

The work of the Peace Corps demonstrates an important productive activity that can be carried out by a society like the United States on behalf of the developing countries. By sending educated men and women into the developing countries, where their work in the performance of skilled occupations is bound up with teaching these skills to the people on the spot, the United States has helped to multiply the number of skilled people in each area.

It is entirely possible to make use of the electronic capabilities of the United States to fabricate television transmitters and receivers in large numbers to be located in developing countries for use in accelerating mass education. Large-screen television sets in remote villages could be powered by batteries and/or solar cells. Such networks would not be a substitute for an educational system but could instruct in literacy, personal hygiene, infant care, and agricultural technology. The cost of such prefabricated networks would be small compared to the return that could be expected as a result of greater occupational competence in a population.

One of the key problems that confronts a developing country

is the establishment of autonomous educational systems to enable their people—or those of a regional group of countries—to generate their own corps of teachers. Ultimately this requires the establishment of universities and the training of instructional staffs. This is the sort of thing with which developed countries can assist without undue disruption of their own university systems. The training of small numbers of men and women required for the establishment of university departments is not an overwhelming task for large university systems. The training of these people will have a large multiplying effect when they, in turn, take up posts in their own countries and operate local universities.

One problem that agitates governments in the developing countries is how to get along with private firms that make investments in their territory. The issue arises because productive investments by private firms usually carry along with them technologically capable staff. Although developing countries very much wish to have this priceless asset, they are invariably wary of large firms linked, as they are, to their own governments. The specter of colonialism is only too real to recently independent societies. Therefore, newly autonomous countries are often ultrasensitive to management by a foreigner, even though he may formally represent a firm rather than a government.

There is another side to this same coin. Many major American firms, for example, hesitate to invest in developing countries for fear of arbitrary and unpredictable nationalization of their properties. It seems to me that it would be worth while to formulate methods of operation that would satisfy the reasonable requirements of both the investing firms and new nations.

Suppose that an investing firm entered into an agreement with the government of a developing country, authorizing the firm to make investments under the following conditions. During the estimated economic life of the investment, let us say fifteen years, the management of the firm would be obliged to employ an increasing proportion of trained local people in the major occupational ranks within the enterprise. At the same time the agreement can stipulate that local citizens, or banks, or government institutions may purchase an increasing number of shares representing the property of the investing firm, up to 51% of the value of the assets, by the end of the investing period.

By this means the local government and population get reasonable assurance of increased participation in both the operation and the ownership of a new enterprise in their country. At the same time the investing management operates within the framework of a plausible investing period for its enterprise. Successful operation means that this management is at an advantage for further activity in the area because of the knowledge and the contacts built up as a result of the initial investment. A formula along these lines could satisfy the requirements of the developing countries and remove the ambivalence that now freezes investing decisions among many private firms in the industrialized nations.

Often the political boundaries of newly independent states— for example, many of those in Africa—do not correspond to economically viable territorial limits. In these cases it is ultracritical that regional common markets and some sort of economic cooperation be arranged. In that fashion, political autonomy could be assured while the size of markets available to various enterprises could be dramatically enlarged. The effect would be to justify larger investments in the regional economic unit, for then an enterprise could look forward to a broader scope of operation. At the same time, the larger market would open the possibility of earlier transition from importing many classes of manufactured goods to beginnings of local production. In short, the sort of benefits enjoyed by the countries of the European-market area could be matched by the developing countries if they were to enter into regional economic arrangements of a similar sort.

As long as the depletion process fueled by concentration on defense work dominates American life, our country is less than competent to give counsel and assistance to the developing nations. On the other hand, as the United States curtails the parasitic growth within itself, it will be able to advise and assist the developing countries to do the same. The reversal of the depletion process within the United States will not only make possible a process of reconstruction at home; it will also liberate talented men and women from the defense-space complex, some of whom will surely desire to participate as members of the staff of A Bank for Economic Acceleration, as members of the Peace Corps, or as employees of firms that become active in developing areas of the world.

As the United States becomes more competent to participate in these ways in economic development in Asia, Africa, and Latin America, there will be an automatic unfolding of very large markets in these areas for capital goods of every sort. A study performed for the United Nations in 1962 estimated that the requirements of the principal developing countries for industrial equipment, in manufacturing industries alone, would be, in the 12-year period from 1958 to 1970, $50.9 billion. During the 5-year period, 1970 to 1975, when acceleration of industrial growth is expected, the world requirement in the developing countries will reach the level of $44.1 billion. A major part of these requirements necessarily will be met from American sources, because the United States today is one of the few areas of the world with a potential for very large production of surplus capital equipment.

As Americans begin to explore the possibilities of reversing the depletion process and moving toward a productive society, there is a growing awareness of the challenging productive opportunity that awaits us both at home and abroad. As The New York *Times* saw it in an editorial on February 22, 1964:

By a decision now that a large part of the funds released from defense will be earmarked for schools, housing, health and public works, the movement away from military war could be coupled with a movement forward in the war against poverty. By this example, a powerful spur would simultaneously be applied to other governments to make similar commitments for reallocation of their resources to peaceful programs. The campaign against poverty could eventually be turned into the worldwide undertaking it must be for true security and the abolition of want.

15

The Productive Society in Motion

One of the most far-reaching features of the depleted society has been the severe restriction of America's ability to cope with change. The manpower, the money, and the policy innovations needed to solve national problems of undeniable urgency are withheld. Even the act of affirming that important changes are needed in public and private behavior is widely understood as fundamental criticism of policies that have been given the highest status.

Alas, the policies designed to wage the Cold War have reinforced the more militarist and nationalist elements of American society, while weaving a new pattern of self-weakening that depletes our country. At the same time, the self-righteousness that invariably accompanies military-nationalist policies has produced built-in resistance to innovations needed to meet new conditions within the United States, and in our relation to the world.

A productive society emphasizes healthy economic growth and thereby has the competence to initiate and to adapt to change— social and technological. This sort of competence is disappearing in our country.

Military-based policies require enormous budgets. Even out-and-out extravagances in defense and related spheres have long been accepted by many Americans as a part of present day government spending—that bolsters the economy. Now that piling up overkill is preposterous, and there is still a long agenda of depletion to be corrected, all the ideologies—domestic and foreign —of the Cold War and the Cold War Institutional Machine are still around. And they operate to restrain even the necessary planning for shifting men and money to productive use.

Our country has major need for many scientists and engineers in civilian spheres that have been unattended. The control of the lion's share of government research money by the defense agencies and defense industry, however, hold up the transfer process needed for changing our economy to a sound and viable and civilian one that would enable us to excel again as *the* leader of the family of nations.

There are repeated alarms about automation and how man is making himself obsolete. Beyond the sensationalism there is the fact that this problem is highly critical to a depleted society, and would be substantially eliminated or modified if productive investment were given greater priority in our country. The change to new markets and new jobs holds the clue to solving the problems of useful work for all, and not until that change is begun will we be able to handle the problems of individual adjustment to many sorts of desirable technological advance.

Men in declining or stagnating industries resist every sort of change in conditions of employment. Witness, for example, the remarkable resistance to technological change shown by workers in the railroad industry. Similar inflexibility occurs in many areas of livelihood as a result of the depletion process. In an atmosphere of declining activity there is something that causes the people associated with it to be fearful of change; they feel that no change would work to their economic benefit; that any change must threaten job security and established ways of operating. This hostile uneasiness surrounds much of the discussion presented in the preceding pages on technological, economic, and political depletion within American society.

Here is an example of how the depletion process restricts the flexibility of Americans. In May, 1964, oil-industry spokesmen in New York City were confronted with public-health data to the

effect that the sulphur content of the fuel oil used in heating buildings in the city was sufficiently high to be a major factor in air
pollution in the metropolitan area. Medical evidence indicated
that excessive sulphur dioxide in the air has been a cause of pul-
monary diseases and heart trouble. Accordingly, a New York
City Councilman sponsored a bill to lower the permissible limit
of the sulphur content of fuel oil; over a period of 10 years it
would decline from the present limit of 2.5% to 1%. As one
might suspect, the lower the sulphur content, the more costly the
oil. One response to this proposal was made by a Teamsters'
Union local officer on behalf of his 4,000 men. He feared that
requiring the use of the higher-priced oil would drive customers
to use gas for fuel. Unlike oil, gas does not need to be transported
in trucks driven by teamsters. In this case, what is lacking is the
imaginative groundwork needed to produce an orderly arrange-
ment for transferring workers among industries and jobs when,
as is clear, the public welfare requires a change.

It has become obvious that stopping the wholesale discard of
human beings, which we have long practiced, is unmanageable
alongside military priorities for key resources. As long as the
country and the Congress are convinced that there is no way of
organizing for American security except by the defense-space
complex as we have known it, there will be no decisive change
toward useful work for all and a meaningful war on poverty in
the United States.

Americans have been dismayed by the gathering storm around
the international value of the dollar, but there will be no durable
change, giving relief from this problem, until military extravagance
is no longer taken for granted as an immutable condition of life.

Americans must find a way to handle the design of government
in a big society. Will government, especially Federal, evolve
with ever-more-detailed decision-power over individuals, and with
concomitant bureaucratization? That is the present course—accelerated by the $50 to 60 billion defense-space budgets that are
managed out of massive governmental central offices. If we are
not to pay a fearful political penalty for this much centralization

of power, we must find ways to use government together with dispersed control over the investment and management of money for public purposes. But change in this direction is blocked by the overwhelming importance of the defense-space budgets whose control cannot be decentralized because of the very nature of military and allied organization.

The overwhelming majority of Americans would like to see an improvement in the qualities of life that have been impaired during the long Cold War: less powerlessness and more ability to effect our future; a change from sustained threat of no future to confidence in ability to live; a change from justified flaunting of the law in political and personal life to law-abidingness as a reinforced rule of society. All these changes would be cheered by an overwhelming majority of our countrymen. But such changes are stymied by the weight of our commitment to policies that generate powerlessness, no future, and lawlessness.

World underdevelopment must be remedied if there is ever to be a chance for a decent, peaceful life for most of the human race. Politically, it is evident that the failure of the West to make possible rapid economic development is frequently at the root of recourse to authoritarian-type regimes along Bolshevik lines— Russian or Chinese. This dismal prospect will not alter fundamentally until the United States is able to discourage the developing nations' squandering of capital funds on military forces, and until the productive power of the United States is turned to helping eradicate hunger from the earth. None of these changes are feasible until we in the United States move away from primary reliance on military methods in world affairs and toward a productive society at home, and act to encourage such moves in every other country.

In order to begin a serious national discussion of how to solve the problems of moving toward a productive society, we need a change in the status of criticism and dissent. The depleted society has discouraged criticism—even though that is an essential part of replacing poor practices with better alternatives. The long-standing Cold War dictum that the United States must excel and be beyond criticism in all spheres has even produced the absurdity of national self-esteem being gauged by the relative scores of Olympic teams.

In the Cold War environment the tradition of loyal opposition has been largely squelched. To the degree that this standard prevails, virtually every sort of constructive change in American policies and practices is held back. Restoring respect for criticism and dissent is therefore of the utmost importance as part of the movement into a productive society, which takes loyal opposition for granted, as an essential part of the process of generating and adapting to change at home and in the rest of the world.

The military and the political circumstances of Cold War international relations have changed substantially since 1945. In place of the chilling, monolithic, Stalinist vista of 1945, there is a manifest thaw within the USSR; the extremist-terrorist features of Stalinist society have been substantially removed. There is expression of political and economic diversity within the USSR and among the Eastern Bloc states.

The challenge to American policy is how to make these changes in the Soviet sphere into an opportunity for improving American security. But the long habituation to the Cold War has made it hard to respond imaginatively to the Soviet changes. We have built up a Cold War Institutional Machine that confers on our whole country a built-in resistance to changing the ideas and the methods that have so long been highly valued. That is why Senator William Fulbright, Chairman of the Senate Committee on Foreign Relations, did us all a great service when he rose on the floor of the United States Senate, on March 25, 1964, and delivered his "Foreign Policy—Old Myths and New Realities."

First, Senator Fulbright made plain some myths that we have about ourselves:

> . . . we are a people used to looking at the world, and indeed at ourselves, in moralistic rather than empirical terms. We are predisposed to regard any conflict as a clash between good and evil rather than as simply a clash between conflicting interests. We are inclined to confuse freedom and democracy, which we

regard as moral principles, with the way in which they are practiced in America—with capitalism, federalism, and the two-party system, which are not moral principles but simply the preferred and accepted practices of the American people. There is much cant in American moralism and not a little inconsistency. It resembles in some ways the religious faith of the many respectable people who, in Samuel Butler's words, "would be equally horrified to hear the Christian religion doubted or to see it practiced."

Our national vocabulary is full of "self-evident truths" not only about "life, liberty, and . . . happiness," but about a vast number of personal and public issues, including the cold war. It has become one of the "self-evident truths" of the postwar era that just as the President resides in Washington and the Pope in Rome, the Devil resides immutably in Moscow. We have come to regard the Kremlin as the permanent seat of his power and we have grown almost comfortable with a menace which, though unspeakably evil, has had the redeeming virtues of constancy, predictability, and familiarity. Now the Devil has betrayed us by traveling abroad and, worse still, by dispersing himself, turning up now here, now there, and in many places at once, with a devilish disregard for the laboriously constructed frontiers of ideology. . . .

With respect to the entire Cold War period, the Senator explained:

The master myth of the Cold War is that the Communist bloc is a monolith composed of governments which are not really governments at all but organized conspiracies, divided among themselves perhaps in certain matters of tactics, but all equally resolute and implacable in their determination to destroy the free world.

The Senator then went on to state that this "master myth" blocks off fresh political initiatives vis-à-vis the changing Soviet Bloc.

Important opportunities have been created for Western policy by the development of "polycentrism" in the Communist bloc. The Communist nations, as George Kennan has pointed out, are, like the Western nations, currently caught up in a crisis of indecision about their relations with countries outside their own ideological bloc. The choices open to the satellite states are limited but by no means insignificant. They can adhere slavishly to Soviet preferences or they can strike out on their own, within limits, to enter into mutually advantageous relations with the West.

Whether they do so, and to what extent, is to some extent at least within the power of the West to determine. If we persist in the view that all Communist regimes are equally hostile and equally threatening to the West, and that we can have no policy toward the captive nations except the eventual overthrow of their Communist regimes, then the West may enforce upon the Communist bloc a degree of unity which the Soviet Union has shown itself to be quite incapable of imposing—just as Stalin in the early postwar years frightened the West into a degree of unity that it almost certainly could not have attained by its own unaided efforts. . . .

With respect to Cuba, Senator Fulbright explained how it is that an economic boycott, organized by the United States, has not worked:

The boycott policy has not failed because of any "weakness" or "timidity" on the part of our Government. This charge, so frequently heard, is one of the most pernicious myths to have been inflicted on the American people. The boycott policy has failed because the United States is not omnipotent and cannot be. The basic reality to be faced is that it is simply not within our power to compel our allies to cut off their trade with Cuba, unless we are prepared to take drastic sanctions against them. . . . We have asked for the full cooperation of other free world countries and it has been largely denied. It remains for us to decide whether we will respond with a sustained outburst of hollow and ill-tempered threats, all the while comforting ourselves with the myth that we can get anything we want if we only try hard enough—or, in this case, shout loud enough—or we can acknowledge the failure of our efforts and proceed, coolly and rationally, to reexamine the policies which we now pursue in relation to the interests they are intended to serve. . . .

The Cold War has surely taken its toll of depletion within Soviet society, too. From this standpoint the governments of the United States and the Soviet Union have a mutual interest: each stands to gain from international agreements that slow the arms race and thereby curtail the depletion process within each society.

In Vietnam and Cuba and the nations of Latin America, the United States Government has demonstrated a conspicuous incapability for adapting to changes. So great has been the American emphasis on military systems of power as a way of affecting politics, that problems of land reform and economic development —which have become centrally important in Asia, Africa, and Latin America—have found the United States Government virtually without a constructive response. Where local governments have refused to carry out land reform and peasant insistence has finally developed into guerrilla warfare, the American response has been to move in the counterinsurgency forces.

One of the more dangerous effects of the big-power conflict is the instruction that it has given to the smaller and the developing countries on how to become and how to behave as a big power. Soon, with a few million dollars, nuclear warheads can be made and delivered by uncomplicated methods. In that perspective, national security, the likelihood of living and being autonomous, is reduced for all nations. In order to change this perspective national control over major weapons will have to be ended and the autonomy of the nation-state will have to be made subject to supra-national institutions responsible for directing and controlling international disarmament and peace-keeping.

We in America have the strongest sort of security incentive for trying hard to formulate and negotiate competent, imaginative, and successful disarmament treaties. Under foreseeable conditions that is the only strategy open for improving the military security of the United States. The conduct of the disarmament process itself will require close attention to details of technical and political reliability. In this perspective methods for replacing military power as instruments for settling political conflicts have priority importance in international relations. Beginnings have been made in our country toward accumulating knowledge on how to handle international disputes without war. American specialists, Professors Grenville Clark and Louis Sohn, have, in their volume *World Peace Through World Law* (Harvard University Press, 1958), prepared blueprints for strengthening and extending the United Nations. But such studies will surely have to be extended in order to cope with present and foreseeable problems among large and small nations.

The disarmament and the inspection processes have been the subject of considerable literature during the last years. In my book *The Peace Race,* I have outlined, in Chapter 10, some key ideas for operating an international disarmament process so as to improve the security of all concerned. In Chapter 11 of that book I described the technique of "inspection by the people," by which the populations of countries that participate in disarmament arrangements could support the reliability of the disarmament process by frustrating any effort to evade the international treaties. In *Inspection for Disarmament* (Columbia University Press, 1958), which I edited, methods of reliable inspection systems are detailed.

While a depleted society adheres fearfully to obsolescence and dogma, a productive society will be able to cope with change in many forms. The challenges of the productive society are at least as many-sided as the major areas of depletion described in this book. They include both social and technical invention.

A major requirement for social invention is the creation and operation of international institutions through which disputes on self-determination can be settled in an orderly way, without resort to military operations. Small wars, by threatening to involve the major nuclear powers, hold the constant threat of extension into nuclear catastrophe. Preventing small wars is rapidy becoming as important as averting nuclear-power confrontations.

On the technical side the requirements for major development are legion. Consider the mundane business of water-pollution control and the treatment of waste matter from household and industrial sources. The principal methods now in use for water purification are at least a half-century old. There has been no major effort in research and development in this field. The problem of fresh water in the United States is becoming so severe that a major effort will be required to cope with it in altogether new ways.*

A productive society is not Utopia, neither is it a scene of catastrophic transformation. The productive society will not be a single condition, but rather a process of change during which the depletion of many aspects of life is slowed down and a reconstruction process is set in motion.

During 1963 and 1964 the white population of America began to respond with increasing sympathy to the demands of its Negro fellow citizens for civic equality and a major improvement of their lot in life. In New York City, for example, after the turbulent Harlem riots of the summer of 1964, the Government promised emergency jobs for about 20,000 persons. Actually about 1,100 jobs were made available. The depleted society has been able to pass a civil-rights law and legislation to facilitate voting by Negroes. But the capital fund and the corps of technologists that would make possible expanding economic opportunity for Negroes and other deprived Americans continues to be used up in the defense-space complex. The movement toward the productive society is the key for making "freedom" a reality for American Negroes.

* The U.S. Department of Health, Education and Welfare has estimated that by 1970 the total effort to combat pollution and maintain a pure water supply throughout the country will involve more than 9,000 engineers and nearly 12,000 scientists. At this time only about one tenth that many specialists are working in this field and the problems that must be solved are becoming increasingly complex. Competent handling of the water-purification and pollution problems, for example, will make it possible for the people of the New York metropolitan area, and other cities, to enjoy vast waterways for recreational purposes.

In short, the issue has yet to be joined. Neither the Executive nor the Legislative branch of the United States Government has faced this fundamental consideration: The movement into a productive society in the United States will be possible only by curtailing the depletion process, only by transferring money and manpower from the defense-space complex to those areas of American life that have been so long deprived.

I have seen government officials reacting fearfully to proposals for transferring manpower and money from military overkill to productive use. Officials have been fearful of political reaction and adverse economic effects from reduced military spending. The fact is that, in the absence of plausible plans for conversion from military to civilian work, the closing of bases and the termination of military orders *has* caused hardship in many areas of the country. Where this fearfulness in the absence of planning prevails, government officials and their constituents become "locked into" the depletion process.

The politics of a productive society will include increasing competence in the Congress for fulfilling the Constitutional mandate "to provide for the common defense and the general welfare" of the people of the United States. When the competence most highly valued by public servants is the design and deployment of missile forces, then the Members of Congress must necessarily take a back seat and simply sign the blank checks submitted by the Defense Department. On the other hand, when the expertise given greatest value in our country concerns methods of organizing and implementing constructive work of many sorts, then the Members of Congress will be able to participate in significant judgments.

I look forward to the removal of the dead hand of the defense agencies from sponsorship of university research. There will then be a growing opportunity for applying the scientific and technological talents of the university community to the great unsolved problems of our society.

I think that an important part of setting a productive society into motion will include a growing ability to differentiate between pseudo goals and real goals for our country, and between pseudo protests against depletion and action that curtails depletion and replaces it with reconstruction. From 1961 on the Executive branch of the Federal Government has been the source of many proposals in the field of education, medical care, housing, civil rights, and civilian technology programs. The awkward fact, however, is that these proposals never included a definition of the cause of the depletion in each sphere. Neither were sufficient sums requested to make possible a reversal of the depletion in each case. Instead, modest sums were requested for these purposes while the military budgets were swiftly raised and the space marathon was undertaken—all on the assumption that the United States is rich enough to have both guns and butter. The result has been that these proposals for improvement could accomplish little in their respective spheres.

While many Americans have been repelled by particular features of our depleted society, their protest against these features has often been pseudo protest. For example, students at some universities during 1964-65 organized protests against adult society by means of campaigns for the acceptance of language ordinarily regarded as obscene. This was accomplished by posters and publications exemplifying the new "free" usage of the English language. Such protests are pseudo protests because they deflect attention from the causes of depletion in society. Pseudo protests are, in fact, a part of the depletion process itself. The targets of the pseudo protests are not the source of the depletion process, and victories against pseudo targets cannot produce any conversion from depletion to productive competence—either personally or for a larger community.

Moves toward a productive society will open new opportunities for restoring optimism in American life because there will be a future that includes activities in which every person can have a say.

In the perspective of a productive society, the social scientists of American universities will have a unique opportunity. It will fall to them to produce the theories and the social technology of a productive society. Our social scientists should undertake a re-examination of the "value free" fashion of the Cold War period.

In order to curtail the depletion process and set in motion the machinery of a productive society, we shall need many types of social invention. Broadly, the productive society will have to cope repeatedly with these problems: How can we combine large organizations with personal and political freedom? How can we make use of the efficiency of forward planning by many groups in our country, while preserving freedom of initiative for the individual? In order to handle such issues we shall need new knowledge on methods of social organization, on decision processes in industrial and other enterprises. Our social scientists will be able to make a major contribution toward the process of reconstruction by giving us firm grounds of definable cause and effect which we can use for making selections from among alternative policies. Many problems during the next decades will involve the answer to the question: How much decision power should be located in Federal Government as against community and state administrations? The answers that we select will have extensive effect on the quality of life in our country.

I see the beginning of a new kind of criticism, a new tone of constructive rebellion among the young people of our country. By constructive rebellion I mean rebellion with a purpose, criticism of things as they are in our society with a constructive alternative attached. Among the students of American universities there is a new readiness to examine critically our old myths in a search for ways of creating new constructive realities. This, I believe, is the meaning of the interest among American youth in civil-rights issues and antipoverty programs, and in alternatives to military-based foreign policies.

In all of this discussion I am not implying Utopia, a world without problems. We are surely confronted with great and grave issues and their solutions call for creative talent of every sort. In a great community with elaborate division of labor, how is it possible to be socially responsible? We have yet to find a way of creating a connection between individuals, groups of people, and the results of the work that they do.

The meaning of a productive society will extend through the formulation of teaching goals and methods for our schools. The process of reconstruction requires not obedient adjustment to Cold War depletion but training of our children for participation in the challenging endeavors of the productive society.

I expect that diverse groups in American life will discover common ground as they each seek ways to improve their own lot. Americans who suffer directly from the depletion process, or whose prospects for a really better life are held up by the depleted society—all these will be acting in parallel, even in concert, to accelerate the reconstruction of American life. Then only, "we shall overcome."

The Cold War, with its fearsome ultranationalism, military threats, and depletion, can be made to give way at home and abroad to the competence of a productive society—bringing productive power to bear for the solution of man's problems.

This is the American agenda, 1965 to 1985.

Appendix A

NOTE: On August 2, 1963, Senator George McGovern, of South Dakota, delivered a historic address on the floor of the United States Senate. This speech soon became one of the "most widely read documents in official Washington." By questioning fundamental postulates of politics based upon military power, Senator McGovern challenged widely accepted ideas. At the same time this address broke a long silence in the Congress. Thereafter, military policies and budgets were opened, increasingly, to debate.   S.M.

New Perspectives on American Security

Speech of Hon. George McGovern of South Dakota
in the Senate of the United States
Friday, August 2, 1963

Mr. McGOVERN. Mr. President, 18 years ago, as the pilot of an American B-24 bomber, I completed the last of 35 missions in the European theater of World War II. A few days after the completion of that tour of duty the war in Europe ended.

Our crew climbed into a battle-scarred bomber to return to the United States with the grim knowledge that we had used the most devastating weapons in the long history of warfare. Our four-engine bomber had day after day dumped 5 tons of TNT on its targets below.

But we had scarcely reached home before news stories told of a fantastic new bomb that had incinerated 100,000 Japanese men, women, and children in a single searing flash. Suddenly, our 5-ton monster lost its significance in the shadow of that 20,000 ton destroyer of Hiroshima.

287

Although the new dimensions of death were beyond comprehension, book titles in the afterglow of Hiroshima—"One World or None," "Modern Man Is Obsolete," "Five Minutes to Midnight"— attempted to assess the meaning of the nuclear age.

Recognizing that humanity stood in deadly peril, we drew comfort only in the conviction that the new techniques of destruction were so terrifying that man surely would never use them—would he?

Five years later, the A-bomb of Hiroshima passed into obsolescence, not because it was too fearful to use, but because it had been replaced by the H-bomb—a thousand times more powerful than the bomb that had devastated Hiroshima.

Meanwhile, the Soviet Union became a nuclear power, and in 1957, Sputnik I ushered in the space age. Today, the two great powers, America and Russia, have piled up nuclear weapons with an explosive power of 60 billion tons of TNT—enough to put a 10-ton bomb at the head of every human being on the planet.

A single warhead from the American or Russian stockpile if exploded over a great city would instantly transform it into a raging fireball 3 miles in diameter with a direct heat and blast capable of burning human flesh and collapsing buildings 25 miles from its center. Above a smoking crater a mile wide and several blocks deep, a gigantic, poisonous radioactive cloud would rise 20 or 25 miles to rain down torturous death on millions of human beings not fortunate enough to be incinerated quickly in the initial firestorm.

In spite of this grim prospect, the accumulation of more and more devastating weapons continues. The great powers are spending over $100 billion yearly on arms—each side justifying its investment in the name of defense. Yet, modern science supports the ancient Biblical wisdom, "there is no place to hide."

Speaking to the United Nations assembly in 1961, President Kennedy said:

> Today, every inhabitant of this planet must contemplate the day when it may no longer be habitable. Every man, woman, and child lives under a nuclear sword of Damocles, hanging by the slenderest of threads, capable of being cut at any moment by accident, miscalculation, or madness. The weapons of war must be abolished before they abolish us * * * . The risks inherent in disarmament pale in comparison to the risks inherent in an unlimited arms race.

We accept the logic of Mr. Kennedy's words, just as we accepted the earlier warning of former President Eisenhower: "There is no longer any alternative to peace." Why, then, does the arms race with its mounting military budgets continue?

Doubtless, a major factor is the uncertain quest for security through superior military strength. The Congress and the Nation have willingly responded to the architects of our military security and have granted them unprecedented sums to insure the defense of our shores. Americans have felt that the growing technical complexity of the military art has required leaving the main judgments about security to our military officers.

As a freshman Congressman in 1957, I was tempted to raise some questions about what seemed to me to be a staggering military appropriations bill. But I lapsed into silence when one of the most respected Congressmen took the floor to say:

If our military leaders are wrong and we listen to their advice, it will cost us some money. But if these experts are right, and we do not heed their requests, it may cost us our country.

Given that grim choice, it is a reckless man indeed who would challenge the demand for more military spending. Every patriotic citizen desires that his country be prepared to defend itself against attack. Even the most ardent economizers—men who vote with zeal to cut funds for education, conservation and health—are quick to shout "Aye" for more billions for arms.

I share the conviction that America ought to have a defense force which is second to none, and fully adequate to meet any need.

But, Mr. President, has the time not come to question the assumption that we are adding to defense and security by adding more and more to the nuclear stockpile? I suggest that we need to examine carefully the assumptions on which our military budget rests. We need a thoroughly honest discussion and debate, not so much about competing weapons systems, but rather about the basic postulates of our defense strategy.

Have we remembered that the defense of a great nation depends not only upon the quality of its arms, important as that is, but also on the quality of its economic, political, and moral fabric?

Have we considered the impact upon these other sources of strength of our vast military investment?

Is there a point of diminishing returns in the race for security through arms?

Have we made the wisest possible allocation of our material and human resources to insure maximum security?

Are we building national strength by creating a higher pile of nuclear bombs and adding to our overkill capacity while failing to match our millions of idle, untrained youth with the Nation's needs for constructive economic growth?

Is our national security jeopardized by an outflow of gold that weakens the international value of the dollar?

Is the size of our military budget the chief criterion of effective international leadership and national strength in today's world?

What is the mounting arms race doing to our freedom and the quality of our lives?

And most important of all, are we following a blueprint for peace or racing toward annihilation?

For this fiscal year, we are asked to approve a Department of Defense budget of $53.6 billion, plus additional billions for the Atomic Energy Commission and the space program. That is well over half of our entire Federal budget. It represents more than the combined cost of all the social and economic programs of the New Deal period from 1933 through 1940.

Soon, we will be called upon to vote on the appropriation of funds for this enormous arms budget. This is a tremendously important vote for all of us, not only because it represents a great deal of money, but because it can give us an opportunity to examine some of the basic assumptions that now guide our national life. A Federal budget is, after all, a careful listing of the public priorities and goals of the Nation. When we devote more than half of that entire budget to one purpose, we certainly need to be reasonably sure of our ground.

My limited effort to prepare myself for this forthcoming vote as a Senator whose chief concern is the security of our country and the peace of the world has led me to certain tentative conclusions. I set them forth now, not as final judgments, but simply as one person's convictions about a most complex problem. It is my hope that these suggestions may stimulate in some way the larger debate which needs to be waged by those Senators and Representatives having greater experience and knowledge than mine. Perhaps the insights of others may lead me to abandon or modify some of my present judgments.

In that spirit, I suggest the following propositions:

First. The United States now has a stockpile of nuclear weapons in excess of any conceivable need.

Second. Bringing the arms race under control involves risks less dangerous than the proliferation of nuclear warheads and the acceleration of the arms race.

Third. Present levels of military spending and military foreign aid are distorting our economy, wasting our human resources, and restricting our leadership in the world.

Fourth. Diverting some of our present and proposed military spending to constructive investments both at home and abroad will produce a stronger and more effective America, a more secure America, and will improve the quality of our lives and strengthen the foundations of peace.

Current Defense Assumptions

To place these convictions in better perspective, I would like to sketch some of the considerations which seem pertinent to our defense policy decisions.

Those who advocate surrender or passive submission to the forces of international communism will find little or no support in the United States. Most of us are willing to risk death rather than give the world over to a tyranny that is alien to all that we hold of value.

Likewise, few, if any, Americans would support the concept of an all-out military onslaught initiated by ourselves to wipe out the inhabitants of the Communist world. This, in another equally fundamental sense, would be a surrender of our values and traditions.

As a nation we have rejected both the concept of aggressive war and passive surrender. We have operated from the premise that the Communist threat is checked only because of our awesome military machine. This is the theory of deterrence which has guided our thinking for most of the period since World War II. When one looks for a more specific answer as to how that policy would be applied in the form of military strategy, he encounters some rather confusing and conflicting assumptions.

It has generally been believed that the deterrent or retaliatory power of America's strategic airpower was targeted on the great cities of Russia to be used in the event of a major Soviet attack.

On June 16, 1962, however, Defense Secretary McNamara, one of the ablest and most courageous men to come into Government in modern times, made an important speech at Ann Arbor, Mich. In this address Mr. McNamara spelled out the "controlled counterforce" or "no cities" doctrine. The Ann Arbor speech set forth the theory that instead of seeking first the mass destruction of the Russian populace, we would aim our missiles and bombers at Soviet nuclear weapons in an effort to cripple their capacity to hit the United States. Only if the Soviets attacked our cities would we strike at theirs.

This speech touched off a wide-ranging controversy, partly because its success would seem to depend upon the United States launching a first strike against the Soviet Union.

If the United States were aiming at the effective destruction of Russia's nuclear forces, how could we apply such a strategy unless we knocked out the Soviet missiles before they were launched from their silos? What military objective could we achieve by knocking out empty missile launchers after their rockets had hit American targets?

Secretary McNamara flatly denied that the United States has any intention of launching a first strike, but the "no cities" or "controlled counterforce" theory seems a most unlikely and impractical strategy.

In lengthy testimony before the House Armed Services Committee early this year, Mr. McNamara said:

> What we are proposing is a capability to strike back after absorbing a first blow. This means we have to build and maintain a second strike force. Such a force should have sufficient flexibility to permit a choice of strategies, particularly an ability to: (1) strike back decisively at the entire Soviet target system simultaneously; or (2) strike back first at the Soviet bomber bases, missile sites, and other military installations associated with their long-range nuclear forces to reduce the power of any follow-on attack —and then, if necessary, strike back at the Soviet urban and industrial complex in a controlled and deliberate way.

The Secretary's own testimony, then, seems to make the above strategy highly unlikely. Mr. McNamara pointed out that the Soviets have always insisted that their nuclear power is aimed at the great urban, industrial, and government centers of America. He then stressed the virtual impossibility of either side destroying the other's hardened ICBM weapons or Polaris-type submarine missiles. And then the Secretary added a third point which would seem to remove any real feasibility of concentrating our nuclear power on Soviet missile sites rather than cities. In his words:

> Furthermore, in a second strike situation we would be attacking, for the most part, empty sites from which the missiles had already been fired.

It might be reassuring to draw the conclusion from the "no cities" strategy that it is possible to fight a nuclear war centered on destroying missiles rather than people—if only we could build enough missiles to destroy the enemy's nuclear capacity. But anyone who is laboring under the impression that our Defense Department believes this to be feasible should read the congressional testimony of Secretary McNamara of last February. The following brief excerpts from that important 163-page statement should be pondered carefully, especially by the Members of Congress who are responsible with the President for the defense policies of our Nation.

Secretary McNamara said:

> Even if we were to double and triple our forces we would not be able to destroy quickly all or almost all of the hardened (Russian) ICBM sites. And even if we could do that, we know no way to destroy the enemy's missile-launching submarines at the same time. We do not anticipate that either the United States or the Soviet

Union will acquire that capability in the foreseeable future. * * *
We could not preclude casualties counted in the tens of millions.

Secretary McNamara said further:

The expanding arsenals of nuclear weapons on both sides of the
Iron Curtain have created an extremely dangerous situation not
only for their possessors but also for the world. As the arms race
continues and the weapons multiply and become more swift and
deadly, the possibility of a global catastrophe, either by miscalculation or design, becomes more real.

One final quotation from the Secretary of Defense is as follows:

More armaments, whether offensive or defensive, cannot solve
this dilemma. We are approaching an era when it will become increasingly improbable that either side could destroy a sufficiently
large portion of the other's strategic nuclear force, either by surprise or otherwise, to preclude a devastating blow. This may result
in mutual deterrence but it is still a grim prospect. It underscores
the need for a renewed effort to find some way, if not to eliminate
these deadly weapons completely, then at least to slow down or
halt their further accumulation, and to create institutional arrangements, which would reduce the need for either side to resort to their
immediate use in moments of acute international tension.

Realities of Soviet-American Overkill

I think it is imperative that every American fully understand what
our Secretary of Defense has told us. If nuclear war comes—no matter who strikes first—both sides will count their losses in tens of
millions of human lives. There is no such condition as true nuclear
superiority in the sense that either the United States or Russia could
escape mass destruction should it attack the other. Hardened ICBM
sites and nuclear-armed submarines have made the so-called counter-
force and no cities doctrines obsolete before they were fully expressed.

Even before Mr. McNamara spelled out the Ann Arbor doctrine
of a nuclear strike confined to military installations, the distinguished
chairman of the Senate Armed Services Committee warned that this
notion was an empty hope. Said Senator RUSSELL on April 11, 1962:

There have been some estimates and some so-called mathematical computations of the casualties that would result from a nuclear
war under various assumptions, including a positive attempt by

the adversaries to limit targeting to military installations and facilities. I have no hesitancy in saying, however, that to me these extrapolations, or projections, or hypotheses are exceedingly unrealistic.

The highly respected Senator from Georgia concluded:

> In my opinion, if nuclear war begins, it will be a war of extermination.

The unprecedented condition of today's strategic military power is this: neither the United States nor the U.S.S.R. can prevent the other from wielding a society-destroying blow, regardless of who attacks first. Offensive military power has been made so varied and strong that all conceivable defensive systems can be overwhelmed or bypassed by the power of offensive nuclear weapons.

Under these conditions, the classic military task of defending the shores of our country can no longer be performed. The present array of military doctrines gives a design for emerging from a nuclear exchange with more missiles than the opponent. But this sort of win would be paralleled by the loss of our society.

The Russians do not have a nuclear capacity equal to ours, but our superiority is largely a meaningless concept in view of their relative parity. In the days when warfare was limited to rifles and cannons and tanks and conventional aircraft, the side with the most weapons and soldiers had a great military advantage. But in today's age, when a nuclear exchange of a few minutes' duration means instant death and indescribable devastation to both sides, what consolation is there to the dazed survivors to know that there remains under the poisoned skies somewhere in the rubble some unused overkill capacity?

When asked at the congressional hearings what the military situation would be after a nuclear exchange between Russia and the United States, Secretary McNamara replied:

> This is a question we have considered. And I can't answer it. I think probably the fatalities in Western Europe would approach 90 million, the fatalities in the United States would approach 100 million, and the fatalities in the Soviet Union would approach 100 million.
>
> Now when you consider on the order of 300 million people dead in those areas, it is very difficult to conceive of what kind of military weapons * * * would continue to exist. We have nonetheless faced that issue, and we have systems provided that we believe would survive.
>
> But it exceeds the extent of my imagination to conceive of how those forces might be used and of what benefit they would be to our Nation at that point.

It might be argued by some that our excessive nuclear spending serves an indirect purpose in that it forces the Soviets to strain their less affluent economy to match our effort. But the Russians, from all indications, seem to be avoiding construction of highly sophisticated weapons beyond what they regard as enough to destroy the United States in the event of war.

During the late 1950's when the Soviets could have built hundreds of the latest types of long-range bombers they constructed less than 200 as against our more than 1,600. There is no indication that they intend to try to narrow this gap. At the present time, while we have a capability of a thousand ICBM's—perhaps considerably more—and are building many more, the Russians have built only a minor fraction of that number. Indications are that they will improve and replace rather than greatly increase the number of their missiles.

The question is whether the United States can afford the vast "overkill" capacity which seems to underlie much of our military budget.

I want to make it clear I am not underestimating the enormous nuclear power of the Soviet Union. Certainly they have an overkill capacity.

My own conviction is that we cannot afford this policy of adding to overkill capacity economically, politically, or morally and that if we persist in following it we will weaken our Nation both at home and abroad.

The United States has used its great power in the period since World War II with a sense of responsibility and restraint. We have done a remarkable job of providing a defense shield to war-torn Europe and assisting the rebuilding of that continent, whose welfare is so important to our own. We have shared our human and material resources with the developing countries around the world. We have strengthened the peacekeeping functions of the United Nations. There is no parallel in world history for the generous, farsighted manner in which the United States has provided world leadership and assistance since 1945.

But if our leadership is to remain effective, we must make certain that we do not fall into a rigid pattern that ignores new conditions and new challenges in the world. I submit that the continuing quest for an ever larger measure of nuclear overkill capacity makes no sense in the perspective of today.

No informed person doubts that we have the power to destroy Soviet society several times over, or that they have the capacity to destroy us. One recent study concluded that we could now erase the bulk of the Russian populace more than a thousand times. Even if that estimate is 100 times too high, we would be able to destroy the Soviet Union with only a partial use of our existing weapons.

Before the substantial increases in our military power of the past

2 years, Secretary McNamara testified that "there is no question but that today, our Strategic Retaliatory Forces are fully capable of destroying the Soviet target system, even after absorbing an initial surprise attack."

We have been building missiles, bombs, and other weapons steadily since then so that our capacity to destroy is much greater today than when the Secretary made that statement early in 1962.

Speaking of our present capability, Mr. McNamara said, on February 6 of this year:

> Allowing for losses from an initial enemy attack and attrition en route to target, we calculate that our forces today could still destroy the Soviet Union without any help from the deployed tactical air units or carrier task forces or Thor or Jupiter IRBM's.

Now, Mr. President, I ask what possible advantage there can be to the United States in appropriating additional billions of dollars to build more missiles and bombs when we already have excess capacity to destroy the potential enemy? How many times is it necessary to kill a man or kill a nation?

If the Secretary is correct—and I think his estimates are conservative—that one quick nuclear exchange would now leave 100 million Americans dead, an equal number of Russians, and nearly as many West Europeans, is that not enough to deter anyone other than a madman from setting off such a catastrophe?

And if either side yields to madness or miscalculation, can any number of arms save us?

A Proposed Arms Budget Adjustment

I think we need to take another careful look at our enormous arms budget, asking ourselves: What part of this budget represents additions to an already surplus overkill capacity? What alternative uses can be made of surplus military funds for strengthening the economic and political foundations of our society?

Our highly able Secretary of Defense has effected many needed economies and efficiencies in operation of the Defense Department. For that he should have the gratitude and praise of all. Congress can encourage him to make much larger savings by limiting the further pileup of overkill capacity.

I have pored over the complicated tables and charts of the defense budget for hours. I certainly do not pretend to understand all of the implications. Indeed, the data as made available to Congress in the Defense budget does not enable one to perceive the full functional pattern proposed.

But I am fully convinced that there is enough talent and brain-power among our military and civilian arms experts to eliminate $5 billion of proposed spending that goes beyond our real defense needs.

A front-page story in the Sunday New York Times of June 30 reports:

> The administration is giving serious consideration to ordering the first substantial cutback in the production of atomic weapons since the United States began building up its nuclear arsenal after World War II. Behind the current study is a belief that the United States with an arsenal of tens of thousands of atomic weapons has a sufficient and perhaps an excessive number of nuclear arms to meet its military needs.

The same article reports:

> Rising concern is felt in high administration circles over the multiplying number of warheads that have been assigned to the military forces in the last 5 years. The major fear is that continuing profusion would only increase the chances of accidental explosion or unauthorized use of the weapons.

The Times reported a growing fear of the members of the Joint Committee on Atomic Energy that the production of atomic weapons is "coming to be based more on the capabilities of the Atomic Energy Commission to manufacture them than on the actual requirements of the military."

The Atomic Energy Commission now has an annual budget of $1.8 billion to produce new warheads to add to our already enormous stockpile. The Times asserts that at a recent Pentagon press briefing "a highly placed Defense Department official" estimated that it might be desirable to make a $1 billion cut in this expenditure. Another policymaking official said:

> We have tens or hundreds of times more weapons than we would ever drop even in an all-out war, and we have had more than we needed for at least 2 years.

None of the sections in this important news article have been challenged by any administration spokesman so I think it is safe to assume that they are well-grounded.

I believe that, in addition to a cut of $1 billion in the Atomic Energy Commission's weapons procurement program, we could wisely cut an additional $4 billion from the proposed budgets of the Air Force, Navy, and Army without reducing the security of the

Nation. Indeed, such reductions could enable us to strengthen our overall national security. Any such substantial cut should, of course, be applied and administered with the expertise of the Secretary of Defense. I will listen thoughtfully to the presentation of our Appropriations Committee and others. I intend to follow the coming debate and discussion with a frank willingness to change my views if there is compelling contrary evidence.

It may be argued that the economy of many of our communities has become so intertwined with military spending that an arms cut of several billion dollars which I have proposed would result in a painful economic dislocation.

It is true that many American communities have come to lean heavily on the economic stimulus of arms production and military installations. We need to accelerate and expand our efforts on the Federal, State, and local level to prepare these communities for a conversion to a more permanent economy appropriate to the conditions of peace.

Competence for converting from a military to a civilian economy is a basic requirement for the economic and political security of the United States.

Planning the Conversion to a Peace Economy

Capability for economic conversion must be developed at all establishments—manufacturing, research, and others—engaged in fulfilling contracts or otherwise working for the Department of Defense or the Atomic Energy Commission.

In order to minimize dislocation; facilitate industrial expansion; reduce regional dependence on single markets; reduce regional dependence on single government markets; and plan for growth in employment, I recommend the following procedure:

First, all establishments that fulfill Defense Department or Atomic Energy Commission work for at least 1 calendar year and whose personnel are 25 percent or more so engaged, should henceforth be required—as a condition of contract fulfillment and acceptable administration—to establish in their managements an operating conversion committee. This committee should actively engage in planning for conversion of the facility from military to civilian work as required in the event of termination, cutbacks, stretchout, or other curtailment of Defense or AEC requirements.

Second, in order to estimate the support that may be required to complement local and regional conversion, an Economic Conversion Commission should be established by the President under the direction of the Secretary of Commerce and including experts from other concerned Government departments. Our Arms Control and Disarmament Agency already has a small but able group of people giving thought to this matter.

The Economic Conversion Commission shall have responsibility for blueprinting appropriate action by departments and agencies of the Federal Government that are required to facilitate conversion from a military to a civilian economy.

In addition to such activities as it should deem necessary, the Commission would prepare schedules of possible private and public investment patterns and the employment and income effects to be expected therefrom. The information would be reported to the President and to the Congress in preliminary form within 6 months after the enactment of authorizing legislation and in final form within 12 months.

The Commission would take counsel with the Governors of all States to encourage appropriate and timely studies and conferences by the States in support of conversion from a military to a civilian economy.

Third, the Commission would, within 12 months of establishment, convene a National Conference on Economic Conversion and Growth to focus nationwide attention on the problems of conversion and economic growth and to encourage appropriate study and organization in all relevant parts of the Nation's economy. This conference should include invited representatives of trade associations, trade unions, professional societies, representatives of appropriate agencies of the Federal and State Governments, and selected individuals with specialized knowledge.

Through intelligent planning we can make a satisfactory transition to an economy less dependent upon arms spending.

Weaknesses in an Arms Economy

A closer look at our present level of arms spending will show that it is not an unmixed blessing now as a stimulus to our economy.

First of all, we have distorted our economy in allocating such a high percentage of our highly trained manpower, research, and technology to weapons production at the expense of our other industry. Japan and our West European Allies have all modernized their civilian industrial plant at a much higher rate than the United States, largely because of our concentration on arms production. This has added to our civilian production costs, decreased our efficiency, undercut our competitive position in international trade, and aggravated the balance-of-payments problem.

American machine tool production was once the envy of the world, but today we have slipped to fourth or fifth rank among the nations. Our best scientific and technical competence is going into arms, not to the modernization of our civilian plant.

Building weapons is a seriously limited device for building the economy—partly because it cannot be counted upon as a permanent system and partly because a military item leads to no further production; it is an end in itself. Disarmament chief William C. Foster said recently that "defense spending of the type we now have has no intrinsic merit in terms of its ability to create production and income as compared to other forms of demand."

Many U.S. industries are losing their capacity to compete not only in world trade but also in the United States. The concentration of capital and technical skill in arms production is a basic cause of our declining competitive ability.

As matters now stand, the U.S. Government is financing 65 percent of all research and development, and most of that is for military purposes. In Germany, by contrast, 85 percent of research is privately financed, and nearly all of it is being used to modernize civilian industries which compete with ours. Those who view military spending as an unmixed blessing to our economy should take a look at the gleaming up-to-date civilian plants in Germany, Belgium, Holland, Italy, and Japan—plants that are surpassing our own neglected civilian production in both quality and low-cost operation. Where will this kind of imbalance leave us in the toughening competition of international trade?

The U.S. economy is jeopardized further by the flow of our gold overseas and the undermining of the dollar as a unit of international exchange. Today, we have a favorable trade balance, but because of our military investments overseas and the flight of investment capital we are suffering an unfavorable balance of payments. Heavy arms spending has aggravated a U.S. fiscal situation that has led many American investors to seek more attractive oversea outlets for their capital.

Our traditionally strong currency has been a powerful instrument in American economic and political leadership in the world. But the strain imposed on our gold reserves as a result of heavy military commitments abroad and excessive arms spending at home is a threat to our international position. The loss of American gold can be halted by reducing some of the burden we have been carrying for the defense of now prosperous allies and by encouraging the conversion of foreign claims on our gold into investments to modernize our industrial system.

While retaining our massive military power, the overriding present need of American security is prompt reinforcement of the economic and political aspects of security at home and abroad.

The Military-Industrial Complex and American Life

It is admittedly difficult to calculate the impact of the arms budget on our civilian economy. It is even more difficult to measure the impact of what former President Eisenhower called "the military-industrial complex" on our moral strength and the climate of freedom. Americans have always feared that any trend toward militarism was a threat to the quality of our democracy. I believe that this is still a legitimate concern. Mr. Eisenhower, whose life has been devoted to military matters, was so concerned about the growing impact of the military-industrial combination on American institutions that he devoted his farewell address to this danger. "We must never let the weight of this combination endanger our liberties or democratic processes," he warned.

Democracy is based on a fundamental respect for the dignity and worth of human life. Its great strength is that it opens the way for the full flowering of man's intellectual, moral, and cultural development.

When a major percentage of the public resources of our society is devoted to the accumulation of devastating weapons of war, the spirit of democracy suffers. When our laboratories and our universities and our scientists and our youth are caught up in war preparations, the spirit of freeman is hampered.

America must, of course, maintain a fully adequate military defense. But we have a rich heritage and a glorious future that are too precious to risk in an arms race that goes beyond any reasonable criteria of need.

We need to remind ourselves that we have sources of strength, of prestige, and international leadership based on other than nuclear bombs.

Conversely, we need to remember that the greatest Communist victories, including the Chinese Communist takeover, came at the moment of our greatest nuclear superiority.

The global contest raging before our eyes today will doubtless continue for as long as we can see into the future, but it need not, indeed cannot, be settled by nuclear warfare.

The United States must be prepared to lead that contest into areas that draw on our true sources of greatness—politics, economics, and morality. There is a growing indication that the course we follow may play a major part in determining the course which our adversaries take for good or ill.

The self-defeating nature of the arms race is that each side reacts to the other's moves in a constantly rising scale of armaments. In his congressional testimony earlier this year, Secretary McNamara explained how the United States tries to evaluate expected Soviet arms moves so that we can plan to counter their efforts by moves of our own. "We are, in effect," said the Secretary, "attempting to anticipate production and deployment decisions which our opponents themselves may not yet have made."

Is it not reasonable to assume that, just as we attempt to counter arms moves by the Soviets, so do they try to gear their efforts to counter ours? Could we not then well afford to make a serious effort to put the arms race in reverse by carefully calculated moves designed to shift the competition with Russia away from arms spending into more peaceful pursuits?

Our Unmet Public Needs: An Alternative to Overkill

We have millions of idle youth who could be employed in existing job vacancies if only they had sufficient training and education. A sizable proportion of these are Negroes and their idleness is at the base of the explosive civil rights crisis now convulsing the Nation. What better use could we make of some of our excess military spending than to divert it to an expanded program of vocational and technical training?

Our civil rights problems require for their solution a major expansion of employment opportunity. The economically depressed regions of the country require fresh capital and technical talent. Both these basic problems of economic development require sizable productive investment.

We have an urgent need for more classrooms, laboratories, libraries, and capable teachers.

We have millions of citizens, particularly among our older people, who need more adequate hospital and nursing home care.

Some of our present defense installations might in the future be converted into vocational schools, community colleges, or health centers.

We have rivers and streams to be saved from pollution and waste —a task calling for considerable engineering and technical manpower.

We have a growing number of farm youth who can no longer make an adequate living on the farm whose lives would be enriched by an expanded rural area development effort.

And for years to come there will be hungry, afflicted people abroad who look to us for help. As the former director of our Nation's food for peace program, I came to a keen realization that most of the people of the world are undernourished rural families who are trying to scratch an existence from the soil by incredibly primitive methods.

We have an opportunity with our amazing agricultural know-how to use an increased volume of farm products and agricultural assistance as development tools abroad. The recent World Food Congress held in Washington underscored the fact that mankind now has the scientific capacity to eliminate hunger from the world.

I think that we should seriously consider diverting $5 billion of our arms budget into the kind of worthwhile programs at home and abroad which I have just sketched. Perhaps some of the military reductions should be expressed in tax reduction. This move would not only result in a stronger and better America, but it might invite a constructive response from the Soviet Union. The Soviets have more to gain than we from a reduction of military spending. They have deprived themselves of the appliances, automobiles, attractive clothing, and personal comforts which we take for granted.

The cold war is now showing some signs of a possible limited thaw. In his inspired address to the Nation last Friday evening, President Kennedy described in cautious but hopeful terms the larger meaning of the proposed nuclear test ban as a first important step to peace. I trust that after careful consideration the Senate will lend its support to this initiative for peace.

As we weigh the proposed test-ban agreement, we can usefully take into account three factors that I have discussed today.

First, when both sides already possess overkill capacity, that lessens the temptation for either side to break the test ban.

Second, some Americans may wonder if the next steps, after a test-ban agreement, might not mean declining military spending and a sag in our economy. I am confident that practical steps which I have outlined for preparing and supporting economic conversion will reassure our people on this count.

Third, the test-ban agreement can lead to savings of many millions of dollars from the funds hitherto used for large-scale testing.

There are hopeful signs other than the proposed test ban. The myth of a solidly united, monolithic Communist bloc was long ago thrown in doubt by Tito. But how much more significant is the mounting evidence of a major convulsion of the Sino-Soviet bloc. We should watch these new developments with caution, knowing well that while Communist powers may differ with each other, they continue to follow a tyrannical system that is alien to American democracy.

But we must also keep free from a rigid diplomacy or excessive reliance on arms that might jeopardize our capacity to exploit for peace these fast-developing changes in the international climate.

Thirteen years ago, the late Senator Brien McMahon, chairman of the Joint Committee on Atomic Energy, made two memorable addresses from the floor of the Senate. The Connecticut Senator warned that a continuance of the arms race would lead sooner or later to catastrophe, and in any event would induce a climate of fear and a Government-controlled allocation of resources that would dry up the wellsprings of American freedom and dignity. The Senator concluded, on March 1, 1950, with this warning:

Mr. President, the clock is ticking, ticking, and with each swing of the pendulum the time to save civilization grows shorter. When shall we get about this business? Now or when Russia and the United States glower at one another from atop competing stacks of hydrogen bombs?

We have arrived at the point in history where we indeed "glower at one another from atop competing stacks of hydrogen bombs." And if the present trend continues, in a few short years a half dozen, and then a dozen, new powers will climb atop their hydrogen stockpiles to glower at their frightened neighbors.

The clock which Senator McMahon heard ticking 13 years ago is still ticking, but our ears have become so accustomed to the sound that we scarcely hear it. Yet, scientists of our day flatly assert that if we do not reverse the arms race, a major nuclear accident will occur before this decade ends even without the intent of the nuclear powers. And how we rest secure knowing that any one of three, six or a dozen national defense ministries or subordinate military officers could set off a nuclear holocaust through miscalculation, impulsive madness, or simply human wickedness.

There are powerful options of peace as well as options of war. Still alive in the world is a faith that can move mountains if we will only seize upon it. From our own heritage the philosophy of Jefferson and Lincoln speaks with a voice that is more effectively heard in Asia, Africa, and Latin America than any number of nuclear explosions or moon shots. A conscientious effort on our part to eliminate excessive nuclear stockpiling will give that voice of peace and reason an even clearer tone.

I pray that our country will in every possible way use its unique power and influence on the side of peace. I know that is what President Kennedy and his administration seek. I am sure that is the sense of the Congress and the American people. I even dare to believe that is what Mr. Khrushchev and his people have come to accept as the only condition of their survival.

Both Americans and Russians must make a choice between the quick and the dead. Negotiators of the test-ban proposal have cast their lot on the side of hope and life. The further steps to peace will be torturous and hard, but they lead, however, slowly, away from catastrophe toward salvation.

If we hold fast to that course, taking into account the new conditions of American security, generations to come will call us blessed, and, as peacemakers, we shall know the Scriptural promise:

The Lord will give strength unto his people; the Lord will bless his people with peace. . . .

Appendix B

The Structure of Alternative Security Policies and Budgets

by Seymour Melman

What alternative security policies and military budgets are available to the United States? What are the implications for the American economy that stem from the choices in security policies and budgets? The accompanying chart is an experimental estimate of an available range of general security policy alternatives.

For each alternative, the chart defines a general security policy, and the associated economic and military strategies. The character of armed forces derives from military strategy which, in turn, determines the size of the military budget. In the last row of the chart, the domestic effects (economic and political) that flow from each set of policies, strategies, forces, and military budgets are identified.

The defined military forces for each alternative are "principal elements" rather than total descriptions of forces. The men of the Navy and the Marines are not shown separately. Neither is the important factor of organization depicted. One would expect that the variation in military organization, from Alternative 1 to 7, would correspond with variation from "military" to "civilian" control of armed forces.

More Polaris missiles are shown in Alternative 4, even with a reduced military budget, because a Polaris submarine fleet of more than 20 vessels (320 missiles) has already been funded and is under construction. Large civil defense and antimissile programs, because of their ineffectiveness, are part of garrison state strategies only. Each military budget level includes maintenance, modernization, and appropriate production of new equipment.

For each set of policies and budgets, the policy-makers' questions are:

Does the policy provide for economic and political, as well as military, aspects of national security?

Is the military strategy consistent with technological feasibility (e.g.—one cannot "win" a nuclear war)?

Are the forces competent to cope with small, non-nuclear engagements?

Do the domestic effects of the policy strengthen or weaken American society—economically and politically?

The policy problem for the United States is this: Which direction of change will improve the security of the United States—from Alternative 3 to 2, or from 3 to 4?

	Alternative 1	Alternative 2
GENERAL SECURITY POLICY	Total reliance on military power for security, regardless of cost, in a garrison state.	Primary reliance on U.S. military power to contain military and other expansion of Soviet system.
ECONOMIC POLICY	Massive federal control of human and material resources for ever-growing military industry and forces.	Use of Federal power to ration wealth into military industry and armed forces. Economic priorities to military budgets.
MILITARY STRATEGY	Ever-mounting strategic counterforce power, with huge civil defense.	Large strategic counterforce power with major nonnuclear forces. (The Mix.)
MILITARY FORCES —Principal Elements		
STRATEGIC:		
Polaris Missiles	800	448
ICBMs	1,200	950
SAC Planes	2,000	1,500
ARMY DIVISIONS (15,000 men per Div.)	25	20
NAVY SHIPS	1,000	950
NAVY PLANES	11,500	9,600
AIR FORCE PLANES (not including SAC)	20,000	17,000
CIVIL DEFENSE ($ Billions)	$100 Billion	$10 Billion
ANTIMISSILE MISSILES	$10 Billion	—
TOTAL MEN IN ARMED FORCES	10 Million	4.2 Million
MILITARY BUDGET (current dollars)	Over $175 Billion	$75 Billion
DOMESTIC IMPLICATIONS, ECONOMIC and POLITICAL	Unrestricted government control of capital and people including profits, prices, and wages. Severely restricted civilian economy and consumption. Personal freedoms subordinated to the state. Military draft (complete). Guns over butter.	Close government rationing of capital, technology, and skilled occupations for military work. Restricted civilian economy and massive tax burden. Major restraints on personal and political freedom. Military draft (heavy).

Alternative 3 (1964 position)	Alternative 4	Alternative 5
Large and varied military forces, American and allied, for crisis control.	Strong defense, with economic development for building political strength.	Major economic development for political strength, with substantial defense.
Foreign aid and trade development within limits of priority to military budgets. Government intervention in economy as a major tool.	General encouragement to economic growth, with priority to less developed U.S. industries and regions. Stabilization of defense spending.	Heavy civilian investment, domestic and foreign. High growth rate; declining defense spending.
Large strategic "retaliatory" forces with varied nonnuclear capability, including control of "brush" wars. (The Mix.)	Maintenance of strategic forces and limited nonnuclear forces. Reliance on regional self-defense.	Retention of shielded second-strike strategic forces, and limited nonnuclear forces.
240	320	320
700	500	300
1,000	500	250
16	12	8
852	600	350
7,900	5,700	2,800
14,000	10,000	5,000
$0.1 Billion	—	—
—	—	—
2.8 Million	2.0 Million	1.5 Million
$50 Billion	$35 Billion	$25 Billion
Government regulation of capital and technology with military priority. Depleted civilian industrial economy. Affluence and poverty in consumption. Heavy tax burden. Military draft (partial).	Capital investment and new technology oriented to civilian priority. Reduced tax rates to encourage productive investment and consumption. Government planning for economic stability and growth. Substantial foreign capital investments. Stabilization or a modest reduction of debt. Standby draft.	Heavy capital and technological investments in civilian economy. Rising consumption levels and diminution of poverty. Large foreign investment. Some retirement of national debt. No draft.

Alternative 6	Alternative 7	
Primary reliance on economic productivity as instrument for political power with minimum deterrence.	Total reliance on economic and political methods of power, with international military force for peace-keeping.	GENERAL SECURITY POLICY
Heavy civilian investment and high growth rate. Priority to domestic consumption and worldwide development. Minimum defense expenditures.	Full use of productive resources for peaceful purposes, including international peacekeeping machinery.	ECONOMIC POLICY
Retention of selected second strike strategic force, and limited non-nuclear force.	Buildup of international police force. Controlled phase-out of national military establishments.	MILITARY STRATEGY
		MILITARY FORCES —Principal Elements
		STRATEGIC:
320	—	Polaris Missiles
200	—	ICBMs
100	—	SAC Planes
		ARMY DIVISIONS (15,000 men per Div.)
4	2	
150	50	NAVY SHIPS
1,000	500	NAVY PLANES
		AIR FORCE PLANES (not including SAC)
2,000	1,000	
		CIVIL DEFENSE ($ Billions)
—	—	**ANTIMISSILE MISSILES**
		TOTAL MEN IN ARMED FORCES
1.0 Million	.5 Million	
		MILITARY BUDGET (current dollars)
$15 Billion	$5 Billion	
Rapid growth in industrial efficiency and consumption levels. Modest federal tax rates to support extended services. Major retirement of national debt. Expanded social security.	Major economic development in U.S. including restoration of depleted soil, forest, and related resources. Major increased consumption by reduction of work year. Use of federal and local government as back-stopping instrument for economic stability and social security. Butter over guns.	DOMESTIC IMPLICATIONS, ECONOMIC and POLITICAL

Appendix C

100 Companies and their Subsidiary Corporations Listed According to Net Value of Military Prime Contract Awards

Fiscal Year 1964
(July, 1963 – June, 1964)

The 100 companies and their subsidiaries which received the largest dollar volume of military prime contracts of $10,000 or more in fiscal year 1964 accounted for 73.4% of the United States total. This is a decrease of 0.5 percentage points from the 73.9% during fiscal year 1963. The table below shows that the 73.4% of prime contracts awarded to the top 100 corporate groups during fiscal year 1964 was somewhat lower than the average over the last 7 years. The first 10 companies had 1.7% more of the total than in fiscal year 1963, while the remaining companies had an over-all decrease of 2.2%. It should be noted that about one half of the military work of the large concerns is subcontracted with approximately 40% of the amount subcontracted going to small business concerns.

The list for fiscal year 1964 contains 19 companies which did not appear on the fiscal year 1963 list. Of the new names, eleven appear between the 76th and 100th positions. One of the new names on the list, Morrison-Utah-Perini-Leavell, a joint venture with contracts totalling $121.5 million, is in 40th position.

Major corporate changes affecting the list during fiscal year 1964 were as follows: Gilfillan Corp. and Garrett Corp., both of which appeared on the fiscal year 1963 and fiscal year 1962 lists, became subsidiaries of International Telephone & Telegraph Corp. and Signal Oil & Gas Co., respectively. Hiller Aircraft Co., acquired

Percent of U. S. Total

Companies	FY 1958	FY 1959	FY 1960	FY 1961	FY 1962	FY 1963	FY 1964
1st	9.8%	7.2%	6.0%	6.5%	5.6%	5.9%	5.8%
2nd	6.4	5.2	5.1	5.2	4.7	5.2	5.4
3rd	3.6	4.5	4.8	5.2	4.4	4.1	4.6
4th	3.5	4.1	4.6	4.1	4.0	4.0	4.1
5th	3.0	4.0	4.3	3.8	3.8	4.0	3.9
1 - 5	26.3%	25.0%	24.8%	24.8%	22.5%	23.2%	23.8%
6 - 10	12.4	12.0	11.3	11.8	11.1	10.9	12.0
11 - 25	19.1	17.6	17.4	18.2	17.2	17.8	17.1
1 - 25	57.8%	54.6%	53.5%	54.8%	50.8%	51.9%	52.9%
26 - 50	9.1	10.7	11.3	11.0	12.6	13.7	12.9
51 - 75	4.8	5.5	5.4	5.5	6.0	5.5	5.1
76 - 100	2.5	3.0	3.2	2.9	2.9	2.8	2.5
1 - 100	74.2%	73.8%	73.4%	74.2%	72.3%	73.9%	73.4%

by Fairchild Stratos Corp., became a subsidiary in the new Fairchild-Hiller Corp. Minneapolis-Honeywell Regulator Co. changed its name to Honeywell, Inc.

Over half of the companies were engaged in missile-space, aircraft and electronics work in fiscal year 1964. The contract work of many of the companies involved more than one major commodity category. Based on the category representing the largest dollar volume of contracts awarded to each company, there were 24 missile-space, 19 aircraft and 14 electronics firms. The remaining 43 companies fell into the following categories: petroleum (12), services (7), construction (7), tank-automotive (6), ammunition (5), ships (4), weapons (1), and photographic equipment and supplies (1). It is noteworthy that there were only two construction companies in fiscal year 1963.

The six nonprofit contractors (see Index) include one new institution, Stanford Research Institute, which was not on the fiscal year 1963 list. These nonprofit contractors are generally providing research, development, and training services in the missile-space and electronics programs.

Four companies received prime contract awards of more than $1 billion each in fiscal year 1964 compared to 5 companies in fiscal year 1963. These companies and a brief description of their more important contract work are as follows:

Lockheed Aircraft Corp. leads the list for the third consecutive year receiving $1,455.4 million, or 5.8% of the total. The aircraft contracts include the C-141A Starlifter Jet Cargo Transport, C-130E Hercules Turboprop Jet Transport, and the P3A Electra Jet Patrol Bomber. It is a principal prime contractor for the Polaris missile, is an important contractor for military space vehicles, and performs research in conjunction with the satellite-control network. The company and its subsidiaries also receive contracts for shipbuilding and electronics.

Boeing Company in second place with contract awards of $1,365.2 million (5.4%), occupies the same position as in fiscal year 1963. Its contract work was almost entirely in aircraft and missiles. The principal missile project is the Minuteman ICBM Missile. Aircraft projects include KC-135 Troop and Cargo Transports, CH-47A Chinook Troop Transport, CH-46A Sea Knight Assault Transport Helicopters, and modification of B-52 Strato Fortress bombers.

McDonnell Aircraft Corp., whose contracts totalled $1,157.4 million (4.6%), ranks third. This compares with a contract value of $497.0 million and 9th position in fiscal year 1963. The prime contract work of the company is predominantly for the production of the F-4 series of Phantom II fighter-bomber and reconnaissance aircraft for Navy and Air Force.

North American Aviation, Inc. received $1,019.5 million (4.1%) in awards, dropping from 3rd place in fiscal year 1963 to 4th place in fiscal year 1964. Its major projects include research and development of the B-70 aircraft, the production of the A-5 Vigilante and T-39 Sabreliner aircraft, missile propulsion equipment, and a wide variety of electronic equipment, including guidance and control for the Minuteman missile and for ship navigational systems.

INDEX OF 100 PARENT COMPANIES WHICH WITH THEIR SUBSIDIARIES RECEIVED THE
LARGEST DOLLAR VOLUME OF MILITARY PRIME CONTRACT AWARDS IN FISCAL YEAR 1964

Rank	Parent Company	Rank	Parent Company
45.	Aerospace Corp. (N)	34.	Kaiser Industries Corp.
87.	American Bosch Arma Corp.	68.	Kaman Aircraft Corp.
61.	American Machine & Foundry Co.	95.	Kiewit (Peter) Sons' Co.
88.	American Ship Building Co.		
7.	American Telephone & Telegraph Co.	56.	Lear-Siegler, Inc.
64.	Asiatic Petroleum Corp.	100.	Leavell-Kiewit (JV)
69.	Atlantic Research Corp.	22.	Ling-Temco-Vought, Inc.
16.	Avco Corp.	28.	Litton Industries, Inc.
		1.	Lockheed Aircraft Corp.
17.	Bendix Corp.		
85.	Bethlehem Steel Corp.	48.	Magnavox Co.
2.	Boeing Co.	9.	Martin Marietta Corp.
53.	Burroughs Corp.	43.	Massachusetts Institute of Technology (N)
		3.	McDonnell Aircraft Corp.
30.	Chrysler Corp.	77.	Mitre Corp. (N)
75.	Cities Service Co.	54.	Morrison-Perini-Hardeman (JV)
37.	Collins Radio Co.	40.	Morrison-Utah-Perini-Leavell (JV)
47.	Continental Motors Corp.		
72.	Continental Oil Co.	10.	Newport News Shipbuilding & Dry Dock Co.
71.	Control Data Corp.	4.	North American Aviation, Inc.
60.	Curtiss-Wright Corp.	31.	Northrop Corp.
66.	Cutler-Hammer, Inc.		
		52.	Olin Mathieson Chemical Corp.
62.	Day & Zimmerman, Inc.		
29.	Douglas Aircraft Co.	32.	Pan American World Airways, Inc.
49.	du Pont (E. I.) de Nemours & Co.		
97.	Dynalectron Corp.	24.	Radio Corp. of America
		21.	Raytheon Co.
70.	Eastman Kodak Co.	51.	Republic Aviation Corp.
86.	Electronic Communications, Inc.	82.	Richfield Oil Corp.
		96.	Ryan Aeronautical Co.
35.	F M C Corp.		
93.	Fairchild-Hiller Corp.	98.	Sanders Associates, Inc.
89.	Firestone Tire & Rubber Co.	67.	Shell Caribbean Petroleum Co.
27.	Ford Motor Co.	63.	Signal Oil & Gas Co.
		94.	Sinclair Oil Corp.
5.	General Dynamics Corp.	44.	Socony Mobil Oil Co.
6.	General Electric Co.	12.	Sperry Rand Corp.
19.	General Motors Corp.	39.	Standard Oil Co. (California)
38.	General Precision Equipment Corp.	83.	Standard Oil Co. (Indiana)
25.	General Telephone & Electronics Corp.	33.	Standard Oil Co. (New Jersey)
13.	General Tire & Rubber Co.	91.	Stanford Research Institute (N)
50.	Goodyear Tire & Rubber Co.	65.	Sverdrup & Parcel, Inc.
11.	Grumman Aircraft Engineering Corp.	59.	System Development Corp. (N)
90.	Gyrodyne Co. of America, Inc.		
		42.	Texaco, Inc.
74.	Hardeman-Monier-Hutcherson (JV)	80.	Texas Instruments, Inc.
92.	Hardeman-Morrison-Knudsen (JV)	26.	Textron, Inc.
73.	Hayes International Corp.	20.	Thiokol Chemical Corp.
76.	Hazeltine Corp.	46.	Thompson-Ramo-Wooldridge, Inc.
36.	Hercules Powder Co.		
41.	Honeywell, Inc.	84.	Union Oil Co. of California
15.	Hughes Aircraft Co.	8.	United Aircraft Corp.
		79.	United States Steel Corp.
14.	International Business Machines Corp.	99.	Universal American Corp.
57.	International Harvester Co.		
18.	International Telephone & Telegraph Corp.	81.	Vitro Corp. of America
		55.	Western Union Telegraph Co.
58.	Johns Hopkins University (N)	78.	Westinghouse Air Brake Co.
		23.	Westinghouse Electric Corp.

(N) - Non-Profit Contractors.
(JV) - Joint Venture

100 COMPANIES AND THEIR SUBSIDIARIES LISTED ACCORDING TO
NET VALUE OF MILITARY PRIME CONTRACT AWARDS

Fiscal Year 1964
(1 July 1963 - 30 June 1964)

Rank	Companies	Millions of Dollars	Percent of U.S. Total	Cumulative Percent of U. S. Total
	U. S. TOTAL a/	$25,163.7	100.0%	100.0%
	TOTAL, 100 COMPANIES AND THEIR SUBSIDIARIES b/	18,484.8	73.4	73.4
1.	LOCKHEED AIRCRAFT CORP.	1,357.0	5.4	
	Lockheed Air Terminal, Inc.	(-)0.3	-	
	Puget Sound Bridge & Dry Dock Co.	98.7	0.4	
	Total	1,455.4	5.8	5.8
2.	BOEING CO.	1,365.2	5.4	11.2
3.	McDONNELL AIRCRAFT CORP.	1,155.5	4.6	
	Rycon Mfg. Co.	1.9	d/	
	Total	1,157.4	4.6	15.8
4.	NORTH AMERICAN AVIATION, INC.	1,019.5	4.1	19.9
5.	GENERAL DYNAMICS CORP.	986.7	3.9	23.8
6.	GENERAL ELECTRIC CO.	892.6	3.5	27.3
7.	AMERICAN TELEPHONE & TELEGRAPH CO.	155.3	0.6	
	Chesapeake & Potomac Tel. Co.	2.2	d/	
	Mountain States Tel. & Tel. Co.	1.6	d/	
	New England Tel. & Tel. Co.	0.3	d/	
	New Jersey Bell Tel. Co.	0.4	d/	
	New York Telephone Co.	0.1	d/	
	Northwestern Bell Tel. Co.	0.4	d/	
	Pacific Northwest Bell Tel. Co.	0.1	d/	
	Pacific Tel. & Tel. Co.	0.6	d/	
	Southern Bell Tel. & Tel. Co.	1.6	d/	
	Southwestern Bell Tel. Co.	1.2	d/	
	Teletype Corp.	19.4	0.1	
	Western Electric Co.	452.4	1.8	
	Total	635.6	2.5	29.8
8.	UNITED AIRCRAFT CORP.	625.0	2.5	
	Vector Mfg. Co.	0.4	d/	
	Total	625.4	2.5	32.3
9.	MARTIN-MARIETTA CORP.	474.7	1.9	
	Bunker-Ramo Corp.	1.5	d/	
	Total	476.2	1.9	34.2
10.	NEWPORT NEWS SHIPBUILDING & DRY DOCK CO.	400.2	1.6	35.8
11.	GRUMMAN AIRCRAFT ENGINEERING CORP.	395.6	1.6	37.4
12.	SPERRY RAND CORP.	373.9	1.5	38.9

Rank	Companies	Millions of Dollars	Percent of U.S. Total	Cumulative Percent of U. S. Total
13.	GENERAL TIRE & RUBBER CO.	$ 4.3	d/	
	Aerojet-Delft Corp.	0.5	d/	
	Aerojet-General Corp.	345.1	1.4	
	Aerojet-General Shipyards, Inc.	0.9	d/	
	Space Electronics Corp.	0.5	d/	
	Space General Corp.	13.1	0.1	
	Total	364.4	1.5	40.4
14.	INTERNATIONAL BUSINESS MACHINES CORP.	332.0	1.3	
	Science Research Associates	0.1	d/	
	Service Bureau Corp.	0.3	d/	
	Total	332.4	1.3	41.7
15.	HUGHES AIRCRAFT CO.	288.7	1.2	42.9
16.	AVCO CORP.	278.7	1.1	44.0
17.	BENDIX CORP.	248.5	1.0	
	Bendix Field Engineering Corp.	8.2	d/	
	Bendix-Westinghouse Automotive Air Brake Co.	0.2	d/	
	Cleveland Instrument Co.	c/	d/	
	Sheffield Corp.	0.5	d/	
	Total	257.4	1.0	45.0
18.	INTERNATIONAL TELEPHONE & TELEGRAPH CORP.	106.8	0.4	
	Airmatic Systems Corp.	c/	d/	
	American Cable & Radio Corp.	3.2	d/	
	Colorado Research Corp.	0.1	d/	
	Federal Electric Corp.	60.7	0.3	
	International Electric Corp.	57.3	0.2	
	ITT Bell & Gossett, Inc.	c/	d/	
	ITT Cannon Electric, Inc.	0.7	d/	
	ITT General Controls, Inc.	0.7	d/	
	ITT Gilfillan, Inc.	25.0	0.1	
	ITT Intelcom, Inc.	c/	d/	
	ITT Semi-Conductors, Inc.	0.3	d/	
	Jennings Radio Mfg. Corp.	0.2	d/	
	Kuthe Laboratories, Inc.	0.6	d/	
	Mackay Radio & Telegraph Co.	0.2	d/	
	Puerto Rico Telephone Co.	c/	d/	
	Suprenant Mfg. Co.	0.3	d/	
	Total	256.1	1.0	46.0
19.	GENERAL MOTORS CORP.	255.8	1.0	47.0
20.	THIOKOL CHEMICAL CORP.	251.2	1.0	
	Shawnee Industries, Inc.	2.4	d/	
	Total	253.6	1.0	48.0
21.	RAYTHEON CO.	248.8	1.0	
	Machlett Laboratories, Inc.	4.2	d/	
	Total	253.0	1.0	49.0

Rank	Companies	Millions of Dollars	Percent of U.S. Total	Cumulative Percent of U. S. Total
22.	LING-TEMCO-VOUGHT, INC.	$ 231.3	1.0	
	Altec Lansing Corp.	0.1	d/	
	Altec Service Corp.	c/	d/	
	Continental Electronics Mfg. Co.	9.6	d/	
	Continental Electronics Systems, Inc.	1.8	d/	
	F F & M Electronics, Inc.	0.2	d/	
	Kentron Corp.	0.1	d/	
	Temco Electronics & Missiles Co.	3.7	d/	
	Temco Electronics Display Systems	0.7	d/	
	Total	247.5	1.0	50.0
23.	WESTINGHOUSE ELECTRIC CORP.	235.9	1.0	
	Bryant Electric Co.	0.5	d/	
	Thermo King Corp.	0.5	d/	
	Total	236.9	1.0	51.0
24.	RADIO CORP. OF AMERICA	233.5	1.0	
	RCA Defense Electronics Corp.	0.1	d/	
	Total	233.6	1.0	52.0
25.	GENERAL TELEPHONE & ELECTRONICS CORP.	0.0	0.0	
	Automatic Electric Sales Corp.	19.1	0.1	
	General Telephone & Electronics Laboratories, Inc.	0.7	d/	
	General Telephone Co. of the Southwest	c/	d/	
	Lenkurt Electric Co., Inc.	6.6	d/	
	Sylvania Electric Products, Inc.	202.3	0.8	
	Total	228.7	0.9	52.9
26.	TEXTRON, INC.	0.9	d/	
	Accessory Products Corp.	0.1	d/	
	Allegany Instrument Co.	c/	d/	
	Bell Aerospace Corp.	210.2	0.9	
	Dalmo Victor Co.	0.9	d/	
	Jones & Lamson Machine Co.	0.6	d/	
	Nuclear Metals, Inc.	0.2	d/	
	Pittsburgh Steel Foundry Corp.	0.1	d/	
	Speidel Corp.	c/	d/	
	Textron Electronics Inc.	2.3	d/	
	Textron Oregon, Inc.	1.0	d/	
	Townsend Co.	c/		
	Total	216.3	0.9	53.8
27.	FORD MOTOR CO.	66.4	0.3	
	Philco Corp.	144.8	0.5	
	Total	211.2	0.8	54.6

Rank	Companies	Millions of Dollars	Percent of U.S. Total	Cumulative Percent of U. S. Total
28.	LITTON INDUSTRIES, INC.	$ 4.1	d/	
	Adler Electronics, Inc.	13.2	0.1	
	Aero Service Corp.	0.5	d/	
	Airtron, Inc.	0.2	d/	
	Clifton Precision Products Co., Inc.	0.2	d/	
	Emertron, Inc.	0.8	d/	
	Ingalls Shipbuilding Corp.	57.3	0.2	
	Litton Electron Tube Corp.	0.1	d/	
	Litton Precision Products, Inc.	1.0	d/	
	Litton Systems, Inc.	131.6	0.5	
	McKiernan-Terry Corp.	0.4	d/	
	Monroe Calculating Machine Co., Inc.	0.2	d/	
	Westrex Corp.	0.4	d/	
	Winchester Electronics, Inc.	c/	d/	
	Total	210.0	0.8	55.4
29.	DOUGLAS AIRCRAFT CO.	203.2	0.8	56.2
30.	CHRYSLER CORP.	170.2	0.7	56.9
31.	NORTHROP CORP.	136.6	0.6	
	Astro Technology Corp.	0.1	d/	
	Page Communications Engineers, Inc.	28.2	0.1	
	Total	164.9	0.7	57.6
32.	PAN AMERICAN WORLD AIRWAYS, INC.	164.4	0.7	58.3
33.	STANDARD OIL CO. (NEW JERSEY)	0.0	0.0	
	Esso International, Inc.	99.3	0.4	
	Esso Research & Engineering Co.	3.7	d/	
	Esso Standard Eastern, Inc.	0.2	d/	
	Gilbert & Barker Mfg. Co.	c/	d/	
	Humble Oil & Refining Co.	57.9	0.2	
	Jersey Production Research Co.	0.1	d/	
	Total	161.2	0.6	58.9
34.	KAISER INDUSTRIES CORP.	0.1	d/	
	Kaiser Aerospace & Electronics Corp.	1.3	d/	
	Kaiser (Henry J.) Co.	1.0	d/	
	Kaiser Jeep Corp e/	128.9	0.5	
	Kaiser Steel Corp	0.8	d/	
	National Steel & Shipbuilding Co.	19.6	0.1	
	Total	151.7	0.6	59.5
35.	F M C CORP.	130.7	0.5	
	Northern Ordnance, Inc.	10.7	d/	
	Total	141.4	0.5	60.0
36.	HERCULES POWDER CO.	136.9	0.5	60.5
37.	COLLINS RADIO CO.	129.0	0.5	61.0

Rank	Companies	Millions of Dollars	Percent of U.S. Total	Cumulative Percent of U. S. Total
38.	GENERAL PRECISION EQUIPMENT CORP.	$ 0.0	0.0	
	General Precision, Inc.	124.4	0.5	
	Graflex, Inc.	0.8	a/	
	Strong Electric Corp.	c/	a/	
	Total	125.2	0.5	61.5
39.	STANDARD OIL COMPANY (CALIFORNIA)	67.4	0.3	
	American Bitumuls & Asphalt Co.	c/	a/	
	Cal-Ky Oil Co.	8.5	a/	
	California Chemical Co.	0.1	a/	
	California Oil Co.	3.7	a/	
	California Research Corp.	0.1	a/	
	Caltex Oil Products Co. f/	37.5	0.2	
	Caltex Philippines, Inc. f/	0.1	a/	
	Community Oil Co.	0.4	a/	
	Standard Oil Co. of Texas	4.6	a/	
	Total	122.4	0.5	62.0
40.	MORRISON-KNUDSEN COMPANY, INC.; UTAH CONSTRUCTION & MINING CO.; PERINI CORP; and C. H. LEAVELL & CO.	121.5	0.5	62.5
41.	HONEYWELL, INC.	107.5	0.4	62.9
42.	TEXACO, INC.	22.2	0.1	
	Caltex Oil Products Co. f/	37.5	0.2	
	Caltex Philippines, Inc. f/	0.1	a/	
	Paragon Oil Co.	3.4	a/	
	Texaco Experiment, Inc.	2.1	a/	
	Texaco Export, Inc.	37.0	0.2	
	Texaco Puerto Rico, Inc.	1.6	a/	
	Texaco Trinidad, Inc.	0.2	a/	
	White Fuel Co., Inc.	1.6	a/	
	Total	105.7	0.4	63.3
43.	MASSACHUSETTS INSTITUTE OF TECHNOLOGY	98.2	0.4	63.7
44.	SOCONY MOBIL OIL CO.	79.4	0.3	64.0
45.	AEROSPACE CORP.	76.2	0.3	64.3
46.	THOMPSON-RAMO-WOOLDRIDGE, INC.	13.3	0.1	
	Good-All Electric Mfg. Co.	c/	a/	
	Magna Corp.	0.1	a/	
	Marlin-Rockwell Corp.	0.8	a/	
	Pacific Semiconductors	0.1	a/	
	Radio Condenser Co.	0.1	a/	
	Radio Industries, Inc.	0.3	a/	
	Ross Gear & Tool Co. Inc.	0.3	a/	
	Space Technology Laboratories, Inc.	59.3	0.2	
	Total	74.3	0.3	64.6

Rank	Companies	Millions of Dollars	Percent of U.S. Total	Cumulative Percent of U. S. Total
47.	CONTINENTAL MOTORS CORP.	$ 52.4	0.2	
	Continental Aviation & Engineering Corp.	17.6	0.1	
	Gray Marine Motor Co.	0.1	d/	
	Wisconsin Motors Corp.	0.5	d/	
	Total	70.6	0.3	64.9
48.	MAGNAVOX CO.	69.4	0.3	65.2
49.	du PONT (E. I.) de NEMOURS & CO.	9.9	d/	
	Remington Arms Co., Inc.	59.2	0.3	
	Total	69.1	0.3	65.5
50.	GOODYEAR TIRE & RUBBER CO.	27.6	0.1	
	Goodyear Aerospace Corp	39.9	0.2	
	Kelly-Springfield Tire Co.	c/	d/	
	Motor Wheel Corp.	0.9	d/	
	Total	68.4	0.3	65.8
51.	REPUBLIC AVIATION CORP.	66.9	0.3	66.1
52.	OLIN MATHIESON CHEMICAL CORP.	66.2	0.3	66.4
53.	BURROUGHS CORP.	65.0	0.3	
	Burroughs Control Corp.	0.4	d/	
	Total	65.4	0.3	66.7
54.	MORRISON-KNUDSEN CO.,INC.; PERINI CORP.; and HARDEMAN (PAUL), INC.	64.9	0.3	67.0
55.	WESTERN UNION TELEGRAPH CO.	59.0	0.2	67.2
56.	LEAR-SIEGLER, INC.	57.2	0.2	
	Hallamore Electronics Co.	c/	d/	
	Lear-Siegler Services, Inc.	c/	d/	
	Rett Electronics, Inc.	1.7	d/	
	Total	58.9	0.2	67.4
57.	INTERNATIONAL HARVESTER CO.	46.1	0.2	
	Hough (Frank G.) Co.	8.8	d/	
	MacLeod & Co.	0.9	d/	
	Total	55.8	0.2	67.6
58.	JOHNS HOPKINS UNIVERSITY	54.9	0.2	67.8
59.	SYSTEM DEVELOPMENT CORP	53.6	0.2	68.0
60.	CURTISS-WRIGHT CORP.	51.2	0.2	68.2
61.	AMERICAN MACHINE & FOUNDRY CO.	50.4	0.2	
	A M F International Co.	c/	d/	
	Cuno Engineering Corp.	0.2	d/	
	Total	50.6	0.2	68.4

Rank	Companies	Millions of Dollars	Percent of U.S. Total	Cumulati Percent U.S. Tot
62.	DAY & ZIMMERMAN, INC.	$ 48.6	0.2	68.6
63.	SIGNAL OIL AND GAS CO.	6.1	d/	
	Garrett Corp.	41.4	0.2	
	Petroleum Heat & Power, Inc.	c/	d/	
	Southland Oil Corp.	0.1	d/	
	T K M Electric Corp.	0.1	d/	
	Total	47.7	0.2	68.8
64.	ASIATIC PETROLEUM CORP.	45.3	0.2	69.0
65.	SVERDRUP & PARCEL, INC.	0.9	d/	
	A R O, Inc.	44.0	0.2	
	Total	44.9	0.2	69.2
66.	CUTLER-HAMMER, INC.	43.0	0.2	69.4
67.	SHELL CARIBBEAN PETROLEUM CO.	24.4	0.1	
	International Lubricant Corp.	0.7	d/	
	Shell Oil Co.	17.2	0.1	
	Total	42.3	0.2	69.6
68.	KAMAN AIRCRAFT CORP.	42.1	0.2	69.8
69.	ATLANTIC RESEARCH CORP.	40.9	0.2	
	Flight Sciences Laboratory, Inc.	0.1	d/	
	Northeastern Engineering, Inc.	0.5	d/	
	Total	41.5	0.2	70.0
70.	EASTMAN KODAK CO.	39.2	0.2	
	Eastman Chemical Products, Inc.	c/	d/	
	Eastman Kodak Stores, Inc.	1.7	d/	
	Recordak Corp.	0.5	d/	
	Total	41.4	0.2	70.2
71.	CONTROL DATA CORP.	40.4	0.2	
	Control Corp.	0.1	d/	
	Rabinow Electronics, Inc.	0.7	d/	
	Total	41.2	0.2	70.4
72.	CONTINENTAL OIL CO.	34.2	0.2	
	Douglas Oil Co. of Calif.	2.6	d/	
	Malco Refineries, Inc.	1.6	d/	
	Western Oil & Fuel Co.	1.3	d/	
	Total	39.7	0.2	70.6
73.	HAYES INTERNATIONAL CORP.	35.8	0.1	70.7
74.	HARDEMAN (PAUL), INC.; CONCRETE INDUSTRIES (MONIER) LTD.; and HUTCHERSON BROS. PTY., LTD.	35.0	0.1	70.8

Rank	Companies	Millions of Dollars	Percent of U.S. Total	Cumulative Percent of U. S. Total
75.	CITIES SERVICE CO.	$ 0.0	0.0	
	Cities Service Gas Co.	0.5	d/	
	Cities Service Oil Co.	34.2	0.1	
	Total	34.7	0.1	70.9
76.	HAZELTINE CORP.	34.6	0.1	71.0
77.	MITRE CORP.	34.5	0.1	71.1
78.	WESTINGHOUSE AIR BRAKE CO.	0.8	d/	
	George E. Failing Co.	0.3	d/	
	Le Tourneau-Westinghouse Co.	3.5	d/	
	Melpar, Inc.	29.7	0.1	
	Microwave Physics Corp.	0.1	d/	
	Total	34.4	0.1	71.2
79.	UNITED STATES STEEL CORP.	34.0	0.1	71.3
80.	TEXAS INSTRUMENTS, INC.	32.7	0.1	
	Metals & Controls, Inc.	0.3	d/	
	Total	33.0	0.1	71.4
81.	VITRO CORP. OF AMERICA	32.9	0.1	71.5
82.	RICHFIELD OIL CORP.	31.8	0.1	71.6
83.	STANDARD OIL CO. (INDIANA)	0.0	0.0	
	American Oil Co.	34.6	0.1	
	Amoco Chemicals Corp.	(-)3.3	-	
	Total	31.3	0.1	71.7
84.	UNION OIL CO. OF CALIFORNIA	31.3	0.1	
	Collier Carbon & Chemical Corp.	c/	d/	
	Total	31.3	0.1	71.8
85.	BETHLEHEM STEEL CORP.	0.0	0.0	
	Bethlehem Steel Co.	30.0	0.1	
	Bethlehem Steel Export Corp.	0.7	d/	
	Total	30.7	0.1	71.9
86.	ELECTRONIC COMMUNICATIONS, INC.	26.1	0.1	
	Benson Mfg. Co.	c/	d/	
	Standard Precision, Inc.	4.5	d/	
	Total	30.6	0.1	72.0
87.	AMERICAN BOSCH ARMA CORP.	30.0	0.1	72.1
88.	AMERICAN SHIP BUILDING CO.	29.7	0.1	72.2
89.	FIRESTONE TIRE & RUBBER CO.	29.3	0.1	
	Dayton Tire & Rubber Co.	0.3	d/	
	Total	29.6	0.1	72.3

Rank	Companies	Millions of Dollars	Percent of U.S. Total	Cumulative Percent of U. S. Total
90.	GYRODYNE CO. OF AMERICA, INC.	$ 29.2	0.1	72.4
91.	STANFORD RESEARCH INSTITUTE	28.7	0.1	72.5
92.	HARDEMAN (PAUL), INC. & MORRISON-KNUDSEN CO., INC.	27.4	0.1	72.6
93.	FAIRCHILD-HILLER CORP.	15.1	0.1	
	Hiller Aircraft Co.	12.2	d/	
	Total	27.3	0.1	72.7
94.	SINCLAIR OIL CORP.	0.0	0.0	
	Sinclair Refining Co.	26.6	0.1	
	Sinclair Petrochemicals. Inc.	c/	d/	
	Total	26.6	0.1	72.8
95.	KIEWIT (PETER) SONS' CO.	25.9	0.1	72.9
96.	RYAN AERONAUTICAL CO.	25.0	0.1	73.0
97.	DYNALECTRON CORP.	25.0	0.1	73.1
98.	SANDERS ASSOCIATES, INC.	24.5	0.1	73.2
99.	UNIVERSAL AMERICAN CORP.	0.1	d/	
	Amron Corp.	16.4	0.1	
	Hardeman (Paul), Inc.	8.0	d/	
	Total	24.5	0.1	73.3
100.	LEAVELL, C. H., CO. & KIEWIT (PETER) SONS' CO.	22.9	0.1	73.4

a Net value of new procurement actions minus cancellations, terminations and other credit transactions. The data include debit and credit procurement actions of $10,000 or more, under military supply, service and construction contracts for work in the U. S.; plus awards to listed companies and other identifiable U. S. companies for work overseas. Procurement actions include definitive contracts, the obligated portions of letter of intent and letter contracts, purchase orders, job orders, task orders, delivery orders, and any other orders against existing contracts. The data do not include that part of open-end or indefinite quantity contracts that have not been translated into specific orders on business firms. The data do not include purchase commitments or pending cancellations that have not yet become mutually binding agreements between the government and the company.

b The assignment of subsidiaries to parent companies is based on stock ownership of 50% or more by the parent company, as indicated by data published in standard industrial reference sources. The company totals do not include contracts made by other U. S. Government agencies and financed with Department of Defense funds, or contracts awarded in foreign nations through their respective governments. The company names and corporate structures are those in effect as of 30 June 1964. Only those subsidiaries are shown for which procurement actions have been reported.

c Less than $50,000.

d Less than 0.05%.

ᵉ Includes $41.3 million in prime contracts awarded to Studebaker Corp. for 5-ton trucks prior to the acquisition by Kaiser-Jeep Corp. in February 1964 of Studebaker production facilities in South Bend, Indiana.
ᶠ Stock ownership is equally divided between Standard Oil Co. of California and Texaco, Inc.; half of the total of military awards is shown under each of the parent companies.

OFFICE OF THE SECRETARY OF DEFENSE

DEPARTMENT OF DEFENSE

500 Contractors Listed According to Net Value of Military Prime Contract Awards for Experimental, Developmental, Test and Research Work

Fiscal Year 1963

The attached report shows 500 military prime contractors listed according to the net value of awards of $10,000 or more for experimental, developmental, test and research work (EDTR) during fiscal year 1963. The list is arranged in three sections. The first section includes 377 U.S. business firms; the second section includes 119 educational institutions, government agencies and other non-profit institutions, and the third section includes 4 foreign contractors.

Of the 500 contractors on the fiscal year 1963 list, 125, or one out of four, were contractors who did not appear on the fiscal year 1962 list. Of the 377 business firms appearing on the current list, 118, or about one out of three, were small business firms.

In addition to the 500 listed contractors, there were 1,339 other contractors that received prime contract awards of $10,000 or more for EDTR work during fiscal year 1963, making a total of 1,839 contractors in all. Of this total, 324 were U.S. non-profit institutions, 119 were foreign contractors, and 1,396 were U.S. business firms. Of the latter, 565 were large business firms, and 831, or 59.5%, were small business firms.

The contractors with the largest value of awards are engaged in research, development, test or production of missiles, aircraft, ships, and other highly complex military materiel. In fiscal year 1963, 88.6% of all EDTR awards of $10,000 or more to U.S. business firms was for work connected with missiles, aircraft, ships, and electronics programs.

OFFICE OF THE SECRETARY OF DEFENSE

This fiscal year 1963 edition of the 500 largest prime contractors for military experimental, developmental, test and research work (EDTR) has been reproduced from accounting machine tabulations. Because of certain limitations of the machine facilities, it was necessary to use nonstandard abbreviations in some cases, and to use a slant (/) instead of an ampersand (&). However, the basic information is the same as that contained in previous reports; i.e., all prime contracts of $10,000 or more for EDTR work were included.

The presentation of data differs in the following principal respects:

1. In previous reports, a single entry was shown for each contractor and the location was where the largest amount of prime contract work was scheduled to be performed. This report shows all locations where the prime contractor was expected to perform the work. Generally, the location is a contractor's plant, laboratory, or other contractor facility. However, if the work was scheduled to be performed at a Defense activity—such as installation, test and check-out at a missile site—that location is the one given, rather than the contractor's plant.

2. Formerly, contractors were separately ranked in each section so that there was a No. 1 business firm and a No. 1 non-profit institution. In this report contractors in all sections are ranked in a single sequence, so that only one contractor in the report is No. 1. The alphabetical index shows the section in which each contractor is located and his rank.

3. Foreign firms, which formerly were included in the section with government agencies and other nonprofit institutions, have been broken out into a separate section.

INDEX OF 500 LARGEST MILITARY
PRIME CONTRACTORS FOR EXPERIMENTAL, DEVELOPMENTAL,
TEST AND RESEARCH WORK

Fiscal Year 1963

RANK & LIST*		CONTRACTOR	RANK & LIST*		CONTRACTOR
90	B	A C F INDUSTRIES INC	233	B	ASTRODATA INC
466	B	A F N INC	439	B	ASTROPOWER INC
32	B	A R O INC	416	B	ASTROSYSTEMS INTERNATIONAL INC
457	B	A R T ELECTRONICS INC	43	B	ATLANTIC RESEARCH CORP
128	B	ACOUSTICA ASSOCIATES INC	302	B	AUSTIN CO
440	B	ADAPTRONICS INC	250	F	AUSTRALIA COMMONWEALTH OF
346	B	ADCOLE CORP	387	B	AUTOMETRIC CORP
379	B	ADMIRAL CORP	15	B	AVCO CORP
148	B	AERO GEO ASTRO CORP	263	B	AVIEN INC
8	B	AEROJET GENERAL CORP	339	B	BAIRD ATOMIC INC
155	B	AERONCA MANUFACTURING CORP	496	B	BALDWIN ELECTRONICS INC
431	B	AEROPROJECTS INC	401	B	BARKLEY / DEXTER INC
18	N	AEROSPACE CORP	209	B	BARNES ENGINEERING CO
490	B	AEROSPACE RESEARCH CORP	89	N	BATTELLE MEMORIAL INSTITUTE
360	B	AEROSPACE RESEARCH INC	328	B	BAUSCH / LOMB OPTICAL CO
194	B	AIR PRODUCTS - CHEMICALS INC	139	B	BECKMAN INSTRUMENTS INC
377	B	AIR REDUCTION CO INC	152	B	BEECH AIRCRAFT CORP
157	B	AIRCRAFT ARMAMENTS INC	370	B	BELL - HOWELL CO
495	B	AIRTRONICS INC	46	B	BELL AEROSPACE CORP
216	N	ALASKA UNIVERSITY OF	325	B	BELOCK INSTRUMENT CORP
150	B	ALL AMERICAN ENGINEERING CO	25	B	BENDIX CORP
369	B	ALLEGHENY LUDLUM STEEL CORP	347	B	BERGEN RESEARCH ENGINEERING INC
264	B	ALLIED CHEMICAL CORP	136	B	BISSETT BERMAN CORP
198	B	ALLIED RESEARCH ASSOCIATES INC	462	B	BLASS ANTENNA ELECTRONICS CORP
341	B	ALLIS CHALMERS MFG CO	249	B	BLISS E W CO
241	B	ALLIS LOUIS CO	5	B	BOEING CO
319	B	AMCEL PROPULSION INC	234	B	BOLT BERANEK NEWMAN INC
187	B	AMERICAN AIR FILTER CO INC	436	B	BOONSHAFT / FUCHS INC
378	B	AMERICAN ASTROPHYSICS	202	B	BOOZ ALLEN APPLIED RESEARCH INC
44	B	AMERICAN BOSCH ARMA CORP	210	B	BORG WARNER CORP
446	B	AMERICAN BRAKE SHOE CO	278	N	BOSTON COLLEGE
217	B	AMERICAN CYANAMID CO	428	B	BOWLES ENGINEERING CORP
166	B	AMERICAN ELECTRONIC LABS INC	424	B	BRADDOCK DUNN / MCDONALD INC
467	N	AMERICAN INSTITUTE OF RESEARCH	178	N	BROOKLYN POLYTECHNIC INSTITUTE O
38	B	AMERICAN MACHINE - FOUNDRY CO	335	B	BROWN ENGINEERING CO
314	B	AMERICAN OIL CO	130	N	BROWN UNIVERSITY
231	B	AMERICAN OPTICAL CO	227	B	BUDD CO THE
484	B	AMERICAN POWER JET CO INC	388	B	BUDD ELECTRONICS INC
118	B	AMERICAN SCIENCE - ENGINEERING I	235	B	BURNS - ROE INC
189	N	AMERICAN UNIVERSITY	54	B	BURROUGHS CORP
386	B	AMOCO CHEMICALS CORP	229	B	C E I R INC
171	B	AMPEX CORP	477	B	CADILLAC GAGE CO
257	B	AMPHENOL BORG ELECTRONICS CORP	247	N	CALIFORNIA INSTITUTE OF TECHNOLO
220	N	ANALYTIC SERVICES INC	48	N	CALIFORNIA UNIVERSITY
195	B	ANTENNA SYSTEMS INC	398	B	CALLERY CHEMICAL CO INC
402	B	ARGUS INDUSTRIES INC	192	F	CANADIAN COMMERCIAL CORP
260	B	ARINC RESEARCH CORP	437	B	CARBORUNDUM CO
403	N	ARIZONA UNIVERSITY OF	196	N	CARNEGIE INSTITUTE TECHNOLOGY
51	N	ARMOUR RESEARCH FOUNDATION	447	N	CASE INSTITUTE OF TECHNOLOGY
299	B	ASSOCIATED AERO SCIENCE LABS INC	112	B	CATERPILLAR TRACTOR CO

*B = Business Firm
 F = Foreign Contractor
 N = Non-Profit Institution

INDEX OF 500 LARGEST MILITARY
PRIME CONTRACTORS FOR EXPERIMENTAL, DEVELOPMENTAL,
TEST AND RESEARCH WORK
Fiscal Year 1963

RANK & LIST*		CONTRACTOR	RANK & LIST*		CONTRACTOR
373	N	CATHOLIC UNIVERSITY	197	N	DUKE UNIVERSITY
243	B	CELANESE CORP OF AMERICA	204	B	DUNLAP / ASSOCIATES
351	B	CHAMBERLAIN CORP	102	B	DUPONT E I DE NEMOURS / CO
410	B	CHESAPEAKE INSTRUMENT	185	B	DYNALECTRON CORP
214	B	CHICAGO AERIAL INDUSTRIES	313	B	DYNAMICS RESEARCH CORP
106	N	CHICAGO UNIVERSITY	340	B	DYNATECH CORP
69	B	CHRYSLER CORP	182	B	EASTMAN KODAK CO
323	B	CHU ASSOCIATES	375	B	EBERLINE INSTRUMENT CORP
426	B	CINCINNATI MILLING – GRINDING MC	87	B	EDGERTON GERMESHAUSEN GRIER
238	N	CINCINNATI UNIVERSITY	170	B	EDO CORP
357	B	CLARK BROS CO	199	B	EITEL MCCULLOUGH INC
452	B	CLARK DAVID CO INC	300	B	ELECTRO INTERNATIONAL INC
143	B	CLEVITE CORP	344	B	ELECTRO MECHANICAL RESEARCH INC
327	B	COHU ELECTRONICS INC	366	B	ELECTRO MECHANICS INC
50	B	COLLINS RADIO CO	83	B	ELECTRO OPTICAL SYSTEMS INC
237	N	COLORADO UNIVERSITY	481	B	ELECTROMAGNETIC RESEARCH CORP
154	B	COLUMBIA BROADCASTING SYSTEM	294	B	ELECTRONIC COMMUNICATIONS INC
42	N	COLUMBIA UNIVERSITY	359	B	ELECTRONIC ENGINEERING CO OF CAL
256	B	COMPUTER CONTROL CO INC	394	B	ELECTRONIC SPECIALTY CO
321	B	COMSTOCK WESCOTT INC	434	B	ELGIN NATIONAL WATCH CO
121	B	CONDUCTRON CORP	372	B	EMERSON ELECTRIC MANUFACTURING C
368	B	CONSOLIDATED ELECTRODYNAMICS COR	285	B	EMERTRON INC
295	B	CONSOLIDATED SYSTEMS CORP	422	B	ENGELHARD INDUSTRIES INC
100	B	CONTINENTAL AVIATION – ENGR CORP	134	B	ESSO RESEARCH / ENGINEERING CO
86	B	CONTINENTAL ELECTRONICS MFG CO	261	B	ETHYL CORP
91	B	CONTINENTAL MOTORS CORP	107	B	F M C CORP
63	B	CONTROL DATA CORP	113	B	FAIRCHILD CAMERA / INSTRUMENT CO
460	B	CONTROL EQUIPMENT CORP	80	B	FAIRCHILD STRATOS CORP
108	B	COOK ELECTRIC CO	253	B	FEDERAL ELECTRIC CORP
396	N	COORDINATING RESEARCH COUNCIL	391	B	FIELD EMISSION CORP
64	N	CORNELL AERNAUTICAL LABORATORY	248	B	FIRESTONE TIRE / RUBBER CO
92	N	CORNELL UNIVERSITY	454	N	FLIGHT SAFETY FOUNDATION
98	B	CUBIC CORP	283	N	FLORIDA UNIVERSITY
76	B	CURTISS WRIGHT CORP	26	B	FORD MOTOR CO
60	B	CUTLER HAMMER INC	70	N	FRANKLIN INSTITUTE OF PENNSYLVAN
417	N	DARTMOUTH COLLEGE	62	B	GARRETT CORP
316	B	DATA CORP	223	B	GENERAL AMERICAN TRANSPORTATION
330	B	DATA DISPLAY INC	151	B	GENERAL APPLIED SCIENCE LAB
291	B	DATA PRODUCTS CORP	266	B	GENERAL ATRONICS CORP
381	B	DATA TECHNOLOGY	2	B	GENERAL DYNAMICS CORP
173	B	DAYSTROM INC	7	B	GENERAL ELECTRIC CO
153	N	DAYTON UNIVERSITY	438	B	GENERAL INSTRUMENT CORP
114	B	DECO ELECTRONICS INC	84	B	GENERAL MILLS INC
226	B	DEFENSE RESEARCH CORP	16	B	GENERAL MOTORS CORP
116	N	DENVER RESEARCH INSTITUTE	30	B	GENERAL PRECISION INC
161	N	DENVER UNIVERSITY OF	246	B	GENERAL TELEPHONE – ELECTR LAB I
311	B	DEWEY G C CO	444	B	GENERAL TIME CORP
491	B	DIKEWOOD CORP	290	B	GENISCO INC
9	B	DOUGLAS AIRCRAFT CO INC	104	B	GEOPHYSICS CORP OF AMERICA
147	B	DOW CHEMICAL CO	93	N	GEORGE WASHINGTON UNIVERSITY

*B = Business Firm
F = Foreign Contractor
M = Non-Profit Institution

INDEX OF 500 LARGEST MILITARY
PRIME CONTRACTORS FOR EXPERIMENTAL, DEVELOPMENTAL,
TEST AND RESEARCH WORK

Fiscal Year 1963

RANK & LIST*		CONTRACTOR	RANK & LIST*		CONTRACTOR
463	N	GEORGIA INSTITUTE TECH	374	N	IOWA STATE UNIVERSITY OF
279	N	GEORGIA TECH RESEARCH INSTITUTE	476	N	ISOMET CORP
97	B	GEOTECHNICAL CORP	251	B	ISOTOPES INC
215	B	GIANNINI CONTROLS CORP	191	D	ITEK CORP
487	B	GIBBS / COX INC	21	N	JOHNS HOPKINS UNIVERSITY
421	B	GICHNER FRED S IRON WORKS INC	179	B	KAMAN AIRCRAFT CORP
67	B	GILFILLAN CORP	470	B	KENTON ENGINEERING CORP
433	B	GILLILAND INSTRUMENT CO	94	B	KENTRON HAWAII LTD
383	B	GOODRICH B F CO	305	B	KOLLMORGEN CORP
409	B	GOODRICH HIGH VOLTAGE ASTRONS	73	B	KOLLSMAN INSTRUMENT CORP
40	B	GOODYEAR AIRCRAFT CORP	443	B	KORAD CORP
384	B	GOODYEAR TIRE / RUBBER CO	393	N	LABORATORY FOR ELECTRONICS INC
488	B	GRACE W R / CO	79	B	LAND AIR INC
322	B	GRACO ENGINEERING — MFG CO	190	B	LEAR-SIEGLER INC
82	B	GRUMMAN AIRCRAFT ENGINEERING CO	177	B	LEAR SIEGLER SERVICE INC
455	B	GYRODYNE CO OF AMERICA	132	B	LETOURNEAU WESTINGHOUSE CO
111	B	H R B SINGER INC	343	N	LIGHTNING / TRANSIENTS RESRCH IN
122	B	HALLICRAFTERS CO	414	B	LINDBERG ENGINEERING CO
167	B	HARDEMAN PAUL INC	35	B	LING TEMCO VOUGHT INC
498	B	HARSHAW CHEMICAL CO	85	B.	LITTLE ARTHUR D INC
124	N	HARVARD UNIVERSITY	228	B	LITTON ELECTRON TUBE CORP
208	B	HARVEY ALUMINUM INC	144	B	LITTON INDUSTRIES
492	N	HASKIN LABORATORIES INC	52	B	LITTON SYSTEMS INC
458	N	HAWAII UNIVERSITY	1	B	LOCKHEED AIRCRAFT CORP
213	B	HAYES INTERNATIONAL CORP	183	B	LOCKHEED ELECTRONICS CO
159	B	HAZELTINE CORP	259	B	LOCKHEED PROPULSION CO
312	B	HAZELTON LABORATORIES INC	471	B	LOGICON INC
11	B	HERCULES POWDER CO	245	N	LOGISTICS MANAGEMENT INSTITUTE
342	B	HEWLETT PACKARD CO	221	B	LORAL ELECTRONICS CORP
429	B	HIGH VOLTAGE ENGINEERING CORP	419	N	LOUISIANA STATE UNIVERSITY OF
244	B	HILLER AIRCRAFT CORP	461	N	LOVELACE FOUNDATION
160	B	HOFFMAN ELECTRONICS CORP	268	N	LOWELL TECH INSTITUTE
412	B	HORIZONS INC	289	B	M B ASSOCIATES
141	B	HOUSTON FEARLESS CORP	389	B	M H D RESEARCH INC
169	B	HOWARD RESEARCH CORP	465	B	M S A RESEARCH CORP
331	N	HUDSON INSTITUTE	297	B	MACHLETT LABORATORIES INC
17	B	HUGHES AIRCRAFT CO	137	B	MAGNAVOX CO
119	B	HUGHES TOOL CO	405	B	MANAGEMENT SYSTEMS CORP
497	B	HUMAN SCIENCES RESEARCH INC	380	B	MANLABS INC
222	B	HYCON MANUFACTURING CO	255	B	MANSON LABORATORIES INC
365	B	HYDRONAUTICS INC	276	B	MARCHETTI J W INC
332	N	ILLINOIS INSTITUTE TECHNOLOGY	413	B	MARKS POLARIZED CORP
72	N	ILLINOIS UNIVERSITY	47	B	MARQUARDT CORP
303	N	INDIANA UNIVERSITY	3	B	MARTIN MARIETTA CORP
88	N	INSTITUTE FOR DEFENSE ANALYSIS	186	N	MARYLAND UNIVERSITY OF
57	B	INTERNATIONAL BUSINESS MACHINES	20	N	MASSACHUSETTS INSTITUTE TECH
41	B	INTERNATIONAL ELECTRIC CORP	310	B	MATERIALS RESEARCH CORP
358	B	INTERNATIONAL HARVESTER CO	58	B	MAXSON ELECTRONICS CORP
22	B	INTERNATIONAL TELEPHONE / TEL CO	68	B	MCDONNELL AIRCRAFT CORP
277	B	INTERSTATE ELECTRONICS CORP	392	F	MCGILL UNIVERSITY

* B = Business Firm
F = Foreign Contractor
N = Non-Profit Institution

INDEX OF 500 LARGEST MILITARY
PRIME CONTRACTORS FOR EXPERIMENTAL, DEVELOPMENTAL, TEST AND RESEARCH WORK
Fiscal Year 1963

RANK & LIST*		CONTRACTOR	RANK & LIST*		CONTRACTOR
162	B	MCGRAW HILL PUBLISHING CO INC	404	B	PACIFIC CAR FOUNDRY CO
473	B	MECHANICAL TECHNOLOGY INC	390	B	PACIFIC CRANE / RIGGING CO
61	B	MELPAR INC	468	B	PACIFIC SEMICONDUCTORS INC
298	B	METEOROLOGY RESEARCH INC	453	B	PAGE COMMUNICATION ENGINEER INC
205	N	MIAMI UNIVERSITY OF	13	B	PAN AMERICAN WORLD AIRWAYS INC
53	N	MICHIGAN UNIVERSITY OF	435	B	PARAMETRICS INC
174	B	MICROWAVE ASSOCIATES INC	362	B	PARKE DAVIS / CO
286	B	MICROWAVE ELECTRONICS CORP	66	B	PARSONS CO INC RALPH M
138	N	MIDWEST RESEARCH INSTITUTE	317	B	PENNSALT CHEMICALS CORP
350	B	MILGO ELECTRONICS CORP	96	N	PENNSYLVANIA STATE UNIVERSITY
269	B	MINE SAFETY APPLIANCES CO	99	N	PENNSYLVANIA UNIVERSITY OF
34	B	MINNEAPOLIS HONEYWELL REG CO INC	181	B	PERKIN ELMER CORP
175	N	MINNESOTA UNIVERSITY OF	288	B	PFIZER CHAS — CO
472	N	MISSISSIPPI STATE UNIVERSITY	28	B	PHILCO CORP
33	N	MITRE CORP	475	B	PHYSICS INTERNATIONAL CO
145	B	MONSANTO CHEMICAL CO	385	B	PICKARD / BURNS INC
395	B	MONSANTO RESEARCH CORP	367	N	PITTSBURGH UNIVERSITY OF
349	B	MORSE INSTRUMENT CO	101	B	PLANNING RESEARCH CORP
56	B	MOTOROLA INC	287	B	PLASMADYNE CORP
133	B	N T W MISSILE ENGINEERING INC	275	B	PNEUMODYNAMICS CORP
156	N	NATIONAL ACADEMY OF SCIENCES	267	B	POLARAD ELECTRONICS CORP
193	B	NATIONAL CASH REGISTER CO INC	459	B	POLYTECHNIC ENGINEERING CO
201	B	NATIONAL CO INC	486	B	POWER GENERATORS INC
345	B	NATIONAL ENGINEERING SCIENCE CO	140	N	PRINCETON UNIVERSITY
315	B	NATIONAL RESEARCH CORP	425	N	PUERTO RICO UNIVERSITY
308	B	NATIONAL SCIENTIFIC LABS INC	212	N	PURDUE RESEARCH FOUNDATION
382	N	NEW MEXICO SCHOOL OF MINES	371	N	PURDUE UNIVERSITY
165	N	NEW MEXICO STATE UNIVERSITY	500	B	R C A SERVICE CO
356	N	NEW MEXICO UNIVERSITY OF	482	B	R F COMMUNICATIONS ASSOCIATES IN
442	N	NEW YORK STATE UNIVERSITY OF	282	B	RADIATION AT STANFORD
109	N	NEW YORK UNIVERSITY	142	B	RADIATION INC
4	B	NORTH AMERICAN AVIATION INC	483	B	RADIATION SYSTEMS INC
432	N	NORTH CAROLINA STATE COLLEGE	14	B	RADIO CORP OF AMERICA
219	N	NORTHEASTERN UNIVERSITY	45	N	RAND CORP
296	B	NORTHERN ORDNANCE INC	376	B	RAVEN INDUSTRIES INC
36	B	NORTHROP CORP	274	B	RAYMOND ENGINEERING LAB INC
135	N	NORTHWESTERN UNIVERSITY	31	B	RAYTHEON CO
361	N	NOTRE DAME UNIVERSITY OF	469	B	REEVES INSTRUMENT CORP
354	B	NUCLEAR METALS INC	406	N	RENSSELAER POLYTECHNIC INSTITUTE
493	B	OCEANICS INC	158	B	REPUBLIC AVIATION CORP
117	N	OHIO STATE UNIVERSITY	258	B	REPUBLIC STEEL CORP
336	N	OHIO STATE UNIV RESERCH FOUNDATI	78	N	RESEARCH ANALYSIS CORP
353	N	OKLAHOMA STATE UNIVERSITY OF	450	N	RESEARCH TRIANGLE INSTITUTE
304	N	OKLAHOMA UNIVERSITY OF	280	N	RHODE ISLAND UNIVERSITY
149	B	OLIN MATHIESON CHEMICAL CORP	200	B	RICHARDSON MERRELL INC
203	B	OPERATIONS RESEARCH INC	499	B	ROCKET POWER INC
485	B	OPTICS TECHNOLOGY INC	105	B	ROHM — HAAS CO
464	B	OREGON METALLURGICAL CORP	415	N	RUTGERS UNIVERSITY
355	N	OREGON STATE COLLEGE	126	B	RYAN AERONAUTICAL CO
418	B	P R D ELECTRONICS INC	172	B	S F D LABORATORIES INC

* B = Business Firm
F = Foreign Contractor
N = Non-Profit Institution

INDEX OF 500 LARGEST MILITARY
PRIME CONTRACTORS FOR EXPERIMENTAL, DEVELOPMENTAL, TEST AND RESEARCH WORK

Fiscal Year 1963

RANK & LIST*		CONTRACTOR	RANK & LIST*		CONTRACTOR
407	N	SAINT LOUIS UNIVERSITY	270	B	TEXTRON ELECTRONICS INC
77	B	SANDERS ASSOCIATES INC	448	B	TEXTRON INC
399	B	SARGENT – GREENLEAF INC	23	B	THIOKOL CHEMICAL CORP
489	B	SCANWELL LABORATORIES INC	324	B	THOMPSON JOHN I CO
293	B	ECOPE INC	55	B	THOMPSON RAMO WOOLDRIDGE INC
211	B	SHELL OIL CO	265	B	TRACERLAB INC
326	B	SIERRA RESEARCH CORP	240	B	TRACOR INC
445	B	SMITH H C CONSTRUCTION CO	329	N	TRAVELERS RESEARCH CENTER
400	N	SMITHSONIAN INSTITUTE	423	N	TUFTS COLLEGE
129	B	SOLAR AIRCRAFT CO	163	B	TYCO INC
224	N	SOUTHERN CALIFORNIA UNIVERSITY	75	B	UNION CARBIDE CORP
318	N	SOUTHERN RESEARCH INSTITUTE	24	B	UNITED AIRCRAFT CORP
123	N	SOUTHWEST RESEARCH INSTITUTE	301	B	UNITED ELECTRODYNAMICS INC
71	B	SPACE GENERAL CORP	479	F	UNITED KINGDOM ADMIRALTY
364	B	SPACE SCIENCES INC	348	B	UNITED NUCLEAR CORP
27	B	SPACE TECHNOLOGY LABS INC	427	N	UNITED STATES ATOMIC ENERGY COMM
184	B	SPARTON CORP	127	N	UNITED STATES COMMERCE DEPT
10	B	SPERRY RAND CORP	59	N	UNITED STATES NATL AERO SPACE AG
39	N	STANFORD RESEARCH INSTITUTE	309	N	UNITED STATES PUBLIC HEALTH SERV
65	N	STANFORD UNIVERSITY	284	B	UNITED STATES RUBBER CO
363	B	STELMA INC	292	B	UNTED STATES STEEL CORP
252	N	STEVENS INSTITUTE OF TECHNOLOGY	242	B	UNITED STATES UNDERSEAS CABLE CO
164	B	SUNDSTRAND CORP	29	B	UNITED TECHNOLOGY CORP
19	B	SYLVANIA ELECTRIC PRODUCTS INC	334	B	UNIVERSAL CYCLOPS STEEL CORP
225	N	SYRACUSE UNIVERSITY	420	B	UNIVERSAL MATCH CORP
176	N	SYRACUSE UNIVERSITY RESEARCH COR	207	N	UTAH STATE UNIVERSITY
74	N	SYSTEM DEVELOPMENT CORP	188	N	UTAH UNIVERSITY OF
408	B	SYSTEMS RESEARCH GROUP	474	N	VANDERBILT UNIVERSITY
236	B	SYSTEMS RESEARCH LABORATORIES IN	430	N	VARE INDUSTRIES INC
320	B	SYSTEMS TECHNOLOGY INC	131	B	VARIAN ASSOCIATES
168	B	T R G INC	494	N	VIRGINIA MEDICAL COLLEGE OF
271	B	TASKER INSTRUMENT CORP	281	N	VIRGINIA UNIVERSITY OF
451	B	TE CO	37	B	VITRO CORP OF AMERICA
478	N	TEAGUE WALTER DORWIN	480	B	WARNER – SWASEY CO
333	B	TECHNICAL APPLIANCE CORP	441	B	WASHINGTON TECHNOLOGICAL ASSOC
103	B	TECHNICAL OPERATIONS	95	N	WASHINGTON UNIVERSITY OF
337	B	TECHNICAL RESEARCH	125	B	WATKINS JOHNSON CO
206	B	TECHNITROL ENGINEERING CO	232	N	WENTWORTH INSTITUTE
239	B	TECHNOLOGY INC	6	B	WESTERN ELECTRIC CO
120	B	TELECOMPUTING CORP	411	N	WESTERN RESERVE UNIVERSITY
273	B	TELEDYNE SYSTEMS INC	12	B	WESTINGHOUSE ELECTRIC CORP
146	B	TEMCO ELECTRONICS – MISSILES CO	218	B	WHIRLPOOL CORP
449	N	TENNESSEE UNIVERSITY	180	N	WISCONSIN UNIVERSITY OF
115	N	TENNESSEE VALLEY AUTHORITY	397	B	WOLF RESEARCH – DEVELOPMENT COR
230	B	TEXACO EXPERIMENT INC	81	N	WOODS HOLE OCEANOGRAPHIC INST
272	B	TEXACO INC	306	B	WYLE LABORATORIES
262	N	TEXAS A – M RESEARCH FOUNDATION	254	N	YALE UNIVERSITY
49	B	TEXAS INSTRUMENTS INC	456	B	YARDNEY ELECTRIC CORP
110	N	TEXAS UNIVERSITY OF	307	B	ZENITH RADIO CORP
338	N	TEXAS WESTERN COLLEGE	352	B	ZIMNEY CORP

*B = Business Firm
 F = Foreign Contractor
 M = Non-Profit Institution

SECTION I - U.S. BUSINESS FIRMS
Fiscal Year 1963

RANK	NAME OF CONTRACTOR AND LOCATION		THOUSANDS OF DOLLARS
1	LOCKHEED AIRCRAFT CORP		547,824*
	BURBANK	CALIFORN	5,227
	LOMPOC	CALIFORN	89
	LOS ANGELES	CALIFORN	249
	MAYWOOD	CALIFORN	17-
	PALMDALE	CALIFORN	136
	PALO ALTO	CALIFORN	722
	REDLANDS	CALIFORN	3,021
	SUNNYVALE	CALIFORN	536,692
	COCOA BEACH	FLORIDA	47
	MARIETTA	GEORGIA	1,034
	NETUCHEN	NEW JERS	23
	PLAINFIELD	NEW JERS	323
	CLARK	NEW JERS	264
	WRIGHT PATTERS	OHIO	14
2	GENERAL DYNAMICS CORP		519,314*
	LOMPOC	CALIFORN	22,995
	POMONA	CALIFORN	63,952
	SAN DIEGO	CALIFORN	337,546
	GROTON	CONN	1,724
	COCOA BEACH	FLORIDA	11,263
	ROCHESTER	NEW YORK	5,338
	JOHNSVILLE	PA	21
	DAINGERFIELD	TEXAS	5,334
	FORT WORTH	TEXAS	71,048
	CAMP MCCOY	WISCONSI	93
3	MARTIN MARIETTA CORP		457,891*
	TUCSON	ARIZONA	114,613
	CHICO	CALIFORN	2,600
	LOMPOC	CALIFORN	19,220
	DENVER	COLORADO	99,187
	LITTLETON	COLORADO	141,553
	COCOA	FLORIDA	24
	ORLANDO	FLORIDA	15,282
	WICHITA	KANSAS	31
	BALTIMORE	MARYLAND	53,294
	MIDDLE RIVER	MARYLAND	1,910
	FORT MONMOUTH	NEW JERS	20
	WRIGHT PATTERS	OHIO	150
	RAPID CITY	SDAK	10,007
4	NORTH AMERICAN AVIATION INC		394,373*
	ANAHEIM	CALIFORN	15,832
	BURBANK	CALIFORN	59
	CANOGA PARK	CALIFORN	36,331
	DOWNEY	CALIFORN	162,776
	EL SEGUNDO	CALIFORN	39
	INGLEWOOD	CALIFORN	98
	LOS ANGELES	CALIFORN	174,395
	NEOSHO	MISSOURI	977
	RENO	NEVADA	1,112
	COLUMBUS	OHIO	1,621
	MCGREGOR	TEXAS	1,133
5	BOEING CO		363,701*
	LOMPOC	CALIFORN	14,877
	SANTA MARIA	CALIFORN	3,200
	COCOA BEACH	FLORIDA	40
	WICHITA	KANSAS	8,707
	KNOB NOSTER	MISSOURI	860
	GREAT FALLS	MONTANA	3,006
	MINOT	NDAK	1,160
	MORTON	PA	622
	RAPID CITY	SDAK	77
	RENTON	WASHINGT	53
	SEATTLE	WASHINGT	329,509
	CHEYENNE	WYOMING	1,390
6	WESTERN ELECTRIC CO		273,959*
	LOMPOC	CALIFORN	574
	SANTA MONICA	CALIFORN	77,186
	COCOA BEACH	FLORIDA	943
	ORLANDO	FLORIDA	2,368
	KEARNY	NEW JERS	303
	MONMOUTH	NEW JERS	10,568
	MURRAY HILL	NEW JERS	692
	WHIPPANY	NEW JERS	193,738
	LAS CRUCES	NEW MEXI	418
	WHIPPANY	NEW JERS	190
	NEW YORK	NEW YORK	8,773
	BURLINGTON	NCAR	32,099
	WINSTON SALEM	NCAR	4,639

RANK	NAME OF CONTRACTOR AND LOCATION		THOUSANDS OF DOLLARS
6	WESTERN ELECTRIC CO		*
	ALLENTOWN	PA	52
		T T PAC	1,416
7	GENERAL ELECTRIC CO		255,792*
	HUNTSVILLE	ALABAMA	22-
	PHOENIX	ARIZONA	99-
	LAYTONVILLE	CALIFORN	92
	LOMPOC	CALIFORN	3,506
	LOS ANGELES	CALIFORN	136
	PALO ALTO	CALIFORN	579
	PLEASANTON	CALIFORN	793
	SAN JOSE	CALIFORN	285
	SANTA BARBARA	CALIFORN	2,720
	WASHINGTON	DC	143
	DAYTONA BEACH	FLORIDA	78
	OWENSBORO	KENTUCKY	454
	BALTIMORE	MARYLAND	25
	BETHESDA	MARYLAND	100
	FITCHBURG	MASS	40
	HOLYOKE	MASS	113
	LYNN	MASS	1,533
	PITTSFIELD	MASS	11,434
	WEST LYNN	MASS	8,536
	BALLSTON SPA	NEW YORK	16
	BUFFALO	NEW YORK	42
	ITHACA	NEW YORK	922
	JOHNSTON CITY	NEW YORK	1,694
	SCHENECTADY	NEW YORK	31,283
	SYRACUSE	NEW YORK	44,477
	UTICA	NEW YORK	3,758
	CINCINNATI	OHIO	11,898
	EVENDALE	OHIO	7,101
	W P A F B	OHIO	148
	OKLAHOMA CITY	OKLAHOMA	911
	ERIE	PA	363
	KING OF PRUSS	PA	271
	PHILADELPHIA	PA	110,486
	PITTSBURGH	PA	450
	VALLEY FORGE	PA	1,137
	IRMO	SCAR	79
	BURLINGTON	VERMONT	4,509
	LYNCHBURG	VIRGINIA	5,714
	ROANOKE	VIRGINIA	16
	WAYNESBORO	VIRGINIA	21
		B W INDI	100
8	AEROJET GENERAL CORP		202,177*
	YUMA	ARIZONA	677
	AZUSA	CALIFORN	38,711
	DOWNEY	CALIFORN	10,356
	EL MONTE	CALIFORN	76
	SACRAMENTO	CALIFORN	150,953
	VALPARAISO	FLORIDA	1,406
9	DOUGLAS AIRCRAFT CO INC		159,471*
	EL SEGUNDO	CALIFORN	495
	LOMPOC	CALIFORN	21,645
	LONG BEACH	CALIFORN	1,920
	SANTA MONICA	CALIFORN	131,267
	TORRANCE	CALIFORN	369
	COCOA BEACH	FLORIDA	623
	CHARLOTTE	NCAR	328
	TULSA	OKLAHOMA	2,824
10	SPERRY RAND CORP		134,195*
	PHOENIX	ARIZONA	1,573
	EDWARDS	CALIFORN	198
	SAN DIEGO	CALIFORN	78
	SAN FRANCISCO	CALIFORN	30
	NEW LONDON	CONN	1,494
	SOUTH NORWALK	CONN	41-
	WATERBURY	CONN	16
	CLEARWATER	FLORIDA	705
	COCOA BEACH	FLORIDA	140
	GAINESVILLE	FLORIDA	86
	OLDSMAR	FLORIDA	422
	BEDFORD	MASS	24
	SUDBURY	MASS	90
	DETROIT	MICHIGAN	59
	ST PAUL	MINNESOT	21,524
	FORT MONMOUTH	NEW JERS	32
	ALAMOGORDO	NEW MEXI	27
	CARLE PLACE	NEW YORK	271
	GARDEN CITY	NEW YORK	179

S = Small Business

SECTION I - U.S. BUSINESS FIRMS
Fiscal Year 1963

RANK	NAME OF CONTRACTOR AND LOCATION		THOUSANDS OF DOLLARS
10	SPERRY RAND CORP		*
	GREAT NECK	NEW YORK	56,764
	ILION	NEW YORK	327
	LONG ISLAND CI	NEW YORK	4,200
	SYOSSET	NEW YORK	43,009
	TULSA	OKLAHOMA	17
	BLUE BELL	PA	279
	PHILADELPHIA	PA	39
	SALT LAKE CIT	UTAH	1,667
	CHARLOTTESVILL	VIRGINIA	1,026
11	HERCULES POWDER CO		132,722*
	WILMINGTON	DELAWARE	19,748
	KENVIL	NEW JERS	32
	PORT EWEN	NEW YORK	31
	BACCHUS	UTAH	3,000
	MAGNA	UTAH	79,515
	ROCKET CENTER	WVA	30,396
12	WESTINGHOUSE ELECTRIC CORP		130,952*
	NEWBURY PARK	CALIFORN	327
	SUNNYVALE	CALIFORN	31,023
	WASHINGTON	DC	501
	BALTIMORE	MARYLAND	29,335
	ELKRIDGE	MARYLAND	370
	WINTHROP	MASS	31
	DETROIT	MICHIGAN	97
	BLOOMFIELD	NEW JERS	50
	RED BANK	NEW JERS	43
	BUFFALO	NEW YORK	90
	ELMIRA	NEW YORK	601
	HORSEHEADS	NEW YORK	127
	DAYTON	OHIO	269
	LIMA	OHIO	474
	BLAIRSVILLE	PA	170
	CHESWICK	PA	62
	LARGE	PA	82
	EAST PITTSBURG	PA	18
	FOREST HILL	PA	40
	LESTER	PA	124
	PHILADELPHIA	PA	50
	PITTSBURGH	PA	65,985
	SHARON	PA	116
	TRAFFORD	PENNSYVA	366
	YOUNGWOOD	PA	661
13	PAN AMERICAN WORLD AIRWAYS INC		121,215*
	TUCSON	ARIZONA	9,705
	COCOA BEACH	FLORIDA	109,836
		CANADA	1,674
14	RADIO CORP OF AMERICA		111,389*
	FORT HUACHUCA	ARIZONA	83
	TUCSON	ARIZONA	21
	PASADENA	CALIFORN	102
	VAN NUYS	CALIFORN	320
	WASHINGTON	DC	1,564
	COCOA BEACH	FLORDIA	1,502
	BETHESDA	MARYLAND	36
	FORT MEADE	MARYLAND	1,768
	BURLINGTON	MASS	265
	WINTHROP	MASS	25,557
	CAMDEN	NEW JERS	180
	HARRISON	NEW JERS	30,746
	MOORESTOWN	NEW JERS	1,659
	MORRISTOWN	NEW JERS	26,652
	PRINCETON	NEW JERS	450
	SOMERVILLE	NEW JERS	12,447
	NEW YORK	NEW YORK	465
	CROYDON	PA	4,329
			63
	LANCASTER	PA	1,447
	PHILADELPHIA	PA	1,642
	ALEXANDRIA	VIRGINIA	114
25	AVCO CORP		104,692*
	NEW LONDON	CONN	26
	STRATFORD	CONN	25,026
	CONNERSVILLE	INDIANA	26
	RICHMOND	INDIANA	1,784
	EVERETT	MASS	5,431
	LOWELL	MASS	16
	WILMINGTON	MASS	71,195
	WINTHROP	MASS	90
15	AVCO CORP		*
	CINCINNATI	OHIO	730
	EVENDALE	OHIO	60
	TULSA	OKLAHOMA	78
	WILLIAMSPORT	PA	235
16	GENERAL MOTORS CORP		86,819*
	EL SEGUNDO	CALIFORN	29
	GOLETA	CALIFORN	1,554
	SANTA BARBARA	CALIFORN	295
	PANAMA CITY	FLORIDA	30
	ANDERSON	INDIANA	283
	INDIANAPOLIS	INDIANA	6,057
	KOKOMO	INDIANA	397
	DETROIT	MICHIGAN	219
	FLINT	MICHIGAN	54
	MILFORD	MICHIGAN	76
	PONTIAC	MICHIGAN	88
	WARREN	MICHIGAN	346
	CLEVELAND	OHIO	17,627
	HUDSON	OHIO	27
	MILWAUKEE	WISCONSI	57,477
	OAK CREEK	WISCONSI	2,260
17	HUGHES AIRCRAFT CO		80,044*
	FORT HUACHUCA	ARIZONA	68
	TUCSON	ARIZONA	121
	CULVER CITY	CALIFORN	65,871
	EL SEGUNDO	CALIFORN	131
	FULLERTON	CALIFORN	9,160
	INGLEWOOD	CALIFORN	152
	LOS ANGELES	CALIFORN	3,225
	MALIBU	CALIFORN	874
	NEWPORT BEACH	CALIFORN	191
	OCEANSIDE	CALIFORN	202
	FLOYD	NEW YORK	49
19	SYLVANIA ELECTRIC PRODUCTS INC		71,331*
	MOUNTAIN VIEW	CALIFORN	29,153
	NEEDHAM HEIGH	MASS	3,941
	WALTHAM	MASS	15,448
	WOBURN	MASS	201
	ANN ARBOR	MICHIGAN	12
	LAS CRUCES	NEW MEXI	245
	BUFFALO	NEW YORK	22,268
	TOWANDA	PA	63
22	INTERNATIONAL TELEPHONE / TEL CO		65,334*
	LOMPOC	CALIFORN	3,864
	SAN FERNANDO	CALIFORN	710
	CHICAGO	ILLINOIS	5,149
	FORT WAYNE	INDIANA	271
	TOPEKA	KANSAS	70
	L.NCOLN	NEBRASKA	31
	OMAHA	NEBRASKA	67
	CLIFTON	NEW JERS	16
	NUTLEY	NEW JERS	10,610
	PARAMUS	NEW JERS	44,074
	ROSWELL	NEW MEXI	100
	ALTUS	OKLAHOMA	250
	SPOKANE	WASHINGT	42
	CHEYENNE	WYOMING	80
23	THIOKOL CHEMICAL CORP		62,542*
	HUNTSVILLE	ALABAMA	5,769
	LOS ANGELES	CALIFORN	26
	BALTIMORE	MARYLAND	75
	ELKTON	MARYLAND	1,410
	DENVILLE	NEW JERS	6,649
	TRENTON	NEW JERS	261
	BRISTOL	PA	183
	BRIGHAM CITY	UTAH	47,958
	LOGAN	UTAH	11
24	UNITED AIRCRAFT CORP		57,031*
	EDWARDS A F B	CALIFORN	2,570
	SAN DIEGO	CALIFORN	269
	SUNNYVALE	CALIFORN	534
	BROAD BROOK	CONN	56
	EAST HARTFORD	CONN	37,752
	HARTFORD	CONN	2,963
	MIDDLETOWN	CONN	40
	NORWALK	CONN	500
	STRATFORD	CONN	10,328

S = Small Business

SECTION I - U.S. BUSINESS FIRMS
Fiscal Year 1963

RANK	NAME OF CONTRACTOR AND LOCATION		THOUSANDS OF DOLLARS
24	UNITED AIRCRAFT CORP		*
	WINDSOR LOCKS	CONN	887
	WEST PALM BEAC	FLORIDA	1,032
	FORT BENNING	GEORGIA	100
25	BENDIX CORP		93,118*
	EDWARDS	CALIFORN	31
	LOS ANGELES	CALIFORN	18
	NORTH HOLLYWOO	CALIFORN	2,813
	SYLMAR	CALIFORN	21
	VAN NUYS	CALIFORN	483
	MISHAWAKA	INDIANA	11,201
	SOUTH BEND	INDIANA	49
	DAVENPORT	IOWA	147
	BALTIMORE	MARYLAND	14,426
	TOWSON	MARYLAND	7,292
	ANN ARBOR	MICHIGAN	10,263
	DETROIT	MICHIGAN	207
	SOUTHFIELD	MICHIGAN	835
	EATONTOWN	NEW JERS	122
	TETERBORO	NEW JERS	3,528
	SIDNEY	NEW YORK	196
	YORK	PA	695
		CANADA	491
26	FORD MOTOR CO		53,055*
	NEWPORT BEACH	CALIFORN	50,278
	DEARBORN	MICHIGAN	2,082
	DETROIT	MICHIGAN	617
	ALEXANDRIA	VIRGINIA	76
27	SPACE TECHNOLOGY LABS INC		52,691*
	CANOGA PARK	CALIFORN	35
	LOS ANGELES	CALIFORN	27,641
	REDONDO BEACH	CALIFORN	16,364
	SAN BERNARDINO	CALIFORN	8,638
	COCOA BEACH	FLORIDA	13
28	PHILCO CORP		51,777*
	CHINA LAKE	CALIFORN	23
	MENLO PARK	CALIFORN	26
	PALO ALTO	CALIFORN	43,000
	FORT MEADE	MARYLAND	181
	BLUE BELL	PA	805
	LANSDALE	PA	268
	PHILADELPHIA	PA	6,132
	WILLOW GROVE	PA	592
		UN KINGD	750
29	UNITED TECHNOLOGY CORP		51,720*
	SUNNYVALE	CALIFORN	51,720
30	GENERAL PRECISION INC		47,715*
	CHINA LAKE	CALIFORN	82
	FLORIN	CALIFORN	250
	GLENDALE	CALIFORN	1,046
	SAN MARCOS	CALIFORN	325
	SUNNYVALE	CALIFORN	48
	SILVER SPRING	MARYLAND	70
	CLIFTON	NEW JERS	29
	LITTLE FALLS	NEW JERS	44,375
	BINGHAMTON	NEW YORK	1,170
	NEW YORK	NEW YORK	43
	PLEASANTVILLE	NEW YORK	277
31	RAYTHEON CO		44,654*
	GOLETA	CALIFORN	293
	OXNARD	CALIFORN	468
	SAN FRANCISCO	CALIFORN	10
	SANTA BARBARA	CALIFORN	275
	MAKU	HAWAII	18
	BEDFORD	MASS	22,082
	BOSTON	MASS	190
	BURLINGTON	MASS	1,042
	LEXINGTON	MASS	5,844
	NEWTON	MASS	80
	NORWOOD	MASS	5,058
	SUDBURY	MASS	2,422
	WALTHAM	MASS	4,049
	WAYLAND	MASS	2,087
	FORT MONMOUTH	NEW JERS	36
	NEWPORT	RI	294
	PORTSMOUTH	RI	1,970
	FORT BLISS	TEXAS*	181
		CANAL ZO	255

RANK	NAME OF CONTRACTOR AND LOCATION		THOUSANDS OF DOLLARS
32	A R O INC		38,497*
	TULLAHOMA	TENNESSE	38,497
34	MINNEAPOLIS HONEYWELL REG CO INC		31,874*
	DUARTE	CALIFORN	804
	LOS ANGELES	CALIFORN	382
	WEST COVINA	CALIFORN	26
	DENVER	COLORADO	75
	ST PETERSBURG	FLORIDA	12,515
	BOSTON	MASS	80
	HOPKINS	MINNESOT	10,612
	MINNEAPOLIS	MINNESOT	6,484
	NEW BRIGHTON	MINNESOT	22
	SEATTLE	WASHINGT	874
35	LING TEMCO VOUGHT INC		30,739*
	EL CENTRO	CALIFORN	99
	LOMPOC	CALIFORN	282
	LOS ANGELES	CALIFORN	435
	DETROIT	MICHIGAN	6,554
	MOUNT CLEMENS	MICHIGAN	6,000
	ARLINGTON	TEXAS	15
	CORPUS CHRIST	TEXAS	40-
	DALLAS	TEXAS	17,285
	GARLAND	TEXAS	39
	HAMPTON	VIRGINIA	41
		THAILAND	29
36	NORTHROP CORP		28,641*
	ANAHEIM	CALIFORN	6,106
	HAWTHORNE	CALIFORN	15,456
	NEWBURY PARK	CALIF	1,979
	PALOS VERDES	CALIFORN	191
	VAN NUYS	CALIFORN	464
	NEEDHAM HEIGHT	MASS	1,240
	NORWOOD	MASS	3,205
37	VITRO CORP OF AMERICA		25,456*
	VALPARAISO	FLORIDA	7,209
	SILVER SPRING	MARYLAND	17,481
	WEST ORANGE	NEW JERS	671
	NEW YORK	NEW YORK	95
38	AMERICAN MACHINE - FOUNDRY CO		23,389*
	CHICO	CALIFORN	3,700
	CULVER CITY	COLORADN	248
	LOMPOC	CALIFORN	1,720
	MARYSVILLE	CALIFORN	8,401
	SANTA BARBARA	CALIFORN	2,534
	DENVER	COLORADO	400
	GREENWICH	CONN	1,057
	STANFORD	CONN	2,949
	NILES	ILLINOIS	106
	BUFFALO	NEW YORK	1,951
	VANDALIA	OHIO	33
	RAPID CITY	SDAK	24
	ALEXANDRIA	VIRGINIA	264
40	GOODYEAR AIRCRAFT CORP		21,798*
	LITCHFIELD PAR	ARIZONA	4,525
	AKRON	OHIO	17,273
41	INTERNATIONAL ELECTRIC CORP		19,982*
	PARAMUS	NEW JERS	19,982
43	ATLANTIC RESEARCH CORP		17,487*
	FORT HUACHUCA	ARIZONA	382
	TUCSON	ARIZONA	634
	ARCADIA	CALIFORN	3,530
	DUARTE	CALIFORN	3,010
	EL MONTE	CALIFORN	3,380
	SAUGUS	CALIFORN	154
	WASHINGTON	DC	125
	WEST HANOVER	MASS	69
	GREEN RIVER	UTAH	700
	ALEXANDRIA	VIRGINIA	5,303
44	AMERICAN BOSCH ARMA CORP		17,353*
	GARDEN CITY	NEW YORK	17,023
	PHILADELPHIA	PA	330
46	BELL AEROSPACE CORP		15,336*
	FORT HUACHUCA	ARIZONA	142
	BUFFALO	NEW YORK	10,681

S = Small Business

SECTION I - U.S. BUSINESS FIRMS
Fiscal Year 1963

RANK	NAME OF CONTRACTOR AND LOCATION		THOUSANDS OF DOLLARS	RANK	NAME OF CONTRACTOR AND LOCATION		THOUSANDS OF DOLLARS
46	BELL AEROSPACE CORP		*	60	CUTLER HAMMER INC		*
	NIAGARA FALLS	NEW YORK	2,841		LONG ISLAND C	NEW YORK	64
	NORTH TONAWAND	NEW YORK	98		MELVILLE	NEW YORK	1,492
	WHEATFIELD	NEW YORK	22		MINEOLA	NEW YORK	14-
	FORT WORTH	TEXAS	1,528		NEW YORK	NEW YORK	1,195
	HURST	TEXAS	24		VERONA	NEW YORK	27
47	MARQUARDT CORP		13,313*	61	MELPAR INC		9,250*
	VAN NUYS	CALIFORN	13,313		DUGWAY	UTAH	150
					FALLS CHURCH	VIRGINIA	9,100
49	TEXAS INSTRUMENTS INC		12,062*	62	GARRETT CORP		9,014*
	FORT HUACHUCA	ARIZONA	27		PHOENIX	ARIZONA	7,369
	ATTLEBORO	MASS	130		LOS ANGELES	CALIFORN	1,645
	FORT MONMOUTH	NEW JERS	13	63	CONTROL DATA CORP		8,860*
	DALLAS	TEXAS	11,892		WASHINGTON	DC	267
50	COLLINS RADIO CO		11,733*		MINNEAPOLIS	MINNESOT	8,593
	BURBANK	CALIFORN	100	66	PARSONS CO INC RALPH M		8,768*
	POINT ARGUELLO	CALIFORN	957		LOS ANGELES	CALIFORN	8,571
	NEWPORT BEACH	CALIFORN	884		PASADENA	CALIFORN	197
	POINT MUGU	CALIFORN	46	67	GILFILLAN CORP		8,690*
	SANTA ANA	CALIFORN	40		AZUSA	CALIFORN	54
	CEDAR RAPIDS	IOWA	2,593		LOS ANGELES	CALIFORN	8,636
	DALLAS	TEXAS	1,722	68	MCDONNELL AIRCRAFT CORP		8,546*
	RICHARDSON	TEXAS	5,391		BURBANK	CALIFORN	21
52	LITTON SYSTEMS INC		11,352*		ST LOUIS	MISSOURI	8,525
	BEVERLY HILLS	CALIFORN	492	69	CHRYSLER CORP		8,493*
	CANOGA PARK	CALIFORN	3,356		CENTER LINE	MICHIGAN	2,261
	WOODLAND HILLS	CALIFORN	5,400		DETROIT	MICHIGAN	5,186
	COLLEGE PARK	MARYLAND	315		STERLING	MICHIGAN	238
	SILVER SPRING	MARYLAND	62		WARREN	MICHIGAN	740
	WALTHAM	MASS	444		FORT BELVOIR	VIRGINIA	68
	HARRISON	NEW JERS	729	71	SPACE GENERAL CORP		8,110*
	NEW YORK	NEW YORK	409		EL MONTE	CALIFORN	7,921
	JOHNSVILLE	PA	55		GLENDALE	CALIFORN	95
54	BURROUGHS CORP		11,232*		LOS ANGELES	CALIFORN	94
	COLORADO SPRIN	COLORADO	936	73	KOLLSMAN INSTRUMENT CORP		7,608*
	WINTHROP	MASS	16		ELMHURST	NEW YORK	7,608
	DETROIT	MICHIGAN	1,200	75	UNION CARBIDE CORP		7,400*
	BROOKLYN	NEW YORK	161		SANTA MONICA	CALIFORN	193
	JOHNSVILLE	PA	14		INDIANAPOLIS	INDIANA	266
	PAOLI	PA	8,823		KOKOMO	INDIANA	143
	PHILADELPHIA	PA	112		BOUND BROOK	NEW JERS	232
	MYRTLE BEACH	SCAR	70		NEWARK	NEW JERS	17
55	THOMPSON RAMO WOOLDRIDGE INC		10,326*		NEW YORK	NEW YORK	308
	FORT HUACHUCA	ARIZONA	2,929		TARRYTOWN	NEW YORK	720
	ANAHEIM	CALIFORN	210		TONAWANDA	NEW YORK	828
	CANOGA PARK	CALIFORN	4,361		CLEVELAND	OHIO	495
	REDONDO BEACH	CALIFORN	401		FOSTORIA	OHIO	28
	SUNNYVALE	CALIFORN	17		PARMA	OHIO	435
	CLEVELAND	OHIO	2,408		LAWRENCEBURG	TENN	1,647
56	MOTOROLA INC		10,275*		TULLAHOMA	TENN	876
	PHOENIX	ARIZONA	2,159		AUSTIN	TEXAS	38
	SCOTTSDALE	ARIZONA	4,197		BENNINGTON	VERMONT	32
	RIVERSIDE	CALIFORN	1,061		SOUTH CHARLEST	WVA	1,102
	CHICAGO	ILLINOIS	2,754	76	CURTISS WRIGHT CORP		7,015*
	FRANKLIN PARK	ILLINOIS	21		UTICA	MICHIGAN	6
	FORT MONMOUTH	NEW JERS	83		CALDWELL	NEW JERS	2,407
57	INTERNATIONAL BUSINESS MACHINES		9,999*		EAST PATERSON	NEW JERS	157
	CHINA LAKE	CALIFORN	32		WOOD RIDGE	NEW JERS	3,798
	LOS ANGELES	CALIFORN	80		WOODBRIDGE	NEW JERS	647
	SAN JOSE	CALIFORN	47	77	SANDERS ASSOCIATES INC		6,956*
	WASHINGTON	DC	1,241		BURLINGTON	MASS	152
	BETHESDA	MARYLAND	2,428		NASHUA	NH	6,749
	ROCKVILLE	MARYLAND	1,573		AVA	NEW YORK	55
	CAMBRIDGE	MASS	16	79	LAND AIR INC		6,323*
	KINGSTON	NEW YORK	959		CHICAGO	ILLINOIS	75
	NEW YORK	NEW YORK	22		HOLLOMAN AFB	NEW MEXI	19
	OWEGO	NEW YORK	972		LAS CRUCES	NEW MEXI	6,229
	POUGHKEEPSIE	NEW YORK	51	80	FAIRCHILD STRATOS CORP		6,262*
	YORKTOWN HGTS	NEW YORK	2,578		MANHATTAN BEAC	CALIFORN	93
58	MAXSON ELECTRONICS CORP		9,916*		HAGERSTOWN	MARYLAND	5,672
	LONG ISLAND CI	N Y	30				
	NEW YORK	NEW YORK	1,131				
	OLD FORGE	PA	8,755				
60	CUTLER HAMMER INC		9,529*				
	DEER PARK	NEW YORK	6,765				

S = Small Business

SECTION I - U.S. BUSINESS FIRMS
Fiscal Year 1963

RANK	NAME OF CONTRACTOR AND LOCATION		THOUSANDS OF DOLLARS
80	FAIRCHILD STRATOS CORP		*
	BAY SHORE	NEW YORK	497
82	GRUMMAN AIRCRAFT ENGINEERING CO		5,967*
	BETHPAGE	NEW YORK	5,967
83	ELECTRO OPTICAL SYSTEMS INC		5,940*
	PASADENA	CALIFORN	5,940
84	GENERAL MILLS INC		5,838*
	MINNEAPOLIS	MINNESOT	2,875
	ST PAUL	MINNESOT	2,963
85	LITTLE ARTHUR D INC		5,734*
	LOMPOC	CALIF	450
	SAN FRANCISCO	CALIFORN	149
	CAMBRIDGE	MASS	5,135
86	CONTINENTAL ELECTRONICS MFG CO		5,624*
	DALLAS	TEXAS	5,624
87	EDGERTON GERMESHAUSEN GRIER		5,427*
		CLASSIFI	68
	GOLETA	CALIFORN	251
	BOSTON	MASS	5,108
90	A C F INDUSTRIES INC		4,903*
		CLASSIFIED	93
	HYATTSVILLE	MARYLAND	698
	RIVERDALE	MARYLAND	3,486
	PARAMUS	NEW JERS	541
	ALEXANDRIA	VIRGINIA	85
91	CONTINENTAL MOTORS CORP		4,890*
	DETROIT	MICHIGAN	4,808
	MUSKEGON	MICHIGAN	82
94	KENTRON HAWAII LTD		4,700*
	POINT MUGU	CALIFORN	4,700
97	GEOTECHNICAL CORP		4,443*
	FORT SILL	OKLAHOMA	397
	DALLAS	TEXAS	853
	GARLAND	TEXAS	3,193
98	CUBIC CORP		4,439*
	SAN DIEGO	CALIFORN	4,439
100	CONTINENTAL AVIATION - ENGR CORP		4,317*
	DETROIT	MICHIGAN	4,169
	MUSKEGON	MICHIGAN	79
	TOLEDO	OHIO	69
101	PLANNING RESEARCH CORP　S		4,135*
	LOS ANGELES	CALIFORN	4,135
102	DUPONT E I DE NEMOURS / CO		4,123*
	WILMINGTON	DELAWARE	3,955
	GIBBSTOWN	NEW JERS	150
	POMPTON LAKES	NEW JERS	18
103	TECHNICAL OPERATIONS		3,929*
	FAIRBANKS	ALASKA	59
	WASHINGTON	DC	13
	HONOLULU	HAWAII	203
	BURLINGTON	MASS	2,773
	FORT BELVOIR	VIRGINIA	781
	FORT MONROE	VIRGINIA	100
104	GEOPHYSICS CORP OF AMERICA　S		3,845*
	BEDFORD	MASS	2,295
	BOSTON	MASS	1,323
	LINCOLN	MASS	26
	SALT LAKE CIT	UTAH	201
105	ROHM - HAAS CO		3,799*
	HUNTSVILLE	ALABAMA	3,799
107	F M C CORP		3,756*
	SAN JOSE	CALIFORN	2,610
	SANTA CLARA	CALIFORN	138
	BALTIMORE	MARYLAND	90
	PRINCETON	NEW JERS	864
	NEWPORT	NEW YORK	54
108	COOK ELECTRIC CO		3,733*
	EDWARDS	CALIFORN	73
	EL CENTRO	CALIFORN	43
	MARIANNA	FLA	421
	MORTON GROVE	ILLINOIS	2,886
	DAYTON	OHIO	310
111	H R B SINGER INC		3,663*
	FORT MONMOUTH	NEW JERS	24
	STATE COLLEGE	PA	3,639
112	CATERPILLAR TRACTOR CO		3,625*
	PEORIA	ILLINOIS	3,625
113	FAIRCHILD CAMERA / INSTRUMENT CO		3,525*
	LOS ANGELES	CALIFORN	49
	MOUNTAIN VIEW	CALIFORN	329
	PALO ALTO	CALIFORN	369
	CLIFTON	NEW JERS	122
	SYOSSET	NEW YORK	2,656
114	DECO ELECTRONICS INC　S		3,506*
	WASHINGTON	DC	482
	BEDFORD	MASS	29
	LEESBURG	VIRGINIA	2,995
118	AMERICAN SCIENCE - ENGINEERING I　S		3,426*
	HONOLULU	HAWAII	30
	CAMBRIDGE	MASS	3,396
119	HUGHES TOOL CO		3,342*
	CULVER CITY	CALIFORN	3,342
120	TELECOMPUTING CORP		3,280*
	LOS ANGELES	CALIFORN	50
	NORTH HOLLYWOO	CLAIFORN	19
	SAN DIEGO	CALIFORN	738
	VAN NUYS	CALIFORN	299
	ALAMOGORDO	NEW MEXI	520
	LAS CRUCES	NEW MEXI	1,516
	PLAINVIEW	NEW YORK	138
121	CONDUCTRON CORP　S		3,119*
	ANN ARBOR	MICHIGAN	3,119
122	HALLICRAFTERS CO		3,072*
	SAN BERNARDINO	CALIFORN	155
	SANTA ANA	CALIFORN	57
	CHICAGO	ILLINOIS	2,761
	DES PLAINES	ILLINOIS	99
125	WATKINS JOHNSON CO		2,991*
	PALO ALTO	CALIFORN	2,991
126	RYAN AERONAUTICAL CO		2,918*
	SAN DIEGO	CALIFORN	2,836
		THAILAND	82
128	ACOUSTICA ASSOCIATES INC		2,830*
	LOS ANGELES	CALIFORN	2,830
129	SOLAR AIRCRAFT CO		2,810*
	SAN DIEGO	CALIFORN	2,810
131	VARIAN ASSOCIATES		2,783*
	PALO ALTO	CALIFORN	2,649
	BEVERLY	MASS	134
132	LETOURNEAU WESTINGHOUSE CO		2,779*
	PEORIA	ILLINOIS	2,779
133	N T W MISSILE ENGINEERING INC　S		2,718*
	LOS ANGELES	CALIFORN	2,718
134	ESSO RESEARCH / ENGINEERING CO		2,686*
	LINDEN	NEW JERS	2,686
136	BISSETT BERMAN CORP		2,626*
	SANTA MONICA	CALIFORN	2,626
137	MAGNAVOX CO		2,619*
	LOS ANGELES	CALIFORN	40
	TORRANCE	CALIFORN	323

S = Small Business

SECTION I - U.S. BUSINESS FIRMS
Fiscal Year 1963

RANK	NAME OF CONTRACTOR AND LOCATION		THOUSANDS OF DOLLARS
137	MAGNAVOX CO		*
	URBANA	ILLINOIS	451
	FORT WAYNE	INDIANA	1,805
139	BECKMAN INSTRUMENTS INC		2,605*
	FULLERTON	CALIFORN	2,388
	RICHMOND	CALIFORN	217
141	HOUSTON FEARLESS CORP		2,517*
	BERKELEY	CALIFORN	554
	LOS ANGELES	CALIFORN	1,380
	TORRANCE	CALIFORN	272
	WASHINGTON	D C	311
142	RADIATION INC		2,503*
	MELBOURNE	FLORIDA	2,114
	ORLANDO	FLORIDA	134
	PALM BAY	FLORIDA	147
	VERONA	NEW YORK	88
143	CLEVITE CORP		2,464*
	PALO ALTO	CALIFORN	435
	CLEVELAND	OHIO	2,029
144	LITTON INDUSTRIES		2,457*
	BEVERLY HILLS	CALIFORN	194
	SAN CARLOS	CALIFORN	2,074
	COLLEGE PARK	MARYLAND	71
	MORRIS PLAINS	NEW JERS	79
	NEW YORK	NEW YORK	21
		CANADA I	18
145	MONSANTO CHEMICAL CO		2,345*
	EVERETT	MASS	1,144
	DAYTON	OHIO	1,201
146	TEMCO ELECTRONICS - MISSILES CO		2,330*
	DALLAS	TEXAS	1,287
	GARLAND	TEXAS	1,019
	GREENVILLE	TEXAS	24
147	DOW CHEMICAL CO		2,315*
	EDWARDS	CALIFORN	36
	MIDLAND	MICHIGAN	2,279
148	AERO GEO ASTRO CORP S		2,306*
	VALPARAISO	FLORIDA	105
	COLLEGE PARK	MARYLAND	172
	ALEXANDRIA	VIRGINIA	2,029
149	OLIN MATHIESON CHEMICAL CORP		2,303*
	NEW HAVEN	CONN	1,454
	EAST ALTON	ILLINOIS	11
	MARION	ILLINOIS	396
	NIAGARA FALLS	NEW YORK	442
150	ALL AMERICAN ENGINEERING CO S		2,295*
	WILMINGTON	DELAWARE	1,992
	LAKEHURST	NEW JERS	303
151	GENERAL APPLIED SCIENCE LAB S		2,287*
	HEMPSTEAD	NEW YORK	300
	WESTBURY	NEW YORK	1,987
152	BEECH AIRCRAFT CORP		2,265*
	WICHITA	KANSAS	2,265
154	COLUMBIA BROADCASTING SYSTEM		2,244*
	STAMFORD	CONN	2,244
155	AERONCA MANUFACTURING CORP		2,195*
	BALTIMORE	MARYLAND	81
	WALDORF	MARYLAND	1,851
	MIDDLETOWN	OHIO	263
157	AIRCRAFT ARMAMENTS INC		2,185*
	NORTHRIDGE	CALIFORN	24
	BALTIMORE	MARYLAND	428
	COCKEYSVILLE	MARYLAND	1,753
158	REPUBLIC AVIATION CORP		2,185*
	FARMINGDALE	NEW YORK	370
	LONG ISLAND	NEW YORK	31
	MINEOLA	NEW YORK	1,784

RANK	NAME OF CONTRACTOR AND LOCATION		THOUSANDS OF DOLLARS
159	HAZELTINE CORP		2,176*
	INDIANAPOLIS	INDIANA	17
	LITTLE NECK	NEW YORK	2,159
160	HOFFMAN ELECTRONICS CORP		2,168*
	EL MONTE	CALIFORN	27
	LOS ANGELES	CALIFORN	1,852
	SANTA BARBARA	CALIFORN	70
	DUGWAY	UTAH	219
162	MCGRAW HILL PUBLISHING CO INC		2,160*
	NEW YORK	NEW YORK	2,160.
163	TYCO INC	S	2,124*
	WALTHAM	MASS	2,126
164	SUNDSTRAND CORP		2,117*
	DENVER	COLORADO	2,086
	ROCKFORD	ILLINOIS	31
166	AMERICAN ELECTRONIC LABS INC	S	2,063*
	COLMAR	PA	1,838
	LANSDALE	PA	191
	PHILADELPHIA	PA	34
167	HARDEMAN PAUL INC		1,986*
	STANTON	CALIFORN	1,986
168	T R G INC	S	1,982*
	PALO ALTO	CALIFORN	123
	BOSTON	MASS	14
	EAST BOSTON	MASS	94
	SYOSSET	NEW YORK	1,751
169	HOWARD RESEARCH CORP	S	1,979*
	BALTIMORE	MARYLAND	22
	ARLINGTON	VIRGINIA	1,957
170	EDO CORP		1,974*
	COLLEGE POINT	NEW YORK	1,974
171	AMPEX CORP		1,958*
	LOS ANGELES	CALIFORN	21
	REDWOOD CITY	CALIFORN	1,937
172	S F D LABORATORIES INC		1,944*
	UNION	NEW JERS	1,944
173	DAYSTRON INC		1,929*
	LA JOLLA	CALIFORN	84
	NEWARK	NEW JERS	282
	POUGHKEEPSIE	NEW YORK	1,046
	ARCHBALD	PA	67
	DUGWAY	UTAH	450
174	MICROWAVE ASSOCIATES INC		1,921*
	BURLINGTON	MASS	1,921
177	LEAR SIEGLER SERVICE INC		1,841*
	ONTARIO	CALIFORN	18
	SANTA MONICA	CALIFORN	66
	ANN ARBOR	MICHIGAN	29
	GRAND RAPIDS	MICHIGAN	1,528
	LONG ISLAND CI	NEW YORK	78
	WRIGHT PATTERS	OHIO	52
	SAN ANTONIO	TEXAS	70
179	KAMAN AIRCRAFT CORP		1,827*
	COLORADO SPRI	COLORADO	1,062
	BLOOMFIELD	CONN	765
181	PERKIN ELMER CORP		1,774*
	COSTA MESA	CALIFORN	189
	LOS ANGELES	CALIFORN	167
	MALIBU	CALIFORN	36
	NORWALK	CONN	1,317
	WILTON	CONN	41
	SILVER SPRING	MARYLAND	24
182	EASTMAN KODAK CO		1,762*
	LOMPOC	CALIFORN	89
	ROCHESTER	NEW YORK	1,673
183	LOCKHEED ELECTRONICS CO		1,753*
	FORT MONMOUTH	NEW JERS	21

S = Small Business

SECTION I - U.S. BUSINESS FIRMS
Fiscal Year 1963

RANK	NAME OF CONTRACTOR AND LOCATION		THOUSANDS OF DOLLARS
183	LOCKHEED ELECTRONICS CO		*
	PLAINFIELD	NEW JERS	1,732
184	SPARTON CORP		1,685*
	JACKSON	MICHIGAN	1,685
185	DYNALECTRON CORP		1,681*
	LAS CRUCES	NEW MEXI	1,608
	GREEN RIVER	UTAH	73
187	AMERICAN AIR FILTER CO INC		1,629*
	ROCK ISLAND	ILLINOIS	356
	ST LOUIS	MISSOURI	1,273
190	LEAR SIEGLER INC		1,613*
	ANAHEIM	CALIFORN	215
	CHINA LAKE	CALIFORN	27
	SANTA MONICA	CALIFORN	393
	DEEP RIVER	CONN	97
	ANN ARBOR	MICHIGAN	170
	GRAND RAPIDS	MICHIGAN	305
	CLEVELAND	OHIO	408
191	ITEK CORP		1,579*
	PALO ALTO	CALIFORN	696
	CAMBRIDGE	MASS	7-
	LEXINGTON	MASS	806
	WALTHAM	MASS	15
	OSSINING	NEW YORK	69
193	NATIONAL CASH REGISTER CO INC		1,571*
	HAWTHORNE	CALIFORN	98
	DAYTON	OHIO	1,473
194	AIR PRODUCTS - CHEMICALS INC		1,535*
	NIMBUS	CALIFORN	71
	SANTA SUSANA	CALIFORN	1,034
	DENVER	COLORADO	59
	ALLENTOWN	PA	80
	FRANKLIN	PA	14
	PHILADELPHIA	PA	84
	TREXLERTOWN	PA	193
195	ANTENNA SYSTEMS INC S		1,526*
	MAITLAND	FLORIDA	448
	HINGHAM	MASS	1,078
198	ALLIED RESEARCH ASSOCIATES INC S		1,452*
	BOSTON	MASS	672
	CONCORD	MASS	780
199	EITEL MCCULLOUGH INC		1,445*
	SAN CARLOS	CALIFORN	1,445
200	RICHARDSON MERRELL INC		1,441*
	SWIFTWATER	PA	1,441
201	NATIONAL CO INC		1,428*
	MALDEN	MASS	1,314
	MELROSE	MASS	114
202	BOOZ ALLEN APPLIED RESEARCH INC		1,411*
	WASHINGTON	DC	104
	CHICAGO	ILLINOIS	195
	BETHESDA	MARYLAND	1,112
203	OPERATIONS RESEARCH INC S		1,389*
	SANTA MONICA	CALIFORN	32
	SILVER SPRING	MARYLAND	1,312
	CARLISLE	PA	45
204	DUNLAP / ASSOCIATES		1,384*
	STAMFORD	CONN	1,384
206	TECHNITROL ENGINEERING CO S		1,359*
	PHILADELPHIA	PA	1,359
208	HARVEY ALUMINUM INC		1,339*
	TORRANCE	CALIFORN	1,339
209	BARNES ENGINEERING CO		1,336*
	STAMFORD	CONN	1,336
210	BORG WARNER CORP		1,301*
	BELLWOOD	ILLINOIS	64
210	BORG WARNER CORP		*
	KALAMAZOO	MICHIGAN	1,237
211	SHELL OIL CO		1,300*
	EMERYVILLE	CALIFORN	571
	SAN FRANCISCO	CALIFORN	76
	HOUSTON	TEXAS	653
213	HAYES INTERNATIONAL CORP		1,263*
	BIRMINGHAM	ALABAMA	1,263
214	CHICAGO AERIAL INDUSTRIES		1,261*
	INGLEWOOD	CALIFORN	85
	BARRINGTON	ILLINOIS	1,176
215	GIANNINI CONTROLS CORP		1,257*
	DUARTE	CALIFORN	854
	SANTA ANA	CALIFORN	144
	BERWYN	PA	259
217	AMERICAN CYANAMID CO		1,241*
	STANFORD	CONN	442
	BOUND BROOK	NEW JERS	51
	WAYNE	NEW JERS	650
	NEW YORK	NEW YORK	98
218	WHIRLPOOL CORP		1,230*
	EVANSVILLE	INDIANA	1,102
	ST JOSEPH	MICHIGAN	128
221	LORAL ELECTRONICS CORP		1,198*
	NEW YORK	NEW YORK	1,198
222	HYCON MANUFACTURING CO S		1,194*
	MONROVIA	CALIFORN	1,159
	PASADENA	CALIFORN	35
223	GENERAL AMERICAN TRANSPORTATION		1,186*
	NILES	ILLINOIS	1,186
226	DEFENSE RESEARCH CORP S		1,166*
	SANTA BARBARA	CALIFORN	1,166
227	BUDD CO THE		1,164*
	LONG ISLAND CI	NEW YORK	340
	PHILADELPHIA	PA	824
228	LITTON ELECTRON TUBE CORP		1,152*
	SAN CARLOS	CALIFORN	1,152
229	C E I R INC		1,144*
	FORT HUACHUCA	ARIZONA	157
	BEVERLY HILLS	CALIFORN	103
	SAN FRANCISCO	CALIFORN	18
	SUNNYVALE	CALIFORN	149
	FORT MONMOUTH	NEW JERS	27
	ARLINGTON	VIRGINIA	690
230	TEXACO EXPERIMENT INC		1,134*
	RICHMOND	VIRGINIA	1,134
231	AMERICAN OPTICAL CO		1,107*
	SOUTHBRIDGE	MASS	557
	KEENE	NH	83
	PITTSBURGH	PA	467
233	ASTRODATA INC S		1,091*
	ANAHEIM	CALIFORN	1,091
234	BOLT BERANEK NEWMAN INC S		1,087*
	CAMBRIDGE	MASS	1,087
235	BURNS - ROE INC		1,085*
	NEW YORK	NEW YORK	817
	FORT BELVOIR	VIRGINIA	268
236	SYSTEMS RESEARCH LABORATORIES IN S		1,083*
	DAYTON	OHIO	1,083
239	TECHNOLOGY INC S		1,058*
	DAYTON	OHIO	986
	SAN ANTONIO	TEXAS	72
240	TRACOR INC S		1,045*
	AUSTIN	TEXAS	1,045

S = Small Business

SECTION I - U.S. BUSINESS FIRMS
Fiscal Year 1963

RANK	NAME OF CONTRACTOR AND LOCATION		THOUSANDS OF DOLLARS
241	ALLIS LOUIS CO		1,042*
	GREENDALE	WISCONSI	74
	MILWAUKEE	WISCONSI	968
242	UNITED STATES UNDERSEAS CABLE CO		1,042*
	WASHINGTON	DC	25
	SEATTLE	WASHINGT	850
		GERMANY	167
243	CELANESE CORP OF AMERICA		1,021*
	SUMMIT	NEW JERS	1,000
	NEW YORK	NEW YORK	21
244	HILLER AIRCRAFT CORP		1,011*
	PALO ALTO	CALIFORN	1,011
246	GENERAL TELEPHONE - ELECTR LAB I		992*
	PALO ALTO	CALIFORN	110
	BAYSIDE	NEW YORK	638
	HICKSVILLE	NEW YORK	244
248	FIRESTONE TIRE / RUBBER CO		964*
	LOS ANGELES	CALIFORN	49
	NOBLESVILLE	INDIANA	98
	CARSON CITY	NEVADA	90
	AKRON	OHIO	727
249	BLISS E W CO		955*
	WOODBINE	NEW JERS	520
	CANTON	OHIO	126
	SALEM	OHIO	309
251	ISOTOPES INC S		934*
	WESTWOOD	NEW JERS	934
253	FEDERAL ELECTRIC CORP		929*
	PARAMUS	NEW JERS	831
	VERONA	NEW YORK	98
255	HANSON LABORATORIES INC S		906*
	STAMFORD	CONN	906
256	COMPUTER CONTROL CO INC		902*
	LOS ANGELES	CALIFORN	267
	FRAMINGHAM	MASS	635
257	AMPHENOL BORG ELECTRONICS CORP		895*
	BROADVIEW	ILLINOIS	214
	CHICAGO	ILLINOIS	681
258	REPUBLIC STEEL CORP		889*
	CANTON	OHIO	16
	CLEVELAND	OHIO	873
259	LOCKHEED PROPULSION CO		888*
	AZUSA	CALIFORN	70
	REDLANDS	CALIFORN	818
260	ARINC RESEARCH CORP		887*
	WASHINGTON	DC	887
261	ETHYL CORP		883*
	BATON ROUGE	LOUISIAN	588
	DETROIT	MICHIGAN	295
263	AVIEN INC		877*
	WOODSIDE	NEW YORK	877
264	ALLIED CHEMICAL CORP		873*
	MORRISTOWN	NEW JERS	873
265	TRACERLAB INC		872*
	RICHMOND	CALIFORN	805
	WALTHAM	MASS	67
266	GENERAL ATRONICS CORP S		871*
	FORT MONMOUTH	NEW JERS	47
	BALA CYNWYD	PA	56
	CONSHOHOCKEN	PA	115
	PHILADELPHIA	PA	395
	WEST CONSHOHO	PA	209
	FORT BLISS	TEXAS	51
267	POLARAD ELECTRONICS CORP		864*
	LONG ISLAND CI	NEW YORK	846
267	POLARAD ELECTRONICS CORP		*
	NEW YORK	NEW YORK	18
269	MINE SAFETY APPLIANCES CO		843*
	CALLERY	PA	259
	PITTSBURGH	PA	584
270	TEXTRON ELECTRONICS INC		840*
	NORTH HOLLYWOO	CALIFORN	49
	SYLMAR	CALIFORN	74
	NEW HAVEN	CONN	717
271	TASKER INSTRUMENT CORP S		834*
	VAN NUYS	CALIFORN	834
272	TEXACO INC		835*
	BEACON	NEW YORK	108
	NEW YORK	NEW YORK	725
273	TELEDYNE SYSTEMS INC		831*
	HAWTHORNE	CALIFORN	831
274	RAYMOND ENGINEERING LAB INC S		826*
	MIDDLETOWN	CONN	826
275	PNEUMODYNAMICS CORP		809*
	EL SEGUNDO	CALIFORN	36
	BETHESDA	MARYLAND	379
	GRAND RAPIDS	MICHIGAN	339
	KALAMAZOO	MICHIGAN	45
	CLEVELAND	OHIO	10
276	MARCHETTI J W INC S		807*
	NATICK	MASS	807
277	INTERSTATE ELECTRONICS CORP		797*
	ANAHEIM	CALIFORN	797
282	RADIATION AT STANFORD		783*
	PALO ALTO	CALIFORN	783
284	UNITED STATES RUBBER CO		772*
	NAUGATUCK	CONN	33
	DETROIT	MICHIGAN	94
	CARSON CITY	NEVADA	89
	WAYNE	NEW JERS	556
285	EMERTRON INC		771*
	JERSEY CITY	NEW JERS	771
286	MICROWAVE ELECTRONICS CORP S		771*
	PALO ALTO	CALIFORN	771
287	PLASMADYNE CORP		764*
	SANTA ANA	CALIFORN	764
288	PFIZER CHAS -. CO		764*
	GROTON	CONN	383
	TERRE HAUTE	INDIANA	125
	NEW YORK	NEW YORK	256
289	H-B ASSOCIATES S		757*
	WALNUT CREEK	CALIFORN	757
290	GENISCO INC S		756*
	ALAMOGORDO	NEW MEXI	756
291	DATA PRODUCTS CORP S		755*
	CULVER CITY	CALIFORN	755
292	UNITED STATES STEEL CORP		754*
	LOS ANGELES	CALIFORN	4
	WORCESTER	MASS	11
	NEWARK	NEW JERS	13
	HOMESTEAD	PA	75
	MONROEVILLE	PA	651
293	SCOPE INC S		748*
	FAIRFAX	VIRGINIA	65
	FALLS CHURCH	VIRGINIA	683
294	ELECTRONIC COMMUNICATIONS INC		741*
	ST PETERSBURG	FLORIDA	60
	TIMONIUM	MARYLAND	681

S = Small Business

SECTION I - U.S. BUSINESS FIRMS
Fiscal Year 1963

RANK	NAME OF CONTRACTOR AND LOCATION		THOUSANDS OF DOLLARS
295	CONSOLIDATED SYSTEMS CORP		734*
	MONROVIA	CALIFOR	734
296	NORTHERN ORDNANCE INC		732*
	FRIDLEY	MINNESOT	114
	MINNEAPOLIS	MINNESOT	618
297	MACHLETT LABORATORIES INC		730*
	SPRINGDALE	CONN	648
	STANFORD	CONN	82
298	METEOROLOGY RESEARCH INC	S	729*
	ALTADENA	CALIFORN	538
	POINT MUGU	CALIFORN	191
299	ASSOCIATED AERO SCIENCE LABS INC	S	728*
	HAWTHORNE.	CALIFORN	728
300	ELECTRO INTERNATIONAL INC		720*
	ANNAPOLIS	MARYLAND	538
	LONG BRANCH	NEW JERS	182
301	UNITED ELECTRODYNAMICS INC		720*
	FORT HUACHUCA	ARIZONA	48
	PAYSON	ARIZONA	306
	PASADENA	CALIFORN	366
302	AUSTIN CO		717*
	NEW YORK	NEW YORK	717
303	KOLLMORGEN CORP		706*
	NORTHAMPTON	MASS	706
306	WYLE LABORATORIES	S	706*
	EL SEGUNDO	CALIFORN	706
307	ZENITH RADIO CORP		701*
	CHICAGO	ILLINOIS	701
308	NATIONAL SCIENTIFIC LABS INC		697*
	WASHINGTON	DC	697
310	MATERIALS RESEARCH CORP	S	691*
	ORANGEBURG	NEW YORK	691
311	DEWEY G C CO	S	690*
	WASHINGTON	DC	89
	NEW YORK	NEW YORK	601
312	HAZLETON LABORATORIES INC	S	687*
	FALLS CHURCH	VIRGINIA	687
313	DYNAMICS RESEARCH CORP	S	681*
	STONEHAM	MASS	681
314	AMERICAN OIL CO		671*
	CHICAGO	ILLINOIS	206
	WHITING	INDIANA	465
315	NATIONAL RESEARCH CORP	S	670*
	CAMBRIDGE	MASS	510
	NEWTON	MASS	75
	NEWTON HIGHLA	MASS	85
316	DATA CORP	S	669*
	DAYTON	OHIO	669
317	PENNSALT CHEMICALS CORP		669*
	KING OF PRUSSI	PA	326
	PHILADELPHIA	PA	343
319	AMCEL PROPULSION INC		666*
	ASHEVILLE	NCAR	666
320	SYSTEMS TECHNOLOGY INC		663*
	INGLEWOOD	CALIFORN	663
321	COMSTOCK WESCOTT INC	S	650*
	CAMBRIDGE	MASS	650
322	GRACO ENGINEERING - MFG CO	S	649*
	GARDENA	CALIFORN	479
	LOS ANGELES	CALIFORN	170
323	CHU ASSOCIATES	S	648*
	SAN DIEGO	CALIFORN	97
	LITTLETON	MASS	551
324	THOMPSON JOHN I CO	S	643*
	WASHINGTON	DC	568
	WALTHAM	MASS	62
	BELLEFONTE	PA	13
325	BELOCK INSTRUMENT CORP		642*
	COLLEGE POINT	NEW YORK	642
326	SIERRA RESEARCH CORP	S	641*
	FORT HUACHUCA	ARIZONA	199
	BUFFALO	NEW YORK	370
	CHEEKTOWAGA	NEW YORK	72
327	COHU ELECTRONICS INC	S	638*
	HINGHAM	MASS	638
328	BAUSCH / LOMB OPTICAL CO		636*
	ROCHESTER	NEW YORK	636
330	DATA DISPLAY INC	S	635*
	ST PAUL	MINNESOT	633
333	TECHNICAL APPLIANCE CORP	S	628*
	SHERBURNE	NEW YORK	628
334	UNIVERSAL CYCLOPS STEEL CORP		625*
	BRIDGEVILLE	PA	625
335	BROWN ENGINEERING CO		623*
	HUNTSVILLE	ALABAMA	623
337	TECHNICAL RESEARCH	S	618*
	SOMERVILLE	MASS	200
	ROME	NEW YORK	175
	SYOSSET	NEW YORK	243
339	BAIRD ATOMIC INC		601*
	BETHESDA	MARYLAND	12
	CAMBRIDGE	MASS	589
340	DYNATECH CORP	S	598*
	CAMBRIDGE	MASS	598
341	ALLIS CHALMERS MFG CO		594*
	NORWOOD	OHIO	53
	MILWAUKEE	WISCONSI	528
	WEST ALLIS	WISCONSI	13
342	HEWLETT PACKARD CO		594*
	PALO ALTO	CALIFORN	594
344	ELECTRO MECHANICAL RESEARCH INC		587*
	SARASOTA	FLORIDA	277
	COLLEGE PARK	MARYLAND	82
	PRINCETON	NEW JERS	228
345	NATIONAL ENGINEERING SCIENCE CO	S	583*
	PASADENA	CALIFORN	583
346	ADCOLE CORP	S	578*
	CAMBRIDGE	MASS	578
347	BERGEN RESEARCH ENGINEERING INC	S	577*
	TETERBORO	NEW JERS	577
348	UNITED NUCLEAR CORP		575*
	WHITE PLAINS	NEW YORK	575
349	MORSE INSTRUMENT CO	S	572*
	HUDSON	OHIO	572
350	MILGO ELECTRONICS CORP	S	567*
	MIAMI	FLORIDA	567
351	CHAMBERLAIN CORP		566*
	WATERLOO	IOWA	566
352	ZIMNEY CORP	S	564*
	MONROVIA	CALIFORN	564

S = Small Business

SECTION I - U.S. BUSINESS FIRMS
Fiscal Year 1963

RANK	NAME OF CONTRACTOR AND LOCATION		THOUSANDS OF DOLLARS	RANK	NAME OF CONTRACTOR AND LOCATION	THOUSANDS OF DOLLARS
486	POWER GENERATORS INC	S	319*			
	LAKEHURST	NEW JERS	121			
	TRENTON	NEW JERS	198			
487	GIBBS / COX INC		318*			
	NEW YORK	NEW YORK	318			
488	GRACE W R / CO		317*			
	BALTIMORE	MARYLAND	92			
	CLARKSVILLE	MARYLAND	225			
489	SCANWELL LABORATORIES INC	S	316*			
	SPRINGFIELD	VIRGINIA	316			
490	AEROSPACE RESEARCH CORP	S	315*			
	ROANOKE	VIRGINIA	315			
491	DIKEWOOD CORP	S	313*			
	ALBUQUERQUE	NEW MEXI	313			
493	OCEANICS INC	S	312*			
	LONG ISLAND	NEW YORK	56			
	NEW YORK	NEW YORK	144			
	PLAINVIEW	NEW YORK	112			
495	AIRTRONICS INC	S	311*			
	WASHINGTON	DC	219			
	BETHESDA	MARYLAND	92			
496	BALDWIN ELECTRONICS INC		311*			
	LITTLE ROCK	ARKANSAS	311			
497	HUMAN SCIENCES RESEARCH INC	S	310*			
	ARLINGTON	VIRGINIA	310			
498	HARSHAW CHEMICAL CO		310*			
	CLEVELAND	OHIO	310			
499	ROCKET POWER INC		309*			
	MESA	ARIZONA	234			
	PASADENA	CALIFORN	75			
500	R C A SERVICE CO		308*			
	CAMDEN	NEW JERS	284			
	ALEXANDRIA	VIRGINIA	24			
			5,569,325			

S = Small Business

SECTION II - NON-PROFIT INSTITUTIONS
Fiscal Year 1963

RANK	NAME OF CONTRACTOR AND LOCATION		THOUSANDS OF DOLLARS
18	AEROSPACE CORP		71,867*
	EL SEGUNDO	CALIFORN	71,853
	LOS ANGELES	CALIFORN	14
20	MASSACHUSETTS INSTITUTE TECH		70,284*
	BOSTON	MASS	11
	CAMBRIDGE	MASS	23,257
	LEXINGTON	MASS	47,016
21	JOHNS HOPKINS UNIVERSITY		65,483*
	BALTIMORE	MARYLAND	3,161
	SILVER SPRING	MARYLAND	62,322
33	MITRE CORP		33,150*
	BEDFORD	MASS	33,150
39	STANFORD RESEARCH INSTITUTE		22,052*
	FORT ORD	CALIFORN	130
	MENLO PARK	CALIFORN	20,765
	SOUTH PASADENA	CALIFORN	20
	STANFORD	CALIFORN	219
	WASHINGTON	DC	690
	HAMILTON	MASS	228
42	COLUMBIA UNIVERSITY		18,731*
	NEW YORK	NEW YORK	18,731
45	RAND CORP		16,849*
	SANTA MONICA	CALIFORN	16,184
	BETHESDA	MARYLAND	665
48	CALIFORNIA UNIVERSITY		12,222*
	BERKELEY	CALIFORN	4,464
	DAVIS	CALIFORN	43
	GOLETA	CALIFORN	38
	LAJOLLA	CALIFORN	4,866
	LOS ANGELES	CALIFORN	1,973
	MOUNT HAMILTON	CALIFORN	15
	RIVERSIDE	CALIFORN	125
	SAN DIEGO	CALIFORN	198
	SAN FRANCISCO	CALIFORN	191
	SANTA BARBARA	CALIFORN	309
51	ARMOUR RESEARCH FOUNDATION		11,564*
	CHICAGO	ILLINOIS	11,564
53	MICHIGAN UNIVERSITY OF		11,246*
	ANN ARBOR	MICHIGAN	7,821
	WILLOW RUN	MICHIGAN	70
	YPSILANTI	MICHIGAN	3,355
59	UNITED STATES NATL AERO SPACE AG		9,796*
	HUNTSVILLE	ALABAMA	186-
	SACRAMENTO	CALIFORN	152
	SANTA MONICA	CALIFORN	2,200
	WASHINGTON	D C	7,083
	CUMBERLAND	MARYLAND	108
	GREENBELT	MARYLAND	28
	PHILADELPHIA	PA	70
	DALLAS	TEXAS	387
	HAMPTON	VIRGINIA	46
64	CORNELL AERNAUTICAL LABORATORY		8,815*
	PATUXENT RIVER	MARYLAND	58
	BUFFALO	NEW YORK	8,337
	FALLS CHURCH	VIRGINIA	420
65	STANFORD UNIVERSITY		8,775*
	PALO ALTO	CALIFORN	172
	STANFORD	CALIFORN	8,603
70	FRANKLIN INSTITUTE OF PENNSYLVAN		8,449*
	PHILADELPHIA	PA	8,429
	SWARTHMORE	PA	20
72	ILLINOIS UNIVERSITY		7,689*
	CHICAGO	ILLINOIS	186
	URBANA	ILLINOIS	7,503
74	SYSTEM DEVELOPMENT CORP		7,501*
	SANTA MONICA	CALIFORN	7,092
	FALLS CHURCH	VIRGINIA	409
78	RESEARCH ANALYSIS CORP		6,631*
	BETHESDA	MARYLAND	6,631

RANK	NAME OF CONTRACTOR AND LOCATION		THOUSANDS OF DOLLARS
81	WOODS HOLE OCEANOGRAPHIC INST		6,057*
	WOODS HOLE	MASS	6,057
88	INSTITUTE FOR DEFENSE ANALYSIS		4,911*
	WASHINGTON	DC	4,911
89	BATTELLE MEMORIAL INSTITUTE		4,909*
	COLUMBUS	OHIO	4,864
		SWITZERL	45
92	CORNELL UNIVERSITY		4,768*
	ITHACA	NEW YORK	3,916
	NEW YORK	NEW YORK	181
		PUERTO R	671
93	GEORGE WASHINGTON UNIVERSITY		4,715*
	WASHINGTON	DC	4,715
95	WASHINGTON UNIVERSITY OF		4,647*
	SEATTLE	WASHINGT	4,647
96	PENNSYLVANIA STATE UNIVERSITY		4,646*
	UNIVERSITY PA	PA	4,646
99	PENNSYLVANIA UNIVERSITY OF		4,423*
	JOHNSVILLE	PA	53
	PHILADELPHIA	PA	4,370
106	CHICAGO UNIVERSITY		3,765*
	CHICAGO	ILLINOIS	3,765
109	NEW YORK UNIVERSITY		3,732*
	NEW YORK	NEW YORK	3,732
110	TEXAS UNIVERSITY OF		3,671*
	AUSTIN	TEXAS	3,425
	DALLAS	TEXAS	112
	GALVESTON	TEXAS	134
115	TENNESSEE VALLEY AUTHORITY		3,454*
	WILSON DAM	ALABAMA	20
	TULLAHOMA	TENNESSE	3,434
116	DENVER RESEARCH INSTITUTE		3,450*
	DENVER	COLORADO	3,450
117	OHIO STATE UNIVERSITY		3,449*
	COLUMBUS	OHIO	3,449
123	SOUTHWEST RESEARCH INSTITUTE		3,072*
	PHILADELPHIA	PA	27
	SAN ANTONIO	TEXAS	3,045
124	HARVARD UNIVERSITY		3,033*
	BOSTON	MASS	68
	CAMBRIDGE	MASS	2,775
	FORT DAVIS	TEXAS	190
127	UNITED STATES COMMERCE DEPT		2,838*
	ARCATA	CALIFORN	100
	BOULDER	COLORADO	787
	WASHINGTON	DC	1,941
	ASHEVILLE	NCAR	10
130	BROWN UNIVERSITY		2,805*
	PROVIDENCE	RI	12
	PROVIDEN-E	RI	2,793
135	NORTHWESTERN UNIVERSITY		2,633*
	EVANSTON	ILLINOIS	2,633
138	MIDWEST RESEARCH INSTITUTE		2,606*
	KANSAS CITY	MISSOURI	2,606
140	PRINCETON UNIVERSITY		2,535*
	PRINCETON	NEW JERS	2,535
153	DAYTON UNIVERSITY		2,253*
	DAYTON	OHIO	2,253
156	NATIONAL ACADEMY OF SCIENCES		2,186*
	LOS ANGELES	CALIFORN	100
	WASHINGTON	DC	2,086

SECTION II - NON-PROFIT INSTITUTIONS
Fiscal Year 1963

RANK	NAME OF CONTRACTOR AND LOCATION		THOUSANDS OF DOLLARS	RANK	NAME OF CONTRACTOR AND LOCATION		THOUSANDS OF DOLLARS
161	DENVER UNIVERSITY OF		2,165*	247	CALIFORNIA INSTITUTE OF TECHNOLO		973*
	DENVER	COLORADO	2,165		PASADENA	CALIFORN	973
165	NEW MEXICO STATE UNIVERSITY		2,096*	252	STEVENS INSTITUTE OF TECHNOLOGY		934*
	LAS CRUCES	NEW MEXI	1,676		HOBOKEN	NEW JERS	934
	UNIVERSITY PA	NEW MEXI	310	254	YALE UNIVERSITY		909*
	UNIVERSITY PAR	NEW MEXI	110		NEW HAVEN	CONN	909
175	MINNESOTA UNIVERSITY OF		1,878*	262	TEXAS A - M RESEARCH FOUNDATION		878*
	MINNEAPOLIS	MINNESOT	1,917		COLLEGE STATI	TEXAS	878
	ROSEMOUNT	MINNESOT	30	268	LOWELL TECH INSTITUTE		848*
	ST PAUL	MINNESOT	69		BEDFORD	MASS	49
176	SYRACUSE UNIVERSITY RESEARCH COR		1,853*		BILLERICA	MASS	20
	SYRACUSE	NEW YORK	1,853		LOWELL	MASS	779
178	BROOKLYN POLYTECHNIC INSTITUTE O		1,840*	278	BOSTON COLLEGE		794*
	BROOKLYN	NEW YORK	1,759		CHESTNUT HILL	MASS	551
	FREEPORT	NEW YORK	81		WESTON	MASS	243
180	WISCONSIN UNIVERSITY OF		1,814*	279	GEORGIA TECH RESEARCH INSTITUTE		788*
	MADISON	WISCONSI	1,684		BOCA RATON	FLORIDA	49
	MILWAUKEE	WISCONSI	130		ATLANTA	GEORGIA	739
186	MARYLAND UNIVERSITY OF		1,670*	280	RHODE ISLAND UNIVERSITY		786*
	WASHINGTON	DC	36		KINGSTON	RI	786
	BALTIMORE	MARYLAND	982	281	VIRGINIA UNIVERSITY OF		786*
	COLLEGE PARK	MARYLAND	652		CHARLOTTESVILL	VIRGINIA	786
188	UTAH UNIVERSITY OF		1,627*	283	FLORIDA UNIVERSITY		776*
	SALT LAKE CIT	UTAH	1,627		GAINESVILLE	FLORIDA	776
189	AMERICAN UNIVERSITY		1,619*	303	INDIANA UNIVERSITY		709*
	WASHINGTON	DC	1,619		BLOOMINGTON	INDIANA	667
196	CARNEGIE INSTITUTE TECHNOLOGY		1,501*		INDIANAPOLIS	INDIANA	42
	PITTSBURGH	PA	1,501	304	OKLAHOMA UNIVERSITY OF		708*
197	DUKE UNIVERSITY		1,487*		NORMAN	OKLAHOMA	708
	DURHAM	NCAR	1,487	309	UNITED STATES PUBLIC HEALTH SERV		695*
205	MIAMI UNIVERSITY OF		1,371*		WASHINGTON	DC	523
	CORAL GABLES	FLORIDA	949		ATLANTA	GEORGIA	105
	MIAMI	FLORIDA	422		SAVANNAH	GEORGIA	22
207	UTAH STATE UNIVERSITY		1,358*		BETHESDA	MARYLAND	45
	LOGAN	UTAH	1,358	318	SOUTHERN RESEARCH INSTITUTE		669*
212	PURDUE RESEARCH FOUNDATION		1,268*		BIRMINGHAM	ALABAMA	669
	LAFAYETTE	INDIANA	1,172	329	TRAVELERS RESEARCH CENTER		636*
	SPRINGFIELD	VIRGINIA	96		HARTFORD	CONN	636
216	ALASKA UNIVERSITY OF		1,255*	331	HUDSON INSTITUTE		630*
	BARROW VILLAGE	ALASKA	864		HUDSON	NEW YORK	630
	COLLEGE VILLAG	ALASKA	391	332	ILLINOIS INSTITUTE TECHNOLOGY		628*
219	NORTHEASTERN UNIVERSITY		1,212*		CHICAGO	ILLINOIS	628
	BOSTON	MASS	1,212	336	OHIO STATE UNIV RESERCH FOUNDATI		621*
220	ANALYTIC SERVICES INC		1,210*		COLUMBUS	OHIO	621
	ALEXANDRIA	VIRGINIA	1,210	338	TEXAS WESTERN COLLEGE		617*
224	SOUTHERN CALIFORNIA UNIVERSITY		1,184*		LAS CRUCES	NEW MEXI	551
	LOS ANGELES	CALIFORN	1,100		EL PASO	TEXAS	66
	PASADENA	CALIFORN	14	343	LIGHTNING / TRANSIENTS RESRCH IN		589*
	POINT MUGU	CALIFORN	70		MINNEAPOLIS	MINNESOT	589
225	SYRACUSE UNIVERSITY		1,175*	353	OKLAHOMA STATE UNIVERSITY OF		563*
	SYRACUSE	NEW YORK	1,127		LAWTON	OKLAHOMA	98
	UTICA	NEW YORK	48		STILLWATER	OKLAHOMA	465
232	WENTWORTH INSTITUTE		1,097*	355	OREGON STATE COLLEGE		560*
	BEDFORD	MASS	408		CORVALLIS	OREGON	560
	BOSTON	MASS	689	356	NEW MEXICO UNIVERSITY OF		558*
237	COLORADO UNIVERSITY		1,072*		ALBUQUERQUE	NEW MEXI	338
	BOULDER	COLORADO	1,006		LAS CRUCES	NEW MEXI	200
	DENVER	COLORADO	66	361	NOTRE DAME UNIVERSITY OF		549*
238	CINCINNATI UNIVERSITY		1,062*		NOTRE DAME	INDIANA	549
	CINCINNATI	OHIO	1,062	367	PITTSBURGH UNIVERSITY OF		538*
245	LOGISTICS MANAGEMENT INSTITUTE		1,010*		WASHINGTON	DC	34
	WASHINGTON	DC	1,010				

SECTION II - NON-PROFIT INSTITUTIONS
Fiscal Year 1963

RANK	NAME OF CONTRACTOR AND LOCATION		THOUSANDS OF DOLLARS	RANK	NAME OF CONTRACTOR AND LOCATION		THOUSANDS OF DOLLARS
367	PITTSBURGH UNIVERSITY OF		*	461	LOVELACE FOUNDATION		350*
	PITTSBURGH	PA	504		ALBUQUERQUE	NEW MEXI	350
371	PURDUE UNIVERSITY		517*	463	GEORGIA INSTITUTE TECH		347*
	LAFAYETTE	INDIANA	517		ATLANTA	GEORGIA	347
373	CATHOLIC UNIVERSITY		510*	467	AMERICAN INSTITUTE OF RESEARCH		338*
	WASHINGTON	DC	510		WASHINGTON	DC	31
374	IOWA STATE UNIVERSITY OF		508*		PITTSBURGH	PA	307
	IOWA CITY	IOWA	508	472	MISSISSIPPI STATE UNIVERSITY		335*
382	NEW MEXICO SCHOOL OF MINES		487*		STATE COLLEGE	MISS	335
	SOCORRO	NEW MEXI	487	474	VANDERBILT UNIVERSITY		334*
396	COORDINATING RESEARCH COUNCIL		455*		NASHVILLE	TENNESSE	334
	NEW YORK	NEW YORK	455	492	HASKIN LABORATORIES INC		312*
400	SMITHSONIAN INSTITUTE		449*		NEW YORK	NEW YORK	312
	WASHINGTON	DC	303	494	VIRGINIA MEDICAL COLLEGE OF		312*
	CAMBRIDGE	MASS	146		RICHMOND	VIRGINIA	312
403	ARIZONA UNIVERSITY OF		447*				
	TUCSON	ARIZONA	447				539,270
406	RENSSELAER POLYTECHNIC INSTITUTE		436*				
	TROY	NEW YORK	436	192	CANADIAN COMMERCIAL CORP		1,576*
407	SAINT LOUIS UNIVERSITY		435*			B W INDI	129
	ST LOUIS	MISSOURI	435			CANADA I	1,447
411	WESTERN RESERVE UNIVERSITY		429*	250	AUSTRALIA COMMONWEALTH OF		940*
	CLEVELAND	OHIO	429			AUSTRALI	940
415	RUTGERS UNIVERSITY		423*	392	MCGILL UNIVERSITY		465*
	NEW BRUNSWICK	NEW JERS	423			CANADA	465
417	DARTMOUTH COLLEGE		418*	479	UNITED KINGDOM ADMIRALTY		325*
	HANOVER	NH	418			UN KINGD	325
419	LOUISIANA STATE UNIVERSITY OF		413*				
	BATON ROUGE	LOUISIAN	330				3,306
	NEW ORLEANS	LOUISIAN	83				
423	TUFTS COLLEGE		406*				
	MEDFORD	MASS	406				
423	PUERTO RICO UNIVERSITY		402*				
		PUERTO R	391				
	RIO PIEDRAS	PUERTO R	11				
427	UNITED STATES ATOMIC ENERGY COMM		398*				
	IDAHO FALLS	IDAHO	100-				
	URBANA	ILLINOIS	50				
	ALBUQUERQUE	NEW MEXI	291				
	ROCHESTER	NEW YORK	99				
	RICHLAND	WASHINGT	58				
432	NORTH CAROLINA STATE COLLEGE		393*				
	RALEIGH	NCAR	393				
442	NEW YORK STATE UNIVERSITY OF		376*				
	ALBANY	NEW YORK	172				
	BROOKLYN	NEW YORK	10				
	BUFFALO	NEW YORK	134				
	OYSTER BAY	NEW YORK	18				
	STONY BROOK	NEW YORK	19				
	SYRACUSE	NEW YORK	23				
447	CASE INSTITUTE OF TECHNOLOGY		369*				
	CLEVELAND	OHIO	369				
449	TENNESSEE UNIVERSITY		365*				
	KNOXVILLE	TENNESSE	220				
	MEMPHIS	TENNESSE	145				
450	RESEARCH TRIANGLE INSTITUTE		364*				
	DURHAM	NCAR	364				
454	FLIGHT SAFETY FOUNDATION		359*				
	NEW YORK	NEW YORK	359				
458	HAWAII UNIVERSITY		355*				
	HONOLULU CITY	HAWAII	355				

Appendix D

A Bank for Economic Acceleration
of Backward Countries

by Morris Forgash

This memorandum by Morris Forgash, President of the United States Freight Company, has been prepared as a policy recommendation for collective action by the West to solve the basic problem of the backward countries.

Five main considerations have dictated its preparation:

1. The conditions of today are not those which obtained when NATO was founded. At that time, exclusive emphasis of joint Western policy was upon common defense of Europe. This is no longer the whole direction of needed strategy. The emergence of newly free but economically backward nations has altered the focus of world affairs;

2. These newly free nations see as their most urgent problem the elevation of their standard of living and the raising of their general social standards. As neutrals in the Cold War, they are less concerned with from whom they receive aid to accomplish this than that they shall receive such aid;

3. Since NATO was founded, the ability of the West to extend such aid has multiplied and its own need for investment opportunities has also grown. The most urgent of Europe's capital needs have been met and some surplus of capital, as shown by under-employment of resources, has developed in the United States. Moreover, capital estimated in the billions of dollars, and as yet uncommitted to long-term employment, has grown to plague the world's monetary system by its rapid migration from financial

center to financial center. The capital resources of the West are thus adequate to meet the capital needs of the backward countries if some satisfactory and safe mechanism can be devised and the West itself needs to create a safe haven for the nervous capital which today disturbs it;

4. The unanimous demand of backward peoples for immediate improvement of their standards of nutrition is now a political problem facing the whole of the West. It is no longer something to be handled unilaterally by a single nation. Nor is it something we can safely leave to the whims or policy changes of governments. Multilateral and continuous action to elevate the social standards of backward peoples, through an autonomous mechanism, not dominated by Great Powers, is a requisite of Western policy posed by the events of our time;

5. The ability of individual governments to handle this growing problem is becoming impaired. No single nation, including the United States, has at its free disposal the capital sums needed to do the job. Nor will the citizens of any one nation permit their government to bear the whole burden even if this were feasible. What is required, therefore, is expansion of the activities of the West in its assistance to backward peoples and, at the same time, reduction of the obligations of governments by attracting private capital through a safe and profitable investment medium. What is today a burden upon taxpayers must be transformed into a profitable and beneficial investment which will relieve governments of excessive drains upon their treasuries.

We have, in short, entered an era in which the world influence of the nations of the West will be measured by what we do, and how we do it, to help the backward countries achieve that economic progress which has so far been denied them and which is the birthright of all mankind.

Our contributions in this direction have been generous. Nevertheless, they have been ill-timed and discontinuous and even, for the most part, insufficient to compensate for the decline in world prices received by countries producing primary products, which are mainly backward countries, in their exchanges for manufactured items produced in the West.

Our efforts have been sincere and humane, yet they have not been addressed to the central problem. In particular, the West has not established an international mechanism for long-term credits to finance general agricultural advancement in backward countries. It has not even contemplated the use of credit to bring about the changes in systems of land tenure which are required if agriculture in back-

ward countries is to yield a produce large enough to sustain the
people at satisfactory standards and to create domestic capitals to
provide for growth.

This proposal that we establish A Bank for Economic Acceleration
is a plan to accomplish these ends at no long-term cost to ourselves,
and at no cost of political freedom to the backward peoples.

This is not foreign to the collective political needs of the West. It
is an extension of joint action into new policy requirements created
by the changing circumstances of our time. One of the principal
objectives of common action by the West is to create conditions of
political stability favorable to the peaceful and democratic defense
of Western institutions. This objective cannot be attained unless we
earn the trust, by our actions and not our words alone, of the newly
emerging nations. This trust must be earned despite the legacy of
mistrust left behind by the colonialism of the past.

What Must Be Done

The first essential step towards alleviation of the poverty of backward countries consists in the transformation of primitive subsistence
farming into a developed incentive system of produce for market.

Such a transformation requires provision of ample credit to achieve
the following:

a. Low-interest financing of farm improvements so as to raise
the productivity of a soil by guaranteeing the farmer a substantial
personal benefit from his improvement of farming methods;

b. Supply of capital for land acquisition, for resale on time payments to individual farmers or to co-operative groups of farmers,
of lands now farmed on insecure or inequitable tenure or now
farmed on terms which deprive the grower of incentive to improve
fertility of the soil, to extend his cultivated acreage, to plant crops
requiring more than one season for their maturation, or to introduce market crops in addition to or instead of subsistence crops;

c. To assist in the establishment of central buying agencies for
farm produce, so as to guarantee the farmer an assured market
and a fair price for his produce, and to secure such concentration
or diversification of crops as conforms to the dietary needs of the
people and to the circumstances of climate, soil chemistry, water
supply, adjacence to transportation, and other factors affecting the
choice of crops by regions;

d. Once land acquisition is under way, to finance the purchase
for co-operative and private use of modern farm equipment, seed,
fertilizers, and crop-storage and transportation facilities, on terms

permitting repayment of the loans and payment of interest out of part of the increased production from the soil after the needs of rising subsistence levels have been met;

e. To assist in the establishment of a system of incentive prices designed to yield cash bonuses to farmers who reach or surpass objectives as to output of farm products and/or a specified yield per acre for stated food items;

f. To finance, over long-term repayment agreements, and at economic but nonusurious rates of interest, the construction of roads, highways, docking and rail facilities, and other means of linking the farming districts and the market centers, so as to create the necessary conditions for transition from nonincentive subsistence farming to incentive market farming;

g. To finance the development of personal skills and the entry into private business by individuals for the supply, maintenance, and repair of vehicles, farm equipment, seed and fertilizer, in order to stimulate extension of such essential services by providing strong personal incentives to private persons to co-operate in raising the productivity and prosperity of backward regions.

Plan for Organization of
the Bank for Economic Acceleration

A soundly functioning Bank for Economic Acceleration working to raise agricultural productivity and food supplies would importantly affect the social and economic standards of backward countries within 10 years, and would decisively transform their economic capacities and their political outlook and influence upon world events within 20 years.

With full knowledge that concepts as novel as those implicit in A World Bank for Economic Acceleration will lead to disagreements, the foundations of a plan for the establishment of such a bank are presented below:

Capitalization: The initial authorized capital of A Bank for Economic Acceleration shall be $10,000,000,000 U.S. Dollars or other hard currency equivalents.

Of the authorized capital, one-half, or $5,000,000,000 equivalent shall consist of noninterest-bearing 50-year notes subscribed by the governments of the NATO nations, said subscriptions to be in the lawful currencies of the High Contracting Parties at the rates of exchange prevailing on the subscription date.

Of the authorized capital, one half or $5,000,000,000 equivalent shall consist of 4% notes of varying maturities issued via public subscription to private citizens, institutions, and business concerns domiciled throughout the Free World.

Whatever the nationality of the private subscriber, his subscription shall be in the lawful currencies of any or all subscribing countries, in whatever proportions the Board of Governors of A Bank for Economic Acceleration shall from time to time deem appropriate upon consultation with the Treasuries of the High Contracting Parties.

Transition to Full Private Subscription: Under such conditions and at such times as are deemed appropriate by the Board of Governors, A Bank for Economic Acceleration shall offer for sale to private investors throughout the Free World any or all of the $5,000,000,000 equivalent of authorized noninterest-bearing capital subscribed by the Governments of the High Contracting Parties. Upon such sale, said noninterest-bearing notes shall commence to bear interest at the rate of 4% per annum. Proceeds of such sale shall be employed to retire the initial investment in the Bank, made by the High Contracting Parties, in proportion to their relative initial investments in the noninterest-bearing capital. Repayment of such capital shall be in the lawful national currencies of the private subscriber at the rates of exchange prevailing at the time initial subscriptions were made.

Tax Exemption: All interest payments on any and all investment instruments issued by A Bank for Economic Acceleration shall be exempt from taxation upon income in all countries signatory to the Treaty whereby the Bank shall be established, in all countries which subsequently shall associate themselves with the Bank, and in all countries to whose nationals or to whose Governments loans are extended by the Bank for whatever purpose, and this exemption from taxation upon income shall be specifically secured by Treaty.

Tax Exemption: Notwithstanding national laws empowering or requiring the governments of nations to levy taxes upon capital gains upon the sale or transfer of property by their nationals, the investment issues of the Bank shall be specifically exempted from such taxation upon capital gains in all countries signatory to the Treaty whereby the Bank shall be established, in all countries which subsequently shall associate themselves with the Bank, and in all countries to whose nationals or to whose governments loans are extended by the Bank for whatever purpose, and this exemption from taxation upon capital gains shall be specifically secured by Treaty.

Guarantees as to Principal and Interest: The High Contracting Parties shall severally and collectively contract to guarantee both principal and interest of all investment instruments lawfully issued by the Bank in accordance with its Charter and with the express authorization of its Board of Governors.

The governments of all countries to whom, or to whose nationals, loans are extended by the Bank shall additionally guarantee repay-

ment of principal and payment of interest upon all such loans as
they fall due, whatever the purposes of such loans, and whatever
changes in government in borrower nations may have occurred subsequent to the signing of the loan agreements and to the implementation of the contracts.

Said guarantee of repayment of face amount of principal and of
payment of accrued interest shall extend to each lawful owner of the
investment instruments issued by the Bank, whether such owner shall
be the original purchaser of these instruments of the Bank or shall
be a successor in interest through purchase, gift, or inheritance.

Arbitration of Disputes: All disputes between contracting parties
incapable of settlement by negotiation shall be submitted to an International Court of Arbitration whose decision shall be binding on all
parties. Such required recourse to arbitration shall be secured by
Treaty.

Central Bank Reserves: It shall be agreed by compact among the
High Contracting Parties that evidences of ownership of noninterest-
bearing notes constituting authorized capital stock of the Bank shall
be counted among the Central Bank reserves of the High Contracting
Parties, in no way distinguishable from lawful currency or from
Central Bank holdings of lawful commercial or governmental paper.

Board of Governors: The Board of Governors of A Bank for
Economic Acceleration shall consist of one representative each of
the High Contracting Parties, one each from designated prospective
borrowing areas of the Free World (e.g., Southeast Asia; India-
Pakistan; North Africa) whose governments are signatories to the
Treaty authorizing establishment and functioning of the Bank.

In addition, the International Monetary Fund, the World Bank,
the Common Market, the European Free Trade Area, and such other
supranational bodies whose functions relate to those of A Bank
for Economic Acceleration shall be represented upon the Board of
Governors.

Lending Policies: A Bank for Economic Acceleration shall supply
capital funds to authorized borrowers for the following purposes
and upon the following express conditions:

a. No loans shall be extended, for any purpose whatever, unless,
in the judgment of the Board of Governors of the Bank, the purposes of the loan, if realized, will contribute directly to enlarging
the national income of the borrower country in measurable degree
and in measurable time;

b. Notwithstanding local availability of loan capital, the Bank
shall extend low-interest loans for worth-while agricultural and
industrial purposes in cases where local rates of interest are so
usurious as to deter private or public borrowing for extension,
expansion, and for improvement of agriculture and industry;

c. No loans shall be extended except of a self-liquidating nature, but sinking fund agreements in all loan contracts shall be of such a nature as not to require commencement of repayment of the capital sum prior to such time as, it is estimated, employment of the loan capital will have begun to bear fruit;

d. It shall be a prime purpose of the lending policy to bring about such changes in systems of land tenure as will contribute to local initiative in the development of resources; the raising of the productivity of labor, capital, and the soil; and the creation of permanent improvements in agricultural, industrial, and commercial practices;

e. Prime among the purposes of loans shall be investments designed to raise the living standards of the people, and to increase the revenues of Governments by increasing the tax-paying ability of their peoples in addition to raising directly both economic and social standards;

f. Purchases of products and capital equipment resulting directly from the extension of loans shall not be permitted to any borrower except from supply sources within the Free World. But the Bank may not specify within the Free World where such purchases may be made by the borrower on credit extended or guaranteed by the Bank;

g. Loans shall be of varying maturities, with a maximum of 50 years in the case of such large installations as irrigation dams; 15-25 years for such investments as electric power and other energy sources; 10-20 years in the case of new mines; 10 years for land acquisition; 5-10 years for direct agricultural improvements; and such shorter-term paper as the purchases at discount of consumer and personal loan paper and approved industrial/commercial paper in more advanced countries

h. No loans shall be extended if, in the judgment of the Board of Governors, the proposed purpose of the loan would result in unrequited increase in living costs or other economic imbalance on the part of borrower countries. For example, loans shall not be extended for the creation of new urban centers and urban industries until it is first demonstrated that the local food supply is sufficient, and is capable of sufficient increase, to prevent a spiraling of food prices as industrial wages are injected into the local economy;

i. Loans shall be extended for the construction of roads, bridges, and highways whereby the interior can be linked with the markets, urban centers, and the seacoast or inland navigation;

j. Sympathizing with the laudable and humane desire of the governments of backward countries to raise their standards of education, medical care, and other aspects of social policy, the Bank shall nevertheless give preference, in extending loans, to projects calculated to increase the national incomes of borrower countries in such ways and in such time as will enable the extension and maintenance of social services to be financed out of the domestic resources of borrower countries;

k. The Bank for Economic Acceleration shall make no grants-in-aid, nor any other advance of funds, not calculated nor designed to be self-liquidating out of the increased national product resulting from wise selection of projects and their capable administration;

l. The Bank shall initiate proposals for the extension of loans, as well as rule upon the merits of loan applications originating with proposed borrowers, and for this purpose, as well as to assist in the supervision of projects for which loans have been granted, shall maintain and staff such regional offices as are deemed necessary;

m. The Bank, in the discretion of its Board of Governors, may create and employ a Portfolio Committee to recommend and supervise such short-term investments in acceptable paper of all descriptions, including discount operations, as will enhance the total yield upon its investments, thereby creating a fund with which to underwrite low-interest rates upon longer-term and desirable projects in underdeveloped or presently unbalanced economic areas of the Free World.

MORRIS FORGASH, 1962

A Bank for Economic Acceleration of Backward Countries

No Duplication of the Functions of Existing International Credit Agencies

It is natural to question whether A Bank for Economic Acceleration would not duplicate the work now being performed by existing agencies. No such duplication is foreseen. The ways in which A Bank for Economic Acceleration would differ crucially from existing agencies are described below.

The International Bank for Reconstruction and Development

1. The World Bank does not concentrate *primarily* on raising the agricultural status and the local food supply of backward peoples;

2. It does not actively seek to extend loans for acquisition of land as the foundation of a rapid, peaceful, and responsible process of changing inequitable and inefficient systems of land tenure into incentive systems;

3. The Board of Governors of the World Bank is controlled through the majority voting rights of the United States and Britain; its operations are therefore subject to an undesirable degree of political control by these two nations. Voting power in the World Bank consists of 250 votes for each member plus 1 additional vote for each

capital share held. In 1954, this meant that the United States voted 32,000 votes (250 votes plus 1 vote for each 31,750 capital shares), the United Kingdom voted 13,250 votes (250 votes plus 1 vote for each of 13,000 shares) and Panama, for example, voted 252 votes (250 votes plus 1 vote for each of 2 capital shares held). The Board of Governors consists of the Governor plus one alternate Governor per member who votes the capital shares of the member nations. In substance, therefore, the Board of Governors of the World Bank is an instrument of the United States and British Governments, which is quite the wrong way to develop a sound international banking agency responsive to the needs of the backward nations as felt by themselves instead of to their needs as imagined by the great powers;

4. Although the World Bank attracts private capital, it possesses no instrumentality whereby the investments of Governments in the World Bank can be converted into private investments and the Government subscriptions returned to the subscribing countries, which would be a feature of A Bank for Economic Acceleration;

5. Despite the operations of the World Bank—and they have indeed been commendable—its inability to meet the needs of the most backward nations is evidenced in the various and costly foreign aid programs of the United States which have been made necessary because no adequate international agency has been created.

The International Finance Corporation

This body was created in 1956 to finance private undertakings of

greater risk than the World Bank was chartered to assume. Permitted to raise funds in the private capital market, it has not yet done so and, until September of 1961, had extended loans of only $45 million (to forty industrial ventures in 18 countries; for an average of $500,000 each) or less than half its $97 million of capital funds.

Its operations are confined to the financing of privately owned and managed enterprises engaged in manufacturing, processing, or mining. It is quite incapable of meeting the capital needs of land reform and acceleration of food production among backward peoples.

The Inter-American Development Bank

1. It is essentially an instrumentality of the United States; as such, it does not truly represent an international effort to solve a manifest world problem;

2. It has been financed, and must continue to be financed by the U. S. Treasury, out of the pockets of United States taxpayers, rather than by private capital brought together for a common end in all parts of the globe;

3. The means whereby its capital is raised contributes in no way to sopping up, and putting to productive use, the billions of dollars of hot money which is endangering the world monetary system;

4. Its capitalization is absurdly small in light even of the limited task assigned to it.

The Overseas Development Fund

1. It functions through gifts, not loans, and therefore carries with it an undesirable degree of political involvement between the recipient and the donor;

2. It is far too small to meet the requirements even of the limited areas in which it operates;

3. There is no guarantee of continuity on its part beyond 1963;

4. The movement of African and Asian countries towards total political independence from their previous colonial ties makes it hazardous to forecast that aid from the Overseas Development Fund may not be halted, perhaps abruptly in some instances.

The International Development Association

1. It is far too small;

2. Its degree of success in future years will be limited (or, at least, determined) by the willingness of Governments to channel some part of their direct foreign aid grants or loans through I.D.A. rather than through the embassies and diplomatic agencies of the various national Governments. In short, I.D.A. will meet the formidable obstacle of power politics, no matter how much its sponsors may wish to avoid this;

3. I.D.A. is to concentrate to some extent, perhaps to a primary extent, on very valuable projects such as housing or sanitation which are absolutely necessary to the social development of backward peoples but will neither increase the food supply nor will be accompanied by insistence upon such increase as a precondition to the creation of urban centers through loans;

Consequently, although I.D.A.'s purposes are of extreme importance, if implemented in areas of limited local supply of food they might cause serious economic dislocation in the countryside and villages by inflating living costs through the injection of undue sums of money into primitive economies without the necessary safeguard of a corresponding increase in local food supply.

A Bank For Economic Acceleration would, therefore, duplicate no important function of existing lending agencies. It would supplement their work by putting, on a continuing basis, the problem of increasing the food supplies of the people of the backward countries in the forefront of economic-social problems to be solved with Western aid, and would do so on a self-liquidating basis.

MORRIS FORGASH, 1962

Sources of
Data

The following notes list all the principal sources of data that were utilized in the preparation of this book. Where particular sources of data are not shown, as in the estimates of capital requirements and employment effects of Chapter 10, the writer is responsible for them. Many of the data sources are United States Government documents. These have a common publisher—the Superintendent of Documents, U.S. Government Printing Office, Washington, D.C.

Chapter 1

National Education Association, Research Division, *Teacher Supply and Demand in Public Schools, April, 1964.*

U.S. Department of Health, Education, and Welfare, *Health Manpower Source Book, Section 18, Manpower in the 1960's,* 1964.

On shipbuilding, The New York *Times,* January 25, 1965.

Atomic Energy Commission Program, The New York *Times,* December 26, 1964.

On shipbuilding during the Second World War, John Gunther, *Inside U.S.A.,* Harper's, 1946.

U.S. Department of Commerce, *Statistical Abstract of the United States, 1964.*

Chapter 2

Basic materials on U.S. forces and strategy are found in the *Statement of Secretary of Defense Robert S. McNamara Before the House*

353

Appropriations Committee on the Fiscal Year 1966–1970 Defense Program and 1966 Defense Budget.

The following sources are also important for estimates of U.S. military forces:

Interview with Secretary McNamara in *U.S. News and World Report,* April 12, 1965.

The Institute for Strategic Studies, *The Military Balance 1964–65,* London, 1964.

Office of Assistant Secretary of Defense (Public Affairs), Washington, D.C., Release No. 308–64, *Department of Defense Statement on U.S. Military Strength,* April 14, 1964. Article by Richard Fryklund in *The Evening Star,* October 1, 1964.

Dispatch by Jack Raymond in The New York *Times,* January 3, 1965.

Washington dispatch to The New York *Times,* April 15, 1964.

Lead article on defense in *Time,* August 23, 1963.

Dispatches by Jack Raymond in The New York *Times,* October 7, 1964 and November 13, 1964.

Article on the TFX (F–111) airplane in The New York *Times,* October 15, 1964.

Report by Karl E. Meyer on overkill, in *New Statesman,* August 9, 1963.

Robert S. McNamara, "Why We Are Stronger Than Russia," *The Saturday Evening Post,* November 7, 1964.

Jerome B. Wiesner and Herbert F. York, "National Security and the Nuclear Test Ban," *Scientific American,* October, 1964.

Testimony in Hearing before the Select Committee on Small Business, United States Senate, 87th Congress, 2nd Session, August 29, 1962.

U.S. Department of Labor, Bureau of Labor Statistics, Bulletin No. 1363, *Employment Outlook and Changing Occupational Structure in Electronics Manufacturing,* October, 1963.

For a summary view of the variety of military systems see *Armed Forces Management,* April, 1964, Military Systems Catalog, also U.S. Department of Defense, Office of the Director of Defense Research and Engineering, *United States Guided Missiles,* 1963.

Washington dispatch on missile scrapping to The New York *Times,* August 22, 1964, and June 12, 1964.

Harold B. Meyers, "The Great Uranium Glut," *Fortune,* February, 1964. Howard Simons, "Our Fantastic Eye in the Sky," The Washington *Post,* December 8, 1963.

Remarks of Secretary of Defense Robert S. McNamara before the Economic Club of New York, Waldorf Astoria Hotel, November 18, 1963.

Department of Defense, Office of Public Affairs, Release No. 1486–63. Text prepared for delivery by Senator Hubert Humphrey, Democratic Vice Presidential Candidate, National Guard Association, Detroit, Michigan, December 30, 1964.

On the power of U.S. tactical nuclear weapons, statement by Secretary McNamara reported in The New York *Times*, August 18, 1964. Report on address by Deputy Secretary of Defense Cyrus R. Vance, The New York *Times*, August 8, 1964.

Memorandum on *United Nations Association and the Committee of 18*, Philip Noel-Baker, M.P., House of Commons, London, England.

On the various weapons gaps, see Charles J. V. Murphy, "The Desperate Drive to Cut Defense Spending," *Fortune*, January, 1964.

On U.S. counterinsurgency technology, article by Hanson W. Baldwin, The New York *Times*, November 6, 1964.

Address by General Dwight D. Eisenhower, Notes for National Association of Manufacturers, New York City, December 7, 1962. *The Budget of the United States Government, Fiscal Year Ending June 30, 1965*, 1964.

Hearings Before a Subcommittee of the Committee on Appropriations, House of Representatives, 88th Congress, 1st Session, *Department of Defense Appropriation for 1964*, Part 1, Secretary of Defense, 1963.

U.S. Senate, *Hearings before the Subcommittee on Department of Defense of the Committee on Appropriations and the Committee on Armed Services*, 88th Congress, 2nd Session, on H.R. 10939, Part 1, 1964.

Paul Kecskemeti, *Strategic Surrender*, Stanford University Press, 1958.

Chapter 3

Business Week, October 24, 1964.

Trains, June, 1964. Articles on the U.S. and Soviet merchant fleets in The New York *Times*, February 19, 1964, and August 13, 1964.

Article on shipbuilding in *Business Week*, February 8, 1964.

U.S. Congress, Joint Economic Committee, Economic Policies and Practices, Paper No. 6, *Subsidies to Shipping by Eleven Countries*, 1964.

Edmund K. Faltermayer, "It's a Spryer Singer," *Fortune*, December, 1963.

Business Week, October 10, 1964.

Seymour Melman, *Report on the Productivity of Operation in the Machine Tool Industry in Western Europe*, Organization for European Economic Cooperation, European Productivity Agency, Paris, France, October 23, 1959.

Article on U.S. cargo fleet in The New York *Times,* November 8, 1964.

Age of U.S. machinery, *American Machinist,* November 17, 1958, June 10, 1963.

On new aircraft development: *U.S. News and World Report,* May 18, 1964; *American Machinist,* June 8, 1964, page 55.

On USSR machine-tool industry, *American Machinist,* July 6, 1964.

On Japanese production of new scientific instruments, The New York *Times,* September 12, 1964, business page.

On the United States merchant marine, statement of Senator Warren G. Magnuson before the Democratic Platform Committee, Washington, D.C., August 18, 1964.

Article on the Singer Company, *The Wall Street Journal,* March 2, 1965.

Chapter 4

On civilian technology, *Science,* June 28, 1963, News and Comment pages.

The Engineers Joint Council, *The Nation's Engineering Research Needs 1965–1985,* Summary Report and Subcommittee Report, May, 1962.

B. K. O. Lundberg, "The Supersonic Threat," *The Observer,* August 25 and September 1, 1963.

Christian Science Monitor, February 21, 1963.

The Wall Street Journal, August 9, 1963.

The Educational Record, April, 1963.

U.S. House of Representatives, Report of the Subcommittee on Science, Research and Development, of the Committee on Science and Astronautics, *Government and Science, No. 2, Fiscal Trends in Federal Research and Development,* 1964.

The Economist, August 1, 1964, on supersonic boom.

Also on the supersonic plane, The New York *Times,* July 7, 1964.

J. Herbert Hollomon, *Technical Policies and Economic Needs,* Office of the Assistant Secretary of Commerce for Science and Technology, September, 1963.

John G. Welles, Robert H. Waterman, Jr., "Space Technology: Pay-Off from Spin-Off," *Harvard Business Review,* 1964.

Robert A. Solo, "Gearing Military R & D to Economic Growth," *Harvard Business Review,* November, 1962.

Verne S. Myers, "The Reversible Relationships between Gross National Product and Research and Development Performed in Industry," *The Journal of Industrial Engineering,* January, 1964.

U.S. House of Representatives, Select Committee on Government

Research, First Progress Report, 1964. *Business Week,* November 2, 1963.

J. Hannifin and Charles J. V. Murphy, "We're Losing the Supersonic Transport Race," *Fortune,* February, 1964.

On successor to DC–3 design, *American Machinist,* September 28, 1964, page 55.

The New York *Times,* July 2, 1964, dispatch on supersonic transport.

National Academy of Sciences, *Federal Support of Basic Research in Institutions of Higher Learning,* 1964.

National Science Foundation, *Reviews of Data on Research and Development,* September, 1963, and May, 1963. Philip A. Abelson (editor of *Science*), *A Critical Appraisal of Government Research Policy,* text of address, undated (1963 or 1964).

Max Tishler, *The Government's Role and the Future of Discovery,* Merck & Company, September, 1963.

On indirect research costs, The Washington *Post,* May 20, 1964, and National Science Foundation, *Reviews of Data on Research and Development,* March, 1962.

U.S. Senate, Hearings before a Subcommittee of the Select Committee on Small Business, *The Role and Effect of Technology in the Nation's Economy,* Part 1 and Part 2, 1963.

American Association for the Advancement of Science, Committee on Science in the Promotion of Human Welfare, *The Integrity of Science,* December 31, 1964.

On civilian aircraft research, The New York *Times,* September 13, 1963.

Carnegie Foundation for the Advancement of Teaching, The Study of the Federal Government and Higher Education, *Higher Education and the Federal Government,* September, 1962.

On trends in national R & D funds, 1953–1962, National Science Foundation, *Reviews of Data on Research and Development,* September, 1963.

James R. Killian, Jr., *The Need for Balance in Our National Research and Development Program,* Sprague Electric Company, North Adams, Mass., October, 1962.

On limits to U.S. research funds, The New York *Times,* October 16, 1963.

National Aeronautics and Space Administration, Office of Legislative Affairs, Statements of NASA Officials, June 11, 1963.

On NASA costs, The Washington *Post,* August 20, 1963.

Space medical problems, The New York *Times,* December 24, 1964.

NASA, *Annual Procurement Report, Fiscal Year 1963.*

U.S. House of Representatives, Report of the Committee on Science and Astronautics, *Posture of the National Space Program,* 1963.

NASA, Appropriation Summary, Fiscal Years 1962, 1963, 1964.

Amitai Etzioni, *The Moon-Doggle,* Doubleday, 1964.
Edwin Diamond, *The Rise and Fall of the Space Age,* Doubleday, 1964.

Chapter 5

U.S. Senate, Permanent Subcommittee on Investigations, Report on the Committee on Government Operations, *Pyramiding of Profits and Costs in the Missile Procurement Program,* March, 1964.
U.S. Senate Subcommittee on Employment and Manpower, Hearings on the Nation's Manpower Revolution, 1963—included here are statements from several major military-industrial managers.
John F. Gorgol (Dept. of Management, Rutgers University), *The Theory of the Military-Industrial Firm in Relation to Conversion Capability,* Paper to Conference of Scientists on Survival, New York, N. Y., June 21, 1964.

Chapter 6

Article by Howard A. Rusk, M.D., The New York *Times,* December 13, 1964.
The Wall Street Journal, January 8, 1965 and January 17, 1965.
Statement by Senator J. W. Fulbright to the National Association of Secondary School Principals, Miami Beach, Florida, January 16, 1965.
On manpower for health, The New York *Times,* January 17, 1965.
Statement by President John F. Kennedy, September 30, 1963.
George Walton, Uncle Sam's Rejects, *The Saturday Evening Post,* December 8, 1962.
The Morningsider, July 9, 1964.
James B. Conant, *Shaping Educational Policy,* McGraw-Hill, 1964.
U.S. House of Representatives, Committee on Education and Labor, *Poverty in the United States,* 1964.
On biological warfare, *Business Week,* December 5, 1964.
On unemployment, James Reston, The New York *Times,* January 27, 1965, and Edwin L. Dale, Jr. in The New York *Times,* August 23, 1964.
On Selective Service rejects, New York *Herald Tribune,* May 18, 1964.
Emile Benoit, "The Economics and Politics of Defense Cutbacks," *War/Peace Report,* June, 1964.
U.S. House of Representatives, Hearings before the Committee on Interstate and Foreign Commerce, *Health Professions Educational Assistance,* February 5, 6, and 7, 1963.
Journal of the American Medical Association, November 16, 1963.

U.S. Department of Health, Education and Welfare, Public Health Service, *Physicians for a Growing America,* October 1959.

J. Robert Moskin, "The Challenge to Our Doctors," *Look,* November 3, 1964.

On physicians' income, *The Economist,* August 29, 1964.

On emergency medical care, The New York *Times,* October 9, 1964.

U.S. News & World Report, March 25, 1963.

Air pollution, New York *World-Telegram and Sun,* June 30, 1964.

Unemployment among Negroes, The New York *Times,* June 14, 1964.

Michael Harrington, *The Other America,* Macmillan, 1962.

U.S. Department of Commerce, *Statistical Abstract of the United States, 1964.* U.S. Department of Health, Education and Welfare, Welfare Administration, *Converging Social Trends, Emerging Social Problems,* 1964.

Chapter 7

U.S. Treasury Department, *Treasury Bulletin,* October, 1964.

U.S. Treasury Department, table on "U.S. Gold Stock and Convertible Foreign Currency Holdings, Gold Reserve Requirement and Foreign Dollar Holdings, 1945."

Business Week, January 16, 1965.

U.S. Congress, Joint Economic Committee, *The United States Balance of Payments,* 1964.

Letter by Robert W. Stevens on military spending abroad, The New York *Times,* September 27, 1963.

On British military sales to West Germany, *The Economist,* July 27, 1963, and August 22, 1964.

Remarks by Robert W. Stevens as a Discussant at the National Foreign Trade Council Economics Round Table, November 20, 1963 [Mr. Stevens is in the General Economics Department, Standard Oil Company (New Jersey)].

Announcement by Secretary of Defense McNamara of U.S.-German military agreements, The New York *Times,* November 15, 1964.

On U.S. forces in Germany, James Reston in The New York *Times,* December 11, 1964.

On Federal Government efforts to check the outflow of gold, dispatch by Edwin L. Dale, Jr. in The New York *Times,* February 14, 1965; also, The New York *Times,* May 24, 1965.

U.S. Department of Commerce, *Statistical Abstract of the United States,* 1961 and 1964 editions.

U.S. Federal Reserve Bank, *Federal Reserve Bulletin,* August, 1964.

Emile Benoit, *Europe at Sixes and Sevens,* Columbia University Press, 1961, Chapter 4.

Economic Report of the President Transmitted to the Congress, 1962, page 158.

On defense of the dollar, *The Wall Street Journal,* January 17, 1963.

The United States Balance of Payments in 1968 (by Walter S. Salant and Associates, The Brookings Institution). Summary Comments on this document by Robert W. Stevens, 1963.

Chapter 8

Dispatch from Buenos Aires in The New York *Times,* March 26, 1965.

Hanson W. Baldwin in The New York *Times,* September 26, 1964.

Dispatch by Jack Raymond in The New York *Times,* August 23, 1964.

Address by Senator Wayne Morse, *Congressional Record,* March 25, 1964.

Dispatch from Korea in The New York *Times,* June 16, 1964.

Charles Abrams, *Man's Struggle for Shelter in an Urbanizing World,* M.I.T. Press, 1964.

The Institute for Strategic Studies (London), Neville Brown, W. F. Gutteridge, *The African Military Balance,* August, 1964.

U.S. Congress, Joint Economic Committee, *The United States Balance of Payments—Perspectives and Policies,* 1963.

U.S. Agency for International Development, *Proposed Mutual Defense and Development Programs, Fiscal Year 1965,* 1964.

U.S. Agency for International Development, *U.S. Economic Assistance Programs,* 1964.

U.S. Congress, Joint Economic Committee, Subcommittee on International Exchange and Payments, *Hearings on Outlook for United States Balance of Payments,* December 12, 13, 14, 1962.

Edwin Lieuwen, *Arms and Politics in Latin America,* Praeger, 1961.

Chapter 9

David Wise, Thomas D. Ross, *The Invisible Government,* Random House, 1963.

David Halberstam, *The Making of a Quagmire,* Random House, 1965.

Life, June 12, 1964.

Address by Senator Gruening, *Congressional Record,* March 10, 1964.

Review of *The Invisible Government,* by Karl E. Meyer in *The New York Review,* September 10, 1964.

Letter to The Washington *Post,* January 24, 1965.

Letter to The New York *Times,* May 29, 1964.

Dispatch by John W. Finney to The New York *Times*, January 16, 1964.

Russell Baker in The New York *Times*, February 14, 1965.

Letter to The New York *Times* on Goldwater, June 11, 1964.

Dispatch by Tad Szulc to The New York *Times*, December 27, 1964.

Address by Senator Wayne Morse, *Congressional Record*, August 5, 1964.

Dispatch on U.S. Information Agency in The New York *Times*, May 3, 1964.

Article on The Kaplan Fund in The New York *Times*, March 3, 1964.

Washington dispatch on the Central Intelligence Agency, The New York *Times*, September 1, 1964.

Dispatch from Tucson, Arizona, The New York *Times*, August 30, 1964.

Dispatch from South Vietnam, *U.S. News & World Report*, May 18, 1964.

Chapter 10

Washington dispatch on automation, The New York *Times*, September 27, 1963.

Senator Eugene J. McCarthy, *A Liberal Answer to the Conservative Challenge*, Macfadden-Bartell, 1964.

Yearbook of Railroad Information, 1964 edition, Eastern Railroad Presidents Conference, 1964.

Article on defending the dollar, *U.S. News & World Report*, February 22, 1965.

On employment in the automobile industry, *Ward's Automotive Reports* and employment statistics from the U.S. Bureau of Labor Statistics.

New York City education budget, The New York *Times*, October 23, 1964.

Report on stream pollution, The New York *Times*, December 28, 1964.

Salaries of public school teachers in the United States, *The Economist*, December 31, 1960; and U.S. Department of Commerce, *Statistical Abstract of the United States, 1964*.

Editorials on mass transit, The New York *Times*, June 22, 29, 1964.

Highway Accidents, The New York *Times*, January 10, 1965.

Computer control of city traffic, *Business Week*, February 3, 1962.

Statement by Stewart L. Udall, Secretary of the Interior, Before the special Subcommittee of the House Education and Labor Committee, on H.R. 10440, April 8, 1964.

Tom Kahn, *The Economics of Equality*, League for Industrial Democracy, 1964.

President Lyndon B. Johnson, State of the Union Message to Congress, The New York *Times,* January 5, 1965.

Employment in New York City, The New York *Times,* December 17, 1964.

Urban transportation trends, *The Wall Street Journal,* June 8, 1964.

The Ralph M. Parsons Company, *North American Water and Power Alliance, Water and Power Plant,* Preliminary Report, April 15, 1964.

U.S. Arms Control and Disarmament Agency, *The Economic and Social Consequences of Disarmament,* 1962.

Emile Benoit and Kenneth E. Boulding, *Disarmament and the Economy,* Harper & Row, 1963.

U.S. Senate, Subcommittee on Employment and Manpower, of the Committee on Labor and Public Welfare, *Towards Full Employment: Proposals for a Comprehensive Employment and Manpower Policy in the United States,* 1964. "Is Automation Really a Job Killer?" *Business Week,* February 24, 1962, and August 22, 1964.

U.S. Bureau of Labor Statistics, Bulletin No. 1287, *Impact of Automation,* 1960.

Business Week, December 14, 1963.

Chapter 11

Irving Bluestone (United Automobile Workers, AFL-CIO), "Problems of the Worker in Industrial Conversion," paper to the International Arms Control Symposium, University of Michigan, December 19, 1962.

John S. Gilmore, "Some Differences Between Defense Firms and Commercial Firms," Denver Research Institute, University of Denver, paper to Conference on New Directions in Engineering, September 25, 1964.

Ben D. Segal, "A Labor Leader's Lament," *War/Peace Report,* June, 1964.

Governor Edmund G. Brown, "How to Put the States Back in Business," *Harper's,* September, 1964.

Hanson W. Baldwin, "Red Flag Over the Seven Seas," *The Atlantic,* September, 1964.

Is There a Future for Our New England Shipyards?, American Friends Service Committee, New England Region (undated, 1963 or 1964).

Yale Brozen, "The New Competition-International Markets: How Should We Adapt?" *The Journal of Business of the University of Chicago,* October, 1960. *Business Week,* November 7, 1964.

U.S. Department of Defense, *Community Economic Adjustment Program,* 1963.

Seymour Melman, "Elements of the Industrial Conversion Problem," *Congressional Record,* February 27, 1964.

Seymour Melman, "Key Problems of Industrial Conversion to the Civilian Economy," in U.S. Senate, Committee on Labor and Public Welfare, Subcommittee on Employment and Manpower, *Convertibility of Space and Defense Resources to Civilian Needs: A Search for New Employment Potentials* (Volume 2), 1964.

Murray L. Weidenbaum, Obstacles to Conversion, *Bulletin of the Atomic Scientists,* April, 1964.

Article by Homer Bigart on Utica, N.Y., The New York *Times,* December 22, 1964.

California conversion project, The New York *Times,* January 10, 1965. "Demand for Engineers, Physical Scientists and Technicians—1964," A Survey Conducted by the Engineering Manpower Commission of Engineers Joint Council, 1964. *The Saturday Evening Post,* September 12, 1964.

On economic development in Japan, The New York *Times* financial page, August 31, 1964.

On the relative growth of government spending in the United States, National Industrial Conference Board, *Business Record,* February, 1963.

U.S. Department of Defense, *Productive Civilian Uses of Former Defense Department Installations,* 1964.

U.S. Senate, Hearings before the Committee on Commerce, 82nd Congress, 2nd Session, on S. 2274, *National Economic Conversion Commission,* May 25 and June 22, 1964.

Article on the aerospace industry in The New York *Times,* August 16, 1964. Education Department, International Union of Electrical, Radio and Machine Workers, AFL-CIO, *Economic Conversion and Your Job,* Washington, D.C., 1964.

Chamber of Commerce of the United States, *The Economics of Defense Spending,* 1965.

Chapter 12

U.S. Congress, House of Representatives, Hearings before a Subcommittee of the Committee on Appropriations, Subcommittee on Department of Defense Appropriations, *Department of Defense Appropriations for 1964,* 88th Congress, 1st Session, Part 1, page 518.

Special Report on California, *Business Week,* December 8, 1962.

Chapter 13

U.S. Senate, Report of the Subcommittee on Retailing, Distribution, and Marketing Practices to the Select Committee on Small Business, *Impact of Defense Spending on Labor Surplus Areas,* 1963.

Harry C. Bredemeier, *Suggestions to Communities for Participation in the War on Poverty*, Urban Studies Center, Rutgers, The State University, New Brunswick, New Jersey.

William B. Shore, *Unemployment: Benefit, Not Burden*, Urban Studies Center, Rutgers, The State University, New Brunswick, New Jersey.

A Statement, Urging a Crash Program of Special Effort to Close the Gap Between the Conditions of Negro and White Citizens, The Board of Trustees of the National Urban League, June 9, 1963.

Dispatch from Durham, North Carolina, The New York *Times*, December 13, 1964.

Report of the Conference on Appalachian Development, The Woodrow Wilson School of Public and International Affairs, Princeton University.

Leon H. Keyserling, *Progress or Poverty*, Conference on Economic Progress, Washington, D.C., December, 1964.

U.S. Senate, *The War on Poverty, The Economic Opportunity Act of 1964*, A compilation of materials relevant to S. 2642, prepared for the Select Subcommittee on Poverty, of the Committee on Labor and Public Welfare, 1964.

Robert Theobald, "The Cybernation Revolution," *New Politics*, Summer 1964.

Michael D. Reagan, "For a Guaranteed Income," The New York *Times Magazine*, June 7, 1964.

On a Fifth of a Nation, *The Economist*, February 1, 1964.

Michael Harrington, "The New Lost Generation: Jobless Youth," The New York *Times Magazine*, May 24, 1964.

"New Deal, New Style," *The Economist*, April 11, 1964. "The War on Poverty: This is War?" *New University Thought*, Summer 1964.

On poverty in New York City, The New York *Times*, November 15, 1964; in West Virginia, The New York *Times*, March 28, 1965.

Chapter 14

Wassily Leontief, Disarmament, Foreign Aid and Economic Development, Peace Research Society (International), Ghent Conference, 1964 (papers published also as issues 3-4, Volume 1, *Journal of Peace Research*), 1965.

U.S. Agency for International Development, Statistics and Reports Division, *Selected Economic Data for the Less Developed Countries*, 1964.

C. L. Sulzberger, The New York *Times*, December 16, 1964.

"Can a Poor Nation Grow on an Empty Stomach?" *Business Week*, December 26, 1964.

Lead article on world hunger, *Newsweek,* June 17, 1963; *U.S. News & World Report,* January 6, 1964.

United Nations on food output, The New York *Times,* October 6, 1964; September 2, 1964.

United Nations, Statistical Office, *World Energy Supplies,* Statistical papers series J, Nos. 1, 2, 4, 6.

Population data in *The World Almanac,* New York *World-Telegram and Sun,* 1964.

Editorial on Poverty and Disarmament, The New York *Times,* February 22, 1964.

U.S. Department of Agriculture, Economic Research Service, Regional Analysis Division, *Man, Land and Food,* Foreign Agricultural Economic Report No. 11, 1963.

U.S. Department of Agriculture, Economic Research Service, Foreign Regional Analysis Division, *The World Food Budget, 1970,* Foreign Agricultural Economic Report No. 19, 1964.

U.S. Senate, 88th Congress, 2nd Session, Report 1188, Part 2, *Foreign Assistance Act of 1964,* Individual Views of Senator Morse, on H.R. 11380, 1964.

United Nations, Department of Economic and Social Affairs, *Industrialization and Productivity,* Bulletin 7, Projection of Demand for Industrial Equipment, 1964.

World Food Congress report, The New York *Times,* June 19, 1963.

Speech of Senator George A. Smathers, World Bank for Economic Acceleration, *Congressional Record,* July 27, 1961. Bernard B. Fall, "A Grain of Rice Is Worth a Drop of Blood," The New York *Times Magazine,* July 12, 1964.

United Nations, Food and Agricultural Organization, Opening address at the World Food Congress in 1963 by President John F. Kennedy.

Seymour Melman, *Aspects of the Design of Machinery Production During Economic Development,* United Nations, Department of Economic and Social Affairs, 1963.

William and Paul Paddock, *Hungry Nations,* Little, Brown & Company, 1964.

On impacts of malnutrition, The New York *Times,* December 12, 1964.

Chapter 15

Senator J. W. Fulbright, "Foreign Policy—Old Myths and New Realities," *Congressional Record,* March 25, 1964.

U.S. Department of Health, Education and Welfare, Public Health Service, Division of Water Supply and Pollution Control, *Career*

Opportunities in Water Supply and Pollution Control, Public Health Service Publication No. 1020, 1963.

On federal housing programs, The New York *Times,* March 4, 1965.

On Negro discontents, The New York *Times,* November 7, 1964.

On regulating the sulphur content of fuels, The New York *Times,* May 14, 1964.

Speech by The Right Hon. Philip Noel Baker, M.P., House of Commons (extract from the Official Report), March 4, 1965.

"Moscow Problem: Food or Weapons," The New York *Times,* March 8, 1962.

On China's nuclear potential, letter to The New York *Times,* November 8, 1964.

Change in Soviet agricultural policy, The Washington *Post,* December 17, 1964.

Change in Czech economic system, The New York *Times,* November 6, 1964.

On trade with China, *The Economist,* February 8, 1964.

Editorial, "The Arms Race," The New York *Times,* December 17, 1964.